BUSINESS IN CONTEMPORARY CHINA

Business in Contemporary China offers a compilation of the best and most relevant articles on Chinese business for use in the classroom or the boardroom. Covering political, economic, and environmental factors, as well as the impact of technological advancements on Asian business, the book provides a well-rounded picture of Chinese enterprise.

Philips and Kim select only the most recent relevant articles, arranged topically with an introduction to each chapter to contextualize and position the content. To further enhance its teaching value, each chapter also includes:

- A "perspectives" opener offering the opinion of a top academic on the topic at hand;
- Practical application exercises and review questions to test the reader's knowledge and understanding;
- Discussion questions to stimulate further analysis;
- Suggested topics for classroom debate; and
- Bibliographic suggestions for future research.

Covering both private and public sector topics, this will be a valuable resource for any student of international business, cross-cultural management, or strategy, especially for those interested in business in Asia or China.

Roger A. Philips teaches international business at Concordia University in Irvine, USA.

Eugene P. Kim is Professor of International Studies and Director of the Master of International Studies at Concordia University in Irvine, USA.

BUSINESS IN CONTEMPORARY CHINA

Edited by
Roger A. Philips
Eugene P. Kim

Routledge
Taylor & Francis Group

NEW YORK AND LONDON

First published 2016
by Routledge
711 Third Avenue, New York, NY 10017

and by Routledge
2 Park Square, Milton Park, Abingdon, Oxon OX14 4RN

Routledge is an imprint of the Taylor & Francis Group, an informa business

Library of Congress Cataloging in Publication Data
Names: Philips, Roger A., author. | Kim, Eugene P., author.
Title: Business in contemporary China / Roger A. Philips, Eugene P. Kim.
Description: New York, NY : Routledge, 2016.
Identifiers: LCCN 2016000875| ISBN 9781138919556 (hbk) |
ISBN 9781138919563 (pbk) | ISBN 9781315687810 (ebk)
Subjects: LCSH: Economic development—China. | China—Commerce. |
China—Economic conditions—2000– | China—Economic policy—2000– |
China—Foreign economic relations.
Classification: LCC HC427.95 .P5195 2016 | DDC 338.951—dc23
LC record available at http://lccn.loc.gov/2016000875

ISBN: 978-1-138-91955-6 (hbk)
ISBN: 978-1-138-91956-3 (pbk)
ISBN: 978-1-315-68781-0 (ebk)

Typeset in Sabon
by Florence Production Ltd, Stoodleigh, Devon, UK

MIX
Paper from
responsible sources
FSC
www.fsc.org   FSC® C013056

Printed and bound in Great Britain by
TJ International Ltd, Padstow, Cornwall

Dedicated to our wives, Antoinette and Eun Chu, who afford us the time and liberty to engage in vocations that are joy-filled and meaningful.

CONTENTS

FOREWORD

China over the past 35 years has assuredly made its existence felt around the world. Just take a moment to look at your material possessions— chances are most of them will carry the inscription 'Made in China'. Indeed, this is a country that is still enjoying one of the fastest growth rates in the world. No other country in recent human history has lifted as many people out of poverty and successfully navigated the largest human migration in these past few decades. Amazing changes have and will continue to take place in the Middle Kingdom—China.

Economics aside, China's influence on politics and culture can be found everywhere across the world. But how much do you actually know about this country? Most people can only name a few cities like Beijing, Shanghai, or Hong Kong. Despite this perceived gap in knowledge, increasing numbers of Westerners visit China to see this incredible and influential country with their own eyes. They are confronted with the reality that China is no longer the same country often portrayed in old Hollywood movies. Sure kung fu, chow mien, red *qipao* dresses and glazed tile roofed palaces all still exist. Now they are accompanied by luxury villas, Michelin-starred restaurants, contemporary art museums, skyscrapers, and the largest shopping malls in the world. The greatest changes however are those that have occurred in the ideas, aspirations and values of the Chinese people.

NewsChina magazine endeavors to show its audience a China in trans- formation. Neither didactic nor moralizing, our approach is one that attempts to present news in an honest and open way. The articles are imbued with real life and authentic narratives, telling the story of China in the present. Panda Express and PF Chang's, successful adaptations of Chinese cuisine in America, present a westernized version of a food tradition that has been around for millennia. Westerners accustomed to this version of our cuisine may not find the original Chinese food palatable or even desirable, and yet one senses a loss, as one would if eating frozen Sara Lee's as opposed to an apple pie from grandma's oven. We at *NewsChina* aspire to bring a taste of authentic China to our readers, a "spiritual food" that will help enlighten and enamor our readers as they grow in their understanding of China.

In the book *Business in Contemporary China*, a systematic compilation of articles from *NewsChina* and other selected periodicals is accompanied by expert insights provided by scholars of contemporary China. With business and education experience on both continents, the editors provide readers with a topical approach to the past years' hottest and most relevant news. Their deep knowledge of China, acute sense of nuance and balanced outlook provides a unique glimpse into the internal and external dialogues that China is presently engaged in, while allowing the reader to make up his or her own mind about the veracity and applicability of their claims. Consequently, each chapter concludes with educational applications, the gauntlet being thrown back at the audience, to make the book a launching pad for both scholars and business practitioners alike to dive into their own study of and engagement with these current events of China. It is our hope that many in the West will benefit from this worthy, informed, and eloquent collaboration between these editors and our reporters on the ground in China.

Fred S. Teng, CEO
NewsChina Magazine

INTRODUCTION

The Pacific Century

Measured by purchasing power, China's GDP surpassed that of the US in late 2014[1]. This signal event, occurring years earlier than many had predicted, presaged the beginning of the "Pacific Century." With Europe in seemingly perpetual economic stasis, the age of Atlantic economic dominance has waned. Together, the US and China account for fully one-third of the global economy[2]. For anyone concerned with commerce today, accurate knowledge of Chinese business is essential.

Fortune Magazine calls this shift in economic power "The Great Eastward Migration," and notes that since 2004, 80 Chinese companies have joined its Global 500, which now make up nearly a fifth of the list[3]. In the same ten-year period, 61 US companies and 25 Japanese firms have dropped from the list. China's G500 participants outnumber those from Germany, France, and the UK combined. Three of the top ten G500 are Chinese versus two US firms. And in September 2014, Chinese firm Alibaba completed the largest initial public offering (IPO) in history, raising US$25 billion on the New York Stock Exchange (NYSE), eclipsing the previous record US$22 billion 2010 IPO by the Agricultural Bank of China on the Hong Kong Stock Exchange.

Some of the chief hallmarks of China's phenomenal economic success are:

- A torrid GDP growth rate, averaging over 9 percent annually for the *thirty years* between 1984 and 2014[4], and still around 6 percent as of 2015.
- Meteoric rise in PPP GDP per capita from US$2,860 in 2000 to US$11,900 in 2013[5], a fourfold increase in 13 years. (PPP is Purchasing Power Parity, which means the countries' exchange rates have been adjusted to reflect their relative real purchasing power.) This rate of mass personal enrichment is unequalled in human history. Nevertheless, the average Chinese is not yet even middle class, implying lots of room for growth in the consumer economy.

1

- The largest economy by PPP, *and* the world's leading exporter at US$2.2 trillion for 2013, which exceeded the total exports of the entire European Union[6].
- Importantly for traders all over the world, China also bought an impressive US$1.95 trillion worth of goods and services from abroad in 2013, nearly equaling the imports of the EU[7]. China represents the world's second largest cross-border country market (next to the US) with its population of 1.4 billion[8].
- Aggressive expansion of foreign economic policy toward major investment in natural resources, primarily in Latin America and Africa.
- Vast improvement in economic infrastructure, including as of 2015 the world's longest high-speed rail network with over 19,370 km (12,036 miles) of track, more than the rest of the world combined[9]. According to the 12th Five-Year Plan (FYP), the total number of airports in the country will have expanded from 175 in 2010 to 230 in 2015[10].

The New Normal

But China is changing. The era of torrid growth has come to an end. Miles Yourman of Knightsbridge Asset Management[11] stated that, despite the official 7 percent growth forecast of the notoriously opaque government, real growth was likely only 3–4 percent for 2015. Stock prices fell precipitously in mid-2015 despite frantic government effort to prop up the markets. And an unexpected yuan devaluation in August 2015 following years of slow rises roiled world markets. So growth will settle out to a more normal rate going forward. After all, at a certain point, export-led growth is limited by the growth of buyers' income. US and European markets are only growing a few percent a year at best, and they are China's main markets.

Focus is moving to consumption rather than export. Wholesale foreign direct investment (FDI) is no longer welcomed, but only in those industries that China cannot do well enough itself. Foreign multinationals are facing increasing regulation and government hindrance that has made a once lucrative market more challenging. So if you understood Chinese business ten or even five years ago, that knowledge is, in practice, now outdated.

Understanding business in China isn't always easy. The balance between state and private enterprise there is unique. "Socialism with Chinese characteristics," as Deng Xiaoping (1984) called it, may seem initially more capitalistic than socialistic. Though dominated by a relatively small number of state-owned enterprises (SOEs) that control basic infrastructure, the Chinese economy leaves space for hundreds of thousands of private companies to flourish. SOEs dominate such critical sectors as financial services, telecom, energy, and transportation. But private companies in China accounted for about 75 percent of the nation's 2013 GDP[12] and returned an average of over 9 percent on assets, while SOEs returned an average of less than 5 percent[13].

Unlike Western democracies, which leave industrial policy largely to the industrialists, China's FYPs put forth by the National People's Congress set out economic policy goals for the nation and have great influence. China has a good track record of largely achieving its past five-year goals. The 12th FYP, promulgated in March 2011, prioritizes industrial growth, sustainability and increased domestic consumption[14]. These priorities translate into an emphasis on energy, automotive, IT infrastructure, and biotechnology. Having a blueprint like this publicly available helps make entry into Chinese markets more rational.

Storm Clouds Ahead?

Along with having been the greatest and most rapid engine of economic growth the world has ever seen, China faces a number of serious economic problems. In this book we attempt to illustrate and explain the most pressing of these, as well as offering potential solutions. These problems include:

- Slowdown of economic growth from near double digits annually to "only" around 6 percent or perhaps even less.
- Over-dependence on exports, which is the flip side of an underdeveloped consumer economy. A high personal savings rate, prompted in part by memories of social instability in the past and an inadequate social security system, hinders the growth of consumerism.
- An overextended credit system with bad loans permeating both local government and the banking system.
- Uneven wealth distribution which is growing ever more so. Despite having the world's largest economy, the average PPP per capita income was only US$12,900 in 2013, less even than the world average of US$15,000 and far below the US average of US$53,000[15] (see Table 0.1 below).
- Pervasive corruption at all government levels, although President Xi Jingping is attempting to address this.
- Poor intellectual property (IP) protection. For example, the Business Software Alliance estimates that some 80 percent of business software in China is pirated[16]. Laws are in place, but effective enforcement is rare, and even then, penalties are light. This discourages high tech foreign direct investment as well as domestic innovation.
- A property price bubble leaves most younger workers unable to buy housing. Owning an apartment is usually a *sine qua non* for a Chinese man to propose marriage, yet a city apartment price is far out of reach for most. Ironically, the majority of apartments held for investment by the wealthy are kept empty, as property tax is scarcely known in China and the cost of ownership is minimal.

Table 0.1 PPP GDP *per capita* in USD (IMF 2013)

USA	53,000
World	14,000
Brazil	15,000
China	12,000
India	4,000
Afghanistan	2,000

According to the World Bank, as of November 2014, China is now the world's largest economy on a PPP basis, but its people are, on average, not rich.

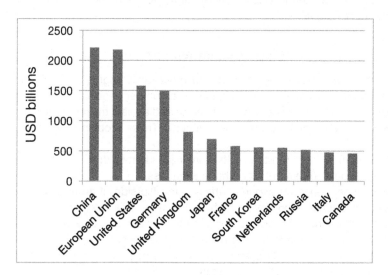

Figure 0.1 World's top exporter
Source: CIA World Factbook 2013.

- An aging population not able to be readily replaced with younger workers due to 35 years of one-child policy. Even with the current two-child policy, China's population has too few females, has nearly peaked and is projected to soon begin a slow decline.
- Lack of a realistic social net for aging citizens forces saving at the expense of consumption.
- An over-aggressive and poorly planned urbanization policy has resulted in "ghost cities" and countless vacant apartments.
- *Hukou* economically disenfranchises millions of migrant workers who so effectively contribute to Chinese productivity. *Hukou* is a system of household registration, a kind of internal visa that affords full social services to permanent residents of a city only. This excludes most migrants and their families from public schools, public housing and any kind of public assistance.

- Loss of farmers' lands through government actions often leaves farmers unfairly compensated.
- Disastrous pollution levels of waterways, farmlands and city skies.
- Poorly built transportation infrastructure that has resulted in numerous casualties.

Stocks and Currency Down

In June 2015, Chinese stock markets, which had reached lofty price levels, began a rapid decline, prompted in part by uncertainty in the ability of the economy to achieve even the official 7 percent growth prediction. By the end of August, the Shanghai SSE Composite Index had lost over 40 percent of its value. During this decline Beijing tried many different tactics to attempt to support the falling market, urging companies to repurchase their shares, jawboning the public not to sell and even going so far as to jail over 100 financial reporters and bloggers who contributed negative news, however factual. (This latter tactic is sure to backfire in the future as it reflects a fundamental lack of understanding about how markets operate. Prospective purchasers will now be even more reluctant to invest, with the facts needed to make informed investments no longer available.) Xiao Qiang, who tracks Chinese censorship, said at the time, that, ". . . in the absence of information about the stock market on official media, Chinese investors are relying on social media, primarily the two 'We's—Weibo and WeChat—to get news about the economy . . ."[17].

On August 11, 2015, the People's Bank of China launched a three-day series of surprise devaluations of the renminbi (RMB), the currency of the People's Republic of China (PRC). This after years of allowing the value of the yuan to slowly appreciate. It once was said that if the US sneezes, the world catches cold. In the Pacific Century, when China sneezes there are colds everywhere. With the Chinese economy cooling off, the demand for all sorts of raw material declines. With the world's largest economy in retreat, investor confidence sagged. The yuan devaluation triggered a precipitous fall in stock markets around the world. The Dow Jones Industrial Average (DJIA) tumbled nearly 2,000 points that week, with similar results in London, Tokyo, and elsewhere.

These problems reflect internally as well. Consumer spending is slowing as consumers worry about the future. "Their angst poses dual problems for China's leadership," wrote New York Times' Edward Wong. "The ruling party bases its legitimacy on delivering high rates of growth and employment. It also hopes to encourage consumer spending as a new engine of growth as the manufacturing sector slows and to nudge the economy away from an investment-driven model. Eroding confidence threatens both goals."[18]

The job market is also suffering. Victor Shih, a political economist at the University of California, San Diego, said, "Highly-paid professional jobs have been scarce for several years now and many young graduates have depended on their parents' connections to obtain entry positions in the government or state-owned enterprises. The current downturn will hit graduates without strong connections or specialized skills."[19]

Going Forward

Any of these issues could halt or even sink the Chinese economic miracle if left unaddressed. Though the 12th FYP addresses many of them, it remains to be seen how effective China is in solving these problems. For foreign business, many of these issues create possibilities for the export of goods or services that would be good for foreign business as well as good for China.

China's PPP GDP surpassing that of the US in 2014 marked a major milestone in world history and even with the recent slowdown should be a wake-up call to every business not fully involved in the export trade. Why? If you take GDP as a rough measure of a country's purchasing power (adding together buying by individuals, companies, and governments) then if you are not selling in China, you may be missing a potential market larger than that of the US.

This Book

Most Westerners likely get the great majority of their information about Chinese business from sources external to China: the "outside-in" view. This book was inspired by the work of Chinese reporters on the ground in China, accessing and interviewing primary sources: the "inside-out" view. This approach gives a more tangible feel and understanding to events in the Chinese economy, and can supplement the "30,000-foot" level view found in most Western business journalism describing Chinese business. Our primary source for the "inside-out" view in this book is *NewsChina*, a monthly publication of *China Newsweek*. Although never sharply critical of the government, the publication doesn't hesitate to forcefully point out missed opportunities, counterproductive policies, inconsistencies, and corrupt and self-serving actions of government bureaucrats. We have found it to be reasonably objective and the best source of accessible "inside-out" Chinese business information available. We believe this is the kind of information that foreign business must have to be successful in China. Here is, somewhat abridged, how *NewsChina* describes itself:

> This monthly magazine is from Beijing and is the English edition of
> *China Newsweek* (Zhong Guo Xin Wen Zhou Kan), one of the most
> influential news magazines on the Chinese mainland. As a matter of
> fact, the magazine itself is the product of China's reform and opening
> up. It was beyond anyone's imagination that such a news magazine

could have been published in China 30 years ago. This magazine, which is geared to investigative reporting, has so far managed to claim a wide circulation, or in other words, secure a big market, taking advantage of the rise of the Chinese middle class.

Based on market-oriented operation and management, *China Newsweek* has grown into a truly progressive modern news magazine. In 2007, we successfully published its Japanese edition. Now, its English edition has come to North America.

This magazine will show you a China in transformation. We are not used to lecturing or moralizing. We like to present news in an honest and open way, crafted as if we were telling a story. . . This may well be the result of a "good combination of Chinese and Western elements." Reading materials in China are called "spiritual food" and it is my hope that *NewsChina* will become "cultural Chinese food" in North America.

Views vary about the name of the English language magazine—News China. Some prefer "China News" to "News China", arguing that the latter sounds like Chinese English. In my view, however, "News China" and "China News" have a different meaning. The latter emphasizes that the news is from China while the former that we decided to adopt indicates that China is news itself.

Compared to the argument about the magazine's name, it is the cover design that may in fact be more illustrative of how the magazine is defined. Instead of the complete red frame as is found on the cover of magazines such as Time, we choose the "two-bar" design as you see it now because simply put, we don't want to be "framed" or "straight-jacketed". News China is an open magazine. Open to the readers! Open to the world!

There have been a good number of excellent books published on Chinese business over the years, including those by McGregor, Inch, Shenkar, Fernandez, Liu, Chao, and Underwood, among others.* But given the rapid pace of change in the Chinese economy, any book on the subject will necessarily have a fairly short useful shelf life. So a second inspiration for this book was to cull the most relevant periodical articles from the past two years into book form, organized by topic. This saves the reader much time as opposed to leafing through many issues to find relevant articles on the topic of interest. We expect to update the book biannually with fresh articles.

In the articles that follow, we attempt to illustrate in detail how some of China's signal economic achievements were accomplished, including, importantly, the kind of private–state interaction that occurs and the unique blend there of command economy and private enterprise. This book is designed to assist your efficient learning of Chinese business in today's world. Each chapter begins with an introduction, encompassing and summarizing the content of the chapter. The chapter bodies are the collection of articles that we have selected, primarily from *NewsChina* magazine, that bear on the chapter topic. The bamboo icon (below) separates our editorial comments from the quoted articles.

You will find learning exercises at the end of each chapter: review questions, discussion topics, suggested research, and related ethical propositions. We hope these will serve to deepen your understanding of Chinese business and provide a gateway to further research.

Prof. Roger Philips—Irvine, California
Dr. Eugene Kim—Shanghai

* Books mentioned above:

• *China's Economic Supertrends* by Inch (2012) InChina Publishing.

Four major economic trends explored.

• *Getting China and India Right* by Gupta & Wang (2009) Jossey-Bass.

Comparative economic treatment of the world's two most populous countries.

• *The Chinese Century* by Shenkar (2006) Wharton School Publishing.

How China will dominate world economics in the 21st century.

• *China CEO—Voices of Experience* by Fernandez and Underwood (2007) Wiley and *China CEO—A Case Guide for Business Leaders* by Fernandez and Liu (2006) Wiley.

Multinational country managers recount their lessons and experiences; accompanying case guide including nine scenarios.

• *One Billion Customers* by McGregor (2005) Wall St. Journal Books.

McGregor was a *Wall St. Journal* Beijing bureau chief.

• *Selling to China* by Chao (2012) iUniverse.

Prof. Roger Philips has over fifteen years' experience in international business and teaches Chinese business at Concordia University Irvine. He is a winner of the President's "E" Award for Export Excellence, given by the US Dept. of Commerce, the highest recognition any US entity may receive for supporting export activity.

He is the author of *Guide to Software Export—A Handbook for International Software Sales*, published by the International Business Press.

Dr. Eugene Kim is Dean of Asia Programs at Concordia University Irvine. He holds a PhD in Education, and has lived and worked in Shanghai for the past six years.

Notes

1 IMF (2014)
2 Ibid.
3 DeCarlo, Scott in *Fortune* (February 1, 2015)
4 *Trading Economics* (2015)
5 World Bank (2015)
6 CIA *World Factbook* (2015)
7 Ibid.
8 National Bureau of Statistics of China (2015)
9 Xinhua (March 3, 2014)
10 FT.com (February 10, 2014)
11 Presentation at "China's Economy in Trouble" seminar, UCLA Anderson Alumni Network, Newport Beach CA (September 25, 2015)
12 Lardy, Nicholas in *Markets over Mao: The Rise of Private Business in China*, the Peterson Institute for International Economics (2014)
13 Gavekal Dragonomics (2014)
14 KPMG (2015)
15 IMF (2013)
16 *8th Annual BSA and IDC Global Software Piracy Study*—Business Software Alliance (2011)
17 August 28, 2015, *New York Times*
18 August 28, 2015, *New York Times*
19 Ibid.

Bibliography

Business Software Alliance (2011). *8th Annual BSA and IDC Global Software Piracy Study.*

Chao, (2012). Selling to China. :iUniverse.

CIA World Factbook (2015). https://www.cia.gov/library/publications/the-world-factbook/

DeCarlo, S. (2015, February 1). *Fortune.*

Fernandez, J. & Liu, S. (2000). *China CEO—A Case Guide for Business Leaders.* Singapore: Wiley

Fernandez, J. & Underwood, L. (2007). *China CEO—Voices of Experience.* Singapore: Wiley.

FT.com (2014, February 10). www.ft.com/home/us

Gavekal Dragonomics (2014). http://research.gavekal.com/content.php/6022

Gupta, A. & Wang, H. (2009). *Getting China and India Right.* San Francisco CA: Jossey-Bass.

Gupta, A., Pande, G. & Wang, H. (2014). *The Silk Road Rediscovered.* San Francisco CA: Jossey-Bass

IMF (2013, 2014). www.imf.org/external/index.htm

Inch, J. (2012). *China's Economic Supertrends.* Victoria BC: InChina Publishing

KPMG (2015).

Lardy, N. (2014). *Markets over Mao:The rise of private business in China.* Peterson Institute for International Economics.

McGregor, J. (2005). *One Billion Customers.* New York: Wall St. Journal Books

National Bureau of Statistics of China (2015). www.stats.gov.cn/english/

Shenkar, O. (2006). *The Chinese Century.* Wharton School Publishing

Trading Economics (2015). www.tradingeconomics.com/china/indicators

World Bank (2015). www.worldbank.org/

Xinhua (2014, March 3). www.xinhuanet.com/english/

Yourman, M. (2015, Sept 25). Presentation at "China's Economy in Trouble" seminar, UCLA Anderson Alumni Network, Newport Beach.

1

THE "NEW NORMAL"

Introduction

Maintaining its position as the largest single-nation contributor to global economic growth, China receives an excessive and undue degree of criticism from its partners, competitors, and even its own citizens. In 2013, China became the world's largest trading nation, with a trade surplus of over $230 billion. The following year, according to the International Monetary Fund (IMF), China surpassed the US as the world's most powerful economy, producing over $17.6 trillion in goods and services. The stellar growth of the Chinese economy over the past few decades, since Deng Xiao Ping ushered in a new economic order in China, is unprecedented in scale and speed. And yet the pundits still ask, "What have you done for me lately?"

When we speak of the "new normal" for China, we are asking an impossible question. Normalcy has defied definition in modern China since the first "free market experiment" or Special Economic Zone in Shenzhen, which transformed a small fishing village into a metropolitan, hyper-urban hub for business, culture, technology, and education—a region that was known as the factory of the world, and is now home to the top domestic and international companies of the world. Based on this model, the free economic zone was extended to all of China, and this policy shift opened the door to spectacular growth across the nation, lifting its population out of poverty into modernity. Each year seemed to outpace the prior, and change was not a contest, rather an assumption.

Nonetheless, economic growth at double digits cannot be sustainable indefinitely, and corrections and market adjustments are inevitable. According to *NewsChina*'s editors[1], China's leadership must disassociate its political legitimacy from quantified objectives, open up space for market forces to act on the economy, establish trust across its international relationships, and redefine fundamental structural assumptions that are no longer applicable in the "new normal".

Disassociation and Recalibration

It has been argued that a steep decline in China's GDP growth rate, even if it has maintained growth year-on-year, could potentially destabilize the country. Citizenry are often willing to accept, or at best overlook, their governments' practices and politics as long as personal prosperity is assured and their future prospects remain optimistic. As Marx and Engels put it, society is governed by class conflict—this assumes the primacy of socio-economic interest as a primary motivator for human impetus. Everyone is patriotic when their portfolios are growing, their grass is greener, and their families are well fed. China's particular challenge is not that of growth, but sufficient growth. Analysts have long imposed a minimum of 8 percent annual growth in China's economy as a requisite for political stability. Currently, GDP growth is at around 7 percent[2], and there are no mass demonstrations or calls for regime change, so these predictions were certainly off base. In addition, as a benchmark, in 2014 and 2015, the GDP annual growth rate for the US averaged around 2.5 percent.

Cheng Siwei, senior economist and former vice-chairman of China's legislature, offers potential strategies for continued growth such as urbanization, land reform, rule of law, environmental protection, mediated investment, and limited regulatory policies towards real estate[3]. He does peg the next GDP growth rate expectation at 7–8 percent, but later indicates that "economic growth of 6 to 7 percent is enough." This is entirely consistent with Cheng's fundamental view that China's economy is in flux and hard targets are not simply unfair, they are unhelpful.

The features of the *new normal* were outlined at China's annual economic conference on December 9–11, 2014. These included consumerism, innovation, urbanization, differentiation, environmental protection, diffuse bubbles, and continued controls[4]. Additionally, clarifications regarding the applications of these normalizations are likely to be determined by near future realities of the market economy. Premier Li Keqiang provided both honest admissions of persistent challenges to economic growth as well as potential solutions to those challenges at the World Economic Forum in September, 2015. Explanations for China's stock market volatility and its sharp reversal of currency valuation—the RMB's greatest loss of value in recent history— provided by Li were appreciated and timely[5]. However, economists and international leaders still remain to be convinced of the story of China's "new normal".

Market Forces

China's Special Economic Zones of the 1980s have been replaced with Free Trade Zones (FTZs), with the first experiment launched in 2013 in Pudong New District, Shanghai[6]. These FTZs allow for a greater range of economic liberalization, including foreign currency exchange, customs and taxes, and incorporation by foreign corporations. With thousands of companies registered in the initial FTZ in Shanghai and additional zones opened up in Pudong, cities across China have clamored for the right to open up their own FTZs, following the historical precedent of the Special Economic Zones that opened China to global market forces. If the same goes for the FTZs, then China may experience significant leaps in economic liberalization in the near future.

In He, Meng, and Zhang's article on the "New Fiscal Faces" of China, we are introduced to a new buzzword coined in 2014 by Chinese economists to describe the "new normal"'s interventionism of China's central government: *micro-stimulus*[7]. Inherent to this new term is a diminishing of government control, systematic investment, and top-down oversight, replaced by a more reflexive, less invasive approach to tinkering with the economic machine. There is accordingly a corresponding rise in the influence from international markets, where interest rates, pricing and capital flow are liberalized. Despite the success story of China's real estate boom over the past three decades, economist Cheng Siwei argues that government investment and real estate interventions need to be moderated, allowing the market and individual choice to govern trends in housing prices. In the worst case scenario, the property market and the banking sector are at serious risk of catastrophic failure, with pessimists comparing this impending economic catastrophe to the 2008 stock market crash in the US. Micro-stimulus, therefore, aims to work alongside market forces, gently nudging the train of progress back on its high-speed tracks, tolerating temporary slowdowns and recognizing that gradual and tempered growth is the new expectation.

International Trust

Transparency and rule of law go hand-in-hand in establishing both domestic consumer confidence and foreign investment. With China's entry into the World Trade Organization (WTO), commitments were made to the international community to establish and safeguard both. Regulatory transparency—access to information on government policy making and participation/input from constituents—is cited as among the top concerns for businesses operating in and with China[8].

From traffic rules to copyright regulations, in China, the enforcement of laws is burdened by historicity and expedience. A 2,500-year-old Confucian tradition of memorization and replication of superior exemplars has frustrated teachers and entrepreneurs alike. Traffic rules are not laws, according to a recent college graduate in Shanghai. A senior partner at a Shanghai-based venture capital firm relates that trademark and copyright infringement is not the problem of young companies trying to overcome diverse barriers to entry; it is the failure of established corporate entities that make it all too easy for their products to be copied and rebranded. Based in Beijing, Xindongfang [New Oriental] is one of the world's largest educational companies and listed on the NY Stock Exchange since 2006. It also gained world-wide publicity from its practice of hiring agents to take and memorize sections of recent Graduate Record Examinations (GREs)—and then passing those same questions on to young Chinese customers, many who went on to earn perfect scores[9,10]. To gain the trust of corporations and consumers around the world, China's companies must sacrifice pragmatics for the cost of building intellectual capacity and a record of integrity.

The threat of debt repudiation has not yet materialized in China, though there are indications that underlying deficits are soon to surface. According to Davis and McMahon[11], debt and guarantees of local governments jumped 67 percent to approximately $3 trillion from 2010 when the figure was closer to $1.7 trillion. Cracks in the walls, seen visibly on China's quickly built, cheaply constructed buildings, are signs of structural weakness and damage. Cheng Siwei claims that "borrowing money to pay old debt is dangerous," like plaster and paint to cover up potential fissures and gaps[12]. Transparency has improved, yet Chinese lenders continue to surreptitiously "sell loans to Chinese trust companies, promising to repurchase the loans any time"[13]. As the public debt of local economies is buried in bureaucracy and as banks camouflage bad debt, these faulty loans will eventually become a burden to the central government[14]. Transparency does not eliminate bad loans, but it forces accountability on those who are participants in that gamble—it appears that the Chinese central government is poised to pursue this strategy to ensure steady and consistent economic growth.

Structural Assumptions

Internally, China attributes some of China's slowdown to factors outside of its control (e.g., international markets) and containment of risk, and consequently growth appears to be a part of China's "new normal". Le Keqiang, China's Premier, confirms that China is "operating in an increasingly unpredictable global environment, but with an improving domestic economy that is stable enough to face external challenges,"[15] expressing confidence that regardless of the environmental conditions, China's economic health remains optimistic. In the same article, Le Keqiang is cited as describing the shift from manufacturing to service industries as central to China's current strategy which will be detailed in its 13th FYP.

Steven Barnett, IMF division chief, describes China's "new normal" as slower but safer, a growth path that is sustainable compared with prior trends[16]. Though economist Paul Krugman, as an external observer, may describe China as a country about to "hit its Great Wall," insiders such as Tsinghua University Professor Hu Angang affirm the "new normal" of "Slower but steadier" growth[17]. Hu cites recent structural changes implemented by the government that have led to 50 million new jobs in China's cities, the increase of service sector contribution to GDP to over 48 percent, and 25 percent increase in GDP allocation to research and development in the years 2010–2014. The prediction is for long-term, sustainable growth through government investment and intervention, albeit of the micro-stimulus variety.

Personality-driven reform, which was ubiquitous in China's past, has the risk of insolvency because of regular rotations of leadership at the city, county, and provincial levels[18]. This system prevents fiefdoms and corruption, but it has resulted in expensive defaults when political leaders who have initiated a portfolio of well-meaning projects move on to other pastures and leave those investments fallow. As we consider the *new normal*, political change is generally off the table; however, adjustments in how politics are played out in China is ever-evolving, a communist ideology engaging in capitalist practices with Chinese characteristics.

ARTICLES

The New Normal

What is the "New Normal"?

There are calls for a "new normal" according to the editors of *NewsChina*, as GDP growth slows to its lowest rate in decades. In fact, the article points out three periods since the establishment of the People's Republic of China: first three decades of economic instability; the following three decades of rapid economic expansion. If each period is consistently three decades in length, then the next 30 years are expected to be challenging ones as the government is confronted with social issues that have arisen out of the previous period's preoccupation with wealth and prosperity.

The article calls for a readjustment of expectation towards annual economic growth; limit the powers of government and liberalize towards a free market system; establish positive relationships with foreign countries; and tackle the problems associated with urbanization and population growth.

China's "New Normal" will be a Long-term Phenomenon

December 2014 Issue of NewsChina | *by* NewsChina Magazine

This period will pose both opportunities and challenges for China and its leadership, as the central authorities are compelled to focus on getting China back on the track of healthy development.

In the past couple of years, China's central leadership has frequently stressed that the country must adapt to a *"new normal"* in terms of the pace of economic expansion, as GDP growth has dropped below 8 percent. As the government shifts its priorities towards legal reforms amid further slowdown, any so-called *"new normal"* will likely be for the long haul.

The 65 years that have passed since the establishment of People's Republic of China in 1949 can be largely divided into two periods. While the first three decades were dominated by devastating political turmoil and economic instability, the latter three have been characterized by rapid economic expansion. It appears that China's *"new normal"* marks a third phase in the short history of the PRC, a period in which China has to tackle a series of looming social crises that many see as systemic in nature, a direct result of a preoccupation with GDP growth ahead of social and civil development.

This period will pose both opportunities and challenges for China and its leadership, as the central authorities are compelled to focus on getting China back on a track of healthy development.

First, and most obviously, the government must adjust its basic attitude towards economic growth. For a long period of time it has been argued that China "must maintain" a growth rate above 8 percent to avoid political instability. Such an approach only serves to exacerbate social problems stemming from economic injustice. It is now a consensus that China must shift priorities from economic growth to social development, a major task for the immediate future.

Second, the leadership must limit its power within the framework of the law, and draw clear boundaries between the government and the market to establish a modern system of governance. The current lack of a free market operating according to the rule of law is the fundamental cause of a variety of social problems.

Thirdly, the leadership must carefully handle its relationships with foreign countries. In recent decades, China's economy has leaned heavily on the global market, with its dependence rate in external markets reaching more than 60 percent. Simultaneously, China's increasing economic, political and military power has exacerbated tensions and confrontations with other countries in the region, which poses a serious threat to future development. The government must seek to establish an effective model for dialog and cooperation with other nations.

Finally, in re-balancing and restructuring the economy, the government needs to address some innate conflicts embedded within the economy itself. For example, as urbanization accelerates, the government should terminate its black-or-white approach to defining urban and rural society, which in practice has uniformly meant benefiting urban residents at the expense of their rural counterparts.

There is no doubt that these problems can only be solved over an extended period. As legal reforms have gained momentum with the recently held Fourth Plenum, the leadership must now demonstrate the political will to push forward relevant reforms to some ambitious goals.

How to Achieve Reform?

Cheng Siwei, senior economist and former vice-chairman of China's legislature, discusses the "new normal" of China and poses both warnings and solutions to the risks inherent to this period. He encourages local governments to take responsibility for their financial health and avoid debt repudiation. Absence of the rule of law is cited as the source of economic waste and lack of innovation. The balance between government and markets, between equity and efficiency, between local and central politics must be appropriately "straightened out." While government investment should be moderated (no more than double the growth rate of GDP), innovation driven by education and training in new industries will be vital to employment and economic growth.

China's stages of economic development are described in 10-year cycles, starting with the Cultural Revolution. Starting in 2013, the present and fourth cycle is described as one of quality and stability of growth. The third cycle, from 2003 to 2012, was marked by rapid economic growth but significant harm to the environment. The current cycle is expected to correct those imbalances and eventually result in higher economic growth—over 8 percent by 2019. To sustain this growth, Cheng proposes urbanization, where rural workers can raise their production rate from $500 to $10,000 per year. Rural collective land should be traded so that their valuations can appreciate. Under-consumption is considered unavoidable, with a weak social security system resulting in public frugality and a Consumer Price Index (CPI) that does not keep pace with their incomes. In addition, the over-inflation of real estate prices prompts less spending and more savings. Cheng suggests government incentives for first-time property buyers, with reductions in down payments and interest rates. He predicts that with urbanization, the real estate boom will be sustained for another 20 years.

Figure 1.1 Cheng Siwei

Reform is so Difficult that its Dividends can only be Attained through Rule of Law

July 2014 Issue of NewsChina | *by Xi Zhigang*

One of China's most respected economists believes that China's future economy must place emphasis on quality and steady growth.

The Chinese economy, the world's second largest, has maintained an average growth rate of nearly 10 percent during the past three decades, but now, the country is witnessing a slowdown throughout its economic structure. In 2014 and beyond, the economy is expected to see a slightly reduced growth rate of 7.5 percent. In the future, how to maximize the dividends of reform, avoid the negative effects of over-investment and cool the real estate market will be issues of growing concern for policy-makers.

Cheng Siwei, senior economist and former vice-chairman of the Standing Committee of the National People's Congress (NPC), China's legislature, shares his views with *NewsChina* on the problems and risks that the Chinese economy may face.

NewsChina: You have recently mentioned that the Chinese economy faces three risks—environmental pollution, local government debt, and overreliance on GDP growth. How do these affect the economy?

Cheng Siwei: There is not much to say about environmental pollution, because economic growth is pointless if public health is under threat. As for local government debt, some have said that as long as it is under control, there is no need to worry. Personally speaking, however, I see it as a serious problem. It was previously reported that the combined public debt of local governments had hit 10.7 trillion yuan (US$1.7tn), but in a recent survey the figure was found to be 20 trillion yuan (US$3.2tn). To make matters worse, it is still growing. If one third of local governments cannot pay the debt, and still more are able but reluctant to do so, the financial risk will grow.

If so, some local government debt will become bad loans for banks—a burden for the central government. I think the central government should not pay the bill, since this would fuel massive defaults. The bad loans will be covered by the gap between loan and deposit interest rate, which will eventually be passed onto the public and enterprises. Obviously, that is unreasonable. Without these bad loans, the deposit interest rate can be raised and loan interest rates can be lowered, which is good for liquidity.

There has not yet been an outburst of debt repudiation, but it is still worth noting that borrowing money to pay old debt is dangerous. In that case, money never plays a role in economic growth. It is a payment delay, and eventually the mess will be shifted to the next government.

More wisdom and different approaches are required to cope with local government debt. Issuing bonds can be encouraged after receiving due credit ratings. Besides, local governments can work out their own ways to raise economic efficiency and production rates to dispose of debt. It is not the responsibility of the central government and banks.

NewsChina: You have said that institutional innovation is the source of reform dividends. What do you mean by that?

Cheng Siwei: In March 2013, I wrote a book with economists Wu Jinglian, Li Yi'ning and Justin Yifu Lin. I wrote the first chapter, titled "Institutional Innovation is the Source of Reform Dividends," wherein I propose points on four key relationships: between the rule of law and the rule of the people; between equity and efficiency; between government and market, and between concentration and decentralization of authority.

Nowadays, a lot of economic waste comes from the absence of rule of law. For example, well-planned projects are liable to be canceled due to the rotation of leadership. I know a city where the leader planned to develop its east side after receiving foreign investment. But later, when he was transferred to another post, the new leader chose to develop the west side—a huge waste of resources.

The lack of rule of law is likely to result in an unhealthy and unstable economic growth. Nowadays, all reform is likely to meet a modicum of opposition, and reform is so difficult that its dividends can only be attained through rule of law.

As for the relation between equity and efficiency, I think that without efficiency, equity is on the low level. On the contrary, without equity, efficiency is unreliable. I do not need to say much about the relation between the government and the market. It is a problem for the concentration and deconcentration of authority. If local governments neglect the central government, it will result in a state in which all sorts of creative ways are proposed to circumvent directives. If the central government fails to take into account the actual conditions of local governments and puts forth one-size-fits-all policies, it will not work either. The above-mentioned factors all make a difference. As a result, reform can only be pushed forward if institutional reform and these four relationships are straightened out.

NewsChina: China's economic cycles are a hot topic. How do you see them?

Cheng Siwei: Generally speaking, China has experienced an economic cycle every 10 years since the end of the Cultural Revolution (1966–76). The first was from 1984 to 1992. The second was from 1993 to 2002. The third was from 2003 to 2012—a period of rapid economic growth with an average growth rate of 10 percent. Now it enters a fourth cycle—the decade following 2013. During this period, the Chinese economy will place its emphasis on the quality and stability of growth.

During the third cycle, inflation climbed to 5.4 percent. Meanwhile, environmental pollution began to take a heavy toll. That does not happen overnight. China's smog dates back to the third economic cycle. We have calculated that the economic loss resulting from low efficiency and environmental pollution was equal to 13.5 percent of GDP in 2005. In 2010, the figure hit 12.3 percent, surpassing China's GDP growth rate.

Now, we have to put priority on environmental protection, and push forward with green GDP growth. During this period, a growth rate of 7 to 8 percent is expected. Premier Li Keqiang has said to keep economic growth above the "lower limit" and inflation below the "upper limit." I think the lower limit is 7 percent and the upper limit is 4 percent. Thus, the economy is currently operating within a reasonable range.

However, economic cycles are in flux. Economic growth is expected to exceed 8 percent in 2019 through structural adjustments. Because China has a large economic aggregate, when the next economic cycle arrives, economic growth of 6 to 7 percent is enough. There is nothing to fear. Take the US for example: its 3 percent growth is equal to China's growth of 6 to 7 percent because of its large economic aggregate.

NewsChina: How can China sustain a growth rate of 7 to 8 percent?

Cheng Siwei: Simply put, the first move is urbanization. The second is the new round of land reform, and the third is innovation. China is urbanizing at a rate of 1 percent every year, and this has huge potential to grow. Actually, rural people's production rate is very low—on average each farmer has an output value of US$300 to 500 annually. But if a farmer works in an urban area, his or her output value can exceed US$10,000, creating more social wealth. The creation of social wealth boosts economic growth on the condition that farmers can land a job in urban areas.

The collectively-owned construction land in rural areas can be traded on the market like State-owned land. This will cause an appreciation of value, and the benefits will be divided between the country and individuals. The possibility of the transference of contracting rights to rural land and the use ownership of rural housing land have also boosted the incomes of rural people working in cities. These reforms will benefit farmers, and consumption can only be driven by rising incomes.

Innovation is the most important. Its core lies in the acceleration of productivity. Investment can boost employment and GDP growth, but it cannot raise productivity. To raise per-capita productivity, technology advancement, vocational education, labor training and scientific management have proven to be essential.

NewsChina: How do you see investment-driven economic growth?

Cheng Siwei: Investment is necessary and it is a crucial factor in driving economic growth, but excessive investment will bring forth several problems. First, some flimsy projects are likely to emerge. Other projects may generate low revenue after completion. Some others, however, depend on financial subsidies—subways are a typical case.

Second, GDP growth is mostly easily driven by investment, and local governments rely heavily on it. The investment rush covers up the problem of low production efficiency. Investment, within a reasonable range, can play a better role, through innovation and raising of productivity.

NewsChina: What is that reasonable range?

Cheng Siwei: The growth rate of investment should never double the growth rate of GDP. It is hard to control. If this happens, it is excessive investment. Some economists may have a different view, though.

NewsChina: How would you see China's investment fields?

Cheng Siwei: The productivity and efficiency of traditional industries must be enhanced through information technology. As for the traditional industries, expanding production should not be encouraged, because they are already over capacity. Great efforts should be made in new industries that have a growth cycle, requiring continuous financial input.

NewsChina: Fueling domestic demand has been discussed for many years, but the public are still cautious about spending money. What's behind that?

Cheng Siwei: As early as 2006, the goal of synchronic growth of the economy and incomes was put forth. To put it differently, the public's slice of the pie should get bigger. Besides, residents' incomes should be linked to CPI, and with a raise in productivity, workers' incomes should grow accordingly.

Raising incomes relies on improving productivity. The per-capita industrial added value in China accounts for only one fifth that of Germany, and one eighth of the US. Raising purchasing power is unrealistic if productivity remains the same.

The public hold their purse strings tight because of a weak social security system. The rising cost of education and house prices are to blame. Social security includes unemployment insurance, senior care and medical insurance. At the current low level of social security, under-consumption is unavoidable.

NewsChina: During this year's CPPCC and NPC [China's two annual high-level government conferences], the government did not unveil regulatory policies on the real estate market as was anticipated. Why?

Cheng Siwei: The real estate market includes commercial property and commercial residential housing. Housing is a basic requirement for livelihood, and it is not only an economic issue, but a political and social one. The government's responsibility is to ensure that the public have shelter, rather than to push forward the idea of home ownership for all. Home ownership for all is a misguided concept, and no country can ensure that. In the US, 70 percent of residents had their own housing before the sub-prime crisis—the figure has dropped to 60 to 65 percent nowadays. In Germany, it is around 50 percent. In China, it is over 80 percent.

The government's responsibility is to provide public rental housing for those who cannot afford commercial apartments. If rent is more than one third of salary, the government should offer subsidies. If incomes grow and exceed this line, the government should not help

For those who want to buy their first apartments, the government ought to incentivize banks to grant loans on favorable terms including down payment cuts, preferential interest rates, and incremental pay. Incremental pay is very important because along with an income raise, equal pay will prove a heavier burden for mortgage debtors. One third of salary is the optimum scale.

As for commercial housing, the market, rather than government interference, should play the key role. Actually, rounds of policies have been made trying to rein in real estate prices, but all to no avail. Commercial housing prices have been growing year-on-year because of high demand, and a growing number of people want to improve their living conditions. China's real estate boom will last at least 20 years, because every year 10 million more rural people flock to cities, and seven million college graduates join the workforce.

As a result, real estate will remain a pillar industry, sustaining the growth of more than 60 other industries including building materials, household appliances and even house-moving services. Like the stock market, the real estate market has price fluctuations but the main trend is ascending. I advise those who need and can afford an apartment to take quick action.

Micro-Stimulus

The "new normal" is described as a change of engine, not merely a change of gear. While command states like China have traditionally wielded significant power and resources to control the direction of their version of the market economy, micro-stimulus is recommended as the approach befitting the "new normal" of China. This would remedy the gross inefficiencies inherent in massive government investment and regulation. A moderation of GDP growth, shifts towards the service sector, stimulation of consumption, and energizing innovation are fundamental to the "new normal." The interpretation of micro-stimulus will determine the success of this impending transition, one which the government hopes will be gradual.

The biggest threat is capital pricing, a distortion of market realities, and a favoring of public vendors over private competitors that are often more effective and efficient. Though short-term risks are cited as barriers to open currency trading and interest rate flexibility, these are key opportunities to liberalization and long-term stability for China. In fact, the article implies that both the internationalization of the RMB and domestic financial restructuring must be advanced together.

New Fiscal Faces

March 2015 Issue of NewsChina | *by He Jun, Meng Shan,*
Zhang Yu

China's economy will not relive the breakneck narrative of the last three decades. It will likely undergo not just a change of gear, but a change of engine. The uncertainty lies in the tempo of these coming changes.

Any predictions concerning China's economic situation and policy in 2015 have to be rooted in understanding of the country's brand new concepts of "the *new normal*" and "micro-stimulus," buzzwords coined in 2014 by both the government's economic planners and international analysts.

In essence, the *"new normal"* refers to a process of economic restructuring. "Micro-stimulus" ensures that this process, which is not without hardship, is neither too volatile nor painful for the national economy to withstand. Instead, this new brand of stimulus, unlike previous tools wielded by China's economic planners, does not seek to remedy outbreaks of boom and bust inherent in any economy.

With its strong grip on economic operations, the Chinese government has huge impact on the path of growth and the performance of the market in both the medium and short term. Therefore, China's economic prospects in 2015 will depend upon how the government will shape the *new normal* and utilize its available micro-stimulus.

The trajectory of both the *new normal* and micro-stimulus is defined by reforms designed to give the market, now generally viewed as the best determining channel, a decisive role in efficiently directing basic production materials to where they are most needed. Currently, the misallocation of financial resources in China's economy is probably more serious and extensive than the misuse of other resources. Nowhere is this problem more apparent than in the present growth model, which is rooted in systematic inefficient investment. Now, the Chinese government is trying to replace this with its vision for a new economic model.

Meanwhile, the international market will increasingly affect the value of the Chinese yuan, as China consolidates her dual role as the world's leading trader and investor. Financial reform to liberalize pricing and capital flow, both within China and across her borders, will continue to be high on the government's agenda in 2015.

The most difficult and most controversial question, therefore, is how to set the right tempo for all these intertwined changes.

BITTER AND SWEET

There is an essential consensus on what China's new economic normal should look like. The term "new normal" itself, first deployed by Chinese

President Xi Jinping in May 2014, is thought to describe the moderation of GDP growth blended with a shift towards a growth powered by an invigorated service sector, more brisk rates of consumption and greater innovation. The country's current growth is thought to be unsustainable and inefficient, as it has been fueled by lavish investment of cheap labor and capital into the country's assembly lines, rather than the efficient allocation of resources to a diverse range of sectors.

Analysts are divided on whether or not the coming transition will be a long, bumpy journey. The gloomy picture painted by pessimists shows China's economy already on the brink of collapse, with both the property market and banking sector at serious risk of replicating the 2008 US subprime crisis and the "Lehman Brothers moment" that engulfed first the US and then the world economy. A rosier future anticipated by optimists entails a swift transition towards a better economic structure. Stimulus policies during the transition will give buoyancy to the national property and stock markets.

Indeed, which scenario is the more likely largely depends on the interpretation of the term "micro-stimulus." It is one of several buzzwords coined by financial institutions or analysts in their interpretation of China's economic policy, words which rarely feature in official documents.

The Financial Times was the first to use the term "micro-stimulus" in reference to the State Council's decision to issue tax rebates and increase investment in the national rail network in July 2013 in a bid to boost growth. This was a correction of the "no stimulus" policy, previously regarded by the international investment bank Barclays Capital as one of the three pillars of Premier Li Keqiang's so-called "Likonomics," the others being deleveraging and structural reform. By stressing the restrained application of pro-growth measures, the concept of micro-stimulus also distinguishes the attempts to boost growth from the "strong stimulus" measures first described by analysts in 2009.

In retrospect, previous cases of government intervention in crucial periods of economic uncertainty have provided important lessons. Some of these interventions began bitterly but had happy outcomes, such as the reform of State-owned Enterprises (SOEs) conducted in 1998. In other examples, the reverse was true, notably the government's 2009 stimulus package. As a consequence, it is clear that the results of reform vary greatly, depending on whether policies tread the right path and are implemented with the right tempo.

The timing and magnitude of micro-stimulus issued in 2014 is evidence of the government's aim to secure a growth rate steady enough not to disturb its *"new normal,"* rather than placing growth back on its former high speed track. It is therefore unlikely that a robust rebound in the growth rate will be seen in 2015. At the same time, it is likely that hardship resulting from a slowdown will be tolerated in a measured way, and that the transition towards a new economic structure will be more gradual than expected.

It is safe to assume that, in 2015, the government will choose to sacrifice short-term comfort for a better future, rather than deploying sweeping stimulus measures for the sake of immediate relief, barring a sudden and major crisis in international or domestic markets. If reform is effective enough to achieve significant progress in economic restructuring, a steady growth rate comparable to the years immediately after 1998 can be maintained.

FLEXIBILITY AND FLOW

Distorted capital pricing is probably the biggest threat to China's market dynamics. Cheap money has been wasted on overcapacity in government-backed projects or government-backed, loss-making "zombie" enterprises, leaving too little access, with too high a price tag, for the more efficient private sector. In addition, with China consolidating her position in the world financial order, reform and opening up of the yuan on the international market will have to be accelerated. Given the possibility of domestic resistance due to concern about the potential risks of a more open Chinese currency, the gap between market expectations and quantifiable breakthroughs may not be significantly narrowed in key areas of financial reform.

In terms of interest rates, the pricing of money on the domestic market, after several years of gradual progress, resulted in mandatory floors for lending rates finally being removed in 2014, leaving only ceilings for deposit rates intact. These ceilings provide cheap deposits for banks, thus guaranteeing their profits even if they lean heavily on lending at very low rates to government-backed projects and enterprises.

On November 30, 2014, a government draft of deposit insurance regulations was opened to public perusal and feedback. Once this system is deployed, there are no technical barriers remaining for the final liberalization of China's interest rate system. Whether or not this can be achieved in 2015 depends on political will, which has to be strong enough to preserve government awareness of the urgency of financial reform, and allow officials to stand their ground in the face of defiance from state-owned banks.

China's status as the world's top trader and investor means that the yuan is increasingly integrated into the international market, for better or worse. Theoretically, a more market-oriented interest rate system will also help avoid drastic cross-border capital flows triggered by more market-oriented future fluctuations in the yuan exchange rate. After 10 years of reforms that have introduced more flexibility into the forex rate system, the yuan has ceased to unilaterally appreciate in value. Instead, China's currency is now typically traded either at a discount or a premium against the parity rate set by China's central bank. Fluctuations have become more frequent, but have also remained within reasonable bands. The pace of China's forex reform has thus been revealed to be basically reasonable, and should be maintained as is.

Division among analysts on pace and path of the internationalization of the yuan, mainly involving the free flow of the capital, however, has made it the most controversial aspect of China's fiscal reform. Advocates of speeding up argue that China has deeply integrated into the global economy to the point that making the yuan an international currency is both an economic and political objective requiring a forceful push.

Opponents, however, have warned that so long as domestic financial reforms, including those of interest rates and the capital market, are yet to be completed, allowing the fully free inflow and outflow of capital, as required by the internationalization of the yuan, could bring a short-term capital flood into China, precipitating property and stock bubbles, or a drastic appreciation in value of the yuan that would hurt Chinese exporters.

Excessive concern about the aforementioned risks has slowed down the opening of the capital account. Anbound Consulting sees progress on the internationalization of the yuan as disproportionately small in relation to China's position as the world's third largest trader (after the EU and the US), and the world's third largest investor. In addition, foreign investment in China's yuan-denominated assets will help underwrite their value. China's local government infrastructure bonds, which will generate or augment future cash flow, for example, might be preferable to foreign investors over unproductive US and European government bonds used to cover government bills. Capital account controls have so far hindered foreign access to China's bond markets.

Speeding up the opening of the capital accounts market would not put the stability of the value of the yuan at risk. Medium- and long-term prospects for steady, reasonable growth in China's economy provide the best guarantee of a general trend of appreciation of its currency. Moreover, there is no lack of successful international examples for China to learn from in putting its cross-border capital flows under proper scrutiny.

China's new strategy for overseas expansion is expected to not only highlight the importance of the internationalization of the yuan and the continued progress of necessary domestic financial reforms, but to accelerate both processes. In 2015, concrete steps will be taken on mega-projects initiated by China or with its joint leadership, including the Maritime Silk Road in Southeast Asia, the New Silk Road in Central Asia, the Asian Infrastructure Investment Bank and the BRICS Development Bank.

The participation of and cooperation between Chinese and foreign financial institutions will probably motivate China to move faster, and with bolder strides, towards its central goals of an internationalized currency and a reformed domestic financial structure.

China's new strategy for overseas expansion is expected to not only highlight the importance of the internationalization of the yuan and the continued progress of necessary domestic financial reforms, but to accelerate both processes

Zhang Yu and Meng Shan are researchers with the China Research Foundation for Economic Reform. He Yun is a senior researcher with Anbound Consulting.

"New Normal" Tasks and Features

The theme of China's annual economic conference, held from December 9 to 11, 2014, is "push the country's economy into a *'new normal'* state." Problems cited include over-reliance on the manufacturing sector, the real estate bubble, imbalanced financial sector, increasing income gap, and environmental issues. With the goal of a stable economy, China hopes to increase consumption, innovation, exports, the service sector, and green technologies. Meanwhile, it will burst bubbles, shift to quality and differentiation, decrease rural surplus labor, and reduce overcapacity.

China to Enter a *"New Normal* Economic State"

February 2015 Issue of NewsChina | *by Dai Min*

The Chinese government held its annual economic conference from December 9 to 11, mapping the country's economic development throughout 2015.

The theme of the conference was defined to "push the country's economy into a *'new normal* state,'" which, according to analysts, is characterized by developing new stimuli for economic growth.

Despite a continually high growth rate, China's economy has been increasingly impeded by overcapacity in the manufacturing industry, the housing market bubble, disproportionate leverage in the financial sector, the widening income gap, and critical levels of environmental pollution.

The so-called *"new normal"* thus aims to push the economy toward a more sustainable model of development with deeper reforms that analysts have said will focus on the faster adjustment of industrial structure, broader access for private investment, tightened supervision on monopolies, harsher controls on pollution, and more attention afforded to low-income groups.

Based on these targets, the Chinese government has emphasized its intention to "maintain stable economic growth" instead of "faster growth." Analysts have predicted that the 2015 GDP growth target might be lowered to around 7 percent.

"Lower growth does not mean economic recession. Instead, it will lead the government and the people to have a clearer and more rational attitude toward economic development," Zhang Zhanbin, economics director of the Chinese Academy of Governance, told Xinhua News Agency.

"[GDP] growth adjustment does not mean the government will make less or no effort toward economic development. The structural adjustment is actually harder and more fruitful [than pure GDP growth]," said Liu Shijin, deputy director of the Development Research Center of the State Council.

FIVE TASKS IN 2015

- maintain stable economic growth;
- develop new growth points;
- quicken the transformation of agricultural development;
- optimize the framework of economic development; and
- further improve quality of life.

FEATURES OF THE *NEW NORMAL*

- increase individualized and diversified consumer demands;
- increase investment in new and creative technologies;
- import of higher-quality and high-tech products, while increasing exports;
- further promote emerging industries, service sectors and small enterprises;
- decrease rural surplus labor and raise quality of human resources;
- shift the focus of market competition to quality and differentiation;
- promote a "green," low-emissions model;
- further de-leverage and "burst" bubbles; and
- control overcapacity and guide industries with the market.

Economic Reform Scorecard

The issue of regulatory transparency, while not the most salient, has for most years remained in the top 10 concerns of US businesses operating in China. The US–China Business Council (USCBC) tracks responses of its member businesses operating in China. This study specifically tracks NPC economic and trade-related laws and policies, and determined a marked decrease between 2013 and 2014 in those that were posted for the legally mandated 30-day period for public comment. Meanwhile, the State Council's record improved by over 50 percentage points. Other ministries, commissions, and administrations had varying degrees of transparency as reported by the study, with the State Administration of Industry and Commerce (SAIC) posting a higher percentage of their broad (28.6 percent) and narrow (61.5 percent) regulatory documents for public comment.

Recent developments revealed progress in a few key areas including comment periods of 60 days for medical devices and pharmaceutical access, public surveys on existing regulations, and expert research, review, and evaluation. Recommendations from the USCBC included a 30-day minimum comment period for all regulations, rules, and documents; clarification of exceptions to the State's transparency requirements; descriptions of the economic methodology and rationale behind policy decisions; centralized database of laws and regulations; and removal of ambiguous wording such as "and other relevant regulations" from policy documents.

USCBC China Economic Reform Scorecard

Impact Unchanged: Still Limited

September 2015

IMPACT OF ECONOMIC REFORM ON FOREIGN COMPANIES (AS OF AUGUST 15, 2015)

*No change since June 2015 report

EXECUTIVE SUMMARY

- The latest US-China Business Council (USCBC) assessment of China's economic reform efforts is unchanged since our June 2015 report, as the impact on the top concerns of US companies remains limited. New policies released since the last scorecard show a few positive signals—and some negative signals—in key areas such as national treatment for foreign companies, market openings, government intervention in markets, and technology and security concerns.

- While China's top-line reform message of "letting the market play a decisive role" is compelling, the slow speed of reform and inconsistent implementation by central-level ministries in key areas cause continued uncertainty about whether policy changes will meaningfully address market access and level playing field concerns of USCBC members.

- Between May and mid-August 2015, China released a number of policies that create narrow openings or operational improvements for companies. Such actions include policies to open areas of the oil and gas industry to private investors (including foreign joint ventures); measures to boost rule of law in environmental protection; openings for foreign central banks to invest in the interbank market using Ren Min Bi (RMB); and policies to promote pharmaceutical drug price reform. Such progress is reflected in data from USCBC's 2015 member company survey, where just over half of respondents indicated they have seen some benefit from economic reform.

- However, these piecemeal steps forward fail to address the systematic issues impacting American companies in China, and are offset by other moves that are more restrictive. For example, one reform area most commonly touted by the Chinese government—streamlining licensing and reducing red tape—77 percent of companies said they'd seen no progress. There have also been troubling trends that spur questions about China's commitment to trade and investment liberalization—the "openings" part of China reform and opening policy Provisions within the National Security Law and the draft Cybersecurity Law restricting cross-border data flows and requiring "secure and controllable" technology standards that effectively exclude foreign suppliers also raise new concerns on whether national security will be used for protectionist purposes.

- Other recent developments, such as old-style government intervention to check volatility in China's stock markets in July 2015 and the sudden devaluation of the RMB in mid-August 2015, have spurred active debate about whether these moves are in line with the speed and direction of reform—and how much they reflect or impact the real economy. These moves have less impact on the business environment than the headlines suggest, but do raise questions about the direction, scope, and pace of reform.

- Looking forward, the next two months provide several opportunities to assess reform prospects: President Xi Jinping will visit the United States in September and deliver a policy address at a USCBC event; a package of reforms is under debate at the highest levels in Beijing, and may come out before the Xi visit; and the Communist Party's annual major meeting will take place in October.

Since President Xi Jinping took office in early 2013, China's senior government officials and central-level agencies have spoken widely about economic reform. The November 2013 Chinese Communist Party (CCP) Third Plenum—the third full meeting of China's top party leadership during the 18th National Congress—was a turning point in the Xi government's early economic reform efforts. Post-plenum documents and official statements said the market should play a "decisive role" in allocating resources—a change from previous statements that the market should play a "basic role." Additionally, these same statements said that reforms should focus on improving the legal system, opening more areas to foreign and private investment, and changing how state-owned enterprises (SOE) are owned and operated.

While China's top-line reform message of "letting the market play a decisive role" remains compelling, more specific signals about reform have been mixed, and few concrete and significant policies have emerged to implement the broad areas laid out for reform. The slow speed of reform, along with inconsistent implementation by central-level ministries, continues to create uncertainty about when—and even whether—policy changes will address the market access and level playing field concerns of USCBC members.

USCBC tracks reform developments to address two major questions:

- What tangible progress have Chinese central government agencies made toward implementing economic reform?
- What impact will reforms have on US companies and their operations in China?

To answer these questions, USCBC has compiled a list of reform-related policies since the start of the Xi administration. The current assessment includes nearly 30 months of data from March 2013 through mid-August 2015. These policies are divided into themes, such as the role of the state and the market, foreign investment, and institutional reforms. Given the stated role of the China (Shanghai) Pilot Free Trade Zone (Shanghai FTZ) as the "test lab" for reforms nationwide, this report also analyzes specific Shanghai FTZ-related policy announcements. USCBC will continue to monitor policies developed for the Shanghai FTZ and the three subsequent free trade zones in Fujian, Guangzhou, and Tianjin.

USCBC's latest assessment of China's economic reform efforts still finds "limited" progress, with no improvement from our June 2015 scorecard. This latest assessment is based on a review of both new policies and a re-examination of previous policies to gauge their ongoing impact.

This report assesses the impact of China's reform efforts on foreign company operations by rating each policy on its direct and immediate impact on foreign company concerns.

- Each policy is assessed as having either a "significant impact" (green), "moderate impact" (yellow), "limited impact" (orange), or "no impact" (red) for foreign company operations in China.
- USCBC's overall assessment uses a three-color dashboard, rating China's reform efforts as either limited, moderate, or significant based on their direct impact on foreign companies.

USCBC ASSESSMENT: IMPACT STILL LIMITED

Between May and mid-August 2015, Chinese government agencies released a number of reform-related policies that address certain foreign company concerns, though in limited fashion. Yet despite such progress, there have also been a series of actions and policies that have raised concern about whether the market is being allowed to play an important role in the economy, as well as the impact of national security considerations in regulating the market. These mixed signals from the Chinese government are creating uncertainty among foreign business about China's reform efforts, while holding China back from achieving its economic and development goals.

Developments in the technology sector raise concerns about the use of "national security" for protectionist purposes. For example, provisions within the recently finalized National Security Law and the draft Cybersecurity Law that restrict cross-border data flows and require "secure and controllable" technology standards for key network infrastructure are concerning trends for China's commitment to opening its market to trade and investment.

Among the reform-related policies tracked during this period, several aim to increase market openings and improve company operations. For example, the People's Bank of China issued new rules to make it easier for international investors to access China's interbank bond market, which was a step toward opening its capital markets and making the RMB an international currency. The oil and gas industry has also seen moderate market-access openings for private capital (and foreign investors through joint ventures) in oil and gas exploration as well as crude oil processing. Both notices create some openings for private capital (including foreign capital) in heavily monopolized sectors.

Other recent developments, such as moves to check volatility in China's stock markets in July 2015 and the sudden devaluation of the RMB in mid-August 2015, have spurred active debate about whether these moves are in line with the speed and direction of reform—and how much these moves reflect or impact the real economy. For companies, these debates only raise questions about the direction, scope, and pace of reform.

The Chinese government also made some strides on legal reform, increasing environmental compliance measures on pollution and providing a legal basis for public monitoring of companies' environmental protection efforts. The tracking period also saw new policies allowing the market to play a more significant role in setting drug prices. Although implementation of the joint agency policy will determine its impact, the potential impact on the pharmaceutical industry as well as the overall health care sector is significant.

From a broad perspective, despite the number of reform policies released by Chinese government agencies since 2013 (more than 400 by USCBC's latest count), many are still not broad enough in scope or specific enough in implementing detail to address foreign company issues. Instead, many of these policies address minor operational issues or are limited to particular sectors. Others do not clearly apply to foreign companies.

Such progress is reflected in data from USCBC's 2015 member company survey, where roughly one-half of respondents indicated they have seen some benefit from economic reform. However, it remains unclear whether this benefit addresses companies' core issues or even areas most commonly touted by the Chinese government: 77 percent of companies, for example, said they'd seen no progress from China's efforts to streamline licensing and reduce red tape.

Senior government officials have stated that China's overall economic reform plans will be implemented through 2020. The Shanghai FTZ was launched in 2013 with a three-year timeframe before its reforms would be implemented nationwide, though some of these policies have already been extended to other designated districts in Shanghai. Reform policies still have the potential to address foreign company issues before the above deadlines are reached, even if the practical progress so far has been scant.

Furthermore, other central government actions call into question China's commitment to market reforms. USCBC encourages Chinese officials to take further steps to issue economic reforms that will benefit the Chinese economy by creating more openings for both foreign and domestic companies. Key steps include establishing concrete policies that liberalize investment, boost the role of the market in the economy, create a level playing field for foreign and domestic firms, and promote further legal reform.

For appendices, see www.uschina.org/sites/default/files/USCBC%20China %20Economic%20Reform%20Scorecard%20Sep%202015%20Final.pdf

FOR FURTHER STUDY

Response Questions

- What is the "new normal?"
- What are China's economic cycles? What stage are they entering into now?
- What is micro-stimulus? How is it different from stimulus?
- How does China's GDP growth in 2015 compare to those of other major countries?
- What are the five tasks in 2015 for China's economy? Explain each one.
- What is Likonomics? Give examples of his three pillars of reform.
- Why is direct government intervention and investment a threat to the "new normal"?
- What are the major barriers to the economic health of China?
- What strategies must the Chinese government implement to ensure a healthy "new normal"?
- Which government agency had the lowest measure of regulatory transparency?

Discussion Questions

- Why does China choose to use the phrase "new normal" to describe its near and present trajectory?
- In discussing the "new normal," what is the overall tone of the articles in this chapter? Optimistic, Pessimistic, Ambiguous? What is your evidence?
- How does the value of the yuan affect China's "new normal"? Is liberalization of its currency exchange rate beneficial or harmful to China's growth? Is it beneficial or harmful to the growth of other large economies (US, Japan, EU)?
- The "new normal" is described as "steady." In relation to the GDP, what does the phrase "steady growth" mean?
- Define transparency. What does transparency mean in the Chinese context? How does transparency act to stabilize or destabilize China's "new normal"?

Research Exercises

- Survey 20 people regarding their views about China's "new normal." Include both demographic questions (gender, age, nationality, SES, education, etc.) and Likert-scale questions (to what degree do you agree/disagree with the following statements?). Create three graphs showing differences between demographics in their responses to Likert-scale questions (e.g., male vs. female views about the expectation that China will see an increase/decrease/no change in GDP this year).

- Interview a company executive or small business-owner. Solicit their predictions for China's "new normal." How will China's "new normal" affect their business/industry (make a list of positive and negative impacts of China on their business/industry)? How will China's *new normal*" affect the US economy (make a list of positive and negative impacts of China on their business/industry)?
- Write a mini-business plan for a new enterprise that capitalizes on China's "new normal." Include a mission statement, description of product/service, market size, competitive analysis, board/management team, SWOT, 5-year timeline/milestones, start-up costs/cash-flow statement, 5-year revenue projections.

Notes

1 China's "New Normal" Will Be a Long-Term Phenomenon. *NewsChina*, December 1, 2014.
2 Magnier, M., Wei, L., & Talley, I. China Economic Growth Is Slowest in Decades: Economy Expanded 7.4 percent in 2014. *Wall Street Journal*, Jan. 19, 2015.
3 Xi, Z. Reform Is So Difficult That Its Dividends Can Only Be Attained Through Rule of Law. *NewsChina*, July 1, 2014.
4 Dai, M. China to Enter a New Normal Economic State. *NewsChina* February 1, 2015.
5 Chen, G. Promoting China's "New Normal" story: Beijing Needs to Reassure the World of Its New Economic Strategy to Restore Investor Confidence. *South China Morning Post*, September 14, 2015.
6 Barboza, D. Experimental Free-Trade Zone Opened in Shanghai. *The New York Times*, September 30, 2013.
7 He, J., Meng, S., & Zhang Y. New Fiscal Faces. *NewsChina*, March 1, 2015.
8 USCBC. China 2015 Regulatory Transparency Scorecard. The US–China Business Council. March 2015.
9 Fang, D. School Told to Pay $9m in row on Copyright: The Beijing Institution Illegally Sold Test Papers for US University Entry Exams. *South China Morning Post*, September 29, 2003.
10 Pan, P. China's Test-Prep Tempest: As Scores Rise, US Group Alleges Cheating. *The Washington Post*, February 21, 2001.
11 McMahon, D. China Banks' Loan Tactic Raises Transparency Issues. *The Wall Street Journal*, December 17, 2009.
12 Xi.
13 McMahon, D.
14 Xi.
15 Work report: A Window to Comprehend China's "New Normal". *China Daily*, March 7, 2015.
16 IMF Official Says China's Growth Slower but Safer. *China Daily*, April 20, 2015.
17 Hu, A. Embracing China's "New Normal". *Foreign Affairs*, *94*, 3 (2015): 8–12.
18 Xi.

Bibliography

Barboza, D. (September 29, 2013). Experimental Free-Trade Zone Opened in Shanghai. *The New York Times*. Retrieved from www.nytimes.com/2013/09/30/business/international/experimental-free-trade-zone-opened-in-shanghai.html

Chen, G. (2015). Promoting China's "New Normal" story: Beijing Needs to Reassure the World of Its New Economic Strategy to Restore Investor Confidence. *South China Morning Post* (September 14). Retrieved from www.lexisnexis.com/hottopics/lnacademic

China Daily (2004). New Oriental Language School Set to Appeal (April 28).

China Daily (2015). Work report: A Window to Comprehend China's "New Normal" (March 7). Retrieved from www.lexisnexis.com/hottopics/lnacademic

China Daily—Africa Weekly (2015). IMF Official Says China's Growth Slower but Safer (April 20). Retrieved from www.lexisnexis.com/hottopics/lnacademic

Dai, M. (2015). China to Enter a New Normal Economic State. *NewsChina* (February 1). Retrieved from www.newschinamag.com/magazine/china-to-enter-a-new-normal-economic-state

David, R. & McMahon, D. (2013). Xi Faces Test over China's Local Debt: Risks from Debt Are Still Controllable, Audit Office Says. *Wall Street Journal* (December 30).

Fang, D. (2003). School told to pay $ 9m in Row on Copyright: The Beijing Institution Illegally Sold Test Papers for US University Entry Exams. *South China Morning Post* (September 29). Retrieved from www.lexisnexis.com/hottopics/lnacademic

He, J., Meng, S., & Zhang Y. (2015). New Fiscal Faces. *NewsChina* (March 1). Retrieved from www.newschinamag.com/magazine/new-fiscal-faces

Hu, A. (2015). Embracing China's "New Normal". *Foreign Affairs*, *94*(3), 8–12.

Magnier, M., Wei, L., & Talley, I. (2015). China Economic Growth Is Slowest in Decades: Economy Expanded 7.4 percent in 2014. *Wall Street Journal* (January 19).

Marx & Engels (1998). *The Communist Manifesto*. New York: Penguin.

McMahon, D. (2009). China Banks' Loan Tactic Raises Transparency Issues. *Wall Street Journal* (December 17).

Pan, P. (2001). China's Test-Prep Tempest; As Scores Rise, US Group Alleges Cheating. *The Washington Post* (February 21). Retrieved from www.lexisnexis.com/hottopics/lnacademic

USCBC (2015). China 2015 Regulatory Transparency Scorecard. The US-China Business Council (March). Retrieved from www.uschina.org/sites/default/files/USCBC%202015%20Regulatory%20Transparency%20Scorecard.pdf

Xi, Z. (2014). Reform Is So Difficult That Its Dividends Can Only Be Attained Through Rule of Law. *NewsChina* (July 1). Retrieved from www.newschinamag.com/-magazine/reform-is-so-difficult-that-its-dividends-can-only-be-attained-through-rule

2

ECONOMIC TRENDS

Introduction

Golden Age to Silver Age? Clearly, the economic situation in China is changing. Whether as called the "New Normal" by China Premier Li Keqiang, or the "Silver Age" by the European Union Chamber of Commerce in China (EUCCC), China's previous exponential rate of growth has now begun to moderate. This emphatically doesn't mean a shrinking market, but it does entail a retreat from the "staggering" 30 percent annual growth rate enjoyed by European companies operating in China between 2001 and 2010.

As the Golden Age matures into the Silver Age for China, many financial institutions are coming under scrutiny for change. From stock exchanges to banks, better-managed process is being mandated. While SOEs stultify, certain private firms are thriving. The examples of Lenovo and Alibaba rising from obscurity to world leadership in their respective fields within a few decades is a message to all. Just consider the consequences to firms in industries around the globe should Beijing eventually go forward with privatization and lift the heavy yoke of political control from its SOEs. One can readily imagine Chinese companies leading most industries worldwide, just as Western ones did in the last century.

Fortune's under-the-covers exploration of Lenovo[1], the world's leading PC manufacturer and perhaps China's best-known privately-run company shows a corporate culture unique to China. Accepting lower margins in exchange for early market dominance, and facing the putative death of the PC, the firm has surged forward with multiple product lines.

As we have seen, certainly China has its problems in the economic sphere, as does any country. But the innate brash, aggressive entrepreneurship of the Chinese commercial soul as displayed by the likes of Alibaba's Jack Ma and Lenovo's CEO Yuanqing Yang lends a good probability of future Chinese global economic dominance.

Other articles in this chapter explore the effects on multinationals of increased regulatory pressure from Beijing while the state simultaneously encourages domestic firms and seeks foreign investment in infrastructure projects. Seeking new development funds, companies are turning to the public but face endemic problems with China's local stock exchanges. As evidence of this, Scott Cendrowski of *Fortune.com*[2] cites the summer 2015 meltdown of the Shanghai stock market, and Beijing's clumsy attempts to shore up share prices, this after urging the populace to invest.

China's new One Belt, One Road (OBOR) initiative, linking Asia and beyond with a "new Silk Road" both by land and by sea is evidence of Beijing's ambition to become the world player its economic status should entitle it to be, out from behind the shadows of the US, Japan, and South Korea.

Much has been made of the weaknesses of the Chinese banking system and the proliferation of unregulated "shadow banking." What is the future of banking in China, and how will banks and the government deal with the massive public debt?

Finally, China's present administration is committed to modernizing the sclerotic state-owned industries that are seen to be holding back economic progress. But many SOE senior executives are also high CCP officials, so reform mandates from Beijing have limited effect. How will Beijing move forward?

ARTICLES

Fundamental Trends

What Follows a Golden Age?

Not only is growth in China leveling off, but foreign investors face much stronger competition from indigenous firms, in both price and quality. Furthermore, seemingly arbitrary regulatory actions have been increasingly directed at foreign firms over the past few years. Zhou Yao, Chen Jiying, and Li Jia's article "A Silver Lining" explores these issues and their likely impact on multinationals as well as national firms in China.

A Silver Lining

January 2015 Issue of NewsChina | *by Zhou Yao, Chen Jiying, Li Jia*

SUSTAINABLE GROWTH IN CHINA IS UNLIKELY TO ARRIVE ON A SILVER PLATTER.

"The 'Golden Age' for business in China is drawing to a close," runs the first sentence of the annual Position Paper released by the EUCCC in September 2014. According to the EUCCC annual confidence survey issued earlier in the year, the number of member companies reporting disproportionately low profit margins for their China operations in the 2013/2014 fiscal year cited in the report outpaced the number of those reporting the opposite for the first time.

Weak financial data have also emerged from US companies operating in China, with the proportion of those claiming a "substantial revenue increase" now in a third year of decline, according to the US Chamber of Commerce in China (AmCham China).

The pinch is felt beyond these companies' account books. At the end of September, 2014, in his first visit to China as CEO of Microsoft, Satya Nadella agreed to cooperate with antitrust investigations launched against his company by Chinese law enforcement agencies. An array of multinationals have been probed, criticized, and fined by Chinese authorities, and investigations have been given plenty of coverage in major State media.

This uncertain atmosphere has bred pessimism regarding the openness of the Chinese market among foreign companies. According to surveys by both AmCham China and the EUCCC, more US companies now classify China as "only one of many foreign direct investment destinations" (the country was top of the list seven years ago), while European companies are also considering other opportunities in Asia.

Besides China's economic slowdown and the rising costs of labor and raw materials, the ever-shifting competitive landscape and an increasingly complicated regulatory environment have been identified by major foreign business communities. The sustainable, innovation-based "silver age" that foreign companies continue to hope for, then, depends on how both multinationals and Chinese regulators respond to the changing marketplace.

ALL THAT GLITTERS

Until 2011, 10 years after China acceded to the WTO, foreign companies in China remitted US$262 billion in profits back to their parent companies, recording staggering average annual growth of 30 percent, according to Chong Quan, deputy international trade representative of China's Ministry of Commerce (MOFCOM) at a press conference in Beijing held in December 2011.

In addition to cheap land and labor costs available to all enterprises during that period, foreign companies also enjoyed preferential tax policies. Foreign companies engaging in productive operations for more than a decade in China were exempted from corporate tax for two years and enjoyed a 50 percent tax cut for the first three years after the year they became profitable. Moreover, tax rebates were granted on profits used to reinvest in China. These, along with a number of other preferential arrangements, were included in the law that was created specifically for the tax structure for foreign companies, which took effect in 1991. In 2003, new regulations extended all these preferential policies to any company with a minimum 25 percent foreign stake after its acquisition by foreign investors—showing an unprecedented welcome to overseas investment.

For ordinary Chinese, working for a foreign company meant a better salary and generally enhanced job security when compared to conditions at either private or State-owned Chinese enterprises (SOEs). In the early 1990s, a Chinese technical professional could expect to earn more than US$500 a month at a foreign company while salaries at SOEs hovered around the US$100 mark. These workers at foreign companies also enjoyed business trips in five-star hotels, were paid annual, sick, and maternity leave, and enjoyed a degree of legal protection that their peers working in Chinese companies could only dream of. This imbalance persisted throughout the labor chain—a young waiter or receptionist with a high school diploma employed by a foreign hotel could earn double the salary of a middle school teacher with a college degree.

This era also ignited China's enduring passion for foreign brand names. At the time, anyone who had the chance to go abroad would typically return laden with purchases for friends and relatives, particularly home appliances like refrigerators, TVs and washing machines, which were hard to come by in China. When China's first McDonald's opened in April 1992, locals lined up round the block. As Chen Tingli, a staff member at that first restaurant, told the *Beijing Daily* in 2009, most customers just asked for "a McDonald's." Few could have identified the items on the menu.

This golden age began to lose its luster in 2006, when foreign companies were required to pay taxes and fees from which they had previously been exempt, including urban land use taxes, urban maintenance fees, and education fees. The preferential law on the taxation of foreign companies was annulled by State legislators in favor of a single taxation law for all businesses in 2008. By the end of 2010, nearly all foreign companies were bound by the same financial requirements as their Chinese equivalents.

COLD SNAP

In early 2013, Samsung and LG became the first foreign-funded companies fined by a Chinese court for price-fixing. The case was followed by several other antitrust investigations into foreign multinationals in various sectors, ranging from infant formula and automobiles to Internet data services and microchip manufacture. In August, 12 Japanese auto parts makers were slapped with US$200 million in fines, the highest levy in the history of Chinese antimonopoly cases.

It was far from rare for foreign companies to be fined by the US authorities over bribery scandals in other markets, including in China. In 2013, a number of international pharmaceutical giants, including GSK, Sanofi, and AstraZeneca, were involved in probes into bribery initiated by the Chinese authorities. Four senior GSK executives were arrested in connection with the case.

Layoffs also became a feature of life in foreign companies in China, when, previously, local staff had been immune from the shockwaves resulting from restructuring or acquisition. Many defected to the less well paid but more secure jobs offered by Chinese private companies, with young Chinese graduates in recent years preferring SOEs over foreign companies.

This phenomenon was recorded right up the corporate ladder. This September, Yaqin Zhang, former vice president of Microsoft, took the reins at Baidu, China's Google equivalent. Peers at Google and Oracle had made similar departures since 2011, betting on a relatively protected domestic sector over embattled multinationals losing faith in China's market potential.

In addition, while foreign brands remain preferred by the wealthy, ordinary consumers in China are overwhelmingly choosing domestic products, from home appliances to fast food and clothing, often due to a combination of low price and the convenience of shopping through the Internet. A recent survey released on September 23 by Strategy&, a consultancy under PWC, showed that 65 percent of executives at foreign companies were surprised to find that their Chinese competitors were equal to them, or even stronger, in terms of innovation in production, service provision, supply chains, and business models.

ADAPTATION

Few doubt that moderate GDP growth in such a large developing economy as China's would still mean huge business opportunities. The EUCCC has defined "a long and sustainable silver period of growth" as "modern, creative and market-oriented."

The arrival of a "silver age", however, is anything but assured. While the claims that Starbucks artificially inflated its prices in China were swiftly exposed as a simple misrepresentation of basic supply and demand economics, complaints about Apple's after-sales service were generally acknowledged by consumers.

China Central Television (CCTV)'s slamming of foreign automakers' high prices, however, sparked a backlash against the government regulations. In June, MOFCOM launched an investigation into local protectionism in the domestic auto market. For example, autos made by local joint ventures were said to enjoy greater market access than those from elsewhere. Moreover, the CCTV reports triggered much attention to what many see as unfair rules that only outlets authorized by a certain auto maker can sell its products, giving them exclusive power over pricing and terms of services. The ongoing investigation by the National Development and Reform Commission on price manipulation by auto giants and their resale agents triggered louder calls to revise these rules. Recently unauthorized sellers in the Shanghai Free Trade Zone have also been allowed to import foreign autos.

This indicates a growing sense among consumers that, while they will be quick to criticize opportunism among profit-hungry multinationals, they also expect regulators to be even-handed, rather than allow Chinese companies to flout regulations while simultaneously launching witch-hunts against foreign brand names.

Teng Binsheng, a professor at the Cheung Kong Graduate School of Business in Beijing, believes the future of foreign companies in China will lie in their efforts to provide better products and services catering to local demand, and to expand outside megacities.

Unlike investors from South Korea, Japan, Hong Kong, or Taiwan, US and European companies in China have long been focused on tapping the Chinese mainland market, rather than exporting China-made products. This has led to disproportionate focus on high-earning local consumers based in major cities. Now, China's growing urban and rural middle class have begun to figure in their expansion strategy, bringing them into more direct competition with local brands. Proctor & Gamble, for example, has begun to offer very cheap shampoo to compete with domestic options, while a report in 2012 by accountancy firm Deloitte showed strong demand for international luxury brands like Gucci and Louis Vuitton in second- or even third-tier cities even as demand dropped off in megacities like Beijing, Guangzhou, and Shanghai. In the auto industry, Chinese automakers remain dominant at the lowest end of the market, though their share is increasingly squeezed by joint ventures which once focused on middle and high-end consumers.

The strategy of France's Scheider Electric is a further example of localization, as the company has explored R&D projects in China for the explicit purpose of selling to the China market, as well as building joint ventures with Chinese partners, according to Zhao Kang, senior deputy president of the company's China operations.

SILVER BULLET

This "silver age" can only be made possible, as the EUCCC has stated, "if broad and decisive reforms are implemented."

Such reforms were already mentioned in the resolution that emerged from the Third Plenum of the Communist Party which was passed in November 2013 and some steps, most notably the removal of certain regulatory barriers, have already been taken. However, achieving the Party's stated goal of "giving the market a decisive role" in the allocation of resources remains a challenge. A free trade zone built in Shanghai to give wider market access to foreign companies is frequently cited as a major step forward. In October, the Party's Fourth Plenum specified a roadmap for legal reform, addressing some concerns about market access barriers and a general lack of the rule of law, but actions, not words, are needed to reassure companies doubtful about the authorities' proclaimed openness to foreign investment.

In its September statement, AmCham China described the progress of reform as "disappointingly slow" due to "still onerous" rules on investment in many sectors. In its statement on the Party's Fourth Plenum resolution, the EUCCC expressed its concerns over whether the principles of rule of law specified in the decision would be implemented effectively and swiftly enough to address the issues of "unpredictable" and "discretionary" legal obstacles for business.

Some recent actions that Chinese regulators have recently claimed are improving market fairness and consumer protection have fueled further anxiety at foreign firms. Although international companies only accounted for 10 percent of the total number of companies investigated in China's recent antitrust law enforcement drive, many felt that the focus has been unfairly trained on them. The US–China Business Council said in a report in September that US companies noticed that cases involving foreign companies were more extensively reported by Chinese media, and US companies were particularly concerned about the weak application of due process, such as company employees being pressured into plea bargains before even being told of the charges against them. Many suspect that the recent antitrust drive is motivated more by protectionism than by genuine enthusiasm for cleaning up China's business environment.

Some new policies are applied equally to all businesses in a sector, but given the market context, foreign companies are more likely to be adversely affected by regulation. For example, pharmaceutical companies have to wait for at least 10 months for approval of clinical trials for new drugs. According to the R&D-based Pharmaceutical Association Commission under the China Association of Enterprises with Foreign Investment, this is already much longer than the four months required in India, two months in Singapore, and one month in the US. In 2014, this waiting period in China was further extended to between 18 and 20 months. This policy has affected originator drugs more, which need stricter clinical trials. In addition, the prices of some originator drugs in the national drug list covered by health care insurance, normally much more expensive than generics, have been capped by Chinese pricing authorities since 2009. Policy now aims to reduce health care costs, with local governments prioritizing low prices—a new policy draft on drug pricing has not even mentioned the concept of originator drugs. All of this is significantly eroding the market access of major foreign pharmaceutical companies that have an unchallenged edge over their Chinese equivalents on the originator drugs market. Many have argued that this policy neither rewards innovation nor respects a patient's right to choose, and that it runs counter to the government's stated claims that it favors greater market openness and competition.

Whatever color association this "silver age" ultimately assumes in the minds of those with a stake in China's business environment, it is unlikely many feel that the current outlook is golden, or even rosy.

Energy and Climate Goals

Though the 12th FYP is nearing its end of implementation, it's the best roadmap we have until early 2016 as to the priorities of the Chinese Communist Party (CPC). Here is an analysis of the energy and climate goals that were articulated in 2011.

Energy and Climate Goals of China's 12th FYP

By Joanna Lewis (March 2011), Center for Climate and Energy Solutions, formerly the Pew Center on Global Climate Change

The 12th FYP adopted by the Chinese government in March 2011 devotes considerable attention to energy and climate change and establishes a new set of targets and policies for 2011–2015.[3] While some of the targets are largely in line with the status quo, other aspects of the plan represent more dramatic moves to reduce fossil energy consumption, promote low-carbon energy sources, and restructure China's economy. Among the goals is to "gradually establish a carbon trade market." Key targets include:

- A 16 percent reduction in energy intensity (energy consumption per unit of GDP);
- Increasing non-fossil energy to 11.4 percent of total energy use;
- A 17 percent reduction in carbon intensity (carbon emissions per unit of GDP).

ENERGY

The relationship between energy and economic growth matters greatly in China; without a reduction in energy intensity since the late 1970s, the country would need to consume three times the energy it does today to sustain its economic growth. At the center of China's 11th FYP (2006–2010) was a target to decrease the overall energy intensity of the economy by 20 percent. This target was implemented in response to increases in energy intensity experienced between 2002 and 2005, the first increase experienced after several decades of rapidly decreasing energy intensity. To reverse the unexpected increases in energy intensity, the government mobilized a national campaign to promote energy efficiency, targeting in particular the largest and least efficient energy-consuming enterprises. The "Top 1,000 Program" targeted approximately 1,000 companies (consuming about one-third of the country's energy) for efficiency improvements.

The 12th FYP builds directly on the 11th FYP energy intensity target and its associated programs, setting a new target to reduce energy intensity by an additional 16 percent by 2015.[4] While this may seem less ambitious than the 20 percent reduction targeted in the 11th FYP, it likely represents a much more substantial challenge. It is likely that the largest and least efficient enterprises have already undertaken efficiency improvements, leaving smaller, more efficient plants to be targeted in this second round. Under preparation is a new Top 10,000 program, which is modeled after the Top 1,000 Program but adds an order of magnitude of companies to the mix. But as the number of plants grows, so do the challenges of collecting accurate data and enforcing targets.

The closure of inefficient power and industrial facilities also helped contribute to the decline in energy intensity during the 11th FYP period, with a reported 72.1 GW of thermal capacity closed.[5] Total plant closures are equivalent to 16 percent of the size of the capacity added over the period. An additional 8 GW of coal plants were reportedly to be shut down in 2011 alone, with further closures no doubt on top over the following five years.

While final data are not yet available, the country likely fell short of meeting its 11th FYP energy intensity target of 20 percent, instead achieving in the range of 19.1 percent. There is no doubt, however, that much was learned though efforts to improve efficiency nationwide. Many changes were made to how such national targets are enforced at the local level, including the incorporation of compliance with energy intensity targets into the evaluation for local officials.

The 12th FYP includes a target to increase non-fossil energy sources (including hydro, nuclear and renewable energy) to 11.4 percent of total energy use (up from 8.3 percent in 2010).[6] While not formally enshrined in the 12th FYP, another recent notable announcement is a cap on total energy consumption of 4 billion tons of coal equivalent (tce) in 2015.[7] To meet the cap on energy consumption, annual energy growth would need to slow to an average of 4.24 percent per year, from 5.9 percent between 2009 and 2010. The government is also trying to slow GDP growth rates, targeting 7 percent per year—far below recent growth rates. Lower GDP growth rates make it even more challenging for China to meet energy and carbon intensity targets, since energy and carbon need to grow more slowly than GDP for the country to achieve declining energy and carbon intensity.

CARBON

In the lead-up to the Copenhagen climate negotiations in the fall of 2009, the Chinese government pledged a 40–45 percent reduction in national carbon intensity from 2005 levels by 2020. To achieve this 2020 target, the 12th FYP sets an interim target of reducing carbon intensity 17 percent from 2010 levels by 2015. Whether this target will result in a deviation from China's expected carbon emissions over this time period depends on the corresponding GDP growth, but many studies have found that this target will be challenging for China to achieve without additional, aggressive policies to promote low carbon energy development.[8]

Also promised in the 12th FYP is an improved system for monitoring greenhouse gas (GHG) emissions, which will be needed to assess compliance with the carbon intensity target, and to prepare the national GHG inventories that, under the Cancún Agreements, are to be reported more frequently to the UNFCCC and undergo international assessment.

The 12th FYP establishes the goal of "gradually establish[ing] a carbon trade market," but does not elaborate. A handful of provinces have announced interest in piloting carbon trading schemes. The Tianjin Climate Exchange, partially owned by the founders of the Chicago Climate Exchange, is positioning itself to be the clearinghouse for any future carbon trading program.[9] While some have suggested that Guangdong Province may be targeted for a pilot program at the provincial level, other reports speculate that the program would begin within a single sector, such as the power sector, or begin by including only state-owned enterprises, which are often the target of early government policy experiments (as was the case with mandatory market shares for renewable energy placed on the large State-owned power companies). Other likely locations for pilots might include China's low-carbon cities and provinces.[10]

Implementing a carbon trading scheme in China, even on a small-scale or pilot basis, will not be without significant challenges. Concerns have already been raised from both domestic and foreign-owned enterprises operating in China about how the regulation could affect their bottom lines. But the key challenge is likely technical, resulting from the minimal capacity currently in place to measure and monitor carbon emissions in China.

INDUSTRIAL POLICY

The 12th FYP also includes many new industrial policies to support clean energy industries and related technologies. Industries targeted include the nuclear, solar, wind and biomass energy technology industries, as well as hybrid and electric vehicles, and energy savings and environmental protection technology industries.[11] These "strategic and emerging" industries are being promoted to replace the "old" strategic industries such as coal and telecom, (often referred to as China's pillar industries),

Table 2.1

The old pillar industries	*The new strategic and emerging industries*
1 National defense	Energy saving and environmental protection
2 Telecom	Next generation information technology
3 Electricity	Biotechnology
4 Oil	High-end manufacturing (e.g., aeronautics, high-speed rail)
5 Coal	New energy (nuclear, solar, wind, biomass)
6 Airlines	New materials (special and high-performance composites)
7 Marine shipping	Clean energy vehicles (PHEVs and electric cars)

Sources: "Decision on speeding up the cultivation and development of emerging strategic industries" (国务院通过加快培育和发展战略性新兴产业的决定), www.gov.cn, September 8, 2010, www.gov.cn/ldhd/2010-09/08/content_1698604.htm; HSBC, *China's next 5-year plan: What it means for equity markets*, October 2010.

which are heavily State-owned and have long benefited from government support (see Table 2.1).[12] This move to rebrand China's strategic industries likely signals the start of a new wave of industrial policy support for the new strategic industries which may include access to dedicated State industrial funds, increased access to private capital, or industrial policy support through access to preferential loans or R&D funds.

Other targets encourage increased innovative activity, including a target for R&D expenditure to account for 2.2 percent of GDP, and for 3.3 patents per 10,000 people. During the 11th FYP period, an estimated 15.3 percent of government stimulus funding was directed towards innovation, energy conservation, ecological improvements, and industrial restructuring.[13]

OTHER TARGETS

The 12th FYP also includes targets to increase the rate of forest coverage by just over 21 percent and the total forest stock by 12.5 million hectares by 2015. Also mentioned are targets for the construction of 35,000 km of high-speed rail and improvements in subway and light rail coverage, as well as a goal to connect every city with a population greater than 500,000.[14]

OUTLOOK

The 12th FYP provides a glimpse into the minds of China's leadership as it lays out a methodological plan for moving the country forward. It includes a strong emphasis on new energy and climate programs and clearly illustrates China's commitment to increased environmental protection. The Plan itself provides a framework for progress, but leaves the details of implementation to policy makers, with many new policies and programs likely to follow in the coming weeks.

Some of the targets will no doubt prove challenging to implement. The national energy and carbon intensity targets will prove particularly difficult if economic growth rates slow in line with targets put forth in the plan. Implementation of energy conservation and efficiency programs at the facility level will prove increasingly demanding as more and more facilities are incorporated into current programs. The non-fossil energy target relies on extensive increases in nuclear energy capacity, but growth in nuclear plants may slow as efforts to improve safety and regulation will be implemented in the aftermath of the recent Japanese nuclear disaster.[15] If nuclear targets are reduced, the share of renewable energy will need to increase even more than current targets propose.

Overall, China's Plan represents many ambitious climate and energy goals, and lays out a strategic roadmap for the county to endeavor to pursue over the next five years.

The Twin Engines of Growth

Responding to China's economic slowdown, Premier Li Keqiang has proposed the twin engines of "popular entrepreneurship and innovation" allied with an "increased supply of public goods and services." Li Jia, in the article "Start Your Engines" details these concepts, their challenges, and possible shortcomings. She mentions a heavy reliance on Internet start-ups, but doesn't mention how being walled off from the best part of the Web will injure these new enterprises. Also mentioned is the hopeful existence of venture capital, angel investment, and crowdfunding. But lack of transparency and a high level of fraud in equity trading in China limits these sources. On the positive side, the second of the twin engines, which basically translates into infrastructure investment, leaves space for foreign firms to compete for some of the substantial spending contemplated.

Start Your Engines

May 2015 Issue of NewsChina | *by Li Jia*

For the new "twin engines" of China's economy, conventional concepts of entrepreneurship like passion, professionalism, and patience are still required.

Forty-one-year-old Ms. Hu always took taxis when working as a PR rep for her previous employer, an Internet company. These days, she takes the subway to meet her clients, but feels much happier. "I was overwhelmed by anxiety at that time, haunted by how much I 'owed' my boss every day; now I am doing what I am really interested in, and pursuing my own dreams," she said to *NewsChina*. Hu is developing a smartphone app for middle-income pensioners in Beijing. "The excitement I feel every day now has even helped me lose weight and look younger than my age," she laughed.

Ms. Yu, a postgraduate student in her late 20s in Beijing, is thinking about starting an online outlet promoting pesticide-free vegetables and fruits, as well as historical tourist attractions of her hometown, a county in relatively underdeveloped Henan Province. She told *NewsChina* she had already received positive responses from several rural cooperatives and friends with IT expertise, and was looking for rural households that could provide accommodation for tourists.

These Internet-based ventures represent the fashionable side of one of the new "twin engines" for China's economy—the engine of "popular entrepreneurship and innovation," as defined as in Chinese Premier Li Keqiang's report to the annual session of the NPC, China's parliament, in March. The other engine is "increased supply of public goods and services" to boost domestic demand. Private investment is also encouraged to fuel this engine.

Several new or revamped concepts were highlighted in the report, which focuses on the new engines driving the "new normal" of the Chinese economy and immediately made headlines in both domestic and international media.

But as the government shows off the blueprints for its shiny new engines, analysts also have reminded that it takes time and effort from various participants to get them under the hood of the economy, and put that power on the road.

GRASSROOTS ECONOMY

For the first time since the Asian Financial Crisis in the late 1990s, deflation, with the specter of systematic business contraction and job losses, has been brought back to the center of debates among domestic and international observers of the Chinese economy. The growth rate target has been set at about 7 percent for 2015, the lowest since 1990. Hitting even this target, as Premier Li acknowledged in his press conference at the conclusion of the NPC session on March 15, is no easy task, given the size of the economy. Moreover, his work report noted that China's growth model remained "inefficient," and the innovation capacity "insufficient."

The "twin engines" are designed to disperse the dark cloud of a continued slowdown in growth rate and uncertainties over structural upgrading in China's economy. They are also endorsed by international analysts. Christine Lagarde, head of the International Monetary Fund, stated in her speech at the China Development Forum in Shanghai on March 20, that if China takes the risk of slower growth to place more importance on innovation and consumption than ever, China's "economic cup of tea" would "end up with a richer taste."

A boom in start-up business among the public, or the "grassroots economy" in the words of Premier Li, is in full swing. In 2014, newly registered companies soared by 47 percent and created more jobs than expected, despite the economic downturn. According to the annual joint survey by State broadcaster CCTV and the National Bureau of Statistics released on March 9, 2015, the group with the strongest desire to open a start-up are married, lower middle-class urban men between the ages of 26 and 35. Those with a higher educational background and higher income seem to be more satisfied with the jobs they have.

INTERNET PLUS

Setting up a business has been made much easier due to the streamlining of registration procedures in the past two years. Technology has provided a seemingly irresistible incentive—Internet-based businesses are the most popular category of start-up. Ms. Hu, for example, had begun to think about her own business three years ago, but did not put her plan into action till recently. "I don't have a glittering background like the superstars of the business world, like a US or European business diploma, or the support of a rich family. But now, the age of mobile Internet gives everyone an equal chance at least to give it a try," she told *NewsChina*.

Premier Li Keqiang, himself an enthusiastic advocate of Internet-based business and consumption, proposed the concept of "Internet-plus," using online services to facilitate offline industries. In cafes in Beijing, it is very common to hear exciting dialogs about Internet business plans. Hu herself spends much of her time meeting with her team and potential users in coffee shops.

Talking and thinking do not cost much. Registering a business is also comparatively easy. However, a lot of money is needed to build both the Internet, and the "plus"—real-world things for consumers to buy.

BELIEVE IN ANGELS

Angel investment, a kind of equity investment that seeks to invest in high-risk, high-return start-up ventures at, or even before, their inception, is widely recognized to have underwritten innovation in the US, the world's most vigorous market for grassroots entrepreneurship. China also hopes to rely on this kind of investment for its Internet-plus boom. Articles and seminars on how to win the favor of an angel are very popular in China—both Hu and Yu, for example, are convinced that somewhere out there, their angels are waiting for them.

Probably not as many as they might imagine. Professor Yao Yang, director of the National School of Development at Peking University, thinks China is still far from being a hotbed of risk-oriented financiers—most of the country's big investors remain preoccupied with bigger, safer projects. In addition, they are heavily concentrated in China's first-tier cities. Chen Zhiyi, director of a local equity exchange for small, unlisted companies in Fujian Province, told *NewsChina* that even in prosperous second-tier cities like Xiamen, such investors are rare.

This means that the small number of angel investors who focus on brand new businesses is even harder to reach. As one of them, Terrence Zhang, told *NewsChina*, while it is true that there are more "angels" out there than ever before—at least in megacities—there is even more competition for their attention. Besides, many of these so-called "angels" themselves have little expertise to offer new companies, and no ability to take the wheel when things go wrong. Experienced angels equate their careful decision making process to "looking for a potential partner in a romantic relationship," according to Zhang.

In the past few years, online crowdfunding or peer-to-peer (P2P) borrowing platforms have mushroomed in China, but a spate of fraud scandals last year dealt a blow to their popularity. By July 2014, founders of about 150 of an estimated 1,200 P2P websites absconded with investors' money, according to the China Banking Regulatory Commission (CBRC). Equity investment platforms are also facing a crisis of creditworthiness. Many crowdfunding investors complain of receiving shoddy products as a reward for their investment.

On March 23, 2015, the State Council declared a roadmap to put an innovation-friendly policy and legal frameworks in place by 2020. Angel investment will enjoy favorable tax conditions, which comes as good news to angel investor Terrence Zhang. CBRC is working on rules governing online lending platforms. It seems angels themselves will have to grow before they can serve as a reliable source of growth for business start-ups on the ground.

MADE IN CHINA 2025

There are also plans to give China's traditional economy a makeover. The "Made in China 2025" strategy has been launched to turn the world's biggest manufacturer into the world's "best," within a decade. "Internet-plus" is also intended to aid this process, with manufacturing serving as the offline "plus." Indeed, the strong German performance in the aftermath of the 2008 Global Financial Crisis has persuaded most Chinese economists that while flashy start-ups may get all the media attention, the so-called "real economy" never goes out of fashion. In an interview with *NewsChina*, Professor Yao Yang expressed his concern about the pervasive "Internet anxiety" in society, and insufficient concentration on small, advanced progress on production lines.

His concern is apparently justified. Terrence Zhang told *NewsChina* he had noticed an obsession with identikit smartphone apps among start-up entrepreneurs, but indifference towards the idea of making something tangible and unique.

Times are tough for small and medium-sized enterprises (SMEs) in the manufacturing sector. Chen Zhiyi has noticed that many local companies cannot afford to hire enough skilled workers, let alone invest in better tech. Though local equity exchanges like Chen's are highlighted in the government roadmap, investors need time to understand the new market and are lukewarm towards buying stakes in SMEs in the current economic downturn, he said.

Various policies have been adopted to address the lingering problem of expensive and restricted access to capital for SMEs. The effect, however, remains limited. Private local banks, with more flexible and robust risk management arrangements than big State-run banks, are regarded as the solution.

Direct subsidies are a much more immediate way of helping enterprises to upgrade. Tens of billions of dollars of public funds have gone to SMEs and hi-tech enterprises, and more investment is planned. However, according to the National Audit Office, some of the money was invested in vineyards in France, rather than for any technical purpose. Party mouthpiece *People's Daily* on March 16 criticized the lack of transparency in reviews of subsidy applications, and the absence of follow-up reviews of how subsidies are used.

Professor Yao does not believe the government is more adept than the market at identifying which industries and companies should get support in the first place. He believes research institutes are a better user of such funds. For enterprises, he explains, bank loans with favorable terms for specific technical upgrading projects would be more helpful, since they would encourage more thoughtful use of funds by putting borrowers under financial pressure, and reduce the risk of corruption among government officials who review applications.

There is another important player whose potential is yet to be exploited in industrial upgrading. Under the existing rules, researchers with universities and institutes, though they possess more cutting-edge, forward-looking know-how than most enterprises, are not entitled to intellectual property rights to their own inventions. Yao proposed that China learn from common practice in the US, whereby researchers share intellectual property rights (IPR) with their institutions, and are permitted to privately monetize the technologies they create. A robust IPR system is also necessary to prevent infringement, he added.

Trials and reforms have been going on to allow private banks to operate, and develop a more diversified and liberalized financial market. The new Budget Law has put public revenues and spending under much stricter scrutiny. According to the State Council's March 23 innovation roadmap, IPR infringements will face tougher legal penalties, while researchers will be allowed to share IPR with their institutions and start their own businesses. In some places, such as Chengdu, capital of Sichuan Province, academic staff at universities have already been encouraged to set up their own businesses implementing the fruits of their research.

None of the above tasks are easy. Ostensibly, since 2014, these tasks are all about money, but in reality, as Professor Yao and Chen Zhiyhi stressed, they are about laws and creditworthiness in the eyes of the law.

HOW TO PARTNER?

As the operator of the other engine, increased public goods and services, the government is also trying out a new strategy. The central government is scheduled to invest US$78 billion this year, and provincial governments' plans made public so far total up to about US$2.3 trillion. Major projects on the list include transportation, power grids, information networks, urban underground pipe networks, agricultural water conservancy, clean energy, and environmental protection. As Premier Li's report described, the government "does not intend to perform an investment soliloquy."

"Public–private partnership" (PPP) has thus become a buzzword since 2014. According to the World Bank definition, the term refers to co-operative contracts on public projects which are long-term, binding commitments with the private party bearing "significant risk and management responsibility." The purpose is to provide public assets and services as professionally and efficiently as possible, and PPPs have been applied in China since the 1980s. However, as Wang Bao'an, Chinese Deputy Finance Minister, acknowledged in an interview with Xinhua News Agency in March 2015, in many cases, Chinese PPPs did not operate as such. A disproportionate amount of credit risk was shouldered by the government. End users were overcharged for the services PPPs provided. Contractors faced government default when new officials took office. The practice shrank greatly after the government's massive 2009 stimulus package to counter the Global Financial Crisis, and reemerged last year when enormous and ill-regulated local government debts in the form of financing platforms, a tool to get around budgetary disciplines to access bank loans, became an alarming risk threatening China's financial system.

A new boom of PPPs seems to be on the horizon. Wang disclosed that local governments had announced more than US$160 billion's worth of PPP projects for 2015. Jin Yongxiang, general manager of Dayue Consulting, a leading Beijing-based PPP consultancy, told *NewsChina* that recently there is now growing interest not only from State-owned, private, and foreign enterprises, but also financial institutions.

In December 2014, the Finance Ministry initiated 30 demonstration PPP projects, 22 of them existing local government financing platforms. This has reinforced the expectation that the model is designed to save local governments from debt.

SOCIAL CAPITAL

Too much emphasis on debt easing, analysts warned, may distort the model once again. Dr Li Kaimeng, Director General of China International Engineering Consulting Corporation, a research center, stressed in an interview with *NewsChina* that efficiency and quality brought by private participation makes much more sense than money in PPP projects.

Unlike in other countries, the "private" in China's PPP refers to "social," and thus also includes SOEs. As private companies have mostly been in competitive sectors and have yet to develop experience in operating infrastructure projects, Dr Li estimated that SOEs, the main existing player, would continue to act as the biggest "social investors" in PPP projects for some time. This, however, has aroused concerns over the efficiency and fairness of PPP projects.

This, Dr. Li noted, has highlighted the importance of following market-oriented and law-based principles in operating PPP projects. For example, he explained, financial analysis has to be taken seriously in feasibility studies which now focus on technical designs and catering to application standards set by different government agencies. The performance of government-SOE cooperative projects, he added, will affect the enthusiasm of private companies joining the game.

Meanwhile, as Jin Yongxiang remarked, the PPP model is also a test for how government carries out its supervising duties, to ensure that quality of public services is not compromised by contractors in their pursuit of cost efficiency, a lesson from other parts of the world.

Policy makers also seem to hope to renovate the model with market-oriented standards. Instructions issued by the Finance Ministry, for example, repeatedly stress that legally based contracts are the core of the whole partnership, and specify every step of the whole process, from feasibility studies and financing, to interest and risk sharing, supervision and dispute settlement. SOEs controlled by local governments are excluded from bidding for local PPP projects.

Another less discussed potential integration of real private participation with PPPs is the plethora of start-ups sprouting up all over the country today. Both Hu and Yu hope that one day they will have the chance to bid for government procurement. Indeed, in developed countries like the UK, Dr Li said, PPPs are more often used in government procurement of public services than in infrastructure projects like construction. He shares Professor Yao's view that this makes it possible to make the two sides of the engine work together, rather than separately.

The twin-engine itself, indeed, is a mega-PPP project. Ways to ensure quality and efficiency have already been made clear. The challenge ahead is to make them not only look shiny, but run smoothly, too.

The RMB as a Reserve Currency

Daili Wanga, Yiping Huanga, and Gang Fan address two frequently asked questions: "Why isn't the RMB an internationally accepted reserve currency?" and "What steps must China take to make it one?" As one of the three dominant world economies, taking the US and the EU as the other two, China naturally desires its currency to be as freely tradable and as widely accepted as are the US dollar and the euro. But clearly, it is not. There are many political implications of becoming a world reserve currency, and Beijing would be forced to give up a large measure of control of the RMB to arrive at that state. Also, confidence in the rule of law and property rights influences this outcome. The authors of this scholarly study explore the measures of a world currency and compare other currencies' histories and management to point to factors involved in answering the above questions.

What follows is an excerpt of the original *China Economic Journal* article. In the interest of brevity we have omitted, among other parts, several tables and the entire data methodology section. The interested reader is encouraged to access and read the entire article.

Will the Renminbi Become a Reserve Currency? (Excerpt)

By Daili Wanga, Yiping Huanga, and Gang Fan

National School of Development, Peking University, Beijing, China;

National Economic Research Institute, Beijing, China March 2015

China Economic Journal, 2015(8), 1, 55–73,
http://dx.doi.org/10.1080/17538963.2015.1001053

In recent years, the authorities in the People's Republic of China (PRC) have made great efforts to internationalize its currency. Will Renminbi (RMB) finally become a reserve currency?

INTRODUCTION

Many policy makers in the People's Republic of China (PRC) believe that the international monetary system dominated by a national currency, the US dollar, is logically inconsistent and unsustainable. The outbreak of the subprime crisis in the United States (US) is evidence of the problem. A possible long-term solution is to create a supranational currency, such as a revamped special drawing right (SDR) of the International Monetary Fund (IMF) (Zhou 2009). In the short run, however, the subprime crisis could lead to weakening demand for the US dollar and create room for the renminbi (RMB) to play some kind of international role.

In 2006, a study group of the People's Bank of China (PBC) published an article titled "The Timing, Path and Strategies of RMB Internationalization," in which it argued that "the time has come for promotion of the internationalization of the RMB" (PBC Study Group 2006). The study group also suggested that internationalization of the RMB could enhance the PRC's international status and competitiveness and would increase the country's influence in the world economy.

The effort to internationalize the renminbi picked up pace in the past five years, and the PRC authorities will likely move ahead more rapidly in the coming years. Will the PRC finally succeed in internationalizing its currency? A growing number of studies have recently addressed this question (Dobson and Masson 2009; Chen and Cheung 2011). Perhaps due to the fascinating growth performance and already gigantic scale of the economy, positive and optimistic views appear to dominate in both press and academic studies. While these optimists believe that the renminbi will soon take a seat among global currency reserves, however, statistics reveal that the percentage of the use of renminbi in international trade and capital transaction is still far behind the use of the Japanese yen, let alone the euro and the US dollar.

In this paper, we tackle the above question by providing an institutional analytical framework. Traditional research on the determinants of reserve currencies mostly concerns economic factors, such as economic scale, financial development and network effects, per se. We call attention to the role of institutional factors in affecting the international use of a currency. After taking account of several important institutional factors, we find the predicted share of RMB in the global currency reserve is more consistent with the actual figure. We thus conclude that despite the fascinating economic growth in the past decades, the PRC is not likely to achieve renminbi internationalization until further progress has been made in improving its institutional environment.

Our work contributes to providing a better understanding of RMB internationalization. The growing international role of the RMB, even if it is a gradual process, should generate significant implications for China, regional economies and rest of the world. On the one hand, the benefits for China are clear—removal of exchange rate uncertainty, generation of seigniorage revenues, and reduction of balance of payment risks (Bowles and Wang 2013). On the other hand, if more central banks intend to hold RMB as a part of their foreign reserves, the Chinese financial system will have to withstand dramatic capital flows (Yu 2012). The ambiguity of the consequence of RMB internationalization calls for further research in the field. As far as we are aware, previous work concerning the future of RMB internationalization has not fully considered the role of the institutional environment. In fact, institutional factors, such as development of the legal system and the increase of economic freedom, are crucial in maintaining the confidence of international investors to hoard a foreign currency and restoring the issuing country's capacity to deal with domestic political tensions. After taking account of these institutional factors, we reach a different yet more realistic conclusion in predicting the outlook of renminbi internationalization.

REVIEW

The literature has identified three key economic determinants of reserve currencies (Tavlas 1997; Lim 2006). The first determinant is pertinent to the confidence of foreign investors to hold a currency. This kind of confidence is inspired if, and sometimes only if, a currency is proven to have a stable value over time, in terms of purchasing power over goods (Tavlas 1997). As Dobson and Masson (2009) suggested, investors' confidence is related to the central bank's ability to deliver low inflation and maintain credibility and independence. Low volatility of currency value is also proven to be crucial in cutting transaction costs (Hartmann 1998). Historically, the internationalization of the Deutsche mark serves as a distinct example suggesting the importance of a stable currency value. The mark was introduced in Ludwig Erhard's currency reform in 1948 and the country's central bank, Bundesbank, was not established until 1957. Despite its short history, the impeccable reputation the Bundesbank built up in keeping the value of the mark strong and stable secured the rise of mark's international status, until the Maastricht Treaty signed in 1992 came to fruition in January 1999, when the Deutsche mark, together with nine other continental currencies, went out of existence in the historic creation of the euro (Frankel 2011).

The second determinant of reserve currencies identified in literature is the existence of well-developed and open financial markets. These markets make the currency an attractive instrument in which to hold assets and to transact, and enable at least some degree of freedom by non-residents to conduct currency conversion (Cohen 2014). Tavlas (1997) pointed to the tight regulation of Japanese financial markets as a factor that has inhibited financial innovation and limited the international role of the yen. Indeed, the yen's share of official foreign exchange reserves remains small despite low inflation and the fact that Japan was the world's second largest economy in the 1980s. In contrast, the US dollar (replacing its precedent sterling) stands as the preeminent international currency ever since the establishment of the Federal Reserve in 1913. The dollar hegemony continues till today, because it has the broadest and deepest financial markets in the world.

The third economic determinant relates to the extensiveness of the issuing country's transactional networks in the world economy, since nothing enhances a currency's appeal more than the prospect of acceptability by others (Krugman 1984). Even when foreigners do not have direct links with the issuing country, they will be tempted to use its currency because the country's worldwide transactional networks guarantee the currency's broad acceptability. Historically, this factor has usually meant a growing economy that is large in absolute size and well integrated into world markets (Eichengreen 2005).

The spectacular rise of international standing of [the] euro provides an important example. At the end of the 20th century, the supranational regional currency came into existence. Naturally the euro started with two advantages: it was the home currency for a bloc that resembled the US in terms of economic scale and it seemed likely to inherit the credibility of the Deutsche mark. As a result, it advanced quickly into the ranks of the top reserve currencies in its first decade and was expected to pose a challenge to the long global supremacy of the greenback.[16]

INSTITUTIONAL DETERMINANT

While traditional wisdom based on the above three economic deter-minants of reserve currencies provides powerful evidence in explaining why a currency comes to be used internationally, it is equally, if not more, important to notice the institutional determinants. Helleiner (2008) proposed a useful framework for such a discussion. Based on his classifi-cation, there are two distinct channels—one indirect and one direct—through which institutional factors function.

With respect to the indirect channel, institutional factors can certainly influence the three economic determinants. First, confidence in a currency is not only derived from economic fundamentals. It may also be affected by the international security power of the issuing state (McNamara 2008), the corruption severity (Barassi and Zhou 2012), and the demo-cratic accountability of the government (Pierpont 2007). Further, poten-tial foreign users are unlikely to be attracted to a currency that is not backed by adequate protection of property rights and genuine respect for the rule of law as well (Cohen 2014). Second, institutional factors cast significant impacts on the development of the financial markets, which help to boost the international standing of a currency. The finance literature has highlighted how financial markets are most likely to emerge in an institutional environment characterized by limited, constitutional government and pro-creditor legal frameworks (Walter 2006). Finally, institutional factors are critical in fostering economic growth, which in turn determines the significance of the currency network effect. Azman-Saini et al. (2010) and Compton et al. (2011) confirmed that economic freedom is a prerequisite of economic growth by analyzing cross-country data and US data respectively. Frank (2003) suggested that the issuing state can use its power to extend trade and financial networks by opening foreign markets for its firms in ways that might boost the attractiveness of its currency.

In addition to the indirect channel, institutional factors can influence international currency standing more directly. As Triffin (1960) argued, reserve currencies face a dilemma between confidence and liquidity. The currency issuing country needs to find the balance between balance of payment deficit (so as to provide global liquidity) and balance of payment surplus (so as to strengthen investor's confidence) concurrently. Following the above discussion, Germain and Schwartz (2014) identified two specific institutional foundations for creating and consolidating an international currency. On the one hand, from an outward-looking perspective, the institutional environment in the issuing country determines its capacity to negotiate international acceptance of the top currency's role and to tackle potential external political tensions. On the other hand, from an inward-looking perspective, the currency issuing country needs to address domestic concerns by ameliorating losses from the trade deficits emerging from use of the top currency and from that recycling of purchasing power.[17] To realize the above two goals, the state emitting a top currency needs to achieve a political compromise externally and domestically at the same time. This is where institutional development kicks in. For those countries with better institutional development (e.g., accountability, quality of its bureaucracy), they should be able to deal with such tensions confidently, and be more likely to promote their currency's internationalization.

The rise of China's economic power has motivated a growing number of studies to discuss the future of its currency. However, as Chey (2013) concluded, most studies of renminbi internationalization share one common limitation—regardless of whether they are positive or negative about the renminbi's future—in that they almost exclusively examine the issue from an economic determinant perspective.

The neglected issue might be of particular importance, since China's institutional environment is very much different from that of other reserve currency issuing countries. In other words, we might expect significant bias in the estimation results which has been derived from a model implicitly assuming China's institutional environment is equivalent to that of such developed countries as United States and Japan. In the following contexts, we follow an institutional analytical framework to overcome such limitation.

BACKGROUND OF RMB INTERNATIONALIZATION

Recent Achievement: In general, China's RMB internationalization strategy could be characterized as a two-track approach (Subacchi 2010). The first track aims at increasing international use of the currency, starting with regional use for trade and investment settlement and establishment of the off-shore market for RMB in Hong Kong. And the second track tackles the capital account convertibility issue, allowing greater cross-border capital mobility, encouraging holding of RMB assets by non-residents and providing instruments for hedging currency risks.

Chinn and Frankel (2005) provided a practical analytical framework for organizing the PRC's recent policy efforts in internationalizing its currency (Table 2.2). An international currency should possess three important cross-border functions: store of value; medium of exchange; and unit of accounting. Each of these functions may be further decomposed into public and private purposes.

Public Sector Achievement: In the public sector, due to long-existing legal and administrative barriers, the PRC's capital market features apparent segmentation. The nonequivalence of the offshore currency (CNH) market with the official or onshore currency (CNY) generates non-negligible

Table 2.2 International use of the Renminbi

Function	Purpose	Date	Event
Store of Value	International reserves (public)	Jul 2012	Indonesia's central bank was allowed to invest in the PRC's interbank bond market
		Apr 2013	Reserve Bank of Australia plans to invest 5% of its foreign reserves in RMB
	Currency substitution (private)	Dec 2002	Provisional Measures on Administration of Domestic Securities Investments of Qualified Foreign International Investors
		Feb 2004	Banks in Hong Kong, China were allowed to open RMB deposit accounts
		Jun 2007	First RMB-denominated bond was issued
		Dec 2012	Qianhai cross-border RMB loan rules were published by the PBC
Medium of Exchange	Vehicle currency (public)	N/A	N/A
	Invoicing currency (private)	Jul 2009	Pilot program for RMB settlement of cross-border trade transactions
		Jan 2011	Domestic enterprises were allowed to invest RMB overseas
		Aug 2011	Cross-border trade settlement in RMB was extended to the whole country
Unit of Account	Anchor for pegging (public)	N/A	N/A
	Denominating currency (private)	N/A	N/A

Note: PBC = People's Bank of China; PRC = People's Republic of China; RMB = renminbi.
Source: Chinn and Frankel (2005), updated by authors.

benefits for foreign investment; while offshore equivalent instruments whose payoff is equivalent in most, if not all, states of the world, investing in the onshore market could yield returns as much as 100–150 basis points higher than the global benchmark (Maziad and Kang 2012). As a result, RMB-denominated assets greatly appeal to foreign central banks that seek high yield yet safe investment to diversify their asset portfolio.

In terms of functioning as medium of exchange, the PRC started signing currency swap agreements with other countries under the framework of the Chiang Mai Initiative (CMI) following the Asian financial crisis. The purpose of such agreements is to improve future financial stability by functioning as an alternative to the individually accumulated foreign exchange reserves, and to promote trade and investment with these countries. As a result of the PRC's involvement in the buildup of the regional financial architecture, the RMB is used as a vehicle currency via the swap agreements and as a denominating currency in the issuance of Asian bonds under the Asian Bond Fund II scheme.

Private Sector Achievement: In the private sector, the authorities took various steps to use the RMB for settlement of international trade and investment, in order to partially replace traditional invoicing currencies such as the US dollar and yen. In July 2009, the PBC and other government departments introduced a pilot program to use RMB in the settlement of cross-border trade. This program aims at facilitating trade and investment for 67,000 enterprises in 16 provinces. Two years later in August 2011, the authorities issued a notice extending the geographical coverage of RMB trade settlement to the whole country. The PBC issued the Administrative Rules on RMB-denominated Foreign Direct Investment in October 2011 and announced in June 2012 that all PRC companies with an import/export license can use RMB to settle cross-border trade.

RMB settlement has grown very rapidly during the past years. According to the PBC data, international trade and foreign direct investment settled in RMB amount to 1 trillion yuan (US$161 billion) and 85.4 billion yuan (US$13.7 billion), respectively, during the first quarter of 2013.[18] One caveat needs to be made, which is that while RMB settlement has increased exponentially, most cross-border activities are still invoiced in other hard currencies such as US dollars. Therefore, the RMB is not yet being used as a true international currency.

In 2010, bond issuance permission was extended to nonfinancial firms and foreign multinationals doing business in the PRC. McDonald's, the well-known fast food chain store, and Caterpillar, the US-based maker of construction equipment, were among the first group of foreign companies to tap into the "dim sum" bond market. HSBC became the first non-Hong Kong, China institution to issue RMB bonds in London in April 2012. Despite its short history, the size of the offshore bond market has expanded rapidly after 2012, with continuous relaxation of restrictions imposed by PRC regulators and strong expectations of RMB appreciation.

Opportunities and Challenges: We summarized before that there are two types of factors in determining reserve currencies—a group of economic fundamentals and a set of institutional determinants. This section briefly describes how these factors look in the context of China today and identifies the opportunities and challenges for China to proceed with RMB internationalization.

Economic Scale: First, we look at the economic scale and the transaction network effects. So far the hope for the RMB to become an international currency is mainly driven by the rapid rise of the Chinese economy. During the first thirty years of economic reform, China maintained an average GDP growth of 10 percent. By the end of 2010, it had already surpassed Japan to become the world's second largest economy. The general expectation is that if strong growth momentum continues, China will likely overtake the US to ascend to the largest economy in the world within the next ten years. [Ed. Note—this actually occurred in 2014 by PPP measurement.]

But sustainability of Chinese growth could be a big question mark. Despite China's strong growth performance, economists and officials have long been worried about its growth model. Some of the key structural problems frequently discussed include unusually high investment share of GDP, heavy dependency on resource consumption, large current account surplus, unequal income distribution and serious pollution. The IMF's latest report on Article IV consultation also confirmed the international community's concern about China's structural problems (IMF 2013).

The good news is that rebalancing the Chinese economy is already underway. And there are at least three pieces of evidence supporting this claim (Huang et al. 2013). One, the current account surplus already narrowed from 10.8 percent of GDP in 2007 to below three percent in recent years. This is the reason why some officials argue that the RMB exchange rate is now close to its equilibrium. Two, recent studies suggest that shares of total and household consumption in GDP started to pick up after 2007 and 2008 (Huang et al. 2013). And three, the official estimate of the Gini coefficient points to continued improvement in income distribution among households after 2008.

Openness and Depth of Financial Markets: The second set of economic fundamentals is the openness and depth of financial markets. Recently, China appears to have accelerated its efforts of capital account liberalization after the new government took office in March 2013. One expectation is that the PBC plans to achieve basic convertibility of RMB under the capital account by 2015 and full convertibility by 2020. Such expectation is certainly consistent with monetary authority's plans to introduce market-based interest rates, adopt the deposit insurance system, strengthen market discipline for financial institutions, and allowing residents to access overseas capital markets.

Huang et al. (2012) assumed complete control of the capital account for 1977, the year before the leaders officially launched economic reform. They then adopted the classifications used by OECD and SAFE, i.e., 11 categories of capital account transactions. For each item, a score of three denotes full control, two for strong control, one for slight control, and zero for liberalized. By updating the index in response to issued legislation, an index ranging from January 1978 to December 2010 is constructed to describe the extensiveof of China's capital control. The results clearly show that capital account liberalization has been going on for some time in China. In fact, the authorities adopted a well-established strategy for liberalization: inflow first, outflow later; long-term first, short-term later; and direct investment first, portfolio investment later. If the index was 100 at the start of economic reform, it has already come down to close to 50 in recent years.

Yet several areas are still under strict regulation. In opening the securities markets to foreign investors, the Chinese government pursued a strategy of "segmenting the markets with different investors." Foreign investors can participate in the transaction of foreign currency denominated shares and debt instruments, such as the B shares, H shares and red chips stocks. However, the RMB-denominated A shares, bonds or other money market instruments are not open to the non-resident investors unless they have a Qualified Foreign Institutional Investor (QFII) quota. Restrictions on Chinese residents are even stricter. Generally, residents cannot purchase, sell or issue capital or money market instruments in the overseas markets outside the Qualified Domestic Institutional Investor (QDII) scheme.

Credibility of Economic and Legal Systems: The transition from planned to market economy necessitates the establishment of an almost entirely new set of institutions. On the positive side, there have been dramatic ideological shifts in China already that have resulted in: the gradual development of legal institutions; the decentralization of political institutions; rapid growth of the private sector; and the development of financial markets (Hasan et al. 2007). However, when talking about renminbi internationalization and development of the institutional environment, lack of credibility of economic and legal systems are still the greatest hurdles that China needs to overcome.

We do not intend to provide a complete list of the challenges faced by Chinese authorities today, but only name a few which we think are the most relevant to the topic of RMB internationalization. One, China needs an independent central bank. While there are many reasons why the PBC is not independent—perhaps there are many good reasons why that is the case—this could seriously affect achievement of monetary policy objectives in an open economy. Two, China needs a fair and transparent legal system to protect property rights and to enforce bankruptcy. An economy with many loss-making state-run enterprises (SOEs) and monopoly state-owned financial institutions could never support an international currency. Non-residents would have confidence in holding RMB assets only if they know that their property rights are effectively protected and they will be fairly treated even if they are involved in economic disputes with Chinese SOEs. And thirdly, political reforms may also be needed to improve the transparency and representativeness of the political system. While we do not have a fixed idea about specific forms of needed political reforms to become a global economic leader, China needs to adopt a political system that the rest of the world trusts.

Investment and Trade

Free Trade Zone Reform

Free trade zones have played an important role in world trade. China's are now being reshaped to help expand trade with non-traditional partners, in part to counter the TransPacific Partnership and the overbalance of the US as an export market.

Free Trade Zones Serve Domestic and International Agendas

April 2015 Issue of NewsChina | *by Sun Xiaolin*

China is preparing for a greater role in reshaping global trade.

On December 27, 2014 the National People's Congress announced that China would dramatically expand the size of the FTZ recently established in Shanghai to include several districts in the city's commercial center which currently host major multinational companies and Chinese banks. Moreover, the NPC announced that it would also establish three new FTZs in Guangdong, Fujian, and Tianjin.

The Guangdong FTZ will include the Nansha New Area in Guangzhou, Shenzhen's Qianhai district, and the Hengqin New Area of Zhuhai, a total area of 116.2 square kilometers. The Tianjin FTZ, with a total area of 119.9 square kilometers, will be comprised of Tianjin Port, Tianjin Airport, and the Binhai New Area industrial park. Finally, the 118.04-square-meter Fujian FTZ will include industrial areas in the provincial capital of Fuzhou, as well as the whole of Xiamen and Pingtan cities.

The major expansion of the FTZ program to include business centers in some of China's most prosperous cities indicates that the leadership sees the scheme as a major policy tool to serve both its domestic and international agendas.

Domestically, it is hoped that by fostering innovation, the establishment of FTZs will help China to push forward the transformation of China's energy-intensive growth model, which has been largely driven by cheap labor and created a nationwide pollution problem.

China launched the Shanghai FTZ in September 2013, and the government has used it to test a number of new economic policies including negative list management of foreign investment, preferential trade and financial policies, and opening up more industries to foreign investors.

By liberalizing government regulation within a series of FTZs, the government also hopes to push forward administrative reforms. As China's international relations adopt a different government and policy framework, particularly in dealings with Western countries, the existence of an FTZ program will help China align its economic and financial policies and practices with international norms.

In recent years, the US has been actively promoting the Trans-Pacific Partnership (TPP), the Transatlantic Trade and Investment Partnership (TTIP), and the Plurilateral Services Agreement (PSA) among its European and Asian allies. As these new initiatives are ultimately designed to replace the framework of the WTO, unless China takes a more active role in studying and participating in the global trade rule-making process, it may find itself marginalized in the long run.

With the expansion of the FTZ program, China can experiment with various different policies and regulations and gain valuable experience in participating in international negotiations.

From this perspective, the expansion of the FTZ scheme is also an integral part of China's global strategy. In 2014, China's leadership adopted the OBOR initiative, meaning its New Silk Road and Maritime Silk Road multilateral trade initiatives, as core elements of its global economic strategy. Through such schemes, which stress international cooperation and greater multilateral market access, China aims to play an active role in facilitating regional integration.

China is currently conducting extensive negotiations with several European countries to reach an agreement on free trade deals. Thus far,

Iceland and Switzerland look like the most likely candidates to first reach consensus with the leadership in Beijing. In Asia, China is negotiating with South Korea and Japan over a free trade area covering all three countries. Beijing has also stepped up its efforts to establish closer economic ties with BRICS (Brazil, Russia, India, China, and South Africa) member states.

Through experience gained in its FTZs, China will be in a better position to participate, or even take a leading role, in rule-making for a new international trade order.

With the expansion of the FTZ program, China can experiment with various different policies and regulations and gain valuable experience in participating in international negotiations.

The author is a researcher and co-founder of the ShiJu Thinktank, an independent Chinese consultancy specializing in finance and economics.

Where is Private Investment?

To understand the direction of the Chinese economy, keep an eye on the National Development and Reform Commission (NDRC), China's top macroeconomic planning body. This powerful agency has lots of clout. In May 2014, in response to falling government revenues, and the fact that Chinese governments have wasted US$6.9 trillion on inefficient investments since 2009, the NRDC opened up 80 infrastructure projects to private investors. Given the pitfalls of often-capricious regulatory action, the response of private money has been tepid at best. Only about half of the projects have attracted much interest from investors. The *NewsChina* article "When We Need Your Money" explores this new approach to getting incompetent governments out of the infrastructure business in China.

When We Need Your Money

February 2015 Issue of NewsChina | *by Sun Zhe, Han Yong*

While the State is calling for more private investment in infrastructure, private enterprises remain skeptical.

In a guideline released late November 2014, China opened seven industrial sectors to private capital, ranging from transport to social services—an extension of a May 2014 invitation to private businesses to invest in 80 pilot infrastructure projects.

This increased openness to the private sector, announced by the NDRC, China's top macroeconomic planning body, is a result of declining growth in the government's fiscal revenue, according to Zuo Xiaolei, chief economist with Beijing-based finance firm Galaxy Securities.

"Also, it is not appropriate for [the government] to invest directly," Zuo said.

ILL-ADVISED

Over the past decade, local governments have repeatedly proved their ineptitude when it comes to investment. According to a report released by a research organization attached to the NDRC, Chinese governments have wasted US$6.9 trillion on inefficient investments since 2009, following a flood of loans for infrastructure projects doled out to local governments and SOEs as part of China's stimulus program during the global recession.

As a result, China used 30 percent more cement from 2011 to 2013 than the US has for the whole of the 21st century, according to data from the US Geological Survey and China's National Bureau of Statistics. Much of this was used to build unnecessary expressways and ill-advised construction developments, creating the much-discussed "ghost-town" phenomenon.

These inefficient investments, many of which had no hope of generating enough profit to cover the interest of the loans used to finance them, accounted for about half of China's total investment over the period 2009–2013. The majority were injected into industries like steel, housing, renewable energy and automobiles, and infrastructure—particularly expressways.

It has become infeasible to rely solely on government spending for infrastructure construction, given that governments themselves are suffering from fiscal strain due to the decline in the land sales that account for more than half their revenues. Outstanding loans accumulated over the past few years only add to their fiscal burden.

Annual growth in fixed investments, or those in infrastructure, topped 25 percent before 2012, but slowed to 20 percent and was expected to drop to 16 percent in 2014. By the end of June 2013, loans to regional governments had reached a total of 11 trillion yuan (US$1.8tn), with 2.4 trillion yuan (US$453bn)—more than a fifth of them—due in 2015.

Bad loans resulting from bad investments on the part of governments and SOEs are now adding to the country's systemic financial risk. The side effects of the stimulus program are also making it difficult for the country to steer itself away from the credit-driven model—bad loans, a slowing housing market, and industrial overcapacity resulting from poor investments during the stimulus are weighing down the economy, and stymieing the country's efforts to carry out economic reform.

In the first half of 2014, GDP growth in more than two-thirds of China's provinces fell short of their targets—a rare occurrence—while fiscal revenue growth in 11 provinces fell below 10 percent, in comparison to the double-digit growth recorded in the past few years.

China's GDP growth fell to 7.3 percent in the third quarter of 2014, a six-year low, causing new fears of further quantitative easing and stimulus. Given that domestic consumption is not expected to grow fast enough to balance out the slowdown in exports, the government is predicted to rely on investment again to boost the economy. Due to the government's cash flow problem, many believe the private sector to be the natural choice.

HESITANCE

So far, however, since the program was launched in May 2014, more than half of the 80 pilot projects open to private capital, including roads, railways, and energy infrastructure, have yet to arouse much interest among private investors.

Their caution is reasonable—in the wake of the stimulus program, when governments were suddenly given easy access to loans from State banks, there were plenty of examples of governments unilaterally canceling private–public partnership projects. While government leaders have repeatedly refuted the idea of another such stimulus program, private investors do not appear to have been convinced.

Premier Li Keqiang has vowed on various occasions that the central government will not launch another stimulus program in pursuit of short-term growth, instead relying more on the improvement of market mechanisms, calling large stimulus packages an "unsustainable" measure that could "sow the seeds of a new risk of relying on government investment to generate economic growth." The central government has repeatedly stated its intention to reform and switch to a more efficient, sustainable and balanced economic growth model.

At a government meeting in early 2014, Xu Shaoshi, director of the NDRC, said that central government investment would mainly be used to build railways in the country's central and western regions, as well as for affordable housing and irrigation projects elsewhere.

But risks exist even for private companies who take on infrastructure projects without partnering with the government.

In one case, a private company in Inner Mongolia took five years to get a three-kilometer branch of railway approved and built. After it was eventually put into use, the company found that all railway transportation was monopolized by a single local State-owned company, locking the private company out of railway cargo quotas.

Moreover, most of the sectors to date open to private investment, such as environmental protection, irrigation, municipal services, transportation, energy infrastructure, and social services, call for long-term investment that will likely only turn a profit after a number of years. Meanwhile, most lucrative sectors such as electricity, telecoms, and banking, remain comparatively closed off to private investment.

Private investors, playing with their own finite resources on an unequal playing field, are bound to be more cautious than governments and SOEs, for whom short-term GDP growth is vital for the promotion of officials.

Projects need a potential minimum profit margin of 5 to 8 percent in order to attract private capital, said Zuo Xiaolei of Galaxy Securities. However, at least in the short term, the seven sectors newly opened to private investment fall far short of this figure, according to a private entrepreneur who asked to remain anonymous. It might take even longer for the NDRC to win the trust of private enterprises.

Status of Foreign Direct Investment

Foreign companies looking to invest on the ground in China face a host of obstacles. Although developed-country members of the WTO are committed to provide domestic treatment to foreign investors, China was not required to meet that standard. There are multiple laws and policies governing foreign direct investors, and pitfalls litter the landscape. In a *NewsChina* interview "Investing in Investment," Professor Sang Baichuan, Dean of the Institute of International Economy at the University of International Business and Economics, lays out the landscape for FDI, as well as the direction China is taking to better encourage the kind of investment it seeks.

Investing in Investment

January 2015 Issue of NewsChina | *by Li Jia*

China's reform of its foreign investment policies matters to all investors, and will set the roadmap for China's ambitions as a new international rule maker.

To inject impetus into its long-stagnant reform agenda, China has once again resorted to boosting the market by further opening it up, a strategy that served the country well after its WTO accession in 2001. Today's China, unlike its pre-WTO incarnation, carries a lot more economic clout, and its leaders are ambitious to participate in shaping the new rules of the international trade and investment game.

Professor Sang Baichuan, Dean of the Institute of International Economy at the University of International Business and Economics, a leading expert of major projects undertaken by China's National Social Sciences Fund, explains to *NewsChina* how the government's investment policies have to be retooled to achieve the leadership's dual goals of greater access alongside broader participation.

NewsChina: China has opened more of its internal market to foreign investment and imposed more market laws and regulations over the years, yet foreign companies in China are today complaining more than ever that their access and legal protection remain limited. Why is this?

Sang Baichuan: Generally, China's investment environment has improved compared with the early years after the WTO accession, but in some aspects it has deteriorated or progressed too slowly. The complaints of foreign investors mainly center on these areas.

Under a new system imposed after China's WTO accession, the review of foreign investment projects is conducted by a committee and based on rules covering national security, antitrust, and industrial policies. This was designed to be a more efficient and rule-based system than the old one in which foreign investors had to deal with more agencies and agree to more detailed checks of their operational affairs at the micro level.

However, without a deadline for such reviews, foreign investors given no response even after a long wait for approval are often told that the committee has yet to convene. If they don't want to wait longer, they have to engage in "public relations" with government agencies responsible for the review process. This has cost foreign investors time and money, and led to corruption. The old system, though more complicated and rigid, set a deadline. As a result, foreign investors feel that progress on paper has been turned into a setback due to opaque implementation.

Recently the NDRC has updated its guidelines determining the commercial sectors in which foreign investment is, variously, encouraged, permitted, restricted, or prohibited. Despite fewer restrictions, this form of market access management is not in line with increasingly uniform international principles and practices set in place after the global financial crisis.

More countries have adopted the condition of pre-access national treatment, which puts foreign investors under the same market access and administrative approval system as their domestic counterparts—

the only way in which foreign investors can benefit from the advantages of reduced red tape enjoyed by Chinese investors. Also, a "negative list," which specifies restrictions on foreign investors, has been used in the Shanghai FTZ launched in September 2013, since China agreed to adopt the negative list model in bilateral investment agreement talks with the US. Though the adopted list was too long, it was regarded as a first step in the right direction and was expected to be shortened in future bilateral negotiations.

The updated guidelines, however, are apparently regarded by foreign investors as showing a lack of will to change old thinking as swiftly as they had expected.

Committing to pre-access national treatment and negative lists also requires a legal framework applicable to all parties on an equal basis. Foreign investment in China is not governed by the country's Corporate Law. Instead, foreign companies are subject to three separate laws: one governing Sino-foreign joint ventures, one governing Sino-foreign cooperative enterprises, and one governing wholly foreign-funded enterprises. Calls to integrate these three into one and ultimately replace this with the Corporate Law have been growing in recent years. However, a timetable for initiating the legislation process has yet to be set. Foreign companies feel they are still being treated differently by [China's] legal system.

NewsChina: Wariness of foreign investment also seems to be growing, though exhorting people to "buy domestic" hasn't persuaded Chinese people to avoid foreign goods. When it comes to foreign investment, however, the rhetoric of "protecting our national brands and security" does have currency. How much does investment affect the market?

SB: Imported products face individual consumers who care more about maximizing the value of their spending, while investors have direct conflicts of interests with better-organized companies. When a company is acquired, its investors will lose their market share, and its managers and employees will lose their positions or even their jobs.

Meanwhile, other companies in the same industry feel the pressure of new competition which could reshape the market. In spite of globalization, the concept of the nation state still prevails in international politics. For example, when Rolls-Royce Motor Cars was sold to Volkswagen in 1998, there was an outcry in the British media about the loss of a national icon, and protests from trade unions fearing job cuts.

Such sentiment is stronger in economies with weaker domestic industries when compared to multinationals. Chinese brands are highly competitive on the consumer products market, but major sectors in the high-end services industry—banking, insurance, securities, accountancy, and legal services—not only involve national economic security but are less developed in an emerging economy like China. In this context, China is more cautious about openness in these areas as opposed to, say, the consumer goods market.

The solution is to improve China's own regulatory competence, and not to overestimate the risks of openness. In insurance, which is probably more open [to foreign investment] than any other financial sector [in China], local insurers are doing better than foreign newcomers. In the banking sector, with its State-backed monopoly and full range of services at nationwide networks, further openness would hardly shake the market structure dominated by Chinese players. This is true in many other service sectors.

NewsChina: There are also growing calls among Chinese officials and analysts that the country should be more selective than ever towards foreign investment. Only investment that will facilitate China's economic restructuring, they said, should be welcome. Do you think China's foreign investment policy should be closely related to the industrial policy?

SB: In many economies, some industries are encouraged to improve competitiveness throughout the whole economy. Moreover, the capital shortage which makes any investment welcome is no longer present in China.

The key point is that such industrial policies should be applied equally to all enterprises. In many sectors where foreign investment is kept outside on the grounds of environmental protection or overcapacity, domestic enterprises are still expanding, making industrial policies aimless.

Indeed, openness towards domestic and foreign investment should go side by side, leading to sweeping reform of the whole investment system. For example, pre-access national treatment requires that administrative approval processes be simplified as much as possible and then applied equally to both domestic and foreign investors. China's recent campaign of streamlining the approval system for domestic businesses is actually a preparatory step towards that.

One of the big problems in integrating openness towards both domestic and foreign investment is the poor coordination between policymakers from different government agencies, and even different offices within the same agency. This is why a unified Corporate Law and pre-access national treatment are urgently needed.

Actually, international investors attach more importance to a transparent and fair regulatory environment than to preferable treatment. In some places in China, local government agency officials whose careers rely on how much investment they attract have appealed to foreign investors with various favorable policies. Then, other agencies without these political interests have imposed annual reviews and huge fines on foreign companies for failing to comply with various rules. Local governments, closely connected to local companies, are frequently overruled by locally based SOEs, leaving foreign companies as sitting targets.

NewsChina: During its WTO negotiations, China, as a developing economy, could ask for certain exceptions to protect domestic industries and enforce more relaxed standards for social responsibility. Is it still possible for China to do this?

SB: This is more difficult to negotiate in bilateral talks than in multinational arenas in which you can find allies to help you resist higher standards. For example, members of the OECD group of industrial economies haven't yet reached an agreement on investment protection.

All global companies want better protection in host countries. The pressure to adopt higher standards is greater in a bilateral setting. The two core issues on foreign investment in China, as elsewhere in the world, are better investor protection and stricter corporate social responsibility standards. The US and the EU have insisted that their level of protection is already higher than China's, and thus demand improvement on China's side on the basis of reciprocal agreements. If Chinese companies want better protection in those markets, China also has to offer something in return. This is a global trend that causes countries to keep improving investor protection to compete for foreign investment which brings advanced management and ideas. China is not short of money, but still needs to import expertise.

There is also the question of a regulatory framework on corporate social responsibility. Multinationals always claim they have the same global policies on environmental and labor protection, but implementation is often different in developed and developing countries. All companies pursue maximum profits. Weak law enforcement in China, combined with the poor corporate social responsibility records of Chinese companies, has incentivized some multinationals to water down their own social responsibility policies with impunity.

It will be hard for China to go against the global trend of moving towards more liberalized investment and stricter social standards in its bilateral negotiations.

NewsChina: China is trying to push forward several regional economic integration projects, notably the Free Trade Area of Asia Pacific

(FTAAP), the New Silk Road initiative, and the Maritime Silk Road project with Southeast Asia. Does this mean, as many analysts believe, that China has the willingness and competence to become an economic rule maker?

SB: The era in which China only accepts whatever international economic rules have been laid down by others has ended. If new rules do not cover the second largest economy in the world, then they will have limited applicability.

In the meantime, China has realized the risk of being marginalized by a future US-led international investment framework. Seven out of China's 10 top trading partners in the Asia-Pacific region have already joined the TPP negotiations. China was not invited to participate in the beginning, then a request to join was refused by the US. The EU and the US, China's top two trading partners, are working on their bilateral TTIP. It is very likely that both the TPP and TTIP could result in a shift of some business that China might have hoped to secure. For example, will foreign investors choose to enjoy easier access and zero tariffs by building a plant in Vietnam and then exporting from there to other TPP member markets, or will they choose to do this in China—which can't offer these benefits?

China does not want to just sit and wait to either accept the new rules or see the loss of trade and investment. This is why the country is trying to push forward its own regional economic integration initiatives. These mechanisms provide a possible way for China to at least become a participant in the drafting of new international economic rules.

However, the FTAAP does not liberalize trade and investment as much as the TPP. Even less-developed economies like Vietnam have joined the TPP negotiations, showing willingness to accept the principles of greater liberalization and stricter social norms. The TPP negotiations are not easy, given resistance from Japanese farmers and difficulty of less-developed economies in meeting the high standard.

However, it might not be very attractive for a country ready to accept high standards to invest a lot of resources in negotiations on more limited liberalization and a less rule-based regulatory agreement like the FTAAP.

The FTAAP initiative may help facilitate regional economic integration, but the prospects may not be as bright as expected.

NewsChina: Foreign companies in China have shown strong interest in seeking business opportunities in China's new initiatives for regional economic integration. Will they have a special role to play?

SB: Foreign companies and China share interests when it comes to regional economic integration. They themselves are part of the global supply chain. Given this, their advantage in experience and expertise in global operations will help them secure a head start in these new opportunities. During this process, Chinese companies, especially those acting as partners in joint ventures, can learn from them and go international with their foreign partners.

In addition, as the supply chain in the Southeast Asian and Central Asian countries is not as developed, these foreign companies still need their Chinese suppliers for parts and logistics. This will create more export orders and new opportunities to invest abroad for Chinese suppliers.

That Troublesome Stock Exchange

A vibrant and reliable stock market is a key factor in capitalizing a country's enterprises. As Beijing and the local governments begin to step back from willy-nilly financing of pet projects, a private equity market is essential to fuel continued growth. Several obstacles have stood in the way: the Shanghai Stock Exchange, the principle mainland bourse, has been plagued by lack of transparency and sound regulation. As a result, there has been a sequence of largely rumor-driven wild swings in share prices over the years. As Li Jia puts it, Chinese stock market investors have even joked that they should have put their money into heart attack pills, simply to turn a profit on the anxiety they have endured.

Also, the yuan is not yet a freely exchangeable international currency, though this is a long-term goal of Beijing. These factors discourage investors, especially foreign ones. China has now taken steps to correct these problems by linking the Hong Kong Stock Exchange, known for good governance and transparency, with the Shanghai Stock Exchange. Li Jia's article, "Bears Meet Bulls," explains the mechanics and ramifications of this important step.

To explain some acronyms used by the author:
QDII = Qualified Domestic Institutional Investor
QFII = Qualified Foreign Institutional Investor
RQFII = Renminbi Qualified Foreign Institutional Investor

Bears Meet Bulls

February 2015 Issue of NewsChina | *by Li Jia*

While some declared the hotly anticipated windfall from the linking up of the Shanghai and Hong Kong stock exchanges over before it began, others argue that it is vital to focus on the scheme's long-term goals.

Chinese stock market investors have joked that they should have put their money into heart attack pills, simply to turn a profit on the anxiety they have endured.

On December 5, 2014, China's stock markets reported the world's largest transaction values, closing at a five-year high. The same markets broke this record in morning trading the following day, before stock prices plummeted that afternoon. The following days saw prices rally, triggering strongly bullish forecasts for 2015. The trading spree, however, seemed to have little to do with the much-hyped Shanghai–Hong Kong Stock Connect, a mutual market access point between the Chinese mainland and overseas investors.

For mainland and Hong Kong investors, mutual market access has held strong appeal since the government's plans to link the two exchanges were revealed in April 2014. Every announcement concerning the deal caused prices to fluctuate based on the assumption that a greater influx of capital would ultimately push prices up.

For China's policymakers, linking the country's two largest stock exchanges was an important bid to inject momentum into the country's growth and reform agenda by further opening up China's markets. Hong Kong's well-established and internationalized trading floor was expected to lend rationality and more efficient regulation to the mainland's chaotic investment environment. Moreover, making the mainland's premium A-shares more accessible to international investors and the further internationalization of the Chinese yuan could cement Hong Kong's position as a leading international financial hub.

However, the huge influx of foreign capital into the mainland anticipated after the link-up simply failed to materialize, leading to pessimism that the linking of the two stock exchanges would, in the long term, prove to be a white elephant, and fail to revitalize China's chaotic stock market.

The madcap purchase of A-shares a few days later was attributed to an unexpected interest rate cut by China's central bank on November 21, 2014, and had little to do with greater international appetite for Chinese assets. The flow of money into Hong Kong from the mainland has been even more underwhelming than the volume of assets traveling the other way. Now, the naysayers are finally being listened to.

ACTION

When Premier Li Keqiang announced the index link plan at the annual Boao Asia Forum on April 10, 2014, it came as a surprise. Barely three hours after the announcement, before analysts could respond to the breaking news, a joint statement on an operational framework for the scheme, including a schedule and an outline of its potential scale, was issued by China Securities Regulatory Commission (CSRC) and the Hong Kong Securities and Futures Commission (SFC). It later emerged that the scheme had been in the pipeline for over two years, but kept secret by its masterminds.

This carefully cloistered preparation has been interpreted as an attempt to avoid the failure of the abortive bid to link the two markets in July 2007. At that time, a liquidity bubble was believed to be threatening China's economy, while Hong Kong's underperforming stock market was in dire need of capital. Chinese mainland investors' access to Hong Kong's stock market could, the theory went, redirect some foreign exchange reserves, a major source of liquidity on the mainland, and at the same time bail out the territory's stock market. Four months after the announcement sent share prices rocketing in Hong Kong, the scheme was shelved over government fears of massive capital flight from the mainland. The advent of the global financial crisis also saw governments turn inward in an attempt to shore up financial defense mechanisms.

While the imminent resurrection of the link-up project has been mooted in some quarters since 2007, economic planners have been careful to manage expectations for fear of a return to the instability of that infamous summer.

As a result, until now, only institutional Chinese and international funds could access one another's capital markets through QDII and QFII schemes. In 2011, RQFII, the yuan-denominated incarnation of the QFII scheme, was initiated. Investor involvement in these schemes is largely restricted to fund managers, and thus they only tap a fraction of the potential market.

WISH LIST

The new, more sophisticated scheme is part of Premier's Li's Boao pledge to combine the further reform and opening up of mainland markets.

Zeng Gang with the research center of the Shanghai Stock Exchange (SSE) explained at a November 20, 2014 forum sponsored by the State Council website gov.cn and the Renmin University of China, that linking the Shanghai index with a Hong Kong market dominated by foreign blue chip investors could bring positive change to the mainland market, where the bulk of capital originates with retail investors speculating on the volatile share prices of generally underperforming companies.

Zeng also argued that the link-up would provide pressure and incentives to improve corporate and regulatory governance in the mainland, seen as a major turn-off for investors.

The other purpose of the scheme is to facilitate the internationalization of the Chinese yuan, a process which has gathered unprecedented momentum in the last few years. Stock transactions which take place between the two markets will be settled in yuan as opposed to Hong Kong dollars. Once a closed currency, the yuan is now becoming an increasingly preferred denomination in China-related international trade. A report by Deutsche Bank in July estimated more than US$400 billion in Chinese yuan had been deposited offshore by the end of 2014, and most of it in Hong Kong. Now, many are clamoring for these reserves to be invested in the Chinese mainland, the world's largest market for yuan-denominated transactions.

As of November 17, 2014, Hong Kong residents have had a former daily foreign exchange limit of 20,000 yuan (about US$3,270) waived, in the words of the Hong Kong Monetary Authority, with regard to "the development of the offshore [yuan] market and the launch of the Shanghai-Hong Kong Stock Connect."

In terms of its architecture, the new scheme is a two-way track open to both institutional and retail investors, with more convenient protocols and better-designed risk control. There is a threshold of US$81,700 minimum balance applied to securities and cash accounts belonging to mainland retail investors, while no restrictions are imposed on mainland institutional investors or overseas investors.

In addition, investors can place orders and obtain settlements through local intermediaries based on their home market, thus eliminating the need to deal with unfamiliar overseas brokers and clearance houses. Quotas are set for daily and total net buying, with more quotas applied to the mainland market, though no limits are placed on daily selling. Capital gains from the sale of shares are immediately repatriated to minimize unwanted impact in the host markets. On November 14, 2014, China's Finance Ministry confirmed that profits made by foreign investors on China's capital market would no longer be subject to Chinese taxation from November 17 that year.

Short-term profits remain the primary concern of stock traders. So far, mid-range and big-cap stocks, including 569 A-shares in Shanghai and 273 in Hong Kong, are on sale to international investors, representing 90 and 82 percent of their respective markets' value. A-share investors were hoping that a foreign preference for blue chips would boost the value of such stocks in Shanghai, particularly those also listed in Hong Kong, as their A-share prices have failed to maintain parity with their alternatives since 2010.

A more internationalized A-share market will also increase the chances that all A-shares will be included on the Morgan Stanley Composite Index (MSCI) list of Emerging Markets Indexes, a benchmark followed by global asset investors. Wang Qing, CEO of China's largest private hedge fund management firm Shanghai Chongyang Investment Management, estimated at the gov.cn forum that the inclusion would bring thousands of billions of US dollars of foreign capital into the mainland capital market. Glowing forecasts like this further fueled expectations of the Shanghai-Hong Kong Stock Connect.

PRECISION STRIKES

Since July 2014, the Hang Seng China AH Premium Index, a comparative index of dual-listed shares, has shown increased convergence, with some A-share prices even creeping up to premium levels. Relevant Hong Kong stocks also rose in price, many in defiance of overall share performance. However, when progress deviated from the schedule set by economic planners, both markets immediately dropped.

Given the already evident market enthusiasm and the significance of the project in terms of China's broader reform agenda, many have argued that the quota system is unworkable. However, in practice, the four weeks preceding December 12, 2014 saw an average of only 25 percent of the daily capital quota used by overseas investors in their Hong Kong—Shanghai trading, and an even lower percentage in transactions heading the other way, according to HKEx data. Aside from one short, lopsided trading frenzy on November 17, 2014, which quickly exhausted the Northbound quota, trading has remained well below the government-approved limits.

Generally, analysts believe that it will take investors time to warm up to this unusual way of doing business, and that an initial "silly season" was inevitable. In a November 23, 2014 article on the HKEx website, the exchange's CEO Charles Li attributed the particularly cold reception from mainland investors to account balance requirements applied to mainland retail investors, a continued lack of access to Hong Kong's small-cap stocks, and the fact that the approval process for mainland institutional investors has yet to be launched.

Indeed, even the total quota for the whole trial project represented only 1.5 percent of the tradable A-share market, and 1 percent of what was available on Hong Kong's main board. Gui Haoming, chief analyst of Shenyin Wanguo Securities, is one of the few analysts who has repeatedly urged caution regarding foreign capital influx, arguing that investor tastes do not change overnight.

In a pre-launch interview with the Communist Party mouthpiece the *People's Daily*, Gui said that net capital flow into the market was "negligible," adding that many foreign investors, already enjoying a presence in China through QFII and RQFII, wouldn't see many advantages in getting involved with this new scheme. The new link-up, Gui told *NewsChina*, would not be "the decisive factor" in whether China's A-shares would be included in international MSCI indexes in 2015.

For the same reasons, financial commentator Ye Tan, writing in the *National Business Daily* on November 17, 2014, does not believe the link-up will dramatically alter the behavior of mainland investors in the near future.

The quota undershoot seems to have undermined analyst confidence, with many now refocusing on long-term goals. Ye is more optimistic when it comes to the scheme's potential impact on the internationalization of the yuan, while Gui told *NewsChina* that the project's initial operational stability is proof that it is "basically sound," predicting a bright future.

Indeed, quotas for existing link-ups with overseas markets like QFII, QDII, and RQFII have all been loosened after a few years' steady operations. Though the scale of net buying has so far been limited, HKEx statistics show active buying and selling for most stocks, indicating robust liquidity.

When the new scheme, along with other existing link-ups, scales up, Gui said, it could help drive forward reforms on several fronts, particularly by granting easier market access to innovative start-ups, giving domestic institutional investors better opportunities to learn from their international counterparts, and making the domestic market big enough for a robust integration into the risk-ridden global capital market. He argued that too much attention has been focused on short-term performance in the early stages of the link-up, causing observers to "miss the real purpose" of the project.

Hu Zhanghong, CEO of Hong Kong-based investment bank CCB International, which is fully owned by the Construction Bank of China, said at a December 10, 2014 forum in Hong Kong that H-shares belonging to mainland companies listed on the HKEx did not attract much interest from international investors early on. Now, 53 percent of total HKEx capitalization comes from mainland stocks, according to HKEx data. Gui and other analysts generally agree that a similar outcome can be expected for the Shanghai–Hong Kong Stock Connect.

There are some long wish lists being drawn up for China's further integration into the global marketplace. However, the sheer size of China's internal market ensures that no external driving force can outmatch that constituted by local investors and regulators who, more than any other interest groups, desperately need to see change.

Banking and Finance

How to Fix the Banks?

Few would argue that China's banking system is in a tenuous position. Many loans made to finance the country's infrastructure have little chance of being repaid on time. Former central banker Wu Xiaoling is in an excellent position to give an insider's view on this issue. In her interview, "Banks Should First Treat Their Borrowers as Enemies, Then Allies," she is asked about "wealth management products" as being especially troublesome. These products, popular with Chinese investors, generally offer a higher yield than bank deposits, but come with a risk of loss that may not be well understood by the investor.

Bloomberg News reported on 14 August 2014 that "the average annualized return was 5.2 percent [for wealth management products], compared with 3 percent for benchmark one-year deposits. . . . Wealth-management products typically require a minimum investment of 50,000 yuan." And according to the *Wall Street Journal* (15 August 2014), "a report issued by China's wealth management product registration platform showed that China's banking system had a total of 12.65 trillion yuan (US$2.04 trillion) of outstanding wealth-management products at the end of June, 2014 up 24 percent from the beginning of the year."

Also addressed in Wu's interview is "shadow banking." Shadow banks are financial institutions that create credit but are not subject to the strict financial regulations that govern banks. Typically, this is because they do not accept deposits and thus have no depositors to protect. Shadow banking may also include unregulated activity by otherwise regulated banks. Again per *Bloomberg News* (14 August 2014), "China's shadow banking, including wealth products, trusts, money-market funds and some interbank lending is estimated at 27 trillion yuan, or about 19 percent of the nation's total banking assets, researchers of the Chinese Academy of Social Sciences said in May." Generally speaking, Ms. Wu is relatively sanguine about the general banking situation, but more concerned with wealth management products and shadow banking, which she believes can be effectively managed through further regulation.

Banks Should First Treat Their Borrowers as Enemies, Then Allies

September 2014 Issue of NewsChina | *by Chen Jiying*

According to former deputy central bank governor Wu Xiaoling, new financial products, shadow banking, and bad debt aren't as problematic as they may seem.

Wu Xiaoling, former deputy governor of the People's Bank of China, the country's central bank, and a major advocate of market-oriented financial reform, speaks to *NewsChina* about China's shadow banking system, and how China's banks can lend enterprises a hand.

NewsChina: The bottom line for the regulation of China's financial sector is the prevention of systemic risk, but while the economy is slowing down, the risk of bad loans is increasing. Do you see any systemic risk there?

Wu Xiaoling: My view is that it has yet to appear. Though the non-performing loan ratio is increasing among Chinese commercial banks, they are much more capable of dealing with risk than they were a few years ago. As of the end of 2013, the capital adequacy ratio of Chinese commercial banks was 12.19 percent, with a 9.95 percent core capital ratio, meaning their capital is of fairly good quality.

Their non-performing loan ratio was 1.49 percent as of the end of last year—for the administrators of foreign banks, a figure below 3 percent is seen as ideal. On the other hand, the provision rate of Chinese commercial banks is as high as 273 percent, way above the international standard of 150 percent. These data indicate that Chinese banks have great capacity to absorb and digest non-performing loans.

NewsChina: Will the clean up of wealth management products exacerbate the funding difficulties experienced by enterprises, and will this harm the real economy?

WX: The wealth management products sold by banks stand for a long funding chain and thus are very expensive sources of funding for enterprises. The clean-up is meant to convert wealth management products into investment business for which the investors themselves shoulder the risk, while currently almost all banks offer implicit guarantee of risk-free fixed yields for wealth management products. The normalization of wealth management products would help bring down the excessively high loan rates. It would shorten the funding chain and thus reduce funding costs for enterprises to rectify interbank deposits and wealth management products. This is unlikely to have any impact on the economy.

NewsChina: A report by the China Academy of Social Sciences revealed that Chinese shadow banking amounts to more than 40 percent of China's GDP. What is your view of shadow banking?

WX: In light of its efficacy in raising funds, shadow banking can be seen to a certain extent as direct financing. It could work as a supplement to bank lending, and could be an appropriate means of direct funding.

Shadow banking should be evaluated objectively and neutrally. One type of shadow banking is within the formal financial system, and the other outside it. The former includes financial institutions such as trust companies that have finance licenses but are under-regulated, which make up the majority of China's shadow banking sector. Chinese shadow banking only boomed after 2006 when the subprime crisis broke out in the US and the Chinese economy was suffering from a decline in global demand, forcing Chinese companies to turn to shadow banking for funding since they could not get loans from banks. In addition, when the stimulus package was launched to cope with the financial recession, it led to a flood of liquidity in the market—another cause for the boom in shadow banking.

NewsChina: What are the risks involved in shadow banking, and how best to regulate it?

WX: Shadow banking primarily involves four problematic risks, namely ambiguity of legal implications, disorganized operation, implicit guarantee of risk-free fixed yields and lack of efficient regulation, with the former being the most pressing risk. Due to the lack of clear information in the sector, investors are willing to share the gains but not the losses and risks, and in order to defend their respective reputations, sellers of financial products try all means to redeem in spite of their own losses. This is no way to maintain market order in the long term.

Excessive regulation exists in some parts of China's shadow banking sector, while insufficient regulation exists in other parts. Along with the development and reform of China's financial sector, we should clarify the boundaries of regulation—we should recognize that we do not have to impose regulation on all credit activities.

First we need to clarify the function of a product, its legal implications, and the breakdown of its yield and risk. We also need to make clear whether a certain financial activity involves a small or a large group of people. If it concerns only a small group who are able to handle relatively high risk, regulation should be moderate. Meanwhile, if the activity involves large numbers of small-time investors, strict regulation should be implemented, given the herd mentality and "free-rider dilemma" that tend to accompany this type of financial activity.

NewsChina: What is the best method to strike a balance between managing financial risk and supporting the real economy, given that many companies are floundering in the current economic downturn?

WX: The enterprises confronted with difficulties fall into two categories, as do their loans. The first type are those burdened with obsolete production capacity—unless they can find an alternative industry to transfer to, their loans can only be written off as bad debt.

The second type are those with good technology in industries suffering from overcapacity. In this case, help would be needed to digest or transfer the excessive production capacity and to expand the market. In these cases, the banks should not call in their loans right away, as this would push enterprises into bankruptcy and potentially harm enterprise, the bank itself or society as a whole.

Banks should first treat their borrowers as enemies, then allies. That is to say, banks must conduct rigorous auditing and risk assessment before lending to ensure security of loans. After lending, banks are obliged to help enterprises with their production, in order to guarantee the safety of lending. It is to the detriment of the bank itself to pull back a loan at the first sign that an enterprise is facing financial difficulty, and the bank should raise its tolerance for bad debt to help enterprises weather the storm.

Thus, banks should closely analyze the causes of bad debts, and should help enterprises through difficulties by solving their problems under the premise of concern for "moral hazards."

Alipay Paves the Way

Jumping into the largely government-controlled banking business, Alibaba in 2013 launched an online offering using Alipay (like PayPal) to allow customers to invest in high-yielding wealth management products. This highly popular service forced many state banks to follow suit. The entertaining account of Jack Ma's successful tilt with the fossilized SOE Chinese banking system is described by Sun Zhe in the article, "Who Needs Banks?"

Who Needs Banks?

March 2014 Issue of NewsChina | *by Sun Zhe*

Alipay is hoping to change the way the finance game is played in China.

The charismatic founder of Chinese e-commerce giant Alibaba, Jack Ma, vowed five years ago that if China's banks didn't change, Alibaba would change the banks.

Now, he looks close to achieving his goal.

Half a year after launching Yu E Bao, or "leftover treasure," a service allowing customers using Alipay (an online payment system similar to PayPal) to convert cash into highly liquid investment products with much higher yields than bank deposits, many Chinese banks have attempted to follow suit.

By the end of 2013, Yu E Bao had gathered a user base of 43 million, with combined deposits of 185 billion yuan (US$30.6bn), making it the second largest single wealth management fund in China.

Since June 2013, when Yu E Bao was launched, its annual returns rose from 4.3 to about 6.5 percent by early January 2014. Considering the tightening liquidity in China's money market towards the end of 2013, this meant the platform offered more than double the ROI of a benchmark one-year fixed-term deposit, and 20 times the interest of a regular checking account.

Predictably, State bankers expressed concerns that Yu E Bao was chipping away at their deposit base. Unlike their international counterparts who mainly profit from investment, Chinese banks, most of them State-run, rely on the State-controlled interest rate margin for the majority of their profits.

Yao Jingyuan, former chief economist with the National Bureau of Statistics, even mocked the banks' inefficiency and reliance on preferential treatment, joking that they could "appoint dogs as their presidents and still make the same amount of money."

As a result, Minsheng Bank, for example, one of China's few privately owned banks, unveiled a product that allowed clients to automatically invest money from deposit accounts into funds and promise a return of 5 percent, while the money could still be withdrawn at any time, an obvious competitor for Yu E Bao.

However, Alipay has retained an edge simply through its liquidity advantage, an area in which State banks struggle to compete. Money can be transferred in real time to an Alipay account for all sorts of payments enabled by the platform—online purchases, taxi fares, water bills, and even the public welfare lottery. Within two hours, money can be transferred from an Alipay account back into a deposit account, whereas most banks freeze any invested deposit for months or even years, charging considerable fees for unscheduled withdrawals.

In addition, Yu E Bao sets no investment limit, allowing customers to invest any amount from 1 yuan (US$0.17) upwards. The average State bank investment product necessitates a minimum investment of 50,000 yuan (US$8,260).

BACK TO THE ROOTS

"Finance used to seem mysterious and remote to the masses," said Alipay CEO Peng Lei. "Now, however, buying and selling financial products is a way of life for most people. The Internet enables us to serve the grassroots."

Due to its convenience and lucrative yields, Yu E Bao has lured a great many customers away from the banks, especially young people. Four out of five Yu E Bao users are aged under 35, investing an average 4,300 yuan (US$710) into the fund, a fraction of the average for bank-held investment products, according to industry consultancy iResearch.

Apart from Yu E Bao, Alibaba has also begun brokering financial products on Tmall, Alibaba's business-to-customer online retailing portal, also the country's largest. Other Internet giants, such as social media icons Tencent, search giant Baidu, and top web-portal Netease, are all competing to offer suspiciously high yields ranging from 8 to even 11 percent.

However, Alipay's expansion in the finance sector has not gone altogether unchecked. In summer 2013, Alipay found it had to remove all its custom POS terminals given to retailers for what it called "reasons known to all" in a statement afterward. It is an open secret that China Unionpay, the State-controlled payment service which provides all the nation's POS devices, was unhappy about losing its monopoly, and pressured the government into forcing Alipay out of the sector.

Alibaba, and other dotcom companies who want to dip their toes into China's hectic but hugely lucrative financial sector, might still need to rely on the mercy of State banks, and their masters, if they are to continue to flourish in one of the world's most tightly restricted financial markets.

Local Government Bond Clean-up

China's debt accumulation at the local level has become unsustainable. Collapse or loss of confidence on the part of investors could be calamitous.

Anxious not to repeat the mistakes made by US regulators leading to the great financial recession of 2008, China is grappling with how to regain control and ultimately ameliorate this looming issue. Here again we see the forces of the center arrayed against local power structures.

Cleaning Balance Sheets

November 2014 Issue of NewsChina | *by Lin Yuzhi and Li Jia*

Will permission to sell bonds reassure the world that indebted local governments in China can get their fiscal affairs in order?

More than half of China's local government borrowing is spent on civic facilities and transportation.

Just as a happy family lives within its means, so should a nation, at least in the view of most Chinese. Legislators received 330,000 responses after opening their second draft of China's amended Budget Law to public comments between July and August in 2012.

Three drafts had been rejected before the final text was endorsed by the Standing Committee of the National People's Congress, China's official legislature, on August 31, 2014, meaning the new Budget Law has been subject to more reviews than almost any other piece of legislation in modern Chinese history. Revision of the law was initiated in 2004, but it took a decade for legislators to agree on a new version.

How best to distribute money and power is rarely an uncontroversial topic. A new item that will appear on the national statute book as a result of the new Budget Law is just one flashpoint. A lack of fiscal discipline in government and unregulated financial innovation were blamed for dragging the world's most developed economies into the Great Recession. Now, China is getting a taste of such potentially dangerous flaws in its vast domestic economy. Colossal debt mountains racked up from the county to the provincial level, mostly secured by unsustainable land revenues, have sown widespread concerns both in China and across the world that the world's number two economy might unleash yet another financial crisis.

The new Budget Law tries to address this issue by allowing local governments to issue their own bonds on the open market while also supervising their debts. While legislators are agreed on what needs to be done, actually doing it is likely to be a mammoth undertaking.

STORMY WATERS

By the end of June 2013, local government debt in China stood at US$2.9 trillion, comprising US$1.8 trillion in outstanding loans and the

US$1.1 trillion that may be needed to bail out loans by other public-funded entities and failing enterprises, mostly local SOEs. Larger than the GDP of France or the UK in 2013, this figure is alarming, but not necessarily the first sign of a looming national default. Given the size of China's GDP and its fiscal revenue, the central government has continuously reassured the world that things remained "generally under control." Both the market and the government, however, understand what might happen if China's local governments default on their debts.

Risk is inherent in the way China's local governments borrow, spend, and repay their debts. Indeed, it is the fiscal irresponsibility of local governments, not the amount of debt, that frightens economic planners. An estimate by CCXI, a Chinese ratings agency partly held by Moody's, shows that more than 50 percent of the outstanding money has gone into civic infrastructure and transportation, areas which usually take five years or more to break even, much less turn a profit. The National Audit Office of China found that a number of local governments have already begun to borrow heavily simply to pay off debts incurred through massive infrastructure projects.

The quickest way for local governments to raise money is land sales, given the State's ability to appropriate or purchase land and sell it on to developers at a markup. Land resources are routinely offered to lenders as direct or indirect collateral for loans. Land transfer fees to local governments, as well as other fees and taxes charged to property developers, is the principal, stable source of local fiscal revenue under the existing public fund system. However, as the property market has cooled and land resources have run out, these revenues have also dwindled. Deng Haiqing, an analyst with CITIC Securities told *NewsChina* that bond investors, mainly financial institutions, are becoming wary of the growing risk of governments defaulting on outstanding bonds.

The behavior of Chinese lenders has exacerbated such jitters. In 2010, the central bank slapped a moratorium on the issuance of new loans to local governments, advocating greater austerity. Banks responded by circumventing procedures and lending through off-balance-sheet quasi-Ponzi schemes, mainly involving the hasty sale of short-term wealth management products to depositors and companies to finance long-term local projects. Other lenders such as trust companies also began to participate in schemes of their own or got involved with banks' schemes. Li Ning, an analyst with the Shanghai-based Haitong Securities, told *NewsChina* that this situation had created a "feedback loop of risk" involving local government debt, local fiscal management, banks, and the property market.

The strong alliance between lenders and local governments has also made any policy aimed at facilitating fundraising for struggling private companies almost impossible to enforce. For example, investors in a private bond market for SMEs launched in 2012 showed much more interest in buying local government debt than investing in private SMEs. This has further concentrated risk in the financial system and distorted to an even greater degree the allocation of financial resources.

FIREWALL

The root cause of all of these messes, as policymakers and analysts have recognized, lies in an obsolete legal and regulatory framework which overlooks weak discipline and disproportionately heavy loaded tasks in the budget operations of local governments, inadvertently incentivizing short-termism and general fiscal irresponsibility.

Local governments in China are desperate for money. Publicly funded investment, though often resulting in long-term losses, can provide a temporary boost to local GDP figures, at least enough to guarantee the officials in charge a promotion. Local governments, particularly at the county level, are required to provide most basic public services, including education, health care and social security. They face increasing pressure from the central government and the public to improve these services, but are also tasked with raising the bulk of local revenue, despite having virtually no taxation power. A penchant for throwing money at grandiose edifices and other prestige projects has further drained government budgets, as has China's ongoing and endemic corruption problem.

Most taxes in China are collected by the central government which then allocates funds back to local authorities from Beijing. Under existing law, local governments are not allowed to borrow from independent financiers. Instead, they have to set up companies, called fundraising platforms, in the process turning government debts into corporate debts, either in the form of bank credits or bonds.

As a result, overseeing and regulating how these loans are spent does not fall under the jurisdiction of legislators and national auditors. Worse still, local land revenues, often used as visible and invisible collateral, are also exempt from government oversight.

The new Budget Law, as Finance Minister Lou Jiwei explained to Party mouthpiece the *People's Daily* on two separate occasions in September, is designed to fix all these problems by "opening the front door, closing the back door and building a firewall." Provincial governments have been granted legal rights to issue their own bonds, also making them, rather than the central government, fully responsible for honoring all terms. Funds raised in this way, Lou said, have to be used for the provision of public goods and services, such as hospitals and roads, not government operations—such as office buildings or banqueting. Caps on issuance will be set, repayment plans determined, and an early-warning system overseeing default risk installed.

Both local government bonds and land revenues will be included in the tightened management of local budgets. Publicized audit reports are also designed to increase transparency, with a sweeping national audit plan concerning the raising of revenue through land sales also on the way.

As Pan Gongsheng, deputy governor of the PBC, noted in a June 30 article in the *People's Daily*, bond issuance will not only give local governments a new source of funds, but push forward transparency and sound public fiscal operations.

DEFICIT

This overhaul of the Budget Law, which looks sound and feasible on paper, cannot work however without overhaul of other systems. Bond issuers, as with companies making IPOs, have to persuade potential investors that their assets will ultimately pay for themselves. Lou Jiwei stressed at a press conference on August 31 that local governments would be legally obliged to open their balance sheets to the public so that their bonds would be rated—a prospect likely to irk officials accustomed to keeping their dealings off the record.

Preparation of balance sheets itself is tricky in a country where the public and independent overseers are generally kept out of the conversation on public spending. As Professor Wang Yongjun at the China Central University of Finance and Economics explained to *NewsChina*, to date governments' fiscal reports only detail annual changes in revenues and spending, and provide no record of the whole picture of assets and liabilities which helps investors judge whether the assets are strong enough to generate cash for all debt repayment in the future.

Most provincial governments have drafted balance sheets in the past three years; some, including Shanghai Municipality, have even rolled out such practices throughout their jurisdiction. However, until some difficult questions are answered, such schemes will remain experimental. In an article in the PBC's *China Finance* journal, Ma Jun, former Deutsche Bank AG Greater China chief economist and current head of the central bank's principal think tank asked whether and how State-owned companies, pensions, landholdings, and even antiques collections and parks should appear on official balance sheets, given their impact on budgets.

A fundamental lack of detailed, transparent accounting in government is one of the two main reasons that media and analysts have questioned the top credit ratings given to nine provinces which currently have approval to issue bonds. The other reason is that China's ratings agencies, with fewer than 20 years' business experience between them, are not well-established enough to have an adequate overview of the national picture. There is reasonable doubt that such rookie organizations can do their job independently, particularly when their clients are China's powerful provincial governments.

The new practice of allowing local government to issue bonds is also a test of the credibility of the central government and potential investors. There is a hidden rule in China's bond market that junk bonds should be quietly cashed by third parties, or erased through a government bailout, in order to avoid scaring investors off.

Local government debts are widely regarded as risk-free because investors believe they are underwritten by the central government—a simplistic misconception that could prove problematic should local governments begin to default en masse.

As Pan Gongsheng has said, only when local governments are required by law to honor their own debts, rather than simply take central government backing for granted, and when investors realize the risks they are running, will discipline govern Chinese fiscal management. It remains to see whether the central government can deliver on its tough talk to put an end to instantaneous bailouts of failing spendthrift local authorities.

The new law is designed to "open the front door, close the back door and build a firewall."

Bank of China Scandal?

The BOC apparently caught in a money-laundering scheme denies everything.

BOC Goes Underground?

September 2014 Issue of NewsChina | *by* NewsChina Magazine

The Bank of China (BOC), one of China's five biggest State-owned banks, has been caught in a trust crisis after claims emerged that the firm was involved in money laundering.

In a news report broadcast on July 9, CCTV revealed that BOC had transferred certain customers' yuan-based assets to its overseas branches before exchanging them into foreign currency in violation of laws restricting the maximum amount of foreign currency Chinese citizens are free to exchange in a year to US$50,000 per capita. The transactions were made via an undeclared emigration service exclusively provided by BOC's Guangzhou branch, the sales volume of which has been recorded as 6 billion yuan (US$1bn).

Despite speculation that this undisclosed service could have led to vast amounts of illegal assets leaving China via the back door, BOC denied the accusation, saying that the service was a "pilot business" approved by regulators and applicable only to Chinese émigrés and real estate investors. The company's statement also claimed that officials could not avail themselves of the service, and that asset transfers were capped at US$300,000 per capita per year.

The investigation continues.

SOEs and the Private Sector

Moving toward Laissez-faire

A fundamental tug of war has raged in China at least since 2003 when the State-owned Assets Supervision and Administration Commission was set up to establish a path to reforming and privatizing SOEs. The Commission became part of the problem rather than part of the solution. In "Absolute Advocate," an interview with Peking University Professor Zhang Weiying, the rift between free marketeers and State-controlled enterprise in China is laid bare. Stakeholders on both sides have much to lose, and the process of reform has essentially stalled over the last 10 years. This interview gives an inside view of how SOEs make a social link with the masses to resist privatization. As Zhang explains, "There is a deep-rooted mentality of hating the rich in Chinese society." The question becomes: should one become rich because of his place in society (the SOE manager and corrupt public official), or should one earn a place in society by having become rich (as a successful entrepreneur)? Zhang, a fervent free market advocate, reveals the fundamental contradictions in this long-standing battle.

Absolute Advocate

October 2014 Issue of NewsChina | *by Zhou Zhenghua*

His full confidence in a self-regulated market has kept Peking University Professor Zhang Weiying controversial.

Among the most well-known Chinese economists, few have advocated laissez-faire market economics so strongly, and so unstintingly, as Zhang Weiying. Zhang is one of an academic minority in China who subscribe to non-Keynesian principles, and has thus been labeled by the media as "spokesperson for vested interest groups," and even, on more than one occasion, "an enemy of the people."

In the context of yet another round of reforms more focused than ever on giving the market, not the State, the decisive role in China's economy, Zhang has gained more support, both among the public and in academia, than ever before. His contribution to making the Guanghua School of Management at Peking University one of the most prominent business schools in China was widely recognized during his tenure as principal of the school between 2006 and 2010.

In 1983, an article by 24-year-old Zhang was published in State newspaper the *China Youth Daily*. The article declared to a society raised from birth to see money and profit as anathema that "making money was a contribution to society."

In 1984, Zhang's notion of giving the market full power to price goods and services became one of the most hotly debated proposals submitted to an historic academic meeting analyzing the potential direction of China's economic reform. In the early 1990s, Zhang's studies at Oxford University, from which he emerged with a PhD, further strengthened his belief in a self-regulated free market. He became an admirer of Ludwig Mises, a prominent proponent of the so-called Austrian School of economics emphasizing individual choice and price signals controlling the marketplace with minimal government intervention.

After returning to China and taking up a post as assistant to the President of Peking University, Zhang's efforts in 2003 to introduce more competitive pressure into academic assessment and to break up alumni monopolies over faculty recruitment encountered strong resistance among his colleagues, and ultimately failed.

This began a series of altercations between Zhang and mainstream Chinese thinking. The next blow came in 2004, when Zhang stood up to defend the private acquisition of State-owned enterprises (SOEs), though the public embraced Hong Kong economist Lang Xianping's sharp criticism of placing State-owned assets in private hands.

In 2006, when China's economic reform program stalled amidst government inertia and public resentment towards corruption and a widening income gap and, Zhang argued in an essay appearing in journal *Money China*, that government officials had lost more from reform than any other group, and claimed they should receive one-off compensation in order to inoculate reformist leaders against an anti-liberalization force.

In his essay, Zhang cited the example of buying out SOE workers in order to liquidate their jobs during privatization in the 1990s, a move strongly resented by those laid off. Zhang's pragmatic solutions, and his position that such short-term pain could prevent long-term agony, drew considerable fire from the Chinese public.

Economic forums in which Zhang participated always saw debates erupt that would make headlines the following day. The most recent example was an encounter between Zhang and his Peking University colleague Professor Justin Yifu Lin, former chief economist with the World Bank. At a July forum held at Shanghai's Fudan University, Zhang insisted on a complete withdrawal of the government from economic management, while Lin took a stance that saw the government as having a positive role in economy.

In an exclusive interview with *NewsChina*, Zhang explains why he has chosen to stand apart from most of his colleagues in espousing his vision of China's economic future.

NewsChina: Why do you describe the past 10 years as a "lost decade?"

Zhang Weiying: Major reforms, like SOE reform, came to a standstill after 2004. The State-owned Assets Supervision and Administration Commission was supposed to be a reformer when it was set up in 2003, but turned into both referee and competitor. Even the direction of reform itself has become inclined in favor of making SOEs bigger and stronger. Some media sources and academics used the new problems arising from the process of SOE management and ownership restructuring to refute the principle of more private investment in SOEs. All of these factors resulted in the stagnation of SOE reform.

NewsChina: Does the media have that much power?

ZW: Egalitarianism has a long tradition in human history, with the desire for fairness and equality embedded in human nature. People have a weakness—envying others their success and blaming others for their own failure.

Unfortunately, there is a deep-rooted mentality in Chinese society of hating the rich. However, the boundary between "proper" and "improper" wealth acquisition sometimes gets blurred.

The biggest problem in realizing SOE reform before 2004 was ideological. Privatization was not regarded as appropriate and so it was done in secret. At the time I called for transparent oversight of the privatization process [but was ignored]. The media was an overwhelming voice opposing the selling off of SOEs, with only a few rational sources supporting it. When competition got fierce in the media market, all sides resorted to currying favor with public opinion.

NewsChina: Do you think that egalitarianism has lost some of its appeal after more than 30 years of reform?

ZW: The situation has changed a lot over the years. A planned economy produces a society entirely based on an official hierarchy. Reform and Opening-up gave legitimacy to the private possession of wealth, and material capital began to gain social power.

    The shift of power from the bureaucracy to capital is a form of progress. There is no such thing as a perfect system for a society. In a "capital centered" society, you can enjoy anything you can afford, while in an "official centered" society you have to hold a bureaucratic position to access anything at all. I agree with [economist] Friedrich August Hayek, who argued that a society in which wealth is the way to social status is better than a society in which social status is the way to wealth. Wealth should not be created either in the process of attaining power, or once one has obtained power. But this is what happens in China.

NewsChina: What do you think of the ongoing SOE reform which promotes the mix of private and State ownership in SOEs?

ZW: Who will mix with whom? Who has the final say in corporate management? Which industries could benefit from this mixed ownership, and which could not? Will the merger process cause corruption? These questions have yet to be answered.

    The transfer to joint ownership, if not handled properly, exposes State assets to private manipulation in some cases, and corruption by officials in others. Given the different motivations of private companies and the government, it is imperative to prevent interested parties from cashing in on investiture of power.

NewsChina: You mean that this mixed ownership lacks stability?

ZW: I think it is just a transitional plan, not a long-term, stable solution. But there are voices claiming that it can be a long-term mechanism. As with many economic issues, people misunderstand it.

NewsChina: Liu Chuanzhi, founder of PC giant Lenovo, has said that family-run enterprises perform the best. Do you agree?

ZW: No one can pass judgment on which form of corporate structure is the "best," In the end the market will choose for itself. With private property rights, people seek efficient ways to engage in transaction and incorporation. Joint-stock limited companies are preferred by big manufacturers, for example, while traditional partnerships still dominate accountancies and law firms. Conglomerates choose to benefit from the economy of scale though internal corruption becomes almost unavoidable in mega-companies.

NewsChina: Then why do you insist that SOEs are not as efficient as private enterprises?

ZW: The de facto absence of owners in SOEs means decision-makers hold power disproportionate to their responsibilities. Private enterprises are actually a way of bonding people together with private property rights together. This doesn't apply to SOEs. Copying the practice of separating ownership from management in private companies does not make sense for State companies. Therefore, efficiency fails to improve because incompatible mechanisms fail beneath a veneer of entrepreneurialism.

NewsChina: There are outstanding managers in SOEs. They are entrepreneurs, aren't they?

ZW: As I said before, some SOE managers have good entrepreneurial qualities. However, a real entrepreneur has to bear the consequences of his or her decisions. In SOEs, even if you are successful, you rarely have the chance to realize your own ambitions as an entrepreneur because you will most likely be promoted out of your business. It is misguided to think that entrepreneurs just want a bigger paycheck. A real entrepreneur puts the health of their business ahead of their personal earnings. The inventor of the Gillette safety razor was likely motivated to make a decent razor before he was concerned with money. The success of an entrepreneur is reflected by the success of their enterprise.

NewsChina: What do you think of those business people who have faced criminal charges because of their close connection to corrupt officials?

ZW: Entrepreneurs are involved in nearly every corruption case that has emerged during the recent anti-corruption campaign. This is the evidence that a good business environment based on the rule of law does not exist.

Entrepreneurs are the group creating wealth. However, in the existing system, the government holds too much power, which motivates some entrepreneurs to give up their job of creating wealth and instead pursue monopolies over resource distribution by accessing and manipulating power.

NewsChina: You and your colleague Professor Lin expressed different views on a government's role in the economy at the Fudan forum. Is that a fundamental division of opinion?

ZW: Yes we are split over the relationship between the government and the market. This division is nothing new in human history, and has lasted for thousands of years. Right ideas do not always prevail. For example, the debate on whether the government is the cause, or the solution, to economic problems continues to rage.

NewsChina: However, classical economics promoting free markets also recognizes that government is a necessary evil.

ZW: 99.9 percent of people would agree. But the question is how to define the role of the government in economics. If government is necessary, then why? A government protects justice and the integrity of a society. However, without a proper property ownership arrangement, neither justice nor integrity is possible. I firmly believe what David Hume believed, that justice does not exist in a society where people believe that the public interest justifies the infringement of individual liberties.

SOE Dinosaur to Greyhound?

China Post Group looks a lot like postal services in the rest of the world: branches everywhere but struggling with the decline of physical mail volume. In their article "Survival for the Fittest," Yang Di and Su Xiaoming describe the attempts of China Post to modernize and succeed in the changing world. Two significant milestones occurred in 2005: the service became a SOE rather than a branch of the government, and it was able to open a bank, the Postal Savings Bank of China (PSBC), which has gone on to become China's seventh largest bank and highly profitable.

Survival for the Fittest

December 2014 Issue of NewsChina | *by Yang Di and Su Xiaoming*

The ossified mega-State-owned Enterprise China Post Group has undergone restructuring to cater to a modern marketplace. But is this enormous entity really able to change?

At 7 PM on September 4, 2014, Wang Xiang sits at her desk in the sorting office of China Post Group in Beijing's Tongzhou District. Wang has worked for this vast government corporation since 1997, her principal job being to sort letters and small packages according to destination.

Though her job is boring and repetitive, Wang takes pride in it, and on a good day can sort some 3,000 letters per hour, making her one of China's most efficient mail sorters—an honor she has had officially recognized by her employer and the State.

"Despite the center being equipped with 20 sorting machines that can each sort 35,000 to 40,000 letters an hour, over 40 percent of mail received still needs to be sorted by hand" said He Huan, head of the Tongzhou center's production and dispatch department. "One reason is illegible handwriting," he added.

As the Internet has become the population's favored communication tool, and courier companies have eaten into the parcel delivery sector, China Post, despite having a virtual monopoly on conventional postal delivery, is struggling to compete.

As a vast enterprise responsible for hundreds of thousands of employees across the whole country, the onus is now on China Post to reform according to the needs of the market.

BUSINESS AS USUAL

Since 1990, faced with increased competition from courier services and the Internet, China Post began to record sustained financial losses for the first time in its history. In a single year (1995), 2 billion yuan (US$326m) was wiped off its books.

Higher consumer demand for express delivery services has driven China Post to attempt to increase efficiency, with each day's mail having to be fully sorted between 7 AM and 4 AM the following day in order to ensure that deliveries make it onto the dozens of postal trains that leave the capital in the early hours of each morning.

By 2013, there were over 954,000 employees working for China Post. To ensure maximum efficiency, the company underwent a massive hardware upgrade, rebuilding its central distribution center in Beijing which today covers an area of about 2,077 acres, or 31 soccer fields.

At peak times, over 1,200 clerks work inside this building, known locally as the "Big Flat," which in 2013 processed a total of 955 million conventional letters, 39 million registered letters, 460 million printed documents, 9.73 million registered printed documents, and 9.14 million parcels. In other words, 20 percent percent of all the mail sent and received in China in that year passed through this single building.

Streamlining has inevitably led to cuts. Between 2002 and 2013, the central authorities cut the number of local post offices in China from 78,000 to 64,000. Nevertheless, China Post is still by far the country's most ubiquitous business, with branches in some of the country's most remote and impoverished areas, providing an essential distribution channel for government welfare to areas lacking even a local bank.

As a result, although savings have been made, profits have remained stagnant.

"According to the common rule established by the Universal Postal Union (UPU)," said Liu Shaoquan, newspaper and periodical distribution bureau chief with China Post Group, "there should be a uniform flat rate to mail a letter to anywhere in the world. Thus, conventional mail services rarely make a profit."

"For example, a letter from Beijing to a remote region in Tibet would cost the consumer a mere 1.2 yuan (19 US cents) to post," Liu continued. The human cost and price of transportation spending has kept increasing as China's economy has expanded and demand has risen. However, prices have remained generally low, as have the wages of postal employees. Even State subsidies have failed to have much of an impact on China Post's declining profitability.

Zhou Huande from the China Post Shanghai Research Institute recalled that at the beginning of the 21st century his company opted for drastic and often misguided measures simply to make ends meet. Beginning in the early 2000s, he told *NewsChina*, local post offices also ran small stores on their premises, selling goods from commemorative stamps and calendars to beer, cake and ramen noodles.

"[China Post] faces both opportunities and difficulties," Zhou told *NewsChina*. "For example, our large number of branches mean operations are expensive, but at the same time it gives us the reach to be able to distribute farming subsidies and agricultural insurance to remote areas," he said.

"To turn disadvantages into advantages, the key is to change our philosophy," Zhou added.

RESHUFFLE MEASURES

In Zhou Huande's opinion, the decade-long reshuffle has been a process of continuous trial and error. Since 2003, the State Council Economic Research Center started to conduct research into reforming China Post. First on the agenda was to attempt to separate its monopolies (conventional mailing) from its competitive services (courier services and financial management) by the end of 2004.

A reform plan was formally issued in September 2005. By November the following year, China Post was formally reclassified as a SOEtate-owned Enterprise (SOE) rather than a branch of the government. The plan also created the Postal Savings Bank of China (PSBC), which today is the nation's seventh-largest bank in terms of holdings. Close ties to the government, an unrivaled network of branches (opened in China

Post's hundreds of thousands of outlets nationwide) and exacting loan application standards have made the PSBC a highly profitable enterprise, with some US$909 billion in total assets and an average default rate of only 0.51 percent.

"It can be said that we are one of the most affluent banks in China," Lü Jiajin, president of the PSBC, told *NewsChina*. According to Lü, the PSBC currently has a total of 390,000 outlets, and enjoys a presence even in the country's most remote locales. "PSBC services cover the largest area and enjoy the largest client base [of any Chinese bank]," he added, with the PSBC's customer base even dwarfing that of the Agricultural Bank of China (ABC), which has nearly 24,000 branches. The company is now preparing to go public.

COMPETITION

In 1980, China Postal Express & Logistics Co., Ltd., the branch of China Post responsible for express mail and courier services, launched EMS, the first courier service in China. EMS enjoyed 97 percent market share until the industry was opened to the private sector in the 1990s, which saw EMS dominance broken in 1995, and its market share sink to 20 percent in recent years (see: "On the Move," *NewsChina*, February, 2013, Vol. 054).

"Compared to private companies, EMS, as an old SOE, faces various restrictions, and is slow and inefficient," said Ma Zhanhong, vice-president of China Postal Express & Logistics Co., Ltd. While some success has been made with international operations, and many online retailers make use of EMS' services, in general private enterprise has cornered the courier market in China.

However, China Post is refusing to give up, and is attempting to secure a share of China's white-hot online marketplace. This June, China Post Group inked a strategic cooperative agreement with Alibaba, announcing that the two parties would "cooperate in various fields including logistics, e-commerce, finance and information security."

Insiders believe that Alibaba's access to big data and cutting-edge Internet technology combined with China Post's network of outlets will help power reform. Six postal services were listed on the Fortune 500 in 2013, and EMS clocked in at No. 196, much higher than its No. 258 ranking in 2012. The company recently opened a vast airmail sorting and distribution center in Nanjing, and processes tens of thousands of letters and packages daily.

However, technology has still proven the biggest competitor to China Post's business operations, with the explosion in the digital sphere taking a heavy toll on its formerly unrivaled position as China's principal distribution network for newspapers and periodicals. Now, this sector of the company runs at a loss. The company's newsstands are also struggling to survive, and despite attempts to diversify by also selling mobile phone credit, SIM cards and soft drinks, this once-familiar sight on Chinese street corners is starting to become less common.

For the first time, China Post has found itself having to engage in marketing in order to retain customers and attract more business. The company has also begun to participate in data analysis in order to make its targeted marketing more sophisticated by establishing a comprehensive subscription database. However, tablet devices and smartphones are both major competitors, and with the trend still being away from print media, China Post is still struggling.

Despite being a household name, China Post's distinctive green and yellow logo, while it may still be seen in every corner of the country, has survived in the modern marketplace only through implementation of a mixed bag of reforms. Its successes continue to be tempered by its need to support a number of loss-making businesses. Unless it can further embrace digital delivery, market competition and the need for efficiency, it is unclear whether this former monopoly will continue to be the powerhouse as it was in its heyday.

Management Compensation

Author Ding Li tackles the long-standing issue of management compensation in "Reform of State-owned enterprises should focus on separating ownership and management." The article was prompted by a January 2015 edict cutting SOE top executive pay by up to 30 percent. Ding looks at the various means that could be used to align executives' incentives with national objectives and priorities. This is just one aspect of dealing with China's problem-ridden paradox of government involvement in capitalism.

Reform of State-owned Enterprises Should Focus on Separating Ownership and Management

February 2015 Issue of NewsChina | *by Ding Li*

When reforming State-owned enterprises, China should learn from the experience of Dongguan farmers in balancing fairness and efficiency.

It was recently reported that the government has approved a plan to reduce the salaries of top executives at State-owned enterprises (SOEs) directly controlled by the central government. Expected to become effective on January 1, 2015, the plan will see pay cuts of up to 30 percent for those affected. The plan has been met with skepticism from economists, many of whom argue that it will lead to further inefficiency within SOEs.

On a smaller scale, the government's current dilemma in reforming SOEs is analogous to the one that faced farmers in Dongguan, Guangdong Province in the 1990s, who had to decide how best to manage their collectively owned rural land in order to maximize their interests. The Chinese government must figure out how best to manage the massive national assets under its control.

Initially, Dongguan farmers resorted to selling their land either to developers or industry, but they soon found that due to their limited land resources, this approach was not sustainable. This approach is equivalent to the idea of privatization of State-owned enterprises, which many worry could lead to the loss of State control over the economy, just as Dongguan farmers worried that selling off their land would lead to them losing control of it.

Therefore, to ensure that they could draw a sustainable income from their land, Dongguan farmers changed tack—instead of selling their land, they offered it to corporations in exchange for stock options. However, as many of these corporations were multinationals, they were able to transfer their profits from the land to overseas subsidiaries in order to minimize the dividends payable to the original owners. This scenario has certain parallels with the current problems embedded within SOEs—on the one hand, they are criticized for not serving their owner, the people, but the managers instead, since profits can be transferred into management costs, leading to low efficiency and corruption within the State sector. On the other hand, reforms to increase tax rates and the ratio of profits turned over to the State have been criticized for hurting efficiency and the morale of management, ultimately harming the economy.

The Dongguan farmers later tried yet another strategy. Instead of insisting on holding a stake in the businesses established on their land, they rented their land for a fixed price that could be renegotiated after a fixed term. By doing this, they could secure their income, while their corporate partners could expect a fixed cost for the land and remain motivated to seek higher profits.

The reform of State-owned enterprises should draw inspiration from this historical example. Instead of resorting to administrative means to slash senior executives' salaries, the reform should focus on separating the ownership and management of national assets. The State can consider the approach of levying a fixed fee on each SOE and allowing management to enjoy the additional profits they earn, ultimately reaching an equilibrium of fairness and efficiency. While the State can generate stable revenue from SOEs, management are thus motivated to work as hard as possible.

Of course, the issue of SOE reform is far more complex than the Dongguan farmers' land sale dilemma. In many fields, such as public utilities, State-owned enterprises should not seek to maximize profits. In these fields, the government should establish mechanisms to allow national assets to change hands between different management organs, encouraging competition to maximize their effective use.

By establishing a system for the effective management of SOEs, the government can also use this as a macroeconomic policy instrument, as with interest rates. By increasing or decreasing fees levied on SOEs, the government will have more tools with which to fine tune the economy. But at the core of its approach, the government must not play a dominant role in the direct management of SOEs—this is the only way the government can balance fairness and efficiency.

The Chinese government must figure out how best to manage the massive national assets under its control.

The author is a senior commentator with *NewsChina*'s sister publication *China Newsweek*.

FOR FURTHER STUDY

Response Questions

- What does the author mean by "Golden Age to Silver Age?" Give numerical support to your answer.
- Define "shadow banking."
- List possible regulatory obstacles a firm might face when establishing a factory in China.
- Name three concerns a foreign investor might have when considering investment in China.
- What obstacles has Beijing placed in the way of domestic companies wishing to do initial public offerings?

Discussion Questions

- Would you invest in a Shanghai exchange-listed stock? Give some reasons for and against.
- Formulate possible solutions to each obstacle you listed in the third item in Response Questions, above.

- What evidence do we have that Chinese economic growth is leveling off?
- What steps should Beijing take to make for a "soft landing?" Which of these steps have been implemented? How successful has each step been?
- What downside consequences do you foresee for Beijing in the case of a "hard landing?"

Research Exercises

- Lenovo is China's most successful "private" multinational. Research its sales penetration and financial condition. Discuss the future of Lenovo. What course should the firm pursue in the face of the changing landscape for computers and phones? Compare Lenovo's marketing methods in China with Apple's. How well does Lenovo deal with IP protection issues in China?
- Compare Alibaba, China's largest online firm to both eBay and PayPal. What obstacles exist for Alibaba to compete successfully in the western world? How should Alibaba proceed as it looks at the worldwide market?
- Compare the Chinese banking system to that of the US, UK, and Japan. How do the systems compare in profitability, risk, regulation, and customer service? Does the US have a shadow banking system?
- What is the trend of SOEs versus private firms in China? Compare over the last five years: total assets, number of enterprises, profitability, number of employees.

Notes

1 *Fortune* June 2013 "Can Lenovo Do It?"
2 Fortune.com August 3, 2015
3 A full version of the plan (in Chinese) is available at http://news.xinhuanet.com/politics/2011-03/16/c_121193916.htm, or at www.chinacleanenergydb.com/general-strategic-plans/Five-Year-Plans/3–2011China12thFive-YearPlanonNationalEconomicandSocialDevelopment-Chinese.pdf?attredirects=0&d=1
4 "Key Targets of China's 12th Five-Year Plan," *Xinhua*, March 5, 2011. www.chinadaily.com.cn/xinhua/2011-03-05/content_1938144.html
5 Wen Jiabao. *Report on the Work of the Government*. Delivered at the Fourth Session of the Eleventh China National People's Congress, March 5, 2011. http://blogs.wsj.com/chinarealtime/2011/03/05/china-npc-2011-reports-full-text/
6 "China Announces 16 pct cut in Energy Consumption Per Unit of GDP by 2015," *Gov.cn*, March 5, 2011. www.gov.cn/english/2011–03/05/content_1816947.htm; "Zhang: 'Twelfth Five' push to Non-fossil Energy to Account for 11.4 Percent Share of Primary Energy" (张国宝: "十二五"末力争非化石能源占一次能源比重11.4%), people.com.cn, January 6, 2011. http://energy.people.com.cn/GB/13670716.html
7 Fellman, Joshua. "China to Hold Primary Energy Use to 4.2 Billion Tons in 2015, Xinhua Says." *Bloomberg*, October, 20, 2010. www.bloomberg.com/news/2010-

10-30/china-to-hold-primary-energy-use-to-4-2-billion-tons-in-2015-xinhua-says.html

8   See, e.g., Cohen-Tanugi, David. "Putting it into Perspective: China's Carbon Intensity Target." NRDC White Paper, October 2010.

9   The Tianjin Climate Exchange (TCX) is a joint venture of China National Petroleum Corporation Assets Management Co. Ltd. (CNPCAM), the Chicago Climate Exchange (CCX) and the City of Tianjin.

10   In July 2010, NDRC announced the selection of official low-carbon pilot provinces and cities, including the provinces of Guangdong, Liaoning, Hubei, Shaanxi and Yunnan, and the cities of Tianjin, Chongqing, Shenzhen, Xiamen, Hangzhou, Nanchang, Guiyang, and Baoding.

11   "Decision on speeding up the cultivation and development of emerging strategic industries" (国务院通过加快培育和发展战略性新兴产业的决定), www.gov.cn, September 8, 2010, www.gov.cn/ldhd/2010–09/08/content_1698604.htm

12   Over 70 percent of SOE assets and profits are concentrated in the "old" magic seven strategic industries. HSBC, *China's next 5-year plan: What it means for equity markets*, October 2010.

13   HSBC, China's Next 5-Year Plan: What it Means for Equity Markets, October 2010.

14   Seligsohn, Deborah and Angel Hsu. "How Does China's 12th Five-Year Plan Address Energy and the Environment?" *China FAQs*, March 7, 2011. www.china faqs.org/blog-posts/how-does-chinas-12th-five-year-plan-address-energy-and-environment

15   Yue, Yang. "China May Revise Nuclear Power Target." *Marketwatch.com* from *Caixin Online*, March 29, 2011. www.marketwatch.com/story/china-may-revise-nuclear-power-target-2011–03–29

16   Whether the euro will displace the US dollar as the main international currency is far from unambiguous. See McNamara (2008) for a detailed discussion.

17   Among others, Frankel (2011) and Cohen (2014) provide extensive reviews on the internationalization of the US dollar and Japanese yen, which offered convincing evidence of the importance of domestic and external tensions in determining currency internationalization.

18   See www.pbc.gov.cn/publish/english/955/2013/20130417083528793671703/20 130417083528793671703.html

References to "Will the Renminbi Become a Reverse Currency"

Azman-Saini,W., A. Baharumshah, and Law, S. 2010. "Foreign Direct Investment, Economic Freedom and Economic Growth: International Evidence." *Economic Modelling* 27(5), 1079–1089.

Barassi, M. R. and Zhou, Y. 2012. "The Effect of Corruption on FDI: A Parametric and Nonparametric Analysis." *European Journal of Political Economy* 28(3), 302–312.

Beck, T., Demirguc-Kunt, A., and Levine, R. 2000. "A New Database on the Structure and Development of the Financial Sector." *The World Bank Economic Review* 14(3), 597–605.

Bowles, P. and Wang, B. 2013. "Renminbi Internationalization: A Journey to Where?" *Development and Change* 44(6), 1363–1385.

Chen, H., Peng, W., and Shu, C. 2012. "The Potential of the Renminbi as an International Currency." In Currency Internationalization: Lessons from the Global Financial Crisis and Prospects for the Future in Asia and the Pacific, BIS Paper, No. 61.

Chen, X., and Y. Cheung. 2011. "Renminbi Going Global." *China & World Economy* 19(2): 1–18.

Chey, H. 2013. "Can the Renminbi Rise as a Global Currency? The Political Economy of Currency Internationalization." *Asian Survey* 53(2), 348–368.

Chinn, M., and Frankel, J. 2005. "Will the Euro Eventually Surpass the Dollar as Leading International Reserve Currency?" NBER Working Papers, No. 11510.

Chinn, M. and Ito, H. 2008. "A New Measure of Financial Openness." *Journal of Comparative Policy Analysis: Research and Practice* 10(3), 309–322.

Cohen, B. 2014. "Will History Repeat Itself? Lessons for the Yuan." Asian Development Bank Institute Working Paper No. 453.

Compton, R., Giedeman, D., and Hoover, G. 2011. "Panel Evidence on Economic Freedom and Growth in the United States." *European Journal of Political Economy* 27(3), 423–435.

Dobson, W. and Masson, P. 2009. "Will the Renminbi Become a World Currency?" *China Economic Review* 20(1),124–135.

Eichengreen, B. 1998. *Globalizing Capital: A History of the International Monetary System.* Princeton, NJ: Princeton University Press.

Eichengreen, B. 2005. "Sterling's Past, Dollar's Future: Historical Perspectives on Reserve Currency Competition." NBER Working Paper No. 11336.

Frank, E. 2003. "The Surprising Resilience of the US Dollar." *Review of Radical Political Economics* 35(3), 248–254.

Frankel, J. 2011. "Historical Precedents for Internationalization of the RMB." Paper Presented to the Council on Foreign Relations and China Development Research Foundation, Beijing, October 31–November 1.

Germain, R., and Schwartz, H. 2014. "The Political Economy of Failure: The Euro as an International Currency." *Review of International Political Economy* (ahead-of-print), 1–28.

Hartmann, P. 1998. *Currency Competition and Foreign Exchange Markets: The Dollar, the Yen and the Euro.* Cambridge: Cambridge University Press.

Hasan, I., Wachtel, P., and Zhou, M. 2007. "Institutional Development, Financial Deepening and Economic Growth: Evidence from China." *Journal of Banking and Finance* 33(1), 157–170.

Helleiner, E. 2008. "Political Determinants of International Currencies: What Future for the US Dollar?" *Review of International Political Economy* 15(3), 354–378.

Huang, Y., Wang, X., Gou, Q., and Wang, D. 2012. "Achieving Capital Account Convertibility in China." *China Economic Journal* 4(1), 25–42.

Huang, Y., Cai, F., Peng, X., and Gou, Q. 2013. "New Normal of Chinese Development." In *China: A New Model for Growth and Development*, edited by R. Garnaut, F. Cai, and L. Song. Canberra: ANU E-Press.

International Monetary Fund. 2013. "People's Republic of China: Article IV Consultation". Washington, DC, July 17.

Krugman, P. 1984. "The International Role of the Dollar: Theory and Prospect." In *Exchange Rate Theory and Practice*, edited by J. Bilson and R. Marston, 261–278. Chicago, IL: University of Chicago Press.

Lane, P. and Milesi-Ferretti, G. 2007. "The External Wealth of Nations Mark II: Revised and Extended Estimates of Foreign Assets and Liabilities, 1970–2004." *Journal of International Economics* 73(2), 223–250.

Lee, J. 2010. "Will the Renminbi Emerge as an International Reserve Currency." Manuscript, Korea University.

Li, D. and Liu, L. 2008. "RMB Internationalization: An Empirical Analysis." *Journal of Financial Research* 11, 1–16.

Lim, E. 2006. "The Euro's Challenge to the Dollar." IMF Working Paper No. 06/153.

Maziad, S. and Kang, J. 2012. "RMB Internationalization: Onshore/offshore Links." IMF Working Paper WP/12/133.

McNamara, K. 2008. "A Rivalry in the Making? The Euro and International Monetary Power." *Review of International Political Economy* 15(3), 439–459.

People's Bank of China Study Group. 2006. "The Timing, Path, and Strategies of RMB Internationalization." *China Finance* 5, 12–13.

Pierpont, B. 2007. "Democracy, Property Rights and FDI in Developing Countries: A Regional Analysis." Honors Project Paper No. 4.

Prasad, E. and Ye, L. 2012. "The Renminbi's Role in the Global Monetary System." Brookings Discussion Paper No. 6335.

Subacchi, P. 2010. "One Currency, Two Systems: China's Renminbi Strategy." International Economics Briefing Paper, Vol. 1. 72 D. Wang et al.

Tavlas, G. 1997. "The International Use of the US Dollar: An Optimum Currency Area Perspective." *The World Economy* 20(6), 709–747.

Triffin, R. 1960. *Gold and the Dollar Crisis: The Future of Convertibility*. New Haven, CT: Yale University Press.

Walter, A. 2006. "Domestic Sources of International Monetary Leadership." In *International Monetary Power*, edited by D. Andrews. Ithaca, NY: Cornell University Press.

Yu, Y. 2012. "Revisiting the Internationalization of the RMB." Asian Development Bank Institute Working Paper No. 366.

Zhou, X. 2009. "Reform of the International Monetary System." Accessed February 7, 2015, www.bis.org/review/r090402c.pdf

Bibliography

Chen, J. (2014, September). Banks Should First Treat Their Borrowers as Enemies, then Allies. *NewsChina*.

Cendrowski, S. (2015, August 3). China Looks for Scapegoats in Continued Stock Market Decline. Fortune.com

Daili, W., Yiping, H., & Gang, F. (2015, March 17). Will the Renminbi Become a Reserve Currency? *China Economic Journal*.

Ding, L. (2015, February). Reform of State-Owned Enterprises. *NewsChina*

Helft, M. (2013, June). Can Lenovo Do It? *Fortune*.

Lewis, J. (2011, March 1). Energy and Climate Goals of China's 12th Five-Year Plan. Center for Climate and Energy Solutions, formerly the Pew Center on Global Climate Change.

Li, J. (2015, January). Investing in Investment. *NewsChina*.

Li, J. (2015, February), Bears Meet Bulls, *NewsChina*.

Li, J. (2015, May). Start Your Engines. *NewsChina*.

Li, J. & Lin, Y. (2014, November). Local Government Bonds: Cleaning Balance Sheets. *NewsChina*.

NewsChina Magazine (2014, September). BOC Goes Underground? *NewsChina.*

Sun, X. (2015, April). Free Trade Zones Serve Domestic and International Agendas. *NewsChina.*

Sun, Z. (2014, March). Alipay—Who Needs Banks? *NewsChina.*

Sun, Z. & Han, Y. (2015, February). When We Need Your Money. *NewsChina.*

Yang, D. & Su, X. (2014, December). Survival for the Fittest. *NewsChina.*

Zhou, Z. (2014, October). Zhang Weiying—Absolute Advocate. *NewsChina.*

Zhou, Y., Chen, J., & Li, J. (2015, January). A SILVER LINING Sustainable Growth in China is Unlikely to Arrive on a Silver Platter. *NewsChina.*

3

POLITICAL ENVIRONMENT

Introduction

In the modern context, domestic and international politics are as bilateral as trade agreements. It is not unexpected for countries to pursue self-interest and domestic agendas, rather it is the obligation of each government to the people it represents. With nations interconnected through global supply chains and online marketplaces, the existence of hermit kingdoms—even North Korea and Iran must parlay with their neighbors—is questionable. Those who hold a zero-sum view of global economics would argue that my neighbor's loss is my gain. However, that particular approach is no longer viable, even if one secretly ascribes to that economic formulation. In Asia, the region's players are testing one another, forging agreements, leveraging competitors, and vying for advantage. Much of this is action and reaction, with the smaller nations in the region responding to the movements of the two super-powers.

Command states such as China practice forward planning and coordination of resources: their multilateral strategy for the region is like a chess game played simultaneously with and against multiple opponents. Two of these multilateral strategies, The New Silk Road and High Speed Rail Diplomacy, cut across land and sea into every continent. By design, these policies start with domestic infrastructure development and capacity building. A significant initial investment is made in order to promote domestic economic growth (e.g., a high-speed rail network connecting every major city in China), but as a result, deposits are made towards future international returns (e.g., high-speed rail expertise and technology transferable to other nations for economic gain and as political capital). China's dual synchronous approach to domestic and foreign affairs is evidenced in its policies of "Harmonious Society" and "Soft Power Politics"—a unified domestic front and consensus building at APEC (Asia-Pacific Economic Cooperation), ASEAN (Association of Southeast Asian Nations), and other international bodies; the OBOR strategy of domestic, international, and intercontinental construction of rail, road, and maritime channels; and FTZs—the alignment of domestic financial policies to international norms.

Prudential Diplomacy

With China's rise, suspicions of a new imperialism are escalating and a new balance between domestic priorities and international relations is being called for[1]. Particularly alarming to its neighbors are territorial disputes including the Diaoyu Islands with Japan, the Kashmir region with India and Pakistan, and the maritime lanes in the South China Seas with the Philippines, Vietnam, Malaysia, and other Southeast Asian countries. Increased military spending, especially naval expansion, in addition to China's dredging to create artificial islands in the South China Sea, has acerbated tensions in the region[2,3].

Though China propounds a win-win solution to every diplomatic conflict and claims a "Soft Power" approach to international relations, there is wary suspicion from both the developing nations to which China is providing assistance, such as those in Africa, as well as economic partner-competitors such as the US. Blue water forays into international territories justified as necessary—and oftentimes heroic—protection of domestic interests, such as the Chinese Navy's antipiracy missions off the coast of Africa, have been viewed by many US analysts as precursors to "broader international security objectives"[4] consistent with the West's insistence on the China Threat[5]. In Southeast Asia, China's implementation of its Charm Offensive and Peaceful Rise rhetoric[6] are pragmatic as much as they are ideological, to reduce the prevalence of China Threat Theory and to consequently gain confidence and trustworthiness among its neighbors to the south. Through the use of soft power such as media, with billions spent on CCTV translation and transmission across the globe, and education, sponsoring over 450 Confucius Institutes worldwide that teach Mandarin and Chinese culture[7,8,9] it is successful in this regard, and is even securing supporters among traditional US allies[10].

In 1972, China welcomed Nixon—the first US president to visit the People's Republic of China—to dialogue with Chairman Mao Zedong in Beijing, and since that time, it has pursued an open door approach to international politics and economic partnerships[11]. By 1989, China had established diplomatic relations with 133 countries. In 2001, China joined the WTO, a move that heralded its official association with global economic cooperation. During November 10–12, 2014, with the APEC Meeting as backdrop, Barack Obama made his second visit to China as US President—the first visit occurring during President Obama's inaugural year on November 15–18, 2009. Yu Xiaodong reports on the success of the APEC meeting, a milestone among a series of political accomplishments made through progressive leadership and harmonious development over the past 37 years of international engagement[12]. With 20 signed agreements, a diplomatic victory was claimed by both US and Chinese leaders. Tourists and businesspeople from both nations now consequently enjoy diverse benefits, including elimination of tariffs on 200 categories of products, capping of carbon dioxide emissions, and 10-year tourist and business visas—increased from 1-year visas prior to the agreement[13,14,15] Representing the two great economic and political superpowers, contentions between the US and China created a range of uneven partisanship, representing ongoing competitive interests in the region. Looking for a win-win scenario that supports China's economic interests while preserving those of its neighbors, advances were made in issues ranging from Southeast Asian sea territory disputes, a regional development bank sponsored by China, and a new free trade agreement. The US opposed each of these, and though not unequivocally, by doing so lost ground and influence with its allies in the region[16]. Through diplomacy and reciprocity, China has galvanized the region's shift away from US dominance even with its new "pivot to Asia", resulting in a new balance of power in the region[17].

Throughout the region, new lines have been drawn and alliances established and contested. To the east, South Korea, which is historically allied with the US, has developed closer economic and political ties to China, somewhat a result of an emboldened Japan that is realigning its military strategy through constitutional amendment[18]. To the north, an old adversary, Mongolia, has signed on with China's One Belt, One Road initiative and is a founding member of China's Asia Infrastructure Investment Bank[19]. To the south, China has seen a traditional ally, Vietnam, militarily contest its claims on maritime lanes in the South China Seas[20,21]and as a result has doubled its efforts to diplomatically re-establish friendly relations. Similarly, India is pursuing a US–military alliance as a potential foil to Chinese expansion in the south[22]. To the west, China is revisiting an old friend, with meetings between Xi Jinping and Vladimir Putin at the 2014 Winter Olympics in Sochi, Russia[23]. Across other continents, China has made significant investments into Africa[24] and to a lesser extent, Latin America[25], following an established pattern that has been successful in other developing regions: "make loans, build infrastructure, cement diplomatic ties . . . and be in a prime position for the resource contracts to come"[26].

China's official, self-described status as a *non-aligned* nation is recently coming under scrutiny by Chinese advisors who believe this approach to international relations, which China has implemented successfully since 1982 to avoid international conflict, is now hampering China's political clout. At the same time, China is mindful of the potential ramifications of the growing rumors across the international grapevine of the China threat and the rise of the Chinese Hegemony (Staff, May 27, 2015). With forays into Latin America, the US is wary of the dragon in its backyard, much as it was when Russia was building its presence in Cuba. Southeast Asia, likewise, has its apprehensions towards the expansion of China into the region. Working through diplomatic channels, such as the UN, and establishing common financial interests with neighboring countries, China is taking an approach that attempts to first and foremost build trust through open communication and prudent engagement[27].

Political Investments

The Marshall Plan, aimed at boosting US influence in a reconstruction Europe after World War II, served the Containment Strategy used against the USSR and its communist allies. China's OBOR Initiative is being compared to the Marshall Plan, and along with the comparisons come claims of the expansion of China's perimeter[28,29]. In support of the OBOR Initiative, China has invested $40 billion into its Silk Road Fund[30], an intercontinental transportation corridor that will increase trade, communication, cultural exchange, and political cooperation between Europe and Asia and the countries joined by the new Silk Road trade belt[31,32]. Chinese analysts point out that there are major differences between the Marshall Plan and the OBOR Initiative[33]. In their perspective, the Marshall Plan supported reconstruction; the OBOR Initiative drives economic development and cooperation. In addition, they claim that The Marshall Plan weakened the political autonomy of its recipient countries; the OBOR Initiative sees partnering nations as equals without one dominant authority. Finally, they argue that the Marshall Plan benefited the US over its recipient countries; the OBOR Initiative will cause economic stimulus in the nations along the Silk Road that will eventually benefit them more than it will China.

As the blueprint for the Silk Road is being laid out, a key link in the ancient Silk Road is conspicuously missing—the Middle East. The threat of violence and terrorism in the region has resulted in its omission from the planning documents China has put forth. In addition, there are suspicions that the volatile region with heavy US military presence is being avoided by the Chinese, who prefer to "minimize direct competition with its main strategic rival[34]". This may simply be rhetoric, as China has invested heavily in Cuba, a politically sensitive region that directly threatens US security interests and has influenced US relations with the neighboring island nation[35]. As Latin America's second largest trading partner, China is contributing $250 billion over the next 10 years to the region in preferential loans and funds towards joint projects including solar power generators and high-tech manufac-turing facilities. Though the political motivations for Chinese expansion in every continent are unknown, at minimum, they advance domestic economic growth by fostering long-term ties with nations that share common interests.

China's developmental path in the early 2000s was carved by intentional government expenditures and public policy. This secured for China its consistent double-digit GDP growth while the US and the global economy struggled with negative or near-zero growth during the same period. Among these public works projects, the high-speed rail network, urban subways, and freeway construction were the most demonstrable. For example, Shanghai had two subway lines by the end of 1999 which were expanded to 14 lines in 2013, with a total combined length of 548 km of track, which makes it currently the longest system in the world[36]—with plans to expand to outlying cities such as Suzhou and Wuxi. Across China there are currently 2,735km of subway rail, with a further 2,853km under construction[37]. China's first high-speed rail was completed in 2008, with technology and expertise originally imported from Germany and Japan. Within six years, China's high-speed rail network surpassed 11,000 km of track and, by the end of 2015, it expects to complete a total of 18,000 km[38]. These projects, through large government investitures, not only support the rapid and inexpensive delivery of people and product over long distances, they employ workers who earn a living and gain vocational skills, develop local economies wherever stations are built, and drive consumption of raw and manufactured goods—these in turn accelerate economic growth, consumer spending, infrastructure, and capacity building.

These political investments have now been commoditized, their conversion into diplomatic currency undertaken across developing nations and more recently in economic peers. Premier Li Keqiang has been promoting High-speed Rail (HSR) during his diplomatic missions overseas, resulting in contracts and plans for HSR development in Thailand, Romania, Hungary, Serbia, the UK, Russia, and countries in the Middle East, Central Asia, and Africa[39,40]. Taking its cues from the Marshall Plan, the intention is to wed international and intercontinental transportation networks to political and economic solidarity. There are ambitions to link China to the Middle East and Europe through the OBOR Initiative[41] that is a re-envisioning of a modern-day Silk Road connecting multiple continents through rail and road. The promotion of a HSR connecting Beijing to Moscow is a contemporary Trans-Siberian Express[42]. Even Boston and California have entered into discussions with Chinese HSR companies to explore potential contracts. In cases like the UK and US, the deals are primarily financially motivated, with profits to be garnered. Meanwhile, pending agreements with Thailand, Russia, and Africa have both economic and political benefits, with China's influence in those regions galvanized by these strategic partnerships. China's clout in ASEAN is strengthened with projects such as the China–Thailand–Singapore HSR System and Pan-Asia Railway Project[43]. Billions of dollars of capital investment and years of construction projects in mainland China are now evolving into what is deemed a "truly trans-global" political strategy, or "High Speed Rail Diplomacy," [44] a potential game-changer across every continent (and interconnecting continents) with Chinese HSR projects being discussed, developed, planned, and implemented around the world.

ARTICLES

International Relations

The Past is Prologue

Any brief undertaking of history is inherently confounded by oversimplification and gross omission. Nonetheless, the accounting of China's foreign policy by the editors of *NewsChina* has several key takeaways. First of all, a stable relationship with its Soviet neighbor to the north has been elusive, with an early alliance based on mutual ideologies and interests replaced by competition and distrust. The Soviets and the Chinese continue to maintain a united front politically, though China has certainly outgrown its former mentor, expanding its international relations to both its neighbors as well as its historic rivals such as the US. Yet, as China leapfrogs over the world's largest economies and pursues strategic goals that would ensure sustained growth, even its new relationships are suspect, with competitive forces tearing at the seams of these uneasy friendships.

A Brief History of China's Foreign Policy

February 2015 Issue of NewsChina | *by* NewsChina Magazine

To understand the mentality of the current Chinese leadership and the rationale behind its foreign policy, it is necessary to look at the drastic changes that have marked the last 65 years of Chinese diplomacy.

1950s: LEANING TO ONE SIDE

After winning the Chinese Civil War and establishing the People's Republic of China in 1949, the Communist Party of China immediately aligned publicly with the Soviet Union. With the onset of the Cold War, and particularly the outbreak of the Korean War (1950–1953), China placed itself firmly in the Soviet camp.

1960s: ANTI-SOVIET AND ANTI-US

China's honeymoon with the Soviet Union soured in the late 1950s and early 1960s as the two countries engaged in an ideological debate on the interpretation of Marxism. Launching political movements in alignment with "traditional" Marxism, Chairman Mao Zedong condemned the Soviet Union's policy of "peaceful coexistence" with the US as "revisionism."

In this period, China adopted hard-line policies towards both the Soviet Union and the US, resulting in diplomatic isolation from both powers. At the height of the Sino-Soviet Split in late 1960, territorial disputes between the two countries led to border skirmishes. In 1962, China also fought a brief border conflict with India.

1970s: 'ONE-LINE' POLICY

As Soviet invasion appeared imminent against the backdrop of deteriorating Sino-Soviet relations, China adjusted its policy towards the West. After President Richard Nixon's landmark visit to China in 1972, China began to adopt a "one-line" policy, uniting with other countries along the same latitude to form a united front against the Soviet Union. It was in this period that China began to normalize relations with the US, Japan, and European countries.

1980s: BEYOND IDEOLOGY

After the death of Mao Zedong in 1976 and the launch of Reform and Opening-up in 1978 under the leadership of Deng Xiaoping, China began to adopt a more pragmatic approach to diplomacy, abandoning political ideology as its guiding doctrine. By 1989, China had established diplomatic relationships with 133 countries. In this period, China embraced policies of setting aside disputes and promoting joint development regarding its territorial disputes in both the East China Sea and the South China Sea.

1990s: BIDING ONE'S TIME

With the collapse of the Soviet Union in early 1991, China faced a great political challenge, especially given the sanctions on China by the West after the Tian'anmen Square Incident in 1989. The easy US military victory in the First Gulf War in 1991 also had a significant psychological impact on Chinese leaders.

As a US-led world began to take shape, Deng Xiaoping raised his famous policy of "hiding our capacities, biding our time and doing something worthwhile." In this period, China adopted a rather passive foreign policy and focused primarily on domestic issues such as economic reform.

2000s: GOING OUT

In 2001, China joined the World Trade Organization, allowing it to seek economic cooperation with other countries on a larger scale. China's foreign policy became more and more centered around ensuring a friendly international environment so that China could focus on economic development.

This period was marked by increasing interdependence between China and the rest of the world, as China became "the world's factory," leading to rapid economic growth. In the meantime, the US' focus on global terrorism also allowed China to begin subtly exerting more influence in the Asia-Pacific region.

2010s: GREAT POWER DIPLOMACY

After decades of economic growth, the relationship between China and Western countries has become unprecedentedly complex. On one hand, China has begun to seek a greater role on the international stage, which it considers a reasonable expectation given its status as the world's second largest economy.

But given China's political system and distinctive development path, the West has become increasingly weary of China's increasing influence. China's aspirations are to some extent considered a threat to the Western-controlled global order.

Since Xi Jinping assumed power in 2013, China has adjusted its policy toward the US and Russia, and become more assertive in territorial disputes with Japan while devoting more diplomatic resources to other parts of the world, possibly hailing a new era for Chinese diplomacy.

Agreements Between Rivals

The APEC summit, hosted by Beijing on November 11, 2014, was a resounding international relations success for China. Though several agreements involving the US were approved, such as environmental protections and trade pacts, the mood of the summit between the superpowers was decidedly competitive. Even prior to the summit, the US had drawn a line in the sand, but most chose to play with China, supporting China's version of the FTAAP instead of the one promoted by the US (TPP). The report describes collaborations with Korea, Japan, ASEAN countries, and Central Asia that China has developed; meanwhile the US is described as taking a zero-sum approach to its international affairs in the Pacific, with its pivot to Asia representing a challenge to China's rise in the region.

Partisan Partnerships

January 2015 Issue of NewsChina | *by*
Yu Xiaodong

Despite landmark deals reached between the US and
China during the recent APEC summit in Beijing, the
world's two largest economies remain in competition
for leadership in East Asia.

When Barack Obama left Beijing on November 11, 2014 in the wake
of the Asia Pacific Economic Cooperation (APEC) summit, he had every
reason to claim an unexpectedly productive diplomatic victory.

UNEXPECTED

Among some 20 agreements signed with China was a landmark deal on
climate change. While the US promised to accelerate its plan to cut carbon
dioxide emissions to 26–28 percent of its 2005 levels by 2025, China,
now the world's number one polluter, made its first-ever commitment to
cap its own emissions by 2030, an abrupt departure from its previous stance.

Moreover, the US and China also agreed to expand the scope of the
global Information Technology Agreement (ITA) pact to reduce tariffs
on 200 categories of products to zero. According to the US authorities,
the agreement, if implemented, could support up to 60,000 new American
jobs and eliminate tariffs on nearly US$100 billion of made-in-America
products.

The two sides also agreed to extend the length of tourist and business
visas granted to each other's citizens to ten years from the current limit
of one year. Analysts believe the development could not only remove some
long-standing impediments to exchanges between the two countries, but
could also pave the way to a bilateral investment treaty, which both
countries have made a priority. Furthermore, to avert potential military
clashes in the waters off the Chinese coast, the two sides also signed a
military accord to "regulate behavior" for encounters in the air and at
sea, and to notify each other of major military activities, such as military
exercises. But for all the talks of collaboration between Washington and
Beijing, the two countries clearly continued to compete for the supreme
leadership role in the Asia-Pacific region.

COMPETITION

As the host country of this year's APEC summit, China's agenda was to
push forward the Free Trade Area of the Asia Pacific (FTAAP), a trade
liberalization framework first proposed in 2006, which includes all 21
APEC member countries.

Despite its initial support for the FTAAP, the US later shifted focus to the smaller Trans-Pacific Partnership (TPP), which aims to adopt "higher standards" in establishing a trading bloc of 12 countries including Japan, Australia, Canada and Mexico, but notably excluding China.

According to a report in the *Wall Street Journal*, during negotiations prior to the summit, the US successfully pressured China to drop two provisions regarding the FTAAP from its draft APEC communiqué. One provision called on the APEC bloc to launch a feasibility study on the FTAAP, which would be the first formal step towards kicking off negotiations on the framework. The other provision was a target date of 2025 for cementing the deal.

Despite these concessions, however, it seems that China won enough support by the end of the conference to claw back some of the ground lost to Washington.

During his closing remarks at APEC to an audience that included President Obama, President Xi Jinping announced that member states had reached an agreement to launch a two-year feasibility study on the FTAAP. Calling the agreement "an historic step," though making no mention of the previous 2025 target China had pushed for, Xi urged members to speed up talks and to "turn the vision into reality as soon as possible."

China has long considered the TPP an attempt to check China's growing economic power, as many in the US have claimed that the existing multilateral trade order favors China over the US. For example, according to estimates from the Peterson Institute of International Economics cited by *The Wall Street Journal*, the US would gain about US$191 billion in export volume under the TPP, much less than it would gain under the FTAAP (US$626bn). In comparison, China would stand to lose about US$100 billion in exports if the TPP were agreed, but would gain US$1.6 trillion under the FTAAP.

From China's perspective, the US preference for the TPP over the FTAAP indicates that Washington has increasingly adopted a "zero-sum" mentality as it becomes more sensitive about its economic gains relative to China, and is willing to forego profits so long as Beijing ultimately loses more. From a US perspective, China's firm advocacy for its own agreement over the TPP at a time when TPP negotiations have stalled, is tantamount to directly challenging US free trade supremacy in the Asia-Pacific region.

NEW APPROACH

However, in contrast to its increasing confidence in pushing forward trade and financial initiatives in recent months, China appears to have taken measures to reduce tensions regarding its territorial disputes with surrounding countries during these various international summits, which many analysts see as an obvious and unexpected departure from its earlier assertiveness.

Besides a military accord with the US designed to avert conflicts, Xi met with Japanese Prime Minister Shinzo Abe in Beijing during the APEC summit, their first meeting in two years. The two countries earlier reached a four-point consensus within which Japan acknowledged the dispute between China and Japan over the sovereignty of the Diaoyu/Senkaku island chain for the first time since 2009.

During the ASEAN summit in Myanmar, directly after APEC, in which President Obama also took part, Chinese Premier Li Keqiang said China and ASEAN are working towards the "earliest possible" consensus on a code of conduct in the South China Sea, something Beijing has been trying to avoid in recent months.

Li also raised a seven-point proposal on a framework for China-ASEAN cooperation in the next ten years, which includes the signing of a treaty of "good-neighborliness and friendly cooperation" with ASEAN countries, establishing mechanisms for meetings between China-ASEAN defense ministers and improved maritime cooperation.

Then, in a speech to the Australian parliament in Canberra on November 17 following the G20 Summit, Xi reasserted that China is "committed to peace and peaceful development." "China will not develop at the expense of others," Xi said. Stressing that China has settled land boundary issues with "12 of its 14 neighbors" through "peaceful consultation," Xi said China will continue to work in this direction in its territorial disputes with other nations. The new approach may indicate a policy adjustment in response to a more serious and assertive stance taken by the US to counter an ascendant China.

Besides the FTAAP, the US effort also extends to a variety of China-led initiatives. Earlier in October, for example, three of Asia's biggest economies—South Korea, Indonesia, and Australia—were absent when China announced the establishment of the Asian Infrastructure Investment Bank (AIIB) along with 20 countries, although all three countries had initially expressed interest in the scheme. It is reported that South Korea and Australia at least had withdrawn support under pressure from the US, which sees the AIIB as a direct challenge to both the World Bank and the Asian Development Bank (ADB), which are largely under the control of the US and Japan.

In the meantime, US and Chinese strategists have raised the possibility of potential military clashes between the two rivals. In his speech made at the University of Queensland on November 15, President Obama reasserted that Washington is determined to maintain its military pre-eminence in the Asia-Pacific region. "The US . . . will deploy more of our most advanced military capabilities to keep the peace and deter aggression [in the region]," he said. Although Obama did not mention China in his speech, these remarks were taken as being directed at China. "By the end of this decade, a majority of our Navy and Air Force fleets will be based out of the Pacific, because the United States is, and will always be, a Pacific power," he added.

China has been concerned that the US "Pivot to Asia" is aimed at causing China's territorial disputes with surrounding countries to flare up in order to strengthen US regional alliances and legitimize enhancing Washington's military presence in the region. It is believed that China's new approach aims to limit competition with the US to trade and economics, areas in which it currently has an advantage, and to avoid direct confrontation with the far superior US military machine. With its recent high-profile diplomatic blitz to launch various trade and financial initiatives in the spirit of regional cooperation, China appears to be confident that its initiatives, which advocate "win-win" situations and a "common destiny" will be able to counter the Pivot to Asia.

Although the TPP negotiations are so far still ahead of those on the FTAAP, China can afford to be more flexible than the US in its negotiating position. If the US were to be successful in blocking the FTAAP, China could switch to the Regional Comprehensive Economic Partnership (RCEP), a trade bloc which would include the ASEAN member states plus Australia, China, India, Japan, South Korea, and New Zealand, and is based on the bilateral FTA already signed between these countries.

On November 10, Beijing secured an FTA with South Korea, followed on November 17 by a similar agreement with Australia—both close US military allies. In the meantime, Indonesia, which chose not to become a founding member of the AIIB, has expressed a subsequent interest in joining. Moreover, to reduce US pressure in the Asian-Pacific region, China has begun overtures to the less integrated states of Central Asia with its New Silk Road Initiative which has gained momentum in recent months.

In an interview with the *People's Daily Online*, Zhang Zhaozhong, a military theorist at the PLA National Defense University, said the APEC summit has a symbolic meaning—China's status as a major power has been acknowledged by regional powers including, crucially, the US. Zhang and many other analysts share the same view that economy, definitely not military, will be the major theme of the competition between the world's two major powers for the next decade.

Experts on both sides of the debate are likely to hope that a zero-sum result isn't the only possible outcome of enhanced interaction between the world's two largest economies.

China's Political Balancing Act

The perceived threat of China's rise, as understood by the US, results in a reconsideration of foreign policy that reassures China's rivals and partners of its peaceful intentions. Patience, balance and prudence are recommended to Chinese leadership who must avert the "Thucydides trap," that looms ahead as China's (rising power's) expansion creates competition with US (established power's) interests, which could escalate to military confrontation. To redistribute political capital and diversify interests, periphery diplomacy is pursued with neighboring countries. Often, these relationships are still entangled with that of the US, and China must pursue its interests carefully, treading lightly particularly when it deals with historically grounded conflicts such as territorial disputes—like those in Southeast Asia. Its relationship with Russia is confounded by a historical alliance grounded in shared ideology and the potential that its northern neighbor could become a significant political liability. Each of these periphery relationships are contextualized as challenges or partners in the inevitable rivalry between the US and China.

China Needs to Balance Assertiveness with Prudence in its Diplomacy

February 2015 Issue of NewsChina | by Shi Yinhong

If China is to become a major power in Asia, its leadership must take a more nuanced approach in dealings with neighboring countries.

In recent years, as China has emerged as the world's second largest economy and has aspired to greater influence in the region, potential clashes with the US—the dominant power both in the region and the world—have become one of the most popular topics among Chinese decision makers, analysts and experts.

Some scholars have dubbed the Sino-US relationship, perhaps the world's most important bilateral relationship, "the contest of the 21st century." Many are concerned that the two countries are headed for what is known in diplomacy as the "Thucydides trap," where competition between a rising power and an established power can escalate towards war.

After decades of globalization, today's geopolitical landscape is characterized by a high level of interdependence between countries, and the Sino-US relationship is no exception. The two nations are both rivals and partners, and their bilateral relationship is one of confrontation and competition as much as cooperation and collaboration. To perceive Sino-US ties purely from the perspective of strategic rivalry is misleading, as such a view ignores the complexity of the relationship.

But, given that the world is a metaphorical chessboard of contending rival powers, it is inevitable that these rivalries will be most acute between the rising great power and the incumbent dominant power. To avoid the prospect of the Thucydides trap, decision makers in both China and the US must craft policies based on a sound and solid judgment of each other's core interests, strategic intentions, actual capability and basic national psyche. Any misunderstanding, underestimation, prejudice or misjudgment could have devastating consequences for both countries, and any attempt by one side to coerce the other would be politically reckless and strategically foolhardy.

In recent months, China has made it clear that its goal both in the short and the long term is to "persuade" the US to recognize and respect China's strategic interests in the West Pacific—an objective China considers to be reasonable. However, in pursing this understanding, China needs to adopt a more balanced approach between assertiveness and prudence.

In order to achieve this strategic goal, China needs to have patience in pushing forward its policies and initiatives. A more balanced and prudent approach will allow China and the US a longer period of stability in which to permanently settle their disputes and agree on a new power equilibrium, ensuring the sustainability of China's peaceful rise.

PERIPHERY DIPLOMACY

In the last couple of years, as China has sought to improve and consolidate relationships with neighboring countries, there has been a notable shift in the focus of Chinese foreign policy toward so-called "periphery diplomacy"—a departure from its previous policy prioritizing the relationship with the US.

However, given that the US has an established network of alliances and commitments in the region, the status of China's relationships with its neighbors continues to depend on China's relationship with the US. For example, China's increasing assertiveness in territorial disputes in the East China and South China seas has led to military confrontations with Japan, the Philippines and Vietnam. These maritime disputes have become a deadlock for Chinese regional strategy, especially when the US has taken advantage of these disputes in the context of its "pivot to Asia."

In the meantime, other challenges have emerged along China's borders. In Northeast Asia, China's relationship with traditional ally North Korea has reached its lowest point since President Xi assumed power in 2012. In South Asia, the prospect of greater rivalry with India has also been on the rise since Hindu nationalist Narendra Modi came to power in 2014.

Given the complexity of power rivalries in the region, China must be clear about its strategic priorities in its relationships with neighboring countries and the US. Rather than showing assertiveness on all fronts, China should devote its resources to its chief strategic objective, while adopting a more flexible and pragmatic approach on other fronts.

RUSSIA

Another notable feature of China's diplomatic activities in the past couple of years is its increasingly close relationship with Russia. Sino-Russian ties are not only a key component of China's periphery diplomacy, but also have significant bearing on the Sino-US relationship.

In the past few months, increased Western sanctions on Russia have resulted in strengthened cooperation between China and Russia. As Russia becomes more and more dependent on China for strategic support, China has provided Moscow with key financial assistance in the form of colossal oil and gas deals.

However, despite the importance of the partnership with Russia in countering the US' increasing strategic pressure on China, China has made it clear that a full-blown alliance with Russia is out of the question. China must remain aware that close ties with Russia may become a liability.

For several decades, China has upheld the principles of non-interference, sovereign integrity, and peaceful resolution of international disputes. But following the crisis in Ukraine, China has resorted to these principles less frequently and less determinedly in international diplomacy. As long as the Ukraine issue remains unsolved, it constitutes a diplomatic challenge for China, as it undermines China's integrity in upholding the various international principles that have long been the foundation of its international credibility.

China must handle its relationship with Russia from a broader global perspective. Closer strategic cooperation with Russia will improve China's geopolitical position in the short term, but China must distance itself from Russia regarding Ukraine and other such thorny issues.

ASIA

As recent events have shown—most notably the APEC leaders' summit in Beijing in mid-November—China's leadership has toned down its previous assertiveness in territorial disputes. By signing a military accord with the US designed to avert conflict and reaching a landmark four-point consensus with Japan, China has made efforts to reduce tensions in the region.

The adjustment suggests that China's leadership has realized that its military assertiveness in the region not only undermines its efforts to build soft power, but increases the likelihood of a military clash with the US and its allies, primarily Japan, and has led the US to take a more assertive stance to counter China's influence.

However, a grand Chinese vision for a future role as the region's dominant power remains unchanged. Its policy adjustment will see China focusing on financial and economic competition, manifested in the various initiatives China has launched in the past few months.

In May, for example, President Xi Jinping proposed the slogan "Asia for Asians" at the fourth Conference on Interaction and Confidence Building Measures. In October, 2014, China reached agreements with 20 other countries to establish the Asian Infrastructure Investment Bank (AIIB), and at the APEC summit Xi called on the bloc to begin negotiations on the FTAAP framework. These moves have been seen as a direct challenge to the existing international order under the leadership of the US.

As the US remains extremely sensitive to any challenge to its predominance in the region, the strategic distrust and rivalry between the US and China will persist, if not intensify. While the chances of a direct military clash have decreased, the competition and rivalry between the two countries will likely become more profound and extensive.

As rivalries in the region become more complicated, China's determination, patience and endurance will be tested. On one hand, China should be unwavering in pushing forward the various trade, financial and economic initiatives it has launched, and on the other, China should tone down its hawkishness in its dealings with its neighboring countries to prevent the US from forging a "united front" against China in the region. Only this way can China achieve its peaceful rise.

One Belt, One Road

HSR Diplomacy

The author describes China's HSR diplomacy as China's version of the Marshall Plan. Given the rate of expansion of its technology, expertise, and construction contracts around the world, China's HSR diplomacy is laying the tracks for footholds in every inhabited continent. With 49 domestic HSR projects underway building a network of over 18,000 km across China's vast and diverse territory, plans are now in place to expand north, south, and west with all roads leading to Beijing. To the south, the major project is a HSR line connecting Kunming to Thailand, eventually reaching Malaysia and Singapore and connecting China to ports on the South China Seas.

China has signed agreements with Romania, Hungary, and Serbia to build westbound from Xinjiang province, passing through Central Asia, Turkey, and Bulgaria. A renewed vision of the Trans-Siberian Railroad, a 7,000 km HSR line from Moscow to Beijing, is becoming a reality.

As a corollary to the US' Marshall Plan, a global HSR network would provide China with a transportation system that could move people and product across the Eurasian region and to the world. It would be a major revenue stream for its HSR companies—now merged into a rolling stock manufacturer—as more and more countries adopt the technology and sign contracts. Internationally it promotes a perception of China as a builder and collaborator, as opposed to a colonizer or hegemon. The last hinges upon China's ability to carve out a win-win scenario for each of its partners/customers.

Truly Transglobal

January 2015 Issue of NewsChina | *by Yu Xiaodong*

With its ongoing high-speed rail diplomacy and various international financial initiatives, has China adopted its own version of the Marshall Plan?

When, on November 7, Mexican President Enrique Peña Nieto canceled a high-speed rail (HSR) deal with a Chinese-led consortium including the China Railway Construction Corp and several Mexican firms, many saw the first major blow to China's effort to export its domestically revolutionary HSR technology. The US$3.75 billion contract to build a 210-kilometer (130-mile) line connecting Mexico City with the central city of Querétaro was China's first such deal in Latin America, and prompted an outcry from Mexican lawmakers when it was announced less than a week earlier.

Few, however, believe that this setback will halt what many have termed China's "high-speed rail diplomacy" drive, as the country endeavors to shift its national growth strategy away from labor-intensive, low-end manufacturing to the higher end of the global market.

EXPANSION

With its first HSR line completed in 2008, China's domestic network surpassed 11,000 kilometers of track within just six years, utterly transforming travel in a country heavily dependent on rail to move both its goods and its people. With 49 new projects totaling 7,000 kilometers of track currently underway, it is estimated that China will have an 18,000-kilometer HSR network by the end of 2015.

Besides domestic expansion, China has also endeavored to export HSR technology as part of its diplomatic outreach to other nations. Dubbed China's leading high-speed rail "salesman," Premier Li Keqiang has been actively promoting Chinese HSR technology on his overseas visits.

On an official visit to Thailand in October 2013, Li inaugurated an HSR exhibition in Bangkok alongside then Prime Minister Yingluck Shinawatra, signing a memorandum of cooperation on a US$23 billion project that will link a fledgling Thai HSR network to China's by 2021. Although the project was suspended after Shinawatra was deposed in a bloodless military coup, Thailand's current ruling junta reactivated the project this August.

During a trade forum held in November 2013 in Bucharest, China announced a HSR project in Romania and also inked a partnership agreement with Hungary and Serbia to build a line connecting Budapest to Belgrade.

During an African tour in May 2014, the Chinese Premier attended the World Economic Forum on Africa, joint research projects were announced on HSR technology, with delegates mooting a vast network connecting several African capitals.

China has long been a major player in the market of railway and infrastructure construction in Southeast Asia and Africa. Now, the country has broadened its scope to include Europe and the Americas, hoping that growing demand for HSR networks in developed economies may disperse previous anxieties about welcoming Chinese investment.

In his visit to London in June, Premier Li signed an agreement with British Prime Minister David Cameron to promote bilateral cooperation on the design and expansion of an extended rail network, including HSR, which analysts believe will pave the way for Chinese enterprises to add impetus to HS2 (High Speed 2), a major infrastructure project aimed at establishing an HSR link between London and the north of England.

During his visit to India earlier in September, President Xi Jinping signed an agreement with Prime Minister Narendra Modi, which will see China investing US$20 billion in India's infrastructure over the next five years, including the addition of HSR lines to the country's rail network.

On October 23, the United States approved cooperation between the Massachusetts Department of Transportation and China North Vehicle Group (CNR), China's other rolling stock giant, to purchase 284 subway trains for the Boston area. Although these trains are not technically high-speed, it is the first time that a Chinese rail company has won a bid for a contract in the US. Both China South Locomotive and Rolling Stock Corporation Limited (CSR) and CNR have indicated their interest in supplying rolling stock for California's proposed US$68 billion HSR network, with its first line between Fresno and Bakersfield scheduled to open in 2021.

GLOBAL AMBITIONS

Besides cooperation with individual countries, China has also proposed several international and even intercontinental high-speed railways. The first to open may be a 3,000-kilometer railway line linking Kunming, capital of Yunnan Province in southwestern China, to destinations in Laos, Thailand, Malaysia and Singapore. The high-speed rail project recently restarted by leaders in Bangkok is believed to be phase one of this grand project.

According to Zhao Xiaogang, an adviser to the China Institute for Innovation and Development Strategy and the former chairman of CSR, China aims to finish this transnational project, which will have an estimated cost of US$75 billion, by 2025.

And even more ambitious is a 6,000-kilometer line linking China's Xinjiang Uygur autonomous region with Eastern Europe, passing through Kyrgyzstan, Tajikistan, Uzbekistan, Turkmenistan, Iran, Turkey and Bulgaria. Few proposed projects follow China's global economic strategy as closely as this rail line, which traces almost exactly the investment path of the government's much-vaunted "New Silk Road" initiative launched by the central leadership under President Xi Jinping in 2013.

During Premier Li Keqiang's visit to Moscow in October, China proposed yet another grand project to build a 7,000-kilometer HSR line from Moscow to Beijing, which would cost about US$230 billion and cut the journey time of today's Trans-Siberian Railroad from six days to two. The two sides signed a memorandum of understanding regarding building Phase One of this proposed project—an HSR link between Moscow and Kazan, the first leg of the Trans-Siberian Railroad.

NATIONAL STRATEGY

Many analysts believe that China's "high-speed rail diplomacy" is part of a national strategy inspired by the US Marshall Plan of the 1940s. Officially called the "European Recovery Plan," the Marshall Plan was an unprecedented package of financial, logistical and military aid provided to the devastated nations of Europe in the wake of World War II. A byproduct of the plan, which some claim was its main intention, was establishing strong overseas markets for American goods, securing US influence in most major world markets and placing the dollar at the heart of global trade.

In 2009, Xu Shanda, former director of the State Taxation Administration, proposed that China should learn from this example to engineer a "Chinese version of the Marshall Plan." According to Xu, China is comparable to the postwar US, suffering an excess of production capacity and vast foreign exchange reserves with limited investment channels. By offering financial assistance to infrastructure projects in both developed and developing countries as well as emerging markets, China can achieve multiple strategic objectives.

Not only would building a global HSR network help China absorb its excess capacity and sustain its flagging domestic economic growth, it could also accelerate the pace of the internationalization of China's currency, increasing the yields on its foreign exchange reserves, reducing its holdings of US treasury bonds and guard against long-term depreciation in value of the US dollar. Moreover, with an increased presence in an in-demand high-tech market, China can boost its soft power and enhance political and security cooperation with partner countries. Although Chinese officials have denied that the government has adopted this strategy, many commentators, both domestic and foreign, have made comparisons to the Marshall Plan, pointing to the fact that Chinese financial initiatives are increasingly tied to infrastructure projects.

Besides low cost and rapid construction, a key advantage of Chinese HSR manufacturers is the virtual guarantee of State-backed funding. In the Mexican deal, for instance, the Export-Import Bank of China (EximBank) offered to finance 85 percent of the project. On October 24, 2014, China, along with other 20 countries, established the Asian Infrastructure Investment Bank, with China providing the bulk of an initial fund of US$50 billion, which Chinese officials say will soon reach US$100 billion. On November 9, that same year, during the APEC summit held in Beijing, President Xi Jinping announced that China will invest US$40 billion in establishing a "Silk Road Fund" to finance its Central Asian initiatives. Then, when ASEAN leaders met in Myanmar the weekend after the APEC summit, Premier Li Keqiang announced that China would provide US$10 billion in loans to ASEAN countries, also allocating another US$10 billion fund to EximBank to finance infrastructure projects in the region. Roads, ports and, crucially, HSR projects will be financed by these initiatives.

MERGERS

Under its national strategy, the Chinese government is reported to be encouraging a merger between CNR and CSR in order to boost competitiveness with major international HSR firms such as Bombardier (Canada), Alstom (France) and Siemens (Germany). It is argued that the two Chinese companies have engaged in a fierce price war on overseas markets which has undermined China's overall strategy. In 2011, for example, the two companies undercut one another in bidding for a Turkish contract, which eventually went to a South Korean firm. Then in 2013, after CSR bid for a rolling stock contract in Argentina, CNR offered a vastly lower price, leading the Argentine government to cast doubt on the credibility of both companies.

On October 27, the two State-owned companies suspended the trading of shares. With total annual revenue of 131 billion yuan (US$21.4bn) and 98 billion yuan (US$16bn) respectively and combined profits of US$1.4 billion in 2013, the merger, if successful, would give birth to the world's largest rolling stock manufacturer, fundamentally changing the international market.

CHALLENGES

Regardless of the aims of its policies, however, China also faces serious political and economic challenges in achieving its stated objective of a global HSR network centered on the People's Republic. Industrial analysts are warning that China's high-speed rail diplomacy, along with the proposed merging of CNR and CSR, will inevitably lead to an intensified diplomatic fightback.

Others warn that it would be very difficult for China to replicate the success of the Marshall Plan, given that it is not the sole player in a global market that, while somewhat stagnant, is far from the devastated wasteland left in the wake of WWII. In an article published on political analysis website *The Diplomat*, Dingding Chen, assistant professor of Government and Public Administration at the University of Macau outlined four major differences.

Unlike the US, which was already a global dominant power in the 1940s, China is a rising and developing power, already perceived as a direct challenge to US supremacy, a status which will inevitably be combated by American maneuvering. Moreover, while the Marshall Plan was conducted between the US and its European allies, China's initiatives are open to almost all countries, meaning a "free ride" for those seeking to profit from infrastructure deals while remaining strategically and economically aligned with US interests. In addition, China still faces trust issues in many markets, as evidenced by the collapse of its Mexican rail initiative.

Chen argues however that China's advantage lies in that it understands "the key desire of many developing countries: They want development first, and they want development without the political strings imposed by the West." "China needs to work harder to convince others that its initiative is indeed aimed at achieving a 'win-win' outcome for everyone," he concluded.

The New Silk Road

Chinese have a penchant for numerical slogans. One of the most recent is "One Belt, One Road." The annual gathering of the National People's Congress and the Chinese People's Political Consultative Conference is popularly referred to as the "Two Sessions." Others from the past included "Three Rounds and a Sound," harking back to when Beijing desired all peasant families to have at least a bicycle, a watch, a sewing machine, and a radio. In the article "One Belt, One Road," the Hong Kong Trade Development Council describes an important new initiative: the Silk Road Economic Belt and the 21st Century Maritime Silk Road—as a key part of China's development strategy. The "Vision and Actions on Jointly Building the Silk Road Economic Belt and the 21st Century Maritime Silk Road," issued by the National Development and Reform Commission on March 28, 2015 outlines the initiative's framework, cooperation priorities, and cooperation mechanisms. The OBOR pointedly omits trade with the Americas and US allies Japan and South Korea, furthering China's effort towards self-sufficient hegemony.

As China expands westward in accordance with its OBOR policy, it is carefully navigating what could be a political minefield. Each country that this "one road" passes through is invariably linked to all other countries along that route. With its ever-growing thirst for Middle East oil, China's decision to omit the region from its OBOR policy has been little understood. The article touches on Islamic threats and past losses due to political instability in the region, but sees the omission of the Middle East as a concession to the US which has long-standing vested interests in the region. The premise is that China wants to avoid conflict with the US and will avoid the entire region so as not to antagonize it.

One Belt, One Road will Bypass the Middle East, and for Good Reason

May 2015 Issue of NewsChina | *by Wang Tao*

Past lessons and ongoing concerns over open competition with the US has led China to circumvent the Middle East in its program to expand its global influence.

With a concentrated slew of diplomatic visits in the past couple of years, China has launched its dual-track New Silk Road initiative. The program aims to achieve regional integration along the ancient overland Silk Road trade belt linking Asia and Europe alongside a Maritime Silk Road Belt linking China, Southeast and South Asia. Dubbed One Belt,

One Road, the dual initiative is set to be China's leading foreign policy priority in the coming years.

But in laying out the blueprints for its One Road, One Belt initiative, it is clear that the Middle East, a key link on the ancient Silk Road, is absent from the plan, a seemingly counter-intuitive omission. In the past few years, China has relied on the oil-producing Arab states for much of its oil and gas. Saudi Arabia, for example, is China's biggest source of crude oil. In 2013, oil imports from Saudi Arabia accounted for 20 percent of China's total. In the meantime, Qatar has become China's principal supplier of liquid natural gas. In 2013, some 30 percent of the crude oil consumed in China originated in the Middle East, which supplied more than 50 percent of China's total imported crude that year.

However, in recent years, China seems to have become wary of venturing further into this region when expanding its overseas investment. In 2013, China's total global FDI amounted to US$90 billion, more than half of which was bankrolled by State-owned energy companies. In terms of geographical allocation of FDI, however, Chinese investment in the Middle East lags far behind that in other oil-rich regions. While China has increased its investment in the energy industry in Africa and South America, in the Middle East it has focused mainly on promoting trade.

A major reason for this caution is the volatile political and security situation in many Gulf states, which in the last few years has made Chinese investors more circumspect. China suffered huge losses in Libya as a result of the Arab Spring movement. The rise of the Islamic State in Syria and Iraq also poses a direct threat to recent Chinese investment in Iraq's oil industry. Even in Saudi Arabia, where the political situation is relatively stable, China's success is limited. For example, the China Railway Construction Corporation (CRCC) lost 4.15 billion yuan (US$670m) on a light rail project in Mecca that ended up completing way over budget due to frequent bureaucratic issues. With these lessons in hand, China's leadership appears to be reluctant to venture into the Middle East when promoting its One Belt, One Road project.

Moreover, as One Belt, One Road has been painted as China's first "global" strategy, it is frequently perceived as a concerted effort by China to challenge the global leadership of the US. The deliberate exclusion of the Middle East, a region of major strategic importance for the US, is China's attempt to minimize direct competition with its main strategic rival. Although the rise of the American shale oil and gas industry has diminished the importance of the Middle East to US energy policy, there is little indication that the US will scale back its political and economic presence and influence in the region. To extend its own economic power in the Middle East, China would be seen to be directly challenging Washington's status in a key strategic region, possibly jeopardizing the One Belt, One Road strategy in the process.

As the Middle East will continue to be an important region in terms of meeting China's energy needs, it is in Beijing's interest to promote stability in the region. For this reason, China has supported the ongoing negotiations between Iran and the US over the former's nuclear program. Moreover, with no experience dealing with the complex political and religious landscape of the Middle East, China is simply not ready to attempt to broaden its political influence among Arab States.

To extend its own economic power in the Middle East, China would be seen to be directly challenging Washington's status in a key strategic region.

The author is a resident scholar with the Carnegie-Tsinghua Center for Global Policy.

OBOR Implications for Hong Kong

According to Billy Wong of the Hong Kong Trade Development Council, the OBOR policy refers to two routes, one road running from China through Russia to Europe, one belt running through ancient maritime routes from China's coastal regions to the West. In fact, the article describes several roads that make up the East to West thoroughfare, with routes passing through Mongolia/Russia, Central Asia, and South Asia/Persian Gulf, all starting in China and terminating in Europe. Each of these routes will leverage the advantages of diverse regions in China: Xinjiang in the northwest; Kunming in the southwest; Hong Kong, Macau, and Taiwan in the coastal regions; Chengdu and Chongqing in the inland regions.

The aims of the OBOR policy are to "promote connectivity in five respects: policy co-ordination, facilities connectivity, unimpeded trade, financial integration and people-to-people bonds." With free trade zones, development/investment banks, education exchanges, and international cooperation platforms such as ASEAN, China hopes to implement the OBOR policy to expand its influence across the Eurasian region and establish infrastructure for future development. Subsequent projects include ports, bridges, airports, industrial parks, and energy and communications projects in the countries along the OBOR routes. Hong Kong will play a vital role by providing support for each of the OBOR aims, from investment platforms to logistic links to financial services.

One Belt, One Road Initiative: The Implications for Hong Kong

By Billy Wong (April 16, 2015)

The "*One Belt, One Road*" Initiative—the Silk Road Economic Belt and the 21st Century Maritime Silk Road—is a key part of China's development strategy. The *Vision and Actions on Jointly Building the Silk Road Economic Belt and the 21st Century Maritime Silk Road (the "Vision and Actions")* issued by the National Development and Reform Commission on 28 March 2015 outlines the initiative's framework, co-operation priorities and co-operation mechanisms.

The Belt and Road Initiative aims to promote connectivity in infrastructure, resources development, industrial co-operation, financial integration and other fields along the Belt and Road countries. These strategic objectives are also closely connected to the "*going out*" strategy of many Chinese businesses. In light of the Vision and Actions document, as well as other related information sources, the "One Belt, One Road" initiative, with its extensive reach across a number of regions, represents clear development opportunities for Hong Kong.

VISION AND ACTIONS: THE KEY POINTS

The "One Belt, One Road" initiative aims to promote "connectivity in five respects": policy co-ordination, facilities connectivity, unimpeded trade, financial integration and people-to-people bonds. These may be summed up as follows:

- The Silk Road Economic Belt focuses on bringing together China, Central Asia, Russia and Europe (the Baltic); linking China with the Persian Gulf and the Mediterranean Sea through Central Asia and West Asia; and connecting China with Southeast Asia, South Asia and the Indian Ocean. The 21st Century Maritime Silk Road is designed to go from China's coast to Europe through the South China Sea and the Indian Ocean and from China's coast through the South China Sea to the South Pacific. On land, the initiative will take advantage of international transport routes, rely on core cities along the Belt and Road, and use key economic and trade zones and industrial parks as co-operative platforms. At sea, it will focus on jointly building smooth, secure and efficient transport routes, connecting major seaports along the Belt and Road.
- Facilities connectivity: Priority will be given to removing transport bottlenecks and promoting port infrastructure construction and co-operation in order to deliver international transport facilitation.

Priority will also be given to the construction of regional communications trunk lines and networks in order to improve international communications connectivity.

ECONOMIC CORRIDORS OF THE "ONE BELT, ONE ROAD"

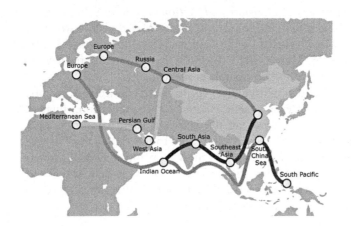

- Investment and trade co-operation: Efforts will be made to resolve the problems of investment and trade facilitation; hold discussions on opening free trade zones; expand traditional trade and develop modern service trade and cross-border e-commerce; promote trade through investment, strengthen co-operation with relevant countries in industrial chains, promote upstream-downstream and related industries to develop in concert, and build overseas economic and trade co-operation zones; and encourage Chinese enterprises to participate in infrastructure construction and make industrial investments in countries along the Belt and Road.
- Financial integration: Efforts will be made to promote the development of the bond market in Asia and push forward the establishment of the Asian Infrastructure Investment Bank, the BRICS New Development Bank and the Silk Road Fund; support the efforts of Belt and Road countries and their companies/financial institutions in issuing RMB bonds in China; encourage Chinese financial institutions and companies to issue bonds denominated in both RMB and foreign currencies outside China; give full play to the role of the Silk Road Fund and that of sovereign wealth funds of the Belt and Road countries, and encourage commercial equity investment funds and private funds to participate in the construction of the key projects of the initiative.

- People-to-people bonds: Efforts will be made to strengthen educational and cultural co-operation, including cross-nation student and education exchanges; enhance co-operation in tourism; and support think tanks in the Belt and Road countries to jointly conduct research and hold forums.
- Fully leverage the comparative advantages of various regions in China:
  - Northwestern and northeastern regions: The initiative will give full scope to Xinjiang's geographical advantages and make it a core area on the Silk Road Economic Belt, while giving full scope to the advantages of Inner Mongolia and Heilongjiang province with regard to their proximity to Russia and Mongolia, as well as improving the rail links connecting Heilongjiang with Russia.
  - Southwestern region: The initiative will give full play to the unique advantages of Guangxi and Yunnan, speed up the opening up and development of the Beibu Gulf Economic Zone and the Zhujiang-Xijiang Economic Zone (also known as the Pearl River-Xijiang Economic Zone), and develop a new focus for economic co-operation in the Greater Mekong Sub-region.
  - Coastal regions and Hong Kong, Macau and Taiwan: The initiative will support the Fujian province in becoming a core area of the 21st Century Maritime Silk Road; give full scope to the roles of Qianhai (Shenzhen), Nansha (Guangzhou), Hengqin (Zhuhai) and other locations in opening up and co-operation, and will help to build the Guangdong-Hong Kong-Macau Big Bay Area; will strengthen port construction in a number of coastal cities, such as Shanghai, Tianjin, Ningbo-Zhoushan, Guangzhou, Shenzhen, Zhanjiang, Shantou, Qingdao, Yantai, Dalian, Fuzhou, Xiamen, Quanzhou and Haikou, and will strengthen the functions of several international hub airports, notably Shanghai and Guangzhou.
  - Inland regions: With a focus on city clusters along the middle reaches of the Yangtze River and around Chengdu and Chongqing, the initiative will establish Chongqing as an important pivot for developing and opening up the western region, while making Chengdu, Xian and Zhengzhou leading areas for opening up in the inland regions, and developing railway transportation in the China-Europe corridor.

Co-operation mechanisms and platforms: The initiative will make full use of existing multilateral co-operation mechanisms, such as the Shanghai Co-operation Organisation (SCO), ASEAN Plus China (10+1), Asia-Pacific Economic Co-operation (APEC), Asia-Europe Meeting (ASEM). In addition to existing forums and exhibitions, it is also proposed that an international summit forum on the Belt and Road Initiative should be established.

INFRASTRUCTURE: TAKING PRECEDENCE IN THE "ONE BELT, ONE ROAD" INITIATIVE

The Asian Development Bank estimated that the Asian economies would need to invest US$8 trillion in infrastructure to bring their facilities up to average world standards between 2010 and 2020. According to reports, China is conducting feasibility studies on four outbound high-speed railways, including the Europe-Asia high-speed rail, the Central Asia high-speed rail, the Pan-Asia high-speed rail and the China-Russia-America-Canada line. The domestic sections of the first three projects are reportedly underway, while negotiations are still being carried out on the last project, as well as on the overseas sections of the first three projects.

Apart from railway networks, other cross-border projects and the building of port facilities, airports, highways, and even electricity and communications projects in the Belt and Road countries are also targets for China's "going out" funds. In addition to investment, there will also be a considerable number of opportunities for the international contracting of construction and machinery exports.

INDUSTRIAL CO-OPERATION: STIMULATING TRADE FLOWS

In terms of resource development, several provinces in China are planning to take advantage of the Belt and Road Initiative in order to encourage competitive industries to go global and undertake co-operation in advanced technologies. Chinese enterprises are also being encouraged to increase overseas investment in the exploitation of mineral resources in order to improve China's supply of energy resources.

According to the Department of Outward Investment and Economic Co-operation of the Ministry of Commerce, China has established 118 economic and trade co-operation zones in 50 countries around the world. (These are set up in the host countries, with Chinese enterprises forming the mainstay based on the market situation, the investment environment, and the host government's policies when it comes to managing investment to attract enterprises to set up production there.) Of these zones, 77 are established in 23 countries along the Belt and Road. These overseas economic and trade co-operation zones have become China's platforms for overseas investment co-operation, as well as platforms for the clustering of industries.

There are 35 co-operation zones in countries along the Silk Road Economic Belt, including Kazakhstan, Kyrgyzstan, Uzbekistan, Russia,

Belarus, Hungary, Romania and Serbia. There are also countless economic and trade co-operation zones along the 21st Century Maritime Silk Road. There are, for example, Chinese industrial parks in Laos, Myanmar, Cambodia, Vietnam, Thailand, Malaysia and Indonesia, and in South Asia, as well as even in Pakistan, India and Sri Lanka. The Belt and Road Initiative, then, will generate more development opportunities, including the building of industrial parks, facilitating investment projects and boosting international trade by the private sector.

SUPPORTING DEVELOPMENT THROUGH FINANCIAL CO-OPERATION

In order to provide financial support for the development of the Belt and Road Initiative, China is actively promoting the establishment of the Asia Infrastructure Investment Bank, the BRICS New Development Bank and the Silk Road Fund. The Silk Road Fund was officially established at the end of December 2014. According to Silk Road Fund chair, Jin Qi, the fund will mainly invest in infrastructure, energy development, and industrial and financial co-operation, and will support the export of high-end technologies and production capacity. The Belt and Road Initiative does not have strict geographical boundaries and the fund will participate in any project relating to connectivity.

The Silk Road Fund may set up sub-funds for investment in particular industries. Some of these sub-funds may have particular industries as entry points. For example, an electricity sub-fund may be established as many companies may choose to invest in electricity projects. Another sub-fund may target particular regions. Where there are enough qualified people well familiar with a particular region, a sub-fund may be established for that region.

According to Zhou Xiaochuan, Governor of the People's Bank of China, the Belt and Road Initiative will generate development and investment opportunities as it has diverse financing needs, with the role of the investment bank being to match investment demand and supply through proper financial arrangements. In terms of the demand for qualified personnel, Zhou said that staff members must have experience in investment and international exposure, in addition to a sound understanding of particular countries. They must also have expertise and social connections, together with an engineering background (especially in financing for engineering projects), possess considerable knowledge or experience in key industries, and speak a relevant foreign language.

DRIVING INCREASED LEVELS OF DOMESTIC INVESTMENT

Chinese provinces are responding positively to the Belt and Road Initiative. According to reports, as of February 5, 2015, more than two-thirds of the 28 mainland provinces that had held their local people's congresses and political consultative conferences have made their own plans for the initiative. In infrastructure planning, for instance, Chongqing has issued its *Opinions on Implementing the Belt and Road Strategy and Building the Yangtze Economic Belt* and is expected to invest RMb1.2 trillion in infrastructure before 2020. This will generate opportunities for co-operation in construction, planning, management, finance and other related fields.

IMPLICATIONS FOR HONG KONG

In terms of industry sector, infrastructure may be the first stage in the development of the Belt and Road Initiative. It requires investment, project contracting and will drive demand for relevant services. In this connection, Hong Kong should be able to find a considerable array of opportunities in financing, project risk/quality management, infrastructure and real estate services (IRES), as well as several other related fields.

A number of Chinese enterprises may become involved in mergers and acquisitions in the course of "going out". According to some analysts, China's aviation industry should also plan to "go out" through mergers and acquisitions. To date, Hong Kong has been the key platform for the mainland's outward investment. By the end of 2013, Hong Kong accounted for 57.1 percent of China's outward investment stock, with the cumulative value standing at US$377.1 billion. The increase of investment and merger and acquisition activities will increase the demand for the respective professional services in Hong Kong.

The launch of the Belt and Road Initiative will increase people-to-people exchanges between China and the countries concerned, as well as boost demand for international logistics. Hong Kong has a leading edge in global logistics links and operation. In addition to freight services, Hong Kong can give further leverage to its functions as a maritime services centre. As Nansha in the Guangdong Free Trade Zone also intends to develop maritime services, Hong Kong may explore co-operation possibilities with the district.

Another area in which Hong Kong can play a substantial role is financial services. Hong Kong can provide additional services here, including fund raising, financing, bonds, asset management, insurance and offshore RMB business. Hong Kong can also seek to play a bigger role in the Asian Infrastructure Investment Bank, BRICS New Development Bank and Silk Road Fund, including encouraging these institutions to set up their headquarters and branches in the territory and make greater use of Hong Kong's international talent, as well as inviting the Silk Road Fund to set up sub-funds in Hong Kong. In addition, passenger and freight transport, aircraft leasing and other aviation-related financial services also represent a considerable number of opportunities.

In terms of industrial co-operation, China's overseas economic and trade co-operation zones will become platforms for overseas investment and co-operation for Chinese enterprises, as well as platforms for the clustering of industries. Southeast Asia, South Asia and Central Asia may further develop into a more extensive network of bases for industrial relocation and even open up as consumer markets. The demand for logistics, supply chain management, consumer products and services may increase with the growth of these regions. Following the opening of logistics hubs in Central Asia, there will be railways linking China with the region. For example, Hong Kong businesses may consider using the Chongqing-Xinjiang-Europe railway to transport goods directly from Chongqing to the Central Asian market, thus saving time and money.

With regard to regional development, apart from Southeast Asia, South Asia, and even Central Asia, Central and Eastern Europe, the demand of mainland provinces for infrastructure investment and logistics services in support of the Belt and Road Initiative will also generate business opportunities for the relevant industries.

Hong Kong can also play a more proactive role in the Belt and Road co-operation platform. For example, Hong Kong may strive to regularly host international summits/forums and work with think tanks and cultural and educational institutions in the Belt and Road countries in conducting research, training, co-operations and exchanges. It could also act as a platform for personnel exchanges/training in relevant fields, such as logistics, infrastructure and finance.

Regional Strategies

Railroad Diplomacy in Africa

China has been active in Africa for decades now, primarily to support its insatiable hunger for natural resources. During that time, it has gained a questionable reputation but has meanwhile avoided the moniker of post-colonial imperialist by keeping its investments confined to specific projects with defined financial goals, such as the Tanzania–Zambia railway that connected Dar es Salaam to the copper fields of Zambia. On November 19, 2014, Nigeria signed a $12 billion contract for an 850-mile railroad built by the Chinese, their largest overseas deal to date. With other railroad lines being initiated from China to Central Asia, Singapore, Turkey, Moscow, and others, China's new Silk Road is being rebuilt and expanded. One concern is the inevitable corruption that follows major railroad construction projects around the world, with criticism coming from Chinese academics who fear that malpractice and corruption are likely to ensue when projects are entirely Chinese run with Chinese money, Chinese companies, Chinese materials, and Chinese workers.

Red Train Rising

December 16, 2014 in Foreign Policy | *by Tom Zoellner*

China's international rail expansion is booming. But not everything is chugging along smoothly.

The railroad barons of China made their largest overseas deal ever on November 19, signing a $12 billion contract with the government of Nigeria to build a train linking the eastern city of Calabar with the economic hub of Lagos. The train, which will travel at a nice clip of 75 miles per hour along the 850-mile route, will outshine anything the British colonialists ever gave to their African stepchild. But it's more of a throwback to Mao Zedong's China than it is to King Edward's England.

China has laid tracks in Africa before—most memorably during the early 1970s, when it built the Tanzania-Zambia Railway Authority train from the Tanzanian capital of Dar es Salaam to the copper fields of Zambia so the ore wouldn't have to cross the soil of the racist government of Rhodesia (now Zimbabwe). This helped establish China's reputation as the new railroad king of Africa, with a little helping of postcolonial glitz.

While so much about China has changed over the last 40 years, there's a surprising amount of consistency in its international rail plans. The Nigerian rail project is firmly in line with China's policy in Africa and other parts of the developing world: make loans, build infrastructure, cement diplomatic ties . . . and be in a prime position for the resource contracts to come. This strategy has played out in such unlikely places as Hungary, Zimbabwe, and Saudi Arabia. A plan to link the capital of

Laos with the Chinese border, for example puts at least 5 million tons of potash per year under control. And it helps business back home: The Nigerian deal sent the stock price of China Railway Construction Corp up 2 percent.

At November's Asia-Pacific Economic Conference, the picture was sunny for rail and its possibilities. Ordinary Beijing commuters—who would have been inconveniently clogging up the city's streets—were offered special vacation deals on high-speed rail so they could evacuate the city and reduce emissions, an instant sky-coloring effect that some called "APEC blue."

Indeed, Beijing has big plans for its rail business. In September, the Chinese business journal *Caixin* uncloaked an ambitious scheme to merge China Northern Locomotive and Rolling Stock (CNR) with its rival, China Southern Locomotive Rolling Stock (CSR), a move that would create the world's largest locomotive builder at a stroke and make the already exclusive bidding club of Siemens, Bombardier, Talgo, and a few select others an even tighter league. *Caixin* reported that executives from the two Chinese companies were "lukewarm" to the idea—which is unsurprising, because nobody likes to see their empire dissolved into a rival's.

But they aren't really in control of their own fate. The China Railway Corporation—the builder of the nation's 7,000-mile spider web of high-speed rail—will be among the prime deciders. Officials there are reportedly upset that price wars between China's twin train set builders (which were, ironically, one company until 2000) were causing lost contracts and market disruption. "It is the state's will," a railway mole told *Caixin*, in a formula that could have summed up China's entire modern railway enterprise at home and across the world. Indeed, the larger purpose of railway-building has always transcended economic rationales.

China's long-term strategy goes far beyond serving its own citizens with gleaming bullet trains and five-hour sprints between Beijing and Shanghai. The real goal is what Chinese leaders have called "high-speed rail diplomacy."

Less alarming than troop movements, and more efficient than trade policy, the extension of Chinese-made and -operated tracks into neighboring countries will solidify its regional influence with a band of iron. Beijing has already tightened its grip on restive Tibet with a stupendous high-altitude train linking the neighboring province of Qinghai with Lhasa, bringing unprecedented levels of Han Chinese migration and cultural Sinification to the plateau. Now there are serious plans to extend the network: Beijing just cut the ribbon on a high-velocity route linking Urumqi, the capital of the wild west region of Xinjiang, with Lanzhou, the capital of the neighboring province of Gansu. Some locals have protested these incursions and the backlash effect has also extended to

Kenya, where a Chinese contractor was forced to halve the number of expatriate workers on a new line from Mombasa to Nairobi.

Next stop: Istanbul? It's possible. Chinese President Xi Jinping likes to talk about a "New Silk Road" of rail that will reach into countries like Kyrgyzstan, Uzbekistan, Iran, and, eventually, Turkey. That this new version of an Orient Express would happen to cross some of the most resource-rich lands in Asia is no coincidence. Another tentacle would reach all the way to Singapore, yet another to Moscow. And there are pharaonic discussions afoot to tunnel under the Bering Strait and connect with the US railway network in Seattle. (One can imagine the horror future passengers will feel as they gallivant off a land-Concorde only to board one of Amtrak's rattletrap coaches.)

Unknown factors lurk within this moonshot, not least of which is the trustworthiness of the engineering. In March I wrote for *Foreign Policy* about some of the construction defects and endemic corruption within the domestic rail buildout, including big kickbacks to high officials and pillars fashioned from weak concrete. The writing was already on the wall: Beijing had sacked a few high-level officials and was in the process of dissolving the perfidious monolith of the Ministry of Railways (nicknamed "Boss Rail") into the new China Rail Corporation. Yet many of the same systemic problems remain. If you'll pardon the expression, meet new Boss Rail, same as old Boss Rail.

The opportunities for railroad self-dealing may be even greater on a frontier—such as Central Asia or Nigeria—when only one supplier is in charge. Rail and mineral resources have been inextricably linked since the first scheduled train chugged up to the mouth of a British coal mine nearly 200 years ago. Sinking that tap into foreign soil means aid deals must be put into place. "Good old-fashioned aid, with China doing everything by itself, meaning Chinese money, Chinese companies, Chinese construction materials and even Chinese workers—frankly speaking, that is an invitation to malpractice and outright corruption," said Zha Daojoing, a professor at Peking University, in response to plans for an international development aid bank.

The temptation is especially great with projects like rail, which involve a magic combination of high budgets, low oversight, bulk materials, and decisions that create instant riches for the well-connected. Railroads everywhere have always been fraught with tawdry deals. One of America's greatest 19th-century achievements, the transcontinental link between the Union Pacific and Central Pacific, was also a spectacular case of high-level corruption that reached into Congress. In this century, Spain built a high-speed network replete with needless stations that enriched local politicians and a payment system that allegedly let contractors go on an overbilling spree. Now China will be entering Nigeria—a country notorious for public money that disappears.

In November, Mexico announced plans to go with CSR as its trainset-maker of choice for a 130-mile line from Mexico City to the manufacturing city of Queretaro. But then President Enrique Peña Nieto canceled the $3.6 billion deal amid charges that the bidding process had been rigged—a temporary setback in North America for China's locomotive shops, which have recently been involved in deals in Boston and California. Mexican newspapers then went on to report that Teya, a local company part of the consortium, may be controlled by a friend—and even landlord—of the President Neito. "Almost all the big companies can be connected to something," said Mexico's transportation minister in a defensive statement, which is also an accurate risk-analysis of China's train ambitions. The Opacity Express keeps on rolling.

Conflict in the South China Sea

On May 2, 2014, the deployment of a Chinese oil rig in Vietnamese-claimed waters alarmed nations in the region and around the world. In the ensuing month, over 1500 collisions occurred between Chinese and Vietnamese ships that had surrounded the oil rig, each nation accusing the other as the aggressor. After anti-China protestors started attacking Chinese factories, killing four and injuring hundreds, Chinese workers fled Vietnam in the thousands out of concern for their safety. Public relations between the two former allies were tentative at best, potentially explosive at worst.

Diplomatic channels have been opened to defuse the conflict, but currently both countries are laying claim to the disputed island in the Paracel Archipelago. Since the vessels involved in the conflict were not military ships, the confrontation remains a largely civilian matter. Nonetheless, both sides are committed to dialogue and seek a diplomatic solution. In 2002 and 2011 China declared a ban on outside arbitration of territorial disputes in the South China Sea, so the matter will eventually be resolved between China and Vietnam.

Holding our Breath

August 2014 Issue of NewsChina | *by Li Jia*

Is there any hope for a peaceful solution to the situation in the South China Sea?

An oil rig deployed by China in the South China Sea on May 2 has made waves throughout the region.

At the Shangri-la Dialog in Singapore on May 31, US Defense Secretary Chuck Hagel labeled the move as one of China's "destabilizing, unilateral actions asserting its claims" in the area, and vowed to strengthen "emerging defense ties" with Vietnam.

The next day Wang Guanzhong, deputy chief of the General Staff of the Chinese People's Liberation Army, slammed Hagel's speech as "the language of hegemonism and words of intimidation." Such blunt exchanges between senior Chinese and US military officials are rarely seen in public.

By mid-June, more than 1500 "collisions" took place between Chinese and Vietnamese flotillas that have gathered around the oil rig, with each side accusing the other of provocation. Both sides published video footage to prove the law was on their side, each depicting the other as sole aggressor. Both countries' officials and observers declared to the rest of the world that their opponent was lying over sovereignty claims and infringing international law in one of the most verbally intense standoffs between China and Vietnam since the end of the Cold War.

Things were no less tense on land. A Chinese manager who gave his surname as Shen, a worker at a private Chinese-invested factory in Vietnam, was advised by his interpreter not to speak Chinese on the street when he arrived in March. Anti-China protesters looted and burned down several factories displaying Chinese-language signage in mid-May, after which Shen was told not to go out at all without a local guide.

According to China's Foreign Ministry, four Chinese were killed in the violence, while 300 more were injured. Thousands were reported to have left the country out of concern for their safety. Shen told *NewsChina* that he had to stay behind only because he spoke no Vietnamese and was unable to guarantee himself safe passage out of the country.

Despite the unprecedented escalation of rhetoric, however, few expect force to be used to resolve this dispute once and for all. Typical of such crises, diplomats have remained cool and collected while the media on both sides have sounded the horn of nationalism. Both China and Vietnam have sent various messages to each other and the rest of the world pledging willingness to explore peaceful solutions. But they remain divided on what such solutions should be and, crucially in China's case, who should be involved in making them.

CONTROLLABLE

The controversial rig is located 17 nautical miles off what China has named Zhongjian Island, a part of the Xisha (Paracel) archipelago, known as Hoang Sa in Vietnam. Both countries claim they hold "indisputable sovereignty" over the islands. While China recognizes the nearby Nansha (Spratly) islands as "disputed," it extends no such terminology regarding the Xisha, which the country is pushing to develop into an inhabited outpost of its southernmost island province of Hainan.

China's Foreign Ministry said that the Chinese company in charge of the rig conducted seismic operations and well site surveys in the area for ten years. Vietnam's response to the rig's launch, however, was far more extreme than even the Chinese had anticipated, seriously hampering its operations.

Wu Shicun, director of the National Institute for South China Sea Studies, told NewsChina that he feels Vietnam is more confident over its claims to the Xisha than the Nansha. In his view, this confidence has made the government in Hanoi reluctant to give any ground whatsoever, which could possibly undermine its claim over the Nansha and fuel a domestic backlash against government "weakness." As it was ordinary citizens, not government agents, who torched Chinese businesses across Vietnam in May, such fears are well-grounded. Emotions in the country over China's perceived encroachment are running high.

As this year marks the 40th anniversary of the naval campaign fought over the Xisha between China and Vietnam in 1974, Wu added, the Vietnamese government has seized a chance to further promote public support for its sovereignty claims. Opponents of Vietnam's ruling Communist Party, meanwhile, see nationalist opposition to China as a boon to creating difficulties for the government in Hanoi.

The sudden appearance of a Chinese oil rig in what Vietnam perceives as its own waters is proof that China is ready and willing to actively conduct oil exploration in disputed territory, further deepening the need for Vietnam to show the strongest possible opposition.

Military conflict, however, is not thought to be an option. Beijing and Hanoi recently confirmed that more than 30 diplomatic communications at various levels have been made since May 2, typically the behavior of countries keen to avoid military incidents.

"Keeping in contact is crucially important in times of crisis; otherwise, even if all parties involved in a crisis agree on peaceful solutions, a lack of communication can still result in misunderstandings heightening the risk of military conflict," said Zhang Tuosheng, chairman of the Academic Committee of the China Foundation for International and Strategic Studies, an expert on international crisis management. In practice, Zhang added, the vessels at the forefront of the ongoing confrontation are not warships and thus the conflict remained largely a civilian matter.

According to English-language reports appearing in Vietnamese state media, criminal charges have been filed in Vietnam against hundreds of looters who took part in the anti-China riots in May. The Vietnamese government also shut down a planned anti-China demonstration. The fact that it did so publicly was an indication that Hanoi is keen to avoid allowing flashpoints to develop on its own turf.

Zhang stressed that since the end of the Cold War, dialog has always been China's first choice for directly resolving territorial disputes with the relevant parties. He argues that this continues to be the case, including in maritime disputes which potentially involve more complex and wide-ranging interests than those based on land. In 1999 and 2000, for example, China and Vietnam successfully reached agreements on land and ocean territory in the Beibu Bay (Gulf of Tonkin) after decades of negotiations.

Both Beijing and Hanoi have repeatedly reaffirmed their long-term commitment to dialog and even cooperation on the South China Sea disputes both before and during the current crisis. During Chinese Premier Li Keqiang's first visit to Hanoi in October 2013, both sides agreed to set up a working group for consultation on joint maritime development.

"The last thing China wants is any turbulence in its neighborhood," ran a Chinese statement to the UN on June 8. Two days later, Vietnam's Ambassador to the UN Le Hoai Trung was quoted in Vietnam's party mouthpiece Nhan Dan Online as having told international media in New York that, after decades of war, the Vietnamese "always want peace."

NAVIGABLE?

Chinese analysts believe there are enough channels in place for China and Vietnam to manage this current crisis without significant escalation. Wu Shicun stressed that disputes over the South China Sea are only one aspect of bilateral ties, and with this in mind, Chinese and Vietnamese leaders have repeatedly pledged to take "strategic and broader relations" into account in solving their maritime disputes.

Chinese Premier Li Keqiang has commented that he expects China's trade with Vietnam to reach US$100 billion in volume by 2017, nearly double the amount in 2013. The Vietnamese government's hardline response to the anti-China riots shows unwillingness to lose foreign investors, including those from China. The sheer number of Chinese who were evacuated from Vietnam in May gives a small indication of the scale of Chinese interests in the country—and thousands more remained behind.

Zhang Tuosheng noted that relations between the two communist parties, though not amiable on the surface, can prove helpful in difficult times. Both parties have a common ancestry and their internal procedures are often complementary. In early 1999, for example, top leaders of both parties agreed to set a deadline on concluding their drawn-out land and maritime demarcation negotiations, giving a crucial boost to a process that stalled in government-to-government talks.

The two sides now are divided on what kind of talks should be conducted and who should be invited to the table. The Philippines have brought their own separate disputes with China to the International Tribunal on the Law of the Sea set up by the UN Convention on the Law of the Sea (UNCLOS). Vietnam is closely following the case and, depending on its outcome, may consider following suit.

China argues that the UNCLOS governs maritime, not littoral, sovereignty—the basis of any claims over maritime sovereignty and interests. Moreover, in 2006 China submitted a declaration to the UN under a relevant article in the UNCLOS, following precedents from other countries such as South Korea, which would prohibit international arbitration in maritime disputes.

Commitment to bilateral consultation on territorial disputes was included in both a Sino-Vietnamese joint statement on maritime issues in 2011 and the Declaration on the Conduct of Parties in the South China Sea signed by China and the Association of South-East Asian Nations (ASEAN) in 2002. These two documents are also frequently cited by China as banning outside arbitration in negotiations.

Although China has stated flatly that it will not discuss the sovereignty of the Xisha Islands as it does not consider them to be in dispute, it has also shown itself to be open to universally accepted principles in international law, including the UNCLOS, in bilateral communications, if not official negotiations. If China was as resolute as it claims to be on such issues, the UNCLOS would be unlikely to have been mentioned in its communications with other parties, nor would it be declaring itself open to dialog.

Yi Xianliang, a senior official with the Chinese Foreign Ministry, indicated at a press conference recently that successful experience built up during previous, lengthy negotiations of land and maritime sovereignty could be useful in bilateral consultations seeking a permanent settlement.

Although plenty of hawks continue to predict a further escalation of tensions, few of these commentators are party to the complex, lengthy and largely amicable discussions continually taking place behind closed doors. Until these doors are opened, therefore, both parties will continue to walk a delicately balanced tightrope between saber-rattling and conciliation.

Warming Relations between China and Vietnam

This article portrays relations between China and Vietnam as warming, with the recent visit by Le Hong Anh, special envoy from Vietnam on August 26, 2014. Prior to Le's visit, in the first eight months of 2014, maritime disputes in the South China Sea had resulted in a flare-up of tensions between the two nations. As a result, Vietnam has been reaching out to the international community, building up its defense capabilities in case the conflict escalates. Though it typically works through the ASEAN apparatus, it has invited India, Japan, and the US to play a greater role in the South China Seas through training, weapons sales, and even international military presence. China is realistic about its relationship with Vietnam, and is making earnest attempts to re-establish friendly relations, often relying on shared political ideology to solidify their ties.

Friends Again?

November 2014 Issue of NewsChina | *by Chen Jun and Li Jia*

Three months after maritime tensions reached boiling point, China and Vietnam appear to have mended relations. But will the peace hold?

According to Vietnam's General Statistics Office, 1.4 million Chinese visitors arrived in Vietnam in the first eight months of 2014, more than the total number of visitors from South Korea, Japan and the US, the next three largest sources of inbound travelers, combined, and twice the number of Chinese that visited the country in July arrived in August. However, it was a Vietnamese visitor to Beijing that attracted the most attention.

On August 26, Le Hong Anh, special envoy of the General Secretary of the Communist Party of Vietnam (CPV) Central Committee Nguyen Phu Trong, became the first senior Vietnamese official to visit Beijing since disputes over maritime territory between the two countries in May and June 2014 caused observers to mutter darkly of a looming regional crisis. By August 27, however, both parties announced a three-point consensus, effectively reaffirming bilateral ties.

"A neighbor cannot be moved away," said Chinese President Xi Jinping during his meeting with Le on August 27, going on to reaffirm solidarity with China's only communist neighbor. Xi went on to appreciate the invitation from Nguyen, his Vietnamese counterpart, who would like to welcome him to Hanoi. Both close geographical proximity and the shared ideologies of the ruling parties in China and Vietnam have played a crucial role in motivating and facilitating efforts to mend ties. However, deep distrust remains on both sides, with Chinese observers accusing Vietnam of hedging its bets when it comes to military strategy.

SAME BOAT

Seeking solidarity through communism is a default position when ties deteriorate between China and Vietnam. Xi Jinping, with his dual role as China's president and General Secretary of the CPC Central Committee, noted that his meeting with Le Hong Anh was "a "high-level meeting between two parties." One of the three points agreed between the two leading Politburo members behind the resultant consensus, Le from the CPV and Liu Yunshan from the CPC, was a pledge to "consolidate inter-party relations." The other two points supported greater engagement between both national leaders and "making the best use of" existing territorial negotiations. In all these areas, the shared political structure of both parties is a significant asset.

China and Vietnam have closely intertwined commercial interests. In the first eight months of 2014, even as tensions over disputed reefs flared, growth in Vietnam-China export volume exceeded growth of Vietnam's total exports to the EU, other Association of Southeast Asian Nations (ASEAN) members and Japan. Vietnam's Ministry of Industry and Trade is optimistic about reaching its target of selling US$15 billion worth of goods to China in 2014, according to national news agency VNA.

Li Yimin, a Chinese investor in Hanoi, was hesitant to commence a planned expansion of his garment factory after it was attacked by anti-China rioters in May. He told NewsChina that he and his friends were talking about whether to relocate to neighboring Thailand or Cambodia. Many observers made dire predictions for the future of cross-border trade, with the Vietnam Ministry of Planning and Investment estimating that the value of new and additional financed FDI projects in 2014 would be down to 80 percent of the value recorded in 2013.

However, the Vietnamese government moved to suppress the riots, compensate foreign business owners and repair trade relations. On August 25, in a statement on the eve of Le Hong Anh's Beijing tour, Le Hai Binh, spokesperson for the Foreign Affairs Ministry of Vietnam, said a delegation from the Vietnam-China Friendship Association would visit China to meet the families of Chinese nationals killed in the rioting, and the government would take measures to help affected Chinese enterprises resume operations and "ensure security and safety for the workers and enterprises of China and other countries in Vietnam."

Vietnam imports more from China than from any other economy. "You don't have to look at any official trade data—just look at how popular Chinese businesses and products are in cross-border trade and in major Vietnamese cities including Hanoi and Ho Chi Minh City," said Nguyen Cao Hung, a manager at a pharmaceutical company in Ho Chi Minh City.

For China, meanwhile, Vietnam is more valuable as a political ally than simply a business partner. Though ASEAN has so far remained neutral in the South China Sea disputes, the attitudes of its various members that are involved in these disputes dramatically influences the organization's China policy. Many Chinese analysts believe that despite

Chinese objection, the South China Sea issue has already spilled beyond bilateral negotiating tables to figure on the ASEAN agenda.

Although ASEAN foreign ministers have always expressed their concerns over the South China Sea issue in their numerous meetings over the past 20 years, they have been cautious about making statements specifically on this issue. The four or five existing statements were almost all made when tensions between China and Vietnam or the Philippines flared. The most recent emerged in May at the height of clashes between China and Vietnam. Hua Chunying, spokesperson for China's Foreign Ministry, responded by criticizing "certain countries' schemes to spoil the atmosphere of friendly cooperation between China and ASEAN by making use of the issue of the South China Sea."

China is well aware that Vietnam is a big hitter in the ASEAN club, and thus friendly relations are essential to avoid having the entire organization, pivotal to China's booming regional exports, turn its back on Beijing. Chinese and Vietnamese efforts to build bridges appear to be paying off. In August, with both countries working hard to fix ties, the joint communiqué issued by the ASEAN Foreign Ministers' Meeting did not even mention the South China Sea issue in its chapter on China.

NEW FRIENDS

While continuing to work towards détente with China, Vietnam has not hesitated to step up efforts to get closer to other major regional players. Vietnam's economic ties with the US are even stronger than those with China, with the US their largest export market. More crucially, ever-closer military cooperation between these two former enemies has also become the focus of China's attention, with the US, which has already outfitted the Philippine navy much to Beijing's chagrin, seemingly on the verge of lifting a 30-year ban on arms sales to Vietnam.

"I think in the near term there will be a discussion on how to lift [the ban]" said Martin Dempsey, Chairman of the Joint Chiefs of Staff, during his historic visit to Ho Chi Minh City on August 16, the first by a US military figure in his position since 1971. He advised that once the ban was lifted, the US would help improve the Vietnamese navy by providing materials for "intelligence, surveillance, reconnaissance and even some weapons [Vietnam] don't yet have for their fleet."

At a series of ASEAN forums in Vietnam as well as during Indian Foreign Minister Sushma Swaraj's visit to Hanoi in August, Vietnam also invited India to play a bigger role in the South China Sea, according to VAN reports. It is widely reported that India has offered a US$100 million line of credit to Vietnam to buy Indian patrol boats. Japan, meanwhile, will deliver a free aid package including six used vessels to Vietnam to be refitted as patrol boats, as well as additional maritime security hardware. The South China Sea dispute between China and some ASEAN members was discussed at the ASEAN-Japan Forum in early September.

Chinese analysts are not particularly worried about Vietnam's moves, for good reasons. Vietnam's strategy is seen as unexceptional by international observers. Murray Hiebert and Phuong Nguyen with the Center for Strategic and International Studies noted in a co-authored article in August that Vietnam often gives "a guarded response" to US initiatives for more military cooperation due to "Hanoi's desire to remain independent in its foreign policy."

Some US officials, the article continued, are concerned that the US could "lose its leverage with Hanoi on human rights" with the lifting of the arms embargo. That Vietnam is reportedly preparing to base submarines purchased from Russia in the South China Sea is further evidence that Hanoi does not expect too much help from any external force and thus is improving her own military power to defend her claims.

While things, at the diplomatic level at least, are all smiles at present, nobody knows when tensions will next flare up, or how far China and Vietnam might go to defend their maritime claims. As Li Yimin, the Chinese investor in Vietnam, told *NewsChina*, the South China Sea disputes will "overshadow business" so long as they remain unresolved. While both parties and governments may be keen to keep the peace, once the forces of nationalism, spurred by the media, have been unleashed among the general public, it's hard to simply muzzle them with diplomatic niceties. The South China Sea disputes will "overshadow business" so long as they remain unresolved.

Relations between China and the Koreas

Seen as a shift in "geopolitical alignment," President Xi Jinping's visit to South Korea on July 3, 2014 came at a time when tensions between China and Japan were escalating over territory disputes in the East China Sea. During his summit with South Korean President Park, Geun-Hey President Xi was accompanied by 250 Chinese business executives including Taobao founder Jack Ma, and Baidu chairman Robin Li. Numerous agreements were signed ranging from tourism to energy to environmental protection to bilateral trade to currency liberalization to denuclearization of the Korean peninsula.

North Korea expressed displeasure with the event by launching missiles into the sea as "warning shots" prior to the visit. Though China's overall policy towards North Korea has not seen any adjustment, peninsular relations with the North and South are generally mutually exclusive. In addition, this first meeting of presidents from South Korea and China potentially brings two countries who share a common experience of suffering under brutal Japanese occupation and oppression during the early 20th century, together in mutual opposition to Abe's nationalistic ambitions. In response to realignment in East Asia, Japan is reaching out to Russia and even North Korea in addition to receiving increased support from the US to take an active military and political role in the region.

Putative Partnerships

September 2014 Issue of NewsChina | *by*
Yu Xiaodong

Xi Jinping's recent visit to South Korea shows common ground between the two countries, which analysts argue may reshape the geopolitical landscape in Northeast Asia.

July 3 saw the first summit between Chinese President Xi Jinping and South Korean President Park Geun-hye since both took office.

While it may seem natural for two close neighbors and stalwart trading partners to convene, Xi's visit to Seoul, amid escalating regional tensions, particularly with Japan, is far more than a mere social call, with some describing it as marking a potentially substantial shift in the region's geopolitical alignment.

"NEW MILESTONE"

Accompanied by 250 business executives including e-commerce billionaire Jack Ma and Baidu chairman Robin Li, Xi signed 12 agreements with Park covering various fields. In the joint statement released by the two leaders, the two countries further agreed to work on over 90 coopera-tive projects in 23 fields ranging from tourism to clean energy and environmental protection.

Among the signature achievements of this most recent visit is China's granting of an 80-billion-yuan (US$12.9bn) RQFII (Renminbi Qualified Foreign Institutional Investors) program to Seoul, which would allow direct yuan-denominated transactions between South Korean and Chinese financial markets.

The two sides also agree to accelerate negotiations on a bilateral FTA expected to be completed by November when China will host the Asia-Pacific Economic Cooperation (APEC) summit in Beijing. In 2013, the volume of bilateral trade between the two countries reached US$274.2 billion, accounting for a quarter of South Korea's total trade volume, making China more valuable to the South Korean economy than the US, Japan and Russia combined.

Besides progress in economic cooperation, the two sides also agreed to launch formal negotiations over a shared maritime boundary in the Yellow Sea in 2015, which has been a thorny issue in bilateral ties.

In summarizing Xi's trip, Chinese Foreign Minister Wang Yi claimed on July 4 that "a new milestone for the future development of bilateral relations" had been reached.

LOOKING NORTH

For many, Xi's visit to South Korea was a snub to its historical ally, North Korea. Ever since China established diplomatic relations with Seoul in 1992, a move called a "betrayal" by the North, new Chinese leaders have always visited Pyongyang before Seoul in a symbolic show of goodwill.

Xi's decision to break with tradition, and the fact that North Korean leader Kim Jong-un has yet to be invited to Beijing, is now seen as a sign of increasing Chinese irritation with Pyongyang's continued belligerence, its nuclear program and ongoing provocations across the DMZ.

The Beijing-Pyongyang relationship appeared further strained in the aftermath of the sudden arrest and execution of Jang Song-thaek, Kim's maternal uncle and previously the second most powerful man in Pyongyang. Jang was seen by many as a political and business intermediary between North Korea and China.

Based on trade data from China's General Administration of Customs, China is believed to have cut oil shipments to Pyongyang from January to at least May 2014, and South Korean media have claimed this has led to the partial grounding of the North Korean air force.

On July 9, North Korea launched two short-range ballistic missiles into the sea off its eastern coast, following similar launches undertaken prior to Xi's visit to Seoul on June 29 and July 2. Although Chinese officials denied any correlation between the launches and Xi's South Korean visits, the routinely symbolic purpose of many North Korean military actions have led to claims that both were "warning shots" showing the North's displeasure with Xi's decision to meet with Park.

As if to further disrupt rapprochement between China and the South, the June 29 launch was followed up with a "special proposal" to Seoul, demanding that both sides "curtail their slander and military hostilities."

Despite a recent rocky period, however, analysts have ruled out any significant changes in China's overall policy towards Pyongyang. Adopting mild language regarding the issue of North Korea, the joint statement issued in Seoul refrained from referring to Pyongyang or the North Korean leadership directly. Instead, the two countries reiterated commitments made at a March nuclear summit in the Netherlands calling for the denuclearization of the Korean Peninsula, while restating the importance of the six-party talks to "defusing regional tensions."

Instead, many analysts have claimed that, in the current political climate, China and South Korea have bonded over a common enemy that both share with Pyongyang—Japan, and what many see as a resurgence of militarism spearheaded by rightwing elements in the administration of Japanese Prime Minister Shinzo Abe.

NEW OLD ENEMY

China and South Korea bore the brunt of Japanese brutality during World War II, and this shared experience, rather than the Korean War, has been the foundation upon which diplomatic relations between Beijing and Seoul have been conducted since formal ties were established in 1992.

Both President Xi and President Park have refused to hold talks with Abe due to his repeated visits to Tokyo's controversial Yasukuni Shrine, where the souls of Japan's war dead, including Class A war criminals, are enshrined. Another factor are territorial disputes—while China is engaged in an increasingly vicious war of words over the Diaoyu/Senkaku island chain in the East China Sea, South Korea remains embroiled in a similarly heated dispute over the Dokdo/Takeshima Islands (Liancourt Rocks) in the Sea of Japan.

On July 4, the *Beijing Youth Daily* published a political advertisement allegedly sponsored by "Southern Korean citizens" that called for the Sea of Japan to be renamed the "East Sea" as it is known in Korea. The ad ran despite an official State ban on Chinese media outlets publishing political propaganda from foreign countries, proving just how central a united front with South Korea has become to China's strategy for counterbalancing Japanese territorial claims.

The meeting of the two leaders also coincided with a highly contentious decision made by the Japanese cabinet to reinterpret Japan's pacifist constitution, enabling the country to project its military power overseas and go into war "in defense of its allies." Vigorously opposed by leftwing political parties and Buddhist organizations in Japan, the move was met with fury in China and South Korea, both of whom have long believed Tokyo has attempted to whitewash Japanese war atrocities and move towards full rearmament.

Despite these developments, however, the two leaders' joint statement on July 3 made no direct references to Japan. When Xi Jinping raised a proposal that, in 2015, China and South Korea should jointly commemorate the 70th anniversary of "China's victory in the anti-Japanese War and the liberation of Korea," President Park avoided giving a direct response. Despite widespread public support in South Korea for a tougher stance on Japan, Seoul's military alliance with the US, which remains firmly in place, restricts Park's ability to form closer political ties with Beijing.

However, closer relations between China and South Korea, once Japan's closest regional partner, are hugely damaging to Tokyo's position. The bilateral FTA between China and South Korea, expected to be finalized in November, will be a blow to Japan's already sluggish economy. As some South Korean industries, particularly automobiles and electronics, are in direct competition with their Japanese counterparts, the bilateral FTA, opening more of China's massive market to South Korea, will further undermine Japan's already shaky economic position in Asia. Political estrangement from Seoul, moreover, further weakens Japan's clout on the Asian mainland, despite its military alliance with the US.

REALIGNMENT

Given the delicate balance of regional power, Xi's visit to South Korea shows a subtle strategic shift in regional geopolitics, blurring lines that had remained ironclad since the Cold War.

Japan and North Korea, formerly inveterate enemies, have appeared to move tentatively towards one another in recent months, commencing negotiations regarding the return of Japanese abductees and even discussing some form of diplomatic rapprochement, a situation unthinkable before both Tokyo and Pyongyang began to become estranged from their historic regional allies. On the same day when Xi met with Park, Japanese Prime Minister Shinzo Abe announced that his government would ease some of its economic sanctions against North Korea.

Despite the two nations appearing to be the most unlikely of partners, analysts believe Japan and North Korea share a similar goal which is to derail attempts by Beijing and Seoul to form a closer diplomatic relationship. To that end, Japan has also made attempts to reach out to Russia, with Shinzo Abe meeting with Vladimir Putin a total of five times in 2013. When Russia annexed Crimea from Ukraine in early 2014, an action condemned by Japan's allies, Shinzo Abe was reluctant to add his voice to the calls for opposition.

North Korea, meanwhile, also appears to be making its own overtures to Russia, a move welcomed by Moscow in its efforts to secure a key strategic economic outlet to the Pacific Ocean. In June, the two countries agreed to boost bilateral trade tenfold by 2020 and it is reported that Pyongyang has granted Russian business executives exclusive privileges to use cellphones and the Internet inside North Korea.

It seems that, however subtly, the geopolitical map that has been largely unchanged in East Asia for over five decades is now beginning to shift. In response to China's rise, the US has encouraged Japan to take a more active role in regional politics, and Tokyo has responded by seeking to wean itself off military dependence on the US Pacific Fleet. For its part, China is increasing cooperation with South Korea and Russia while also attempting to keep relations with Pyongyang on an even keel.

As the US continues to play a major role in the region, a "new order" in East Asia is unlikely in the near future. However, it is clear that old boundaries, once seemingly set in stone, have liquefied in recent years.

Relations between China and Mongolia

Coinciding with the 65th anniversary of the establishment of diplomatic relations between China and Mongolia and the 20th anniversary of their Treaty on Friendly Relations and cooperation, during his speech to the Mongolian Parliament on August 22, 2014 President Xi Jinping proposed a "three-in-one model for economic integration" that includes partnerships in raw materials, infrastructure, and financial cooperation. Couched in terms of assistance and partnership, China pledged its expertise, capital, and cooperation in promoting Mongolian economic development. As a key member of China's Silk Road initiative, Mongolia would receive investment funding from the newly-formed AIIB spearheaded by China.

In addition to the natural resources China hopes to gain access to, Mongolia's importance to China is tied to Sino-Russian relations. As a gateway to the North, the transportation network connecting China to Russia naturally passes through Mongolia. In fact, the visit from President Xi was initially proposed as a trilateral summit, with Russia's President Vladimir Putin scheduled during the same time.

Mongolia has been silent on international debates concerning Russia and China, and has invited both to participate in development, natural resource, and transportation projects on its soil. Similarly, Mongolia has been cementing ties with Japan, South Korea, and the US, diversifying its international relations strategy using its geopolitical and economic significance as leverage in its dealings with these superior economies.

Steppe Forward

November 2014 Issue of NewsChina | *by Ouyang Kaiyu, Xu Fangqing, and Yu Xiaodong*

Despite sharing a vast border, China and Mongolia have had a complicated relationship.

"China welcomes Mongolia to hitch itself to the train of China's rapid development," said President Xi Jinping in his keynote speech to the Mongolian parliament delivered on August 22 during his recent visit to Ulaanbaatar.

Proposing a "three-in-one" model for economic integration, combining mineral resources extraction, infrastructure construction and financial cooperation, President Xi said that China can help Mongolia to deal with developmental challenges such as its limited infrastructure and transportation links with China and a shortage of investment capital. "China has the willingness and capacity to help Mongolia, through close cooperation, to translate its advantages into economic development," said Xi.

The first Chinese head of state to visit Mongolia in 11 years, Xi was warmly received by Mongolian President Tsakhia Elbegdorj, who hosted Xi in his own home, and referred to the Chinese president as "Mongolia's most distinguished guest." Both sides describe the visit as "an historic one."

DISTANT NEIGHBORS

During Xi's trip, timed to coincide with the 65th anniversary of the establishment of bilateral diplomatic relations and the 20th anniversary of the two countries' Treaty on Friendly Relations and Cooperation, both sides agreed to establish a "comprehensive strategic partnership." Both leaders signed more than 30 agreements on trade, infrastructure, energy and financial cooperation. The agreements included a memorandum of understanding on strengthening coal processing cooperation, seen as a precursor for a long-expected coal gas project worth US$30 billion to both economies. In another agreement, Mongolia agreed to extend a bilateral currency swap for a further three years while also increasing its reserves to 15 billion yuan (US$2.4bn).

Mongolia also signed up to China's Silk Road Economic Belt initiative, a centerpiece of Xi Jinping's global economic strategy, simultaneously becoming a founder member of the China-initiated Asian Infrastructure Investment Bank.

Despite sharing a border of more than 4,000 kilometers with China, Mongolia has historically maintained a certain diplomatic and economic distance from its vast and populous southern neighbor. Domestic opinion on China is varied but tends towards wariness—understandably so in a country with a small population dwarfed by that of most second-tier Chinese cities, but which nevertheless constitutes a large geographical area containing an estimated US$1.3 trillion worth of unexplored natural resources.

In 2013, bilateral trade reached US$6 billion, 15 times the volume recorded in 2003, with China accounting for more than 50 percent of

Mongolia's total annual trade volume. China received 90 percent of Mongolian exports, mostly coal, mineral and animal products. The August agreement to further increase bilateral trade volume to US$10 billion by 2020, has led many Chinese observers to conclude that it marks a "qualitative change" in the bilateral relationship.

"What is special about Xi's visit is that it is the first time a Chinese president has made a specific visit to Mongolia alone," Huang Jiakui, former ambassador to Mongolia told *NewsChina*. Many have compared Xi's Mongolian trip to his earlier one-stop visit to South Korea, which saw historic deals signed by both sides. In Seoul, too, Xi talked about bilateral relations in terms of "historic highs."

Since Mongolia gained independence from China in 1911, Chinese leaders have typically only visited Ulaanbaatar as part of a tour of other regional capitals. The change marked by Xi's visit, some believe, represents both the increasing importance of Mongolia to regional economics, but also China's desire to bolster its influence in Asia-Pacific diplomacy.

Indeed, many have pointed to a third party, largely unmentioned during Xi's Ulaanbaatar visit, as the principal reason for China's sudden interest in reinforcing ties with Mongolia—the Russian Federation.

TRILATERAL COORDINATION?

With Russia's relationship with the West increasingly strained over the crisis in Ukraine, Mongolia's strategic position has seen it encircled by two emerging geopolitical heavyweights. Russian interests have figured heavily in Mongolia's China policy for over a century, with Sino-Mongolian relations waxing and waning in tandem with Sino-Russian relations.

In the 1950s, the golden age of Sino-Soviet cooperation, the first ever trans-Mongolian railroad was built with the blessing of the then People's Republic of Mongolia. To this day, the same route still serves as the major commercial rail link between Russia and China. During the Sino-Soviet Split in the 1960s, however, Mongolia fell almost entirely within the Soviet sphere of influence, adopting accordingly hostile policies towards its southern neighbor in exchange for considerable economic aid from the USSR.

After the loss of subsidies from Moscow following the collapse of the Soviet Union in the 1990s, Mongolia embraced parliamentary democracy, a market economy and a more independent foreign policy, reaching out to the rapidly expanding Chinese market. Politically, Mongolia has adopted a "third neighbor" regional strategy which seeks political and strategic support from particularly the United States and Japan to reduce its reliance on its two giant neighbors. Mongolia is also a close partner of NATO, and has committed military personnel to peacekeeping operations in both Kosovo and Afghanistan. In 2012, the country became a full member of NATO's Individual Partnership and Cooperation Program.

However, given its geographic position as being completely surrounded by Russia and China, Mongolia has avoided actions that might bring it into direct conflict with either China or Russia. Mongolia has remained silent regarding Russian actions in Ukraine, and abstained from the March 27 United Nations General Assembly resolution condemning Russia's annexation of Crimea, despite pressure from its NATO partners. Indeed, it seems as if rising tensions between the West and Russia have presented as many opportunities as challenges for Mongolia since Russia is increasingly looking eastward to expand its trade relationship with Asian countries in the face of Western sanctions.

It is against this backdrop that Ulaanbaatar is seeking to establish itself as a new transportation corridor for Sino-Russian trade. In May, the Mongolian government submitted a resolution to Parliament to allow for a mix of Chinese and Russian-gauge railroads in Mongolia, rather than retaining the country's long-standing Russian-gauge-only policy. Analysts see this as the first step towards establishing international-standard narrow-gauge railroad spurs across the Mongolian border with China, which would dramatically facilitate the movement of goods between the two countries.

It is reported that Russian and Mongolian leaders have also held talks on linking up the Trans-Siberian and Trans-Mongolian rail networks in order to allow both to serve as a primary trade route between China and Russia. Some see the development of such an integrated network as a bid to offset the potential impact of Beijing's proposed New Silk Road initiative which, if realized, would establish a high-speed rail link through Central Asia connecting China with key European markets. During his visit, President Xi pledged that China would increase its cooperation with Mongolia under the framework of its New Silk Road initiative, and would remain "open" to Mongolia's initiative of a "Grasslands Road," which many see as a reference to the proposed trans-Mongolian railroad.

Against the backdrop of this emerging commercial partnership with both Russia and China, Mongolian officials labeled Xi's trip a "trilateral summit" as it initially looked set to coincide with that of Russian President Vladimir Putin, scheduled to visit Mongolia to celebrate the 75th anniversary of the Soviet-Mongolian victory over the Japanese at Khalkhin Gol in 1939. Although Putin's visit was later postponed to early September, which some analysts interpreted as a sign that Russia remains wary of China's growing regional influence, Xi personally endorsed Mongolia's proposal to hold a trilateral summit with Russia in the future.

BEYOND CHINA?

Despite the warmth of their rhetoric, Mongolian leaders are likely to be looking further than China and even Russia as this landlocked and often overlooked Asian nation seeks to assert itself on the global stage. In the past, aside from its close cooperation with the US in matters of politics and national security, Mongolia has worked hard to diversify the sources of its foreign investment in order to avoid overdependence on a single power.

Just one month prior to President Xi's visit, Mongolia's President Tsakhia Elbegdorj met with Japanese Prime Minister Shinzo Abe, and the two sides signed a joint statement on July 22 cementing the final roadmap toward instituting a bilateral Economic Partnership Agreement (EPA). Slated for ratification by both respective parliaments in early 2015, this would be the first EPA Mongolia has signed, and is likely to be seen as a major coup for Japan, one of China's principal rivals in Mongolia's resources market.

Earlier in February, Mongolia's Minister of Foreign Affairs Luvsanvandan Bold visited Seoul, marking the first official visit of a Mongolian foreign minister to South Korea in a decade. Both sides agreed to create an inter-governmental mechanism to stimulate Korean investment in Mongolia's largest mining and infrastructure construction projects, as well as planning a State visit to South Korea by President Elbegdorj in 2015. Mongolia has also shown willingness to play a more active role in regional security through its Ulaanbaatar Dialog on Northeast Asian Security, an initiative launched earlier this year which according to Mongolian leaders aims to "facilitate a peaceful solution to the confrontation on the Korean peninsula."

During his visit, President Xi voiced his support for Ulaanbaatar's aspiration to have a more prominent regional role. Among the agreements signed during his trip was a transport deal allowing Mongolian exporters to use China's rail network. According to Mongolian media, Beijing will allow Mongolia to conduct trade via eight sea ports in northern and northeastern China.

"The problems of transit and sea ports, Mongolia's most pressing issues, have now been solved," declared President Xi during his address to the Mongolian parliament. Xi also reiterated his earlier pledge to support Mongolia's bid to enter APEC during the APEC leaders' summit which will be held in Beijing in November. Xi also voiced support for the Ulaanbaatar Dialog, something other regional powers, particularly South Korea, are skeptical of. In return, Ulaanbaatar signed an agreement that neither nation would enter into a military alliance with a country hostile to the other, which some analysts claimed was a swipe at US influence in Mongolian military strategy.

Xi's Mongolian trip was in line with what Qu Xing, president of the China Institute of International Studies, calls China's "peripheral diplomacy," which emphasizes securing a stable political relationship with bordering countries through regional economic integration and interdependence. By offering enhanced trade relations and investment, Beijing hopes to both boost its economic output but, crucially in the case of Mongolia, further secure its land borders to facilitate an increasingly proactive global strategy.

Relations between China and Russia

In affirmation of their long-established friendship, President Xi Jinping attended the Winter Games in Sochi, Russia. Conspicuously missing was a stance on Ukraine, despite pressure from the international community. Instead, President Xi praised Russia for a successful Olympics and indirectly confirmed their political alliance. During the same time, Chinese and Russian warships were escorting confiscated Syrian chemical weapons in the Mediterranean, military cooperation that reifies the ties between them. They are united against the Japanese front, with the joint objective to contain Japan (and by association, the US), both contending territorial disputes with Japan in the Pacific.

The article argues that China needs to delineate between allies and adversaries, that it must reverse its "non-alignment" stance of the past three decades. The authors [?] base this on the view that the US has achieved and sustained its super-power status by establishing secure alliances around the world. During an interview with Dean Yan Xuetong at the Institute of Modern International Relations with Tsinghua University, China's spectrum of major power relations in descending order of friendship included Russia at the top with France, Germany, the UK, and India following. China is deemed to have "competitive relations with global implications" with the US. With Japan, China has confrontational relations. Yan predicts with a strategic alliance signed with Russia, China will have about 20 allies by 2023.

Friends or Allies?

April 2014 Issue of NewsChina | *by Cai Rupeng and Li Jia*

Is China quietly changing its official foreign policy of non-alignment? If so, will Russia prove to be the friend, and more importantly, even the ally, China needs?

Hearing Chinese President Xi Jinping and his Russian counterpart Vladimir Putin refer to each other as "friend" in their recent meeting during the 2014 Winter Olympics in Sochi was not out of the ordinary. This is a regular feature of meetings between world leaders, regardless of the politics underlying the camaraderie.

However, Xi's specific timing seems to have caught the attention of those looking to read the tea leaves when it comes to the direction of the new president's inscrutable foreign policy.

SMILES AND FROWNS

Xi's Sochi appearance marked the first time that a Chinese head of state has ever attended a major international sports event overseas. As in 2012, Russia remains Xi's first choice of overseas destination, indeed, his only choice so far this year. In an exclusive interview with a Russian TV channel, Xi praised the "top-notch preparation and organization" of the Games. Meanwhile, Xi's international counterparts, under pressure from mounting condemnation of Putin's various domestic policies, conspicuously gave Sochi a wide berth. The leaders of the US, UK, France and Germany all sent underlings to the opening ceremonies.

Global media outlets ran reports ranging from investigations into the recent Russian crackdown on LGBT rights to the perceived poor condition of the Olympic site and its press facilities. Security concerns, the arrest and detention of LGBT and environmental activists, and above all the sheer cost of the Games—a cost, many allege, increased tenfold by rampant corruption—were all a feature of international coverage.

China's State media, by contrast, were all smiles, delivering endless glowing reports of Sochi's "exemplary" organization, and slamming the "Western media bias" which sought to "undermine" the Games for political reasons.

The "relentless disparagement" of Sochi, ran a commentary by the English service of China's State-run Xinhua News Agency, is "all too familiar." "[Beijing] faced identical political finger-pointing" six years ago, during the Beijing Olympics, it continued.

As Russia's Prime Minister, Putin attended the Beijing 2008 Olympics opening ceremony despite his country being on the eve of a war with Georgia. As on that occasion, Xi's presence in Sochi was not a goodwill mission. Rather it was designed to show solidarity with another world power which is politically isolated in the international community, and to court Russian support in potential future conflicts.

It seems that after a decade of playing the good guy, China has dropped the pretense of being "everyone's friend," and is instead distinguishing between allies, friends and, potentially, enemies.

Chinese experts have long warned that China is in desperate need of allies. The US secured a virtual monopoly on political support after World War II, and has since deepened its influence with developed nations who preferred American support over the alternative—the Soviet Union.

Now, with both Chinese and international media muttering about a new East-West political divide, China may be explicitly delineating friends and enemies after the fashion of its biggest rival—the US. Xi's rhetoric in Sochi suggests that Russia is a key player in determining a new status quo.

DÉJÀ VU

The Winter Olympics, despite attempts by Russia to tone down the underlying politics, has proven a symbolic battleground between competing ideologies, at least in terms of the associated media coverage.

The theme of the opening ceremonies—"Dreams about Russia"—was designed, as Putin explained at a reception held February 7, to "give people the opportunity to take a new look at Russia, its achievements, distinctiveness and traditions." A similar note was struck during the opening ceremonies of the Beijing Olympics in 2008, framing what would later become Xi Jinping's China Dream ideology in the context of China's oft-repeated desire to throw off imperialist oppression and return, triumphant, to its rightful place at the center of the world. "Mutual support is an important element in the Sino-Russian strategic partnership of cooperation, and evidence of the close friendship between the leaders of the two countries," said Li Jianmin, a research fellow at the Institute of Russian, Eastern European and Central Asian Studies of the Chinese Academy of Social Sciences.

While the world's athletes competed in Sochi, Chinese and Russian warships were on a joint UN mission escorting a shipment of Syrian chemical weapons through the Mediterranean Sea to a US base where they were destroyed. In video addresses alongside their respective naval commanders, Xi and Putin reiterated their commitment to a "political settlement of the Syria crisis." China's State media saw this as a triumph for the Sino-Russian stance on the Syria conflict, favoring diplomacy over military intervention. An editorial in the *People's Daily* on February 8 crowed that, had both nations not stood opposed to military intervention, this international cooperation on destroying Syrian chemical weapons "would not have been possible."

Japan is also a factor that unites China and Russia. Remarking that "history cannot be forgotten," Xi and Putin agreed to hold joint activities in 2015 to commemorate the 70th anniversary of the Chinese victory over Japan and the end of World War II. The Soviet Union never signed a peace treaty with Japan after the war, and today's Russian Federation has its own territorial disputes with Japan in the Pacific, while China's increasingly acrimonious standoff over the Diaoyu (Senkaku) Islands continues to foment.

Professor Jin Canrong, a well-known international relations scholar at the Renmin University of China, thinks that working with Russia to contain Japan's right-wing Abe administration was definitely "on Xi's agenda" during his Sochi visit. Though Japanese Prime Minister Shinzo Abe also exchanged warm words with Putin in Sochi, Jin believes that "shared experiences" in World War II and its resulting treaties (or lack of them, in the case of Russia and Japan) have given China and Russia more incentives to work together to contain suspected Japanese rearmament. "Of the countries which have the potential to become China's allies, Russia is the largest," said Professor Yan Xuetong, dean of the Institute of Modern International Relations with Tsinghua University.

REFRESH OR RESTART?

China's foreign policy discourse has not talked in terms of "allies and enemies" since the country implemented an official non-aligned stance in 1982 to avoid becoming further embroiled in the Cold War. Many Chinese experts think this defensive approach, suitable for weaker countries wishing to appear neutral, has harmed China's global standing, and left the world No. 2 economy lagging far behind smaller countries in terms of diplomatic clout.

China's rise has not helped Beijing's international isolation. Even experts who continue to support the principle of non-alignment agree that at least a more flexible practice is needed to prepare for a day when China may find itself on one side or another of a major international incident or conflict. Yan argues that the number and quality of its allies is an important factor underlying the US victory in the Cold War and securing virtual global hegemony. Despite a number of recessions, including the Great Recession of 2008–09, the US weathers economic storms by shoring up its international network of friends and committed allies. China, meanwhile, has no explicit alliances, and its closest "friends" remain even more politically isolated nations like North Korea, Cuba and, until recently, Myanmar.

"In the context of nuclear weapons and globalization, there is no other way available for the peaceful rise of a big nation with fewer drawbacks than forming alliances," Yan told our reporter. In Yan's "spectrum" of major power relations with China, by descending order in terms of how friendly they are, Russia stands the highest, followed by a raft of "ordinary relations" with major European countries, specifically France, Germany and the UK. After these comes India, and then "competitive relations with global implications" with the US. Bringing up the rear are "confrontational relations" with Japan. "China should take responsibility for protecting allies, winning over the neutrals and punishing opponents," he stressed.

The possibility of an alliance has been discussed more frequently by Chinese and Russian experts since 2010, when both countries chafed at the Obama administration's proposed "pivot to Asia." Despite this, many have pointed out the ideological and cultural differences which could be a sticking point in deepening cooperation. A history of both armed and diplomatic conflict between China and Russia, stretching back into the days of the Qing Empire, the present-day growth gap and the use of mutual antipathy to the US as a basis for friendship have all been seen as problematic. Many observers point out that neither nation trusts the other enough to consider an alliance. Jitters have also surfaced over a potential Cold War II, splitting the world into East and West, and further isolating an ascendant China still dependent on its US trade relations for economic supremacy. Pragmatists also fear that, if China chose an overt alignment with Russia, it would be backing the weaker power.

Yan insists that, unlike in a friendship, shared interests, particularly in terms of security, are a better bond than mutual trust when it comes to political alliances. In his words, "alignment is a rule in the human history of diplomacy," not a "Cold War contingency." Yan's advice is for China to sign a treaty with Russia "guaranteeing strategic commitment," while offering Moscow preferential regional development conditions to balance the economic gap between the two. "If neighbors get economic benefits and, more importantly, security protection, from China, then [Beijing] could have about twenty strategic allies by 2023," he added.

Relations between China and Latin America

Chinese companies have been making inroads in Latin America for the past decade, but only recently have these forays been coordinated and supported by China's Central Government. One potential rationale for the caution exercised thus far is US interests in the region and historical protectionism leading to armed conflict with past communist states in the region. Particularly controversial are Chinese relations with Cuba, which seems to be pre-empted by the Obama administration currently contending with legislators regarding US diplomacy with its neighboring island country.

Meanwhile, China's influence across Central and South America has been diversifying and broadening in scope. As Latin America's second largest trading partner, China has set a goal of $500 billion in annual trade with the region by 2024. Even US analysts and advisors are declaring the era of the Monroe Doctrine, US hegemony over the hemisphere, and the derogatory mention of Latin America as the US' backyard to be gone and replaced by a diversification of trading opportunities and options for countries such as Cuba, Brazil, Venezuela, Bolivia, and others in the region. The author goes to some length to convince the reader that China's intentions are benign and purely driven by economic interests, mentioning Beijing's retreat from Latin American discussions regarding China's potential role as a counterweight to US hegemony in the region.

Finally, from the perspective of Latin American non-governmental organizations (NGOs), trade groups, and officials, Chinese companies have been criticized, often violently, for corruption, exploitation, and unfair practices. These errors are attributed to a lack of sufficient knowledge of local culture and engagement with NGOs and groups. They are advised to consider the lessons learned from Japanese companies who have set up smaller operations in collaboration with local partners while engaging in continuous dialogue with the general populace to encourage transparency and trust. They hope to learn from both the mistakes other countries have made in the region in addition to those made by China in other regions such as Africa and Myanmar.

Buenas Vistas

March 2015 Issue of NewsChina | *by Li Jia*

China and the US seem to have avoided misreading each other's intentions in Latin America. Beijing's interests in the region appear largely economic, and though China has avoided repeating the mistakes of others, it has yet to learn from its own missteps elsewhere.

Several third parties were mentioned in President Obama's December 17, 2014 statement on restoring diplomatic relations with Cuba. China, as "a far larger country also governed by a Communist Party," was referred to as a precedent for the US building normal ties with the Caribbean island nation. Obama's opponents, meanwhile, have also raised China as an example—of how diplomatic engagement does not equal effecting political change.

Given China's special relationship with both the US and Cuba, China's role in this case seems a little more complicated than such claims would suggest. China has long been one of the major providers of political and economic support to the Castro administration. The uncertainty surrounding whether a Sino-US strategic rivalry can avoid the familiar trap of conflict between an emerging and an existing power is probably the biggest concern for today's complex global geopolitics.

From a broader perspective, the US-Cuba détente is widely expected to greatly improve waning US influence in Latin America. Cuban leader Raúl Castro confirmed on December 20, 2014 that he would attend the Summit of the Americas in Panama in April 2015 for the first time since the summit was first organized in 1994 by the Washington-led Organization of the American States (OAS). The OAS suspended Cuba's membership in 1962, and when it attempted to reinstate the country's status in 2009, Cuba rejected the offer.

As the US has struggled to retain its regional influence, China's star in Latin America has been rising in the past decade, a trend that looks set to continue. In early January 2015, Beijing hosted the first ministerial meeting of the Forum of China and the Community of Latin American and Caribbean States (CELAC). The forum is an initiative designed by China to provide a much better platform to get closer to Latin America as a whole, a more efficient alternative to existing country-by-country or less representative regional organizations.

Such moves have aroused questions in the context of a US-Cuba rapprochement. For China, will this breaking of the ice complicate relations with both countries? And has China been factored into US calculations regarding its Cuban and Latin American policies? For now, there seems to be no easy answer.

NEW REALITY

Besides being a communist ally, China is an important economic partner for Cuba. According to US Central Intelligence Agency (CIA) data, China was Cuba's second largest trading partner in 2012 in terms of both exports (behind Canada) and imports (behind Venezuela). The United Nations Economic Commission for Latin America and the Caribbean (UNECLAC, more commonly called by its Spanish-language title, NU CEPAL) estimated in a January 2015 report that China became Cuba's largest trading partner in 2013.

The report detailed how, since 2000, China went from a "minor partner" to a "central actor" in Latin American foreign trade. In his interview with Latin American media on May 31, 2013, just before his first visit to the region as China's head of state, President Xi Jinping announced that China had become Latin America's second largest trading partner in 2012, three years ahead of the UN's previous forecast.

New goals have been set at the first China-CELAC ministerial meeting, including a target of US$500 billion in annual trade volume by 2024, nearly double the current level, along with massively increasing China's total direct investment in Latin America. Xi's remarks suggested that China hoped to contribute a total US$250 billion to the region by 2025, nearly triple its entire US$90 billion contribution to date. China's commitment to providing billions of dollars in preferential loans and funds for joint projects in the region, declared during Xi's second presidential visit to Latin America in July 2014, could help realize these ambitious goals.

The recent forum in Beijing shows that China has completed her global network of "collective cooperation mechanisms to include all developing countries," according to Chinese Foreign Minister Wang Yi, speaking at a seminar in Beijing on December 24, 2014. All 33 countries in the region are members of CELAC, which launched in 2011 to facilitate regional integration and reduce US influence in the region.

The US, by contrast, has seen her position in this region, though still unparalleled, begin to diminish in recent years. While the US remains overwhelmingly the largest trading partner and investor in Latin American countries, with China lagging way behind, the latter is gaining momentum. The US and Latin America may be providing rapidly growing markets for one another, but data in a September 2014 report by NU CEPAL proves the continuation of an upward trend in regional trade volume with China, growth which has outpaced that between Latin America and the US since 2006. Negotiations on the Free Trade Area of the Americas, a US-backed initiative, have made little progress nearly ten years after it missed its main deadline, as a result of strong resistance from many Latin American countries.

"If there was an era of US hegemony in Latin America, it is over," concluded the Council on Foreign Relations (CFR) Task Force led by former US trade representative Charlene Barshefsky and former commander of US Southern Command General James T. Hill in a report issued in 2008. This conclusion was attributed to dramatic political and economic "diversification" within Latin America, and "Americans' lack of interest" in the region. The report called for policy shifts to reflect this "new reality." China, which at the time did not have its current status as the world's second largest economy, was not mentioned.

NO SHOCK

In recent years, any moves made by China or the US in Latin America have begun to be perceived by some analysts as responses to a strategic rivalry between an emerging power and an existing hegemony.

The Obama administration has been trying to rebuild the image of the US in Latin America, and the Cuba deal could help achieve this aim. "The era of the Monroe Doctrine is over," declared US Secretary of State

John Kerry in November 2013. His reference to Latin America as the "backyard" of the US in April that year drew criticism from regional powers. The Monroe Doctrine has been synonymous with US interventionism and hegemony in Latin America since the 1820s. Julia Sweig, a Nelson and David Rockefeller Senior Fellow for Latin American Studies, commented in a recent interview with CFR that the change in its Cuba policy gives the US a chance "to restart a conversation and rebuild its standing in Latin America."

Chinese analysts generally agree that Obama's change of heart on Cuba will improve US relations with Latin America. Professor Wu Baiyi, director of the Institute of Latin America with the Chinese Academy of Social Sciences, explained to *NewsChina* that an improvement in US-Cuban relations will pave the way for Venezuela, whose oil supply has been crucial to Cuba's economy, to improve its own ties with the US—another major customer and a potential investor in the country's newly designed and more relaxed market structure. This would, according to Wu, consequently soften the attitude of the Bolivarian Alliance for the Peoples of Our America, a transnational leftist political camp led by Cuba and Venezuela, towards the US. Wu went on to say that the Cuba issue had long been the "only common source of political criticism" against the US among Latin American countries, and thus rapprochement would "greatly ease" tensions between Washington and Latin America. Wu also stated that, in using the Cuba deal to tell Latin Americans that the US seeks friendship with all countries in the region, the US is trying to counterbalance China's increasing influence there. This stems from a belief that Americans think China has taken advantage of their declining regional influence.

Not everyone agrees with this assessment. While concurring that the new Cuba policy could provide a considerable boost to US-Latin American ties, Professor Shi Yinhong with the Renmin University of China, a prominent figure in the study of Sino-US relations, does not think it necessary to look at each power's every single move in all places and at all times from the perspective of rivalry. President Obama's decision, he told *NewsChina*, has simply written off "an extremely bad policy of hostility" which should have been abandoned long ago, a fact acknowledged in Obama's December 17 announcement. Even without existing competition with China, Shi stressed, Obama's actions would have been the same, as they were taken out of consideration for both long-term US interests and his own political legacy.

Moreover, China does not have to worry about a change of heart towards China on the part of Cuba simply because the US has reached out to Havana. Both Shi and Wu agree that normalized US–Cuba relations will, in fact, alleviate concerns over possible US opposition to its dealings with Cuba. As Shi pointed out, even in the case of Myanmar, which shares a border and a history of uneasy relations with China, improved relations with the West would translate into long-term dividends for Beijing by making it easier for Beijing to balance her ties between former geopolitical outsiders and the West.

Moreover, after decades of enmity and crippling sanctions, Cuba is unlikely to rush to embrace the US at the cost of ties with a long-term ally like China. In Washington, meanwhile, a Republican-dominated Congress is equally unlikely to make it easy for Obama to proceed with his Cuba plans.

NO MORE, NO LESS

In reference to its growing presence in Latin America, China has been repeatedly described by some Western media and analysts as "a dragon in the backyard." Evan Ellis, research professor of Latin American Studies with the US Army War College Strategic Institute recently warned the US government not to give a wrong message to China and Russia that the US "re-engagement" with Cuba was "a retreat from weakness."

An article in June 2014 published by the Council on Hemispheric Affairs, a Washington-based think tank, claimed that "China's attempt to balance US global power is clearly present in Latin America." The launch of the Nicaragua Canal mega-project by a consortium led by a Chinese private company on December 22, 2014 immediately triggered speculation on whether the project was driven by China's strategic, or even military, interests, though US and European companies were also included in the consortium.

Chinese analysts categorically dismiss this vision of China's strategic presence in Latin America. Professor Shi, for example, stressed that China's prevailing interests in Latin America are economic. In addition, he believes that China's economic gains in the region, no matter how significant, are not going to help Beijing "balance the pressure of the US efforts towards strategic rebalancing in East Asia, the area still at the top of China's diplomatic agenda."

Indeed, trade, investment and finance have been identified by the China-CELAC Forum as its three pillars of cooperation. Even in this economic mechanism, Professor Wu said, China bears neither the intent nor the capability to play a politically decisive role in the forum's operations.

Indeed, it is a belief widely held by Chinese analysts that China's political interests in Latin America focus on wresting regional diplomatic ties away from Taiwan and garnering support for China in multinational frameworks on global affairs, for example, climate change action, or unconventional security issues, such as the safety of Chinese citizens living and working in Latin American countries. So far, 12 Latin American states, including Nicaragua, have not established formal diplomatic relations with Beijing, more than in any other region in the world.

Wu noted, reflecting on the Soviet attempt at establishing a military presence in Latin America during the Cold War, that China did not, and would not "make the same mistakes as the former Soviet Union did in this region." Chinese analysts argue that US policymakers, though uncomfortable with increasing competition from China in the Latin American market, are not concerned about China's strategic intentions in the region. Moreover, China and the US have maintained a dialog platform on Latin America since 2006. Generally, Chinese analysts have not seen any sign from the Obama administration of excessive concern regarding China's activities in Latin America.

Indeed, the Renmin University of China's Wang Yiwei, writing for the Singapore-based web journal zaobao.com on January 9, 2015, found that some Latin American countries hoping that China might become a regional counterweight to the US were disappointed by China's consistently reiterated position that it has no intention of challenging the existing world order.

OLD LESSONS

Of course, Beijing's focus on trade does not mean that China and Latin America will immediately become ironclad business partners. Issues yet to be addressed revolve around frictions commonly experienced between industrial and raw material traders, the lingering weakness of China's efforts to go truly global and Latin America's lack of a clear multilateral agenda to promote business opportunities.

At an ECLAC workshop hosted in Chile in September 2014, Latin American experts and government officials expressed concerns over the "risk of deindustrialization" in trade dealings with China, that is, "a return to exports based on natural resources and involving lower productivity." Currently, Latin America mainly sells commodity products to China, particularly oil, gas and copper. China's investment in the region is also heavily concentrated on raw materials exploration and extraction.

Research by Wu's team, compiled in 2013 into the book *Opportunities Along with Transformation*, found that Latin American market demand for imports of labor-intensive products with mid- and low-tech input from China had already reached saturation point. This focus on cheap exports, it says, should be replaced partly by investment in local manufacturing and also by hi-tech exports, both of which are needed by Latin America to build an indigenous value chain.

Diversification of China's trade and investment with Latin America has already begun, and is a trend that looks set to continue. A joint feasibility study has been launched by China, Brazil and Peru on a railway project that would connect the Atlantic and Pacific coasts via both Latin American countries. In the roadmap of cooperation issued by the China-CELAC forum, special emphasis is placed upon Chinese investment in "high-tech and high-value-added manufacturing sectors." Chinese auto and electronics companies are building footholds in Latin America in a view to tapping both local markets and the US market. The CASS [Chinese Academy of Social Sciences] book suggests that, in Brazil at least, petroleum transportation and refinery facilities are possibly an even better area for Chinese investment than exploration. ECLAC, meanwhile, has recommended more exports of Latin American food products and business services to China, which is experiencing strong demand for both.

The complexity of the Latin American business environment is highlighted in the CASS book, including the region's broad political diversity, particularly in terms of political parties, a continent-wide reinforcement of nationalist and populist politics, powerful trade unions and the strong role played in governance by NGOs. Barriers to foreign investment are common in the natural resources sector, including market access restrictions and unpredictably enforced tariffs, taxes and charges on oil exploration. In the manufacturing sector, meanwhile, Latin America's labor markets lag behind most world economies in the international rankings in terms of cost, flexibility and productivity.

These prove the importance of due diligence, particularly concerning the prevailing political climate and operational considerations, for any foreign investors looking to gain a presence in any of Latin America's 33 states. It is implied in the CASS book that Chinese enterprises are at a disadvantage both in their understanding of the importance of regional differentiation in Latin America, and also in their experience of dealing with non-governmental interests. Some try to sidestep these necessities by neglecting trade unions and NGOs and maintaining close contact with senior officials.

Such practices have merely led to the unexpected entanglement of Chinese enterprises in local feuds between different political interest groups, attracting protests against their insufficient contributions to local employment and environmental protection, causing disruptions in production. In Peru, for example, Chinese steel maker Shougang Group has been struggling to cope with frequent strikes at its local iron mining operations for more than 20 years. This case has been repeatedly cited by Chinese media and analysts as an example of Chinese companies' weakness in dealing with labor issues in overseas markets.

In 2012, a mass protest was organized by the Confederation of Indigenous Nationalities of Ecuador (CONAIE) opposing a contract approved by President Rafael Correa that was awarded to the Chinese-funded El Mirador open-pit copper mine project, which was seen as threatening forestry resources belonging to the indigenous Shuar community.

President Correa, who won the election in 2006 largely with the strong support of indigenous minorities, tried to appease campaigners by ordering the Chinese company to surrender half their profits to the national government. Ecuacorriente, the Chinese company, was criticized by local communities for only negotiating with Ecuador's central government and ignoring local interests.

Such examples of underestimating local political risk and shunning talks with non-governmental organizations have been made by Chinese enterprises in other markets, including African states and Myanmar. The report advises Chinese companies to learn from Japanese experience in setting up low-key, small-scale manufacturing plants, collaborating with local or international companies, training local workers and communicating with local media.

The UN report calls on Latin American countries to formulate "active" and "coordinated" policies "overcoming known lags in innovation, competitiveness, science and technology, infrastructure, trade facilitation and business internationalization." For example, it says, the complicated visa application system used in the region could deter Chinese tourists from visiting Latin America.

While trying to avoid balance-of-power game-playing with the US in Latin America, China will find political considerations no less important than the bottom line in terms of pursuing business partnerships.

FOR FURTHER STUDY

Response Questions

- What is High Speed Rail (HSR) diplomacy? What are the goals of HSR diplomacy?
- What is the Marshall Plan? How is it similar/dissimilar to China's High Speed Rail (HSR) diplomacy?
- What is the Thucydides Trap? Does it apply to the US and China?
- What is the One Belt, One Road (OBOR) policy? What countries does OBOR apply to? How?
- What is the significance of the FTAAP and TPP? Who signed on with the FTAAP? Who supported the TPP?
- What is the geopolitical realignment in East Asia? Who are the actors? Which countries are converging politically, economically?

- What major international incident did US Secretary of Defense Chuck Hagel label as one of China's destabilizing, unilateral actions asserting its claims in the area that resulted in the deterioration of diplomatic ties with one of China's traditional allies?
- Which countries did Xi Jinping visit in 2014? What is the significance/outcome of those visits?
- What is Xi Jinping's Three-in-One Model of Economic Integration? Which country does it involve?
- What is soft power? Provide at least three examples of China's exercise of soft power.

Discussion Questions

- In the Wang (2015) article on the One Belt, One Road policy, the premise of omitting the Middle East in their global foreign policy is based on avoidance of conflict with the US. Is this consistent with other articles you have read concerning US–China relations? Does China avoid countries and regions because the US has existing interests there?
- Discuss the current relationship between China and Russia. Are they friends or adversaries? What interest does China have in Russia? What concerns does China have in regards to Russia? What are the reasons for their current state of diplomatic relations?
- What is China's US strategy? What are your predictions for US–China relations based on the reading of the articles in this chapter? How do current or future US–China relations affect international business and commerce in China?
- How do China's relations with one country affect its relations with a third country? For example, how do China's relations with South Korea affect its relations with North Korea?
- China is being confronted with a major international relations decision after three decades of non-alignment. At this juncture, what are the potential benefits and challenges for China of deviating from their non-alignment stance? If it did chose allies, which would be most beneficial for China? Why?
- How do international relations affect business and enterprise? Give some examples from the articles you have read.
- What are the tensions, complications, and challenges of Chinese engagement in Latin America? In your discussion, include the perspectives of Chinese companies, US government, and local NGOs and interest groups in Latin American countries.

Research Exercises

- What are China's economic and political interests with its neighbors to its north, south, east, and west? Create a diagram with China in the center and its neighboring countries around it: up (north), down (south), right (east), and left (west) of China. The thickness of the lines should show China's economic/political distance from each neighboring country (thick lines = strong ties; thin lines = weak ties). Draw a green line for positive economic relations; a black line for negative economic relations; a blue line for positive political relations; a red line for negative political relations. Each country should have a circle around it—inside the circle, write key meetings, events, summits, agreements, partnerships, co-operations, projects that affect its political/economic relations with China. Bonus: draw lines between neighboring countries.
- Conduct a survey of 20 people regarding their perceptions of China as a rising power. Try to get a cross-section of the general population, with a mix of gender, age, education level, ethnicity/nationality, and socio-economic status (these demographics should all be included in the questionnaire as survey questions). Include five Likert-scale questions (i.e., to what degree do you agree/disagree with the following state-ments?) such as: "China's rise is peaceful"; "US–China relations are positive" and graph your results separated by gender, ethnicity/ nationality, age, education level, and socioeconomic status.
- Business opportunities are available during peace as well as conflict. Consider a potential diplomatic conflict (with China) in the Pacific region and come up with a product or service that would capitalize on a unique opportunity born from that conflict. Research the necessary require-ments for conducting your business in that national context. Write up a one-paragraph summary of each conflict, a one-paragraph descrip-tion of your product/service, and a one-paragraph report of the legal/ regulatory rules, policies, and requirements of conducting the business in that country.

Notes

1 Yinhong, S. China Needs to Balance Assertive-ness with Prudence in Its Diplomacy. *NewsChina*, February 2015.
2 Li, J. & Chen, J. China and Vietnam—Friends Again? *NewsChina*. November 1, 2014.
3 Wong, C.H. China Lays Out Its Plans for Harder Military Stand. *The Wall Street Journal Asia Edition*, May 27, 2015.
4 Erickson, A.S. & Strange, A.M. China's Blue Soft Power. *Naval War College Review*, 68, 1 (2015): 71–91.
5 Corkin, L.J. China's Rising Soft Power: The Role of Rhetoric in Constructing China-Africa Relations. *Revista Brasileira De Política Internacional*, 5749 (2014): 72.

6 Tai-Ting, T. & Tung-Chieh, T. Swords into Ploughshares? China's Soft Power strategy in Southeast Asia and Its Challenges. *Revista Brasileira De Política Internacional, 5728* (2014): 48.

7 Burnett, A. China, Russia and the US #124 Juggle Soft and Hard Power. *The Nation (Thailand)*, January 13, 2015.

8 Chen, S.G. The new No. 1 Struggles with Soft Power: As Beijing Shifts Its Economic Focus to Quality, It Needs to Learn That Soft Power Can't Be Bought. *South China Morning Post*, December 8, 2014.

9 Shih, T.H. Hard Investment Versus Soft Power: Experts Disagree on How Successful China Has Been in Building Its Intangible—Non-economic—Influence in Africa. *South China Morning Post*, July 22, 2013.

10 Yu, X Partisan Partnerships. *NewsChina*, January 1, 2015.

11 *NewsChina*. A Brief History of China's Foreign Policy. *NewsChina*, February 1, 2015.

12 Yu.

13 Coonan, C. APEC Summit Dominated by Climate and Trade. *The Irish Times*, November 18, 2014.

14 Jiang, S. FTAAP to Signal Start of New Era: The Free Trade Area of the Asia-Pacific, Which Includes China and the US, Is the Most Extensive Plan for Regional Economic Integration to Date. *South China Morning Post*, January 30, 2015.

15 Shih, T.H., Chen, A., & Zhou, L. Number of US Visas Issued to Chinese Soars; Recent Figures Show 68pc Rise Thanks to 10-year Permits for Business and Leisure Travellers. *South China Morning Post*, February 4, 2015.

16 Callick, R. Australia will join China's Asia bank. *The Australian*, December 8, 2014.

17 Shi, Y. China Needs to Balance Assertive-ness with Prudence in Its Diplomacy. *NewsChina*, February 2015.

18 Yu, X. Putative partnerships. *NewsChina*, September 1, 2014.

19 Ouyang, K., Xu, F., & Yu, X. Steppe Forward. *NewsChina*, November 1, 2014.

20 Li, J. & Chen, J. China and Vietnam—Friends Again? *NewsChina*, November 1, 2014.

21 Li, J. Holding Our Breath. *NewsChina*, August 1, 2014.

22 Bender, J. China's Influence Is Growing So Fast That Two of the World's Biggest Militaries Are Teaming Up to Block It. *Business Insider UK*, June 7, 2015.

23 Cai, R. & Li, J. Friends or allies? *NewsChina*, April 1, 2014.

24 Zoellner, T. Red Train Rising. *Foreign Policy*, December 16, 2014.

25 Li, J. Buena Vistas. *NewsChina*, March 1, 2015.

26 Zoellner.

27 Li, J. Face the Fear. *NewsChina*, September 1, 2014.

28 Liu, Y. Marshall Plan Copycat Allegations Misleading. *Beijing Review, 58*, 6 (2015): 20.

29 Xinhua. Chinese Think Tank Releases Report on the Security of China's Perimeter. *Chinascope, 73* (2014): 20.

30 Danese, P. NPC Could Fire Up RMB Silk Road. *GlobalCapital*, February 27, 2015.

31 Wang, T. One Belt, One Road Will Bypass the Middle East, and for Good Reason. *NewsChina*, May 1, 2015.

32 Wong, B. One Belt, One Road Initiative: The Implications for Hong Kong. Hong Kong Trade Development Council, April 16, 2015.

33 Liu.

34 Wang.

35 Li, 2015.

36 UITP. Statistics Brief World Metro Figures. Union Internationale des Transports Publics (UITP), October 2014.

37 Riedel, H.-U. (2014). Chinese Metro Boom Shows No Sign of Abating. *International Railway Journal*, November 19, 2014.
38 Yu, X. Truly Transglobal. *NewsChina*, January 1, 2015.
39 Ibid.
40 Pu, Z. Diplomatic Touch. *China Daily European Edition*, January 9, 2015.
41 Catanzaro, J., Qi, R., Jia, C., & Han, B. Belt, Road Built on Reciprocity. *China Daily, European Edition*, May 8, 2015.
42 Fu, J. Two-Part Harmony. *China Daily, European Edition*, May 1, 2015.
43 Wade, J. Changing Asia: China's High Speed Railway Diplomacy. *The Strategist*, December 2, 2013.
44 Yu.

Bibliography

Bender, J. (June 7, 2015). China's Influence Is Growing So Fast That Two of the World's Biggest Militaries Are Teaming Up to Block It. *Business Insider UK*, retrieved from http://uk.businessinsider.com/us-and-india-aim-to-block-chinese-influence-2015-6

Burnett, A. (January 13, 2015). China, Russia and the US #124 Juggle Soft and Hard Power. *The Nation* (Thailand), retrieved from www.lexisnexis.com/hottopics/lnacademic

Cai R. & Li Jia (April 1, 2014). Friends or Allies? *NewsChina*, retrieved from www.newschinamag.com/magazine/friends-or-allies

Callick, R. (December 8, 2014). Australia Will Join China's Asia Bank. *The Australian*, retrieved from www.lexisnexis.com/hottopics/lnacademic

Catanzaro, J., Qi, R., Jia, C., & Han, B. (May 8, 2015). Belt, Road Built on Reciprocity. *China Daily European Edition*, retrieved from www.lexisnexis.com/hottopics/lnacademic

Chen, S.G. (December 8, 2014). The new No. 1 Struggles with Soft Power: As Beijing Shifts Its Economic Focus to Quality, It Needs to Learn That Soft Power Can't Be Bought. *South China Morning Post*, retrieved from www.lexisnexis.com/hottopics/lnacademic

Coonan, C. (November 18, 2014). China Improves Trade Links with Nearby Economies. *The Irish Times*, retrieved from www.lexisnexis.com/hottopics/lnacademic

Coonan, C. (November 18, 2014). APEC Summit Dominated by Climate and Trade. *The Irish Times*, retrieved from www.lexisnexis.com/hottopics/lnacademic

Corkin, L.J. (2014). China's Rising Soft Power: The Role of Rhetoric in Constructing China-Africa Relations. *Revista Brasileira De Política Internacional*, 5749–72. doi:10.1590/0034-7329201400204.

Danese, P. (February 27, 2015). NPC Could Fire Up RMB Silk Road. Globalcapital.

Erickson, A.S. & Strange, A.M. (2015). China's Blue Soft Power. *Naval War College Review*, 68(1), 71–91.

Fu, J. (May 1, 2015). Two-Part Harmony. China Daily European Edition, Retrieved from www.lexisnexis.com/hottopics/lnacademic

Jiang, S. (January 30, 2015). FTAAP to signal start of New Era: The Free Trade Area of the Asia-Pacific, Which Includes China and the US, Is the Most Extensive Plan for Regional Economic Integration to Date. *South China Morning Post*, retrieved from www.lexisnexis.com/hottopics/lnacademic

Li, J. (August 1, 2014). Holding Our Breath. *NewsChina*, retrieved from www.newschina mag.com/magazine/holding-our-breath

Li, J. (September 1, 2014). Face the Fear. *NewsChina*, retrieved from www.newschina mag.com/magazine/face-the-fear

Li, J. (March 1, 2015). Buena Vistas. *NewsChina*, retrieved from www.newschina mag.com/magazine/buenas-vistas

Li, J. & Chen, J. (November 1, 2014). China and Vietnam—Friends Again? *NewsChina*, retrieved from www.newschinamag.com/magazine/friends-again

Liu, Y. (2015). Marshall Plan Copycat Allegations Misleading. *Beijing Review, 58*(6), 20.

Ouyang, K., Xu, F., & Yu, X. (November 1, 2014). Steppe Forward. *NewsChina*, retrieved from www.newschinamag.com/magazine/steppe-forward

Pu, Z. (January 9, 2015). Diplomatic Touch. *China Daily European Edition*, retrieved from www.lexisnexis.com/hottopics/lnacademic

Riedel, H.-U. (November 19, 2014). Chinese Metro Boom Shows No Sign of Abating. *International Railway Journal*, retrieved from www.railjournal.com/index.php/metros/chinese-metro-boom-shows-no-sign-of-abating.html?channel=525

Shi, Y. (February 2015). China Needs to Balance Assertive-ness with Prudence in Its Diplomacy. *NewsChina*, retrieved from www.newschinamag.com/magazine/china-needs-to-balance-assertive-ness-with-prudence-in-its-diplomacy

Shih, T.H. (July 22, 2013). Hard Investment Versus Soft Power: Experts Disagree on How Successful China Has Been in Building Its Intangible—Non-economic—Influence in Africa. *South China Morning Post*, retrieved from www.lexisnexis.com/hottopics/lnacademic

Shih, T.H., Chen, A., & Zhou, L. (February 4, 2015). Number of US Visas Issued to Chinese Soars; Recent Figures Show 68pc Rise Thanks to 10-year Permits for Business and Leisure Travellers. *South China Morning Post*, retrieved from www.lexisnexis.com/hottopics/lnacademic

Staff (February 1, 2015). A Brief History of China's Foreign Policy. *NewsChina*, retrieved from www.newschinamag.com/magazine/a-brief-history-of-chinas-foreign-policy

Staff (May 27, 2015). Rise of the Regional Hegemons. *The Wall Street Journal Asia Edition*.

Tai-Ting, T. & Tung-Chieh, T. (2014). Swords into Ploughshares? China's Soft Power Strategy in Southeast Asia and Its Challenges. *Revista Brasileira De Política Internacional*, 5728–48. doi:10.1590/0034–7329201400203.

UITP (October, 2014). Statistics Brief World Metro Figures. Union Internationale des Transports Publics (UITP) (International Association of Public Transport).

Wade, J. (December 2, 2013). Changing Asia: China's High Speed Railway Diplomacy. *The Strategist*, retrieved from www.aspistrategist.org.au/changing-asia-chinas-high-speed-railway-diplomacy/

Wang, T. (May 1, 2015). One Belt, One Road Will Bypass the Middle East, and for Good Reason. NewsChina, retrieved from www.newschinamag.com/magazine/one-belt-one-road-will-bypass-the-middle-east-and-for-good-reason

Wong, C.H. (May 27, 2015). China Lays Out its Plans for Harder Military Stand. *The Wall Street Journal Asia Edition*.

Wong, W. (April 16, 2015). One Belt, One Road Initiative: The Implications for Hong Kong, retrieved from http://economists-pick-research.hktdc.com/business-news/

article/Research-Articles/One-Belt-One-Road-Initiative-The-Implications-for-Hong-Kong/rp/en/1/1X32LK39/1X0A23WV.htm?DCSext.dept=12&WT.mc_id=6111085

Xinhua (2015). Chinese Think Tank Releases Report on the Security of China's Perimeter. *Chinascope*, (73), 20.

Yu, X. (September 1, 2014). Putative Partnerships. *NewsChina*, retrieved from www.newschinamag.com/magazine/putative-partnerships

Yu, X. (January 1, 2015). Partisan Partnerships. *NewsChina*, retrieved from www.newschinamag.com/magazine/partisan-partnerships

Yu, X. (January 1, 2015). Truly Transglobal. *NewsChina*, retrieved from www.newschinamag.com/magazine/truly-transglobal

Zoellner, T. (December 16, 2014). Red Train Rising. *Foreign Policy*, retrieved from http://foreignpolicy.com/2014/12/16/red-train-rising-china-africa-rail/

4

SOCIAL FACTORS

Introduction

Thomas Malthus argued that population growth was a predictor of and would be checked by global problems including famine, war, and disease. He believed that each positive check was a natural consequence of its absence, in other words, long periods of food abundance, peace, and health would lead to geometric population growth which naturally have to be positively checked by their inverse forms resulting in massive deaths. Preventative checks, on the other hand, prevent growth and reproduction—most nations favor these approaches which include birth control, delayed marriages, and inflation. Aldous Huxley presented a version of the future—albeit some of it is already the present—where population growth is strictly controlled by artificial measures and policies. Even with global population growth year-on-year, countries such as Denmark, Russia, Japan, Singapore, and South Korea struggle with extremely low population growth and are implementing tax benefits, propaganda, and prizes to encourage pregnancies[1].

As the world's largest nation by population size, China has been combatting overpopulation for the past three decades, largely a result of Mao's encouragement in the 1950s and 1960s to be fruitful and multiply. At approximately 1.3 billion people, China was been more effective at curbing birth rates than any other modern nation, by a Malthusian–Huxleyan preventative check—the One Child Policy, now broadened to two children. However, the success of draconian birth control has a long shadow that presently threatens to disrupt family structures of second-generation only-children, economic security for a graying China, and a precarious urban–rural equilibrium.

Little Emperors

The Little Emperors (and Empresses) were so dubbed by both Chinese and foreigners[2] who foresaw the potential negative effects of China's One Child Policy first introduced in 1979 to curb rapid population growth and impending food shortage in the world's most populous nation[3]. There were rumors of an impending doom, a social schism across demographics that would deepen and broaden with the first generation of only-children growing into hundreds of millions of potentially maladjusted, socially stunted, psychologically narcissistic adults finding their way into business, medicine, education, politics, and every other trade or vocation. In the US, we would call this same generation the Millennials. Since the baby boomer generation of the 1940s and 1950s, each cohort of adults has provided its expert analysis on their children's generation (Gen X, Gen Y, etc.), dubbing them the "Me" generation[4]. Stein goes on to argue that this perhaps goes back to time of the Reformation when Luther argued on behalf of a generation of Christians that they did not need the Church to talk to God. Likewise, the moniker of Little Emperors comes as no surprise, and it both accurately and inadequately describes a generation of Chinese that are now becoming parents of another second generation of Little Emperors[5] — and we know what typically happens to young liberals who become parents, take on mortgages, and buy memberships at their local gyms. They become their conservative, protective parents who are counting white hairs, miles per gallon (or kilometers per liter), and years to retirement. The difference this time is that the parents were only-children once. Consumerism appears to benefit nicely from the hedonism frequently attributed to only-children[6]. Society and culture may not receive equally polite treatment[7].

Elderly

The 4–2–1 phenomenon, a funnel-shaped family structure, where only-children of only-children have the sole burden of caring for four grandparents and two parents, implies an imbalance in family responsibility which is likely to result in financial stress on public social welfare in addition to psychological stress on the single individual at the bottom of that inverted pyramid. By 2050, more than a quarter of the Chinese population will be over 65, and concerns regarding the Chinese equivalent of social security are rampant[8]. With a growing aged population which threatens the pension system—this should sound familiar to Americans who have been predicting the collapse of Social Security for the past two decades—the Chinese government responded with a selective Two Child Policy starting in 2014 which allows couples to have two children if either is an only child[9]. Though they expected up to four million additional births that year, only 700,000 of the eligible couples applied to have a second child during that period[10], which prompted legislators to call for a complete and permanent overhaul to the One Child Policy. This resulted in a broad Two Child Policy announced in October 2015.

Compounded by a shrinking birth rate, problems of age dependency may adversely affect the macro-economics of China[11]. In pursuit of a better fix, China is now looking to the market economy and the workforce to bear the burden of social welfare for the elderly that accounted for 24 percent of total government revenues in 2013, and will amount to nearly $13 trillion by 2050 or 91 percent of annual GDP[12]. Beijing is taking cues from other nations, and gradually increasing the average retirement age of 55 to 65. The private sector, largely unsuccessful in the Chinese market until recently, is being incentivized and encouraged to increase offerings for the aged, from senior care facilities to retirement planning services. These remain controversial as the quality of care is not sufficiently monitored or regulated[13,14].

Hukou

The One Child Policy is most blatantly visible in the urban centers of China. This is because the countryside has a different set of rules in regards to childbirth—those registered as rural farmers have had the benefit of having more than one child, particularly if their first is a daughter. In addition, minorities whose populations are greatest in the northeast, west, and southwest are typically migrants without permanent residence papers, or Hukou, in the eastern developed cities. These minorities are also provided preferential policies in regards to the number of children that a family may have[15]. This Hukou system is a two-edged sword. Its intention is to control migration and demographic shifts from rural-to-urban and province-to-province[16,17]. The percentage of total population living in urban areas has grown from 25 in 1990 to 54 in 2014[18]. The resulting urbanization is a direct result of uneven regional economic growth which favored the large cities along the east coast of China. Despite the Hukou system, which left illegal migrants without a social safety net, unprecedented human migration has caused the rise of mega-cities like Beijing, Shanghai, and Shenzhen. With urban residents outspending their rural counterparts by over 360 percent, urbanization is now seen as a viable solution to low consumer spending[19].

However, the lack of health care, housing, education, and other social provisions granted to legal residents has sparked unrest and subsequent removal of many migrants from cities that they may have lived in for years[20]. Some provinces have enacted reforms to the Hukou system, granting rural residents the opportunity to gain urban residence permits through a point system[21,22]. Critics and wary migrants believe this to be a government scheme to appropriate rural property in exchange for the promise of the good life[23,24,25]. In theory, by becoming an urban resident, one surrenders the rights, including rural land rights, of a rural resident. Additional concerns include the inability of urban areas to absorb the needs of new residents, including education, clean water, housing, and health care.

Chinese society contends with challenges to stability and harmony, with some of its most demanding issues stemming from the One Child Policy, including generational culture shifts, a gender imbalance, and an aging society[26]. Coming full circle on the Little Emperors debate, the conclusions on the psychosocial health of only children of only children are even less conclusive, with evidence supporting both sides[27,28]. Though the elderly are growing in proportion to the overall population, they are resilient and willing to sacrifice for their only children and only grandchildren as seen in the following response from Mr. & Mrs. Wang, grandparents of only children: "We are good now. We have our pensions and shouldn't need financial support from our son and daughter-in-law in the future. We will try our best not to bother our son and his wife in our old age."[29] With the *Hukou* (or household registration system) undergoing change and experimentation, challenged by the rising perceived value of rural properties, complications to the ebb and flow of human migration across China's regions have defied demographic predictions. As government policies shift to encourage workers to leave farms and villages for jobs in the big city, children are left behind in the care of their grandparents[30,31].

The 4–2–1 phenomenon produced a most fortunate generation, receiving the uncontested care, providence, and attention of four grandparents and two parents whose blessings, like the rivers of Chinese proverbs, always flowed downstream. As those same parents and grandparents enter into an uncertain retirement, the Little Emperors and Empresses may see their fortunes reversed, solely responsible for caring and providing for the welfare and health care of six elderly parents and grandparents. With a graying society, the river, by necessity, must flow upwards.

ARTICLES

Demographics

Second Generation of Only Children

Children are inherently dependent upon their parents, but this dependency has exceeded normal limits in China, with a large proportion of adults remaining financially depending on their elderly parents. The generation of Chinese who grew up as only children—often called *Little Emperors*—are now parents, but supposedly unprepared to do take on that role, and so they delegate parental duties to the grandparents. These second-generation *Little Emperors* are described as entitled, self-obsessed, and intolerant. Sun Yunxiao, deputy director of the China Youth and Children Research Center, claims that young Chinese parents are inadequately prepared to raise children consistent with their values. According to the Academy of Social Sciences, post-80s Chinese parents are utilizing their access to information and educational background to inform themselves of parenting practices for their *Little Emperors*, with over 45 percent referring to online parenting websites and forums. *Little Emperors* are now raising their own *Little Emperors* with good intentions but inherent challenges.

Second-generation Little Emperors

January 2015 Issue of NewsChina | *by Wang Yan*

With the children of China's One Child Policy becoming parents themselves, traditional beliefs clash with modern parenting.

More than thirty years after the introduction of the One Child Policy in 1979, the generation of Chinese people born in the policy's first decade are now fully grown—many of them already married with children. According to official estimates, the coming decade will see another 10 million only-children born to the original generation of only-children.

The "post-80s" generation, a cohort famously known as "little emperors" in their youth, now face the challenge of raising their own children. Variously described as liberal, independent, unruly and selfish in the media, society watches with anticipation to see how these traits will affect their parenting style, and what kind of children they will raise.

DEPENDENT

In October, a middle-aged man in Ningbo sued his daughter for being "*kenlao*," literally "biting the elderly," meaning to be financially dependent on one's parents. Herself the mother of a two-year-old child, she borrowed over 700,000 yuan (US$114,000) from her parents even though she was still living as their dependent. The Chinese Research Center on Aging estimates that a third of Chinese of adult age, mostly the single child generation, still remain in some way financially dependent on their parents.

In China, the tradition of living with one's extended family has endured for thousands of years. But when the policy of Reform and Opening-up in the early 1980s drastically increased mobility, many began to leave their hometowns for big cities in pursuit of jobs or business opportunities. In many cases, their elderly parents offered to accompany them, to help take care of their young children: the post-80s generation. In order to save money and energy, most agreed, often begrudgingly.

Zhao Zhongxin, honorary chairman of the Family Education Committee under the Chinese Society of Education, has noted that a large proportion of the post-80s generation are unable to live independently due to them having been over-indulged by their parents in childhood. "I know a mother who still creeps into her married son's room at night to tuck him in when he's asleep, and a married daughter who still asks her mother to help her put her socks on," Zhao told *NewsChina*: "It is very common to see the elderly do housework for their married children nowadays."

In 2012, a survey of 534 households by research institute the Shanghai Children Nurturing Base (SCNB) found that more than 40 percent of the post-80s generation live with their parents, over 28 percent said their parents would help raise their children, and over 15 percent said the elderly often help with household chores. The elderly also provide financial support. The survey found that more than 50 percent of the post-80s generation had paid for their apartment entirely with their parents' money, and almost zero percent had not accepted any financial help from their parents when buying their house.

Chen Caiyu, the SCNB's deputy director, said: "The reality is that it is very hard for the single-child generation to be independent." Li Yuqin, a Zhengzhou-based pediatrician believes that many Chinese children have been spoiled by their grandparents, causing them to become "selfish, dependent, and inconsiderate of others."

"The first single-child generation are not yet ready to be parents, so it is very common for them to let their parents take care of their kids," said Sun Yunxiao, deputy director at the China Youth and Children Research Center. Sun further explained to the reporter that most parents either ask their elderly parents to look after their child while they're at work, or simply leave their child entirely in the care of grandparents. While taking one's children to work was relatively common in the 1980s, this practice is generally seen as unacceptable in modern workplaces.

COMPENSATION

Having grown up in a comparatively liberal sociopolitical environment under Reform and Opening-up, the post-80s generation witnessed China's transformation from a poor developing country into an economic superpower. During their childhood, however, the spoils of development were yet to materialize—the best most could expect was ample food and clothing.

Wang Lin, an only child, was born in 1981 to a working-class family in a third-tier city in Hubei Province. Like many children of her age, she played with homemade toys, and was occasionally given rock candy as a special treat. Her father made a chessboard and taught her how to play. Now mother to a young daughter, Wang often finds herself comparing her own childhood with her daughter's: "She eats express-delivered organic vegetables, drinks imported baby formula, has piles of toys and books, and her diapers cost us over 1,000 yuan (US$163) a month," Wang told our reporter.

Wang admitted that she tries her best to meet her daughter's material expectations, to provide herself with what she called "mental compensation" for her own relatively underprivileged childhood. Wang buys her daughter snacks whenever she ask for them, and like many parents, she packs her daughter's schedule with extracurricular classes like dance and calligraphy. Having had no opportunity to pursue hobbies when she was young, she told NewsChina she did not want her daughter to have a similarly "depressed and uninteresting" childhood.

Zhu Yuan, a Shanghai-based mother of two, began sending her elder daughter Coco to an early learning center from the age of one. Now, Coco attends a bilingual kindergarten and takes classes in painting, logical thinking, music, ballet, and swimming. Zhu told *NewsChina* that she expected her daughter "to act like a lady" when she grows up.

"ME" GENERATION

"My granddaughter points at me and my wife, and shouts to her brother: 'These are my grandpa and grandma!'" said Zhao Zhongxin. "Apparently she, as a second-generation only child, wants to claim us as her possessions," said Zhao. "This indicates an only child's typical psychology to control, dominate and possess things exclusively." Zhao warns that this second generation of only children may have a tough time getting along with the rest of society.

Chen Caiyu's training course instructs young parents to help children distinguish between "what is yours, what it is you want, and what you can get." Chen is trying to teach post-80s moms and dads that unrestricted acquiescence to a child's demands will result in self-obsession, and, ultimately, another generation of little emperors.

Compared to their parents, most of whom grew up during the Cultural Revolution, the post-80s generation are perhaps most famous for the individualism with which they approach their lives and relationships— a trait that has led to them being called the "me-first" generation. Pediatrician Li Yuqin says he often sees impatient post-80s parents at hospitals shouting at nurses in order to have doctors see their children first. "Rude, undisciplined behavior on the part of some parents might be detrimental to their children's attitudes towards others, and I worry their children will be even less tolerant and even more restless when they grow up," said Li.

Sun Yunxiao noticed that in practice, many young parents—even educated ones—do not know how to raise their children in a way that fosters both freedom and respect. "A successful home education should result in a balance in a child's self-motivation and self-restriction," Sun told *NewsChina*. "A family with both democracy and authority can benefit a child's healthy development."

FREESTYLE

In the 1970s and 80s, most Chinese parents would inquire very little about their child's behavior in school, other than to ask whether they were obedient or not. Now, parents ask their children what they learned in school, and how happy they are.

Many of the post-80s generation, particularly in cities, have received a college education and, through the Internet and overseas travel, have enjoyed relatively easy access to Western culture, as well as modern scientific parenting methods. They are more likely than the previous generation of parents to educate their children with emotional support rather than criticism.

According to a 2005 paper by the Shanghai Academy of Social Sciences, over 45 percent of post-80s parents have looked to the Internet to learn about modern parenting methods, and regularly use online parenting forums. *Babytree.com*, one of China's most popular online parenting communities, has more than 16 million registered members, most of them born in the 1980s. Discussion threads on alternative education methods like Montessori education generate lengthy debates.

Zhang Wen, a mother in Beijing, told *NewsChina* that she prefers what she calls "freestyle" or "natural" parenting. Zhang wants to spare her daughter the overwhelming burden of schoolwork—she may even allow her child a "non-traditional" education, whatever form that may take. "I want her to have a memorable and interesting youth," added Zhang. Yet in reality, adopting a new parenting style might not be as simple as Zhang Wen expects. For most parents of her generation, regardless of their own views on parenting, they still face a perhaps insurmountable obstacle: their own conservative parents.

According to Bao Leiping, a researcher from the Shanghai Academy of Social Sciences, it is still too early to gauge grandparents' influence on the personal development of the new generation of children. "Much previous research on parenting has indicated that while grandparents can help with day-to-day childcare, social and moral guidance [should] remain the responsibility of parents," Bao told *NewsChina*.

(Chen Wei and Ma Haiyan also contributed reporting.)

China's Greying Population

With an aging population, China has reversed its decades-old One Child Policy, allowing for two-child families if either parent is an only child. This policy shift has not had its intended effect, with Chinese parents reluctant to have a second child even without the penalties that were historically assessed on families with more than one child. The rising costs of caring for the elderly, an aging of the overall population because of low birth rates and longer life expectancies, along with a rapidly diminishing pension fund, has forced the government to explore unpopular cost-saving strategies. An expected policy change to the retirement age, currently 50 for women and 60 for men, will result in a new retirement age of 65 for both men and women.

Privatization of the social security market as well as reductions in benefits to public servants are considered inevitable consequences to the changing demography of China.

Dynamic Demography

March 2015 Issue of NewsChina | *by Wu Fan*

Given that China's efforts to tackle its demographic problem in 2014 have brought limited results, the country is gearing up to launch a new policy package this year, billed as its most diverse and comprehensive yet.

When China adopted a selective "two-child policy" in early 2014, allowing couples to have two children if either prospective parent was an only child themselves, experts predicted that it would lead to an additional two to four million births in the first year of the policy. On the contrary, statistics from the National Health and Family Planning Commission (NHFPC) show that only 700,000 of 11 million couples eligible to have a second child under this policy applied to do so in the first ten months of 2014.

With the policy, the NHFPC aimed to increase the birth rate to 1.8 children per couple, but most demographers have conceded that the policy has failed to achieve this goal. The birth rate itself is disputed—although statistics from China's census in 2010 showed a birth rate of about 1.2, the NHFPC has adopted a higher rate of 1.5 and 1.6, due to a belief that many children born in violation of the One Child Policy were not registered during the census.

With evidence of so many parents reluctant to have a second child, it is believed that the birth rate reported in the census is close to accurate, leading many to advocate replacing the One Child Policy with a two-child policy. But according to Zhao Yanpei, a senior NHFPC official, there is currently no timetable for nationwide implementation.

Many attribute the reluctance of the government to replace the One Child Policy with a two-child policy to an earlier report jointly released by more than 20 demographers, which warned that a two-child policy would send the birth rate surging to 4.4 in its first year, decelerating to 2.4 in the long run. However, given the unexpectedly ambivalent response to the policy revision in 2014, there have been growing calls from academics for further relaxation.

PENSION FUND DEFICIT

As China's birth rate has stagnated in recent years, the population of senior citizens has been steadily increasing. In 2013, the number of people over 60 reached 202.43 million, accounting for 14.9 percent of the whole population. According to Vice Premier Ma Kai's report to the National People's Congress (NPC) in December, the proportion of elderly people will have risen to over 19.3 percent by 2020, and to 34.2 percent of the total population by 2050.

The prospect of an aging population not only poses a threat to macroeconomic development, but has become an acute social problem. In recent years, China's pension system has begun to feel the strain, as growth in revenue has lagged behind growth in expenditure. According to a report released by the China Academy of Social Sciences, pension funds in 14 provinces were already running at a deficit in 2011, with a total shortfall of 67.9 billion yuan (US$10.7bn). Since then, the management of China's national pension fund has been under close public scrutiny, as many are concerned about the sustainability of the current social security system.

Under China's existing pension system, the national retirement fund is composed of two accounts, the "social pooling" account, a pay-as-you-go fund paid for by employers at the rate of 20 percent of an employee's salary, and the "individual account," to which each employee is entitled upon retirement, paid for by themselves, at a rate of 8 percent of their salary.

In theory, while funds in the social pooling account can be used to pay the pensions of retirees, the funds in the individual account belong to individual employees, who can make a lump-sum withdrawal upon retirement. In reality, as the funds in the social pooling account have depleted, individual accounts have been tapped to make up the shortfall. In 2013, deficits in the national individual account reached 3.1 trillion yuan (US$535bn), 50 percent more than in 2011.

The authorities have repeatedly reassured the public that rather than a self-sustaining system (such as that in the US), China's social security system is a State-guaranteed fund, and as such, there is no risk of default. However, many are becoming concerned that given the sheer volume of potential deficit, even a State guarantee is shaky. For example, the deficit in the individual account fund in 2013 alone accounted for 24 percent of total government revenue that year. Between 2011 and 2013, the government subsidies provided to the social security fund increased from 227.2 billion yuan (US$36.6bn) to 301.9 billion yuan (US$48.7bn) with an average annual increase of about 15 percent.

According to the estimates of a research team led by Li Yang, deputy president of the Chinese Academy of Social Sciences (CASS), the deficit in China's urban pension fund will reach 80.2 trillion yuan (US$12.9tn) in 2050, expected to account for 91 percent of annual GDP.

On December 28, at a legislative session of the Standing Committee of the NPC, a delegation of several ministers led by Vice Premier Ma Kai outlined a new policy package to address the problems in China's social security programs. Included in the policy package was a plan to include 40 million civil servants, Party officials and staff at public institutions in the public social security program. By contrast, public servants, who pay no pension premiums, currently enjoy an 80 percent replacement ratio on retirement, much higher than that enjoyed under the public pension system, which is estimated to lie somewhere between 40 and 60 percent. The proposed reform is considered a major breakthrough, as earlier efforts to reduce the retirement welfare allotment for public servants have repeatedly stalled.

Another major policy change is a plan to postpone the retirement age. Discussion around taking this step has been underway for years, and has long faced strong public opposition. Under China's current policy, female employees can claim their pension at 50 (55 for female party cadres), while male workers claim theirs at 60. According to research released by CASS on December 26, 2014, China should gradually postpone the retirement age to reduce the societal impact of an aging population. The research advises that China first drop the dual-track retirement age that distinguishes between female party cadres and all other women, to adopt 55 as a unified retirement age. Then, beginning from 2018, the retirement age for both men and women should be postponed by one year every three years, so that by 2045, both men and women will retire at 65.

A similar plan proposed by experts at Tsinghua University in late 2013 proposed that China postpone the retirement age gradually—one year every year for women, and six months every year for men. It is not yet known which plan the government will ultimately adopt, but it has become clear that postponing the retirement age is on the policy agenda. Other policy changes include plans to channel more dividends of State-owned enterprises to social security funds. Currently, State-owned enterprises submit only about 10 percent of their profits to the treasury, a rate that will increase to 30 percent in 2020, according to Finance Minister Lou Jiwei.

Ma also stressed that the government will encourage the private sector to enter the social security market. In November, China launched a series of pilot programs in different localities, whereby the government provides subsidies to encourage a market-oriented approach in senior care. As the government has begun to consider senior care as a new source of GDP growth, it is expected that the government will be more active in pushing forward market-oriented programs. But for demographers, the policy package only addresses the symptoms of the aging population, not the root causes. According to Cai Fang, vice president of the Chinese

Academy of Social Sciences, to deal with China's demographic problem, further relaxation of the One Child Policy is inevitable. Moreover, China needs a systematic approach to policy in various fields like education, health care and social security to prevent or delay the imminent aging population problem.

An End to China's One Child Policy

Underpopulation is an issue for highly developed economies such as Japan and Korea; now it is a recognized social crisis for China, which ironically still is the largest population in the world. According to the National Bureau of Statistics, China's labor force declined by 3.45 million working-age people in 2013; the following year, it dropped by another 2.44 million workers. In November 2013, the Chinese central government allowed couples to have a second child if either mother or father were themselves only-children. Out of 11 million eligible couples, only 6 percent actually applied for a birth permit, highlighting the failure of the intended policy. Academics at top higher education institutions and think-tanks in China have called for a nationwide end to the One Child Policy. Currently, there is resistance to such universal reversals of the policy by legislators who are concerned for uneven population growth between wealthier and poorer regions in China. With national and local data demonstrating significant declines in workforce, aging of the general population and a growing gender divide, the demographic dividends of the One Child Policy are now working against the country's interests.

Call to Cancel

May 2015 Issue of NewsChina | *by Min Jie*

Academics continue to call for an end to the population control policy to address the dual issues of an aging society and a looming labor shortage. Why are their requests still being rebuffed?

2015 marked the fifth consecutive year that school principal He Youlin, also a deputy to the National People's Congress (NPC), China's top legislature, appealed to the government to end China's One Child Policy during its annual sessions in Beijing.

He was not alone. As early as in 2004, a dozen academics including Renmin University of China demographer Gu Baochang signed and delivered a report to the central government calling for adjustment of China's population control policy. Before the opening of the conferences of the NPC and the Chinese People's Political Consultative Conference (CPPCC), China's top advisory body, in March 2015, 39 academics once again petitioned the government to end the current State-enforced family planning policy.

UNEXPECTED

In November 2013, the Chinese central government announced that it would relax the One Child Policy to allow couples to have a second child if either the father or mother was an only child, yet another significant change to a population control policy in effect since the 1970s. That year, China's National Health and Family Planning Commission (NHFPC) predicted that more than 2 million additional babies would be born each year, leading to a birth spike. Nevertheless, statistics issued by the same agency in December 2014 showed that although more than 11 million couples across the country were now entitled to have a second child, only 6 percent of these had applied for a birth permit, a far lower percentage than anticipated. In 2014, only 470,000 Chinese couples had a second child. Zhejiang, the first province to adopt the amended policy, estimated that about 80,000 babies would be born in 2014, but saw only 16,000 registered additional births.

Indeed, across China, and particularly in urban areas, the number of applications for birth permits has been declining, indicating that the birth rate continues to fall despite attempts to shore it up with amended policies.

Wang Feng, a sociology professor with Shanghai Fudan University, was surprised to see that previous projections for China's birth rate from government demographers were nearly 70 percent off the mark. NHFPC spokesman Mao Qun'an said the unexpectedly low rate of second births was probably because the policy was put into practice in 2014 and many couples were still preparing to have a second child. In the same statement, Mao predicted a rise in the rate of second births in 2015.

CRISIS

For He Youlin, the tweaked policy has in effect been a failure, prompting him to "strongly urge" lawmakers for a total relaxation to allow all couples to have a second child. "The policy to allow couples to have a second child if one parent was an only child failed to address China's aging society and labor shortage—especially after its rapid change from a country with a high birth rate to low one," He told *NewsChina*. "The current problem with China's population is the phasing out of the demographic dividend [and emergence of] a low birth rate, an aging society and a gender imbalance."

In December 2014, academics from over 30 institutions across the country discussed China's population problem and agreed that rapid urbanization, growing population mobility as well as the growing number of single-child families have become China's "new demographic normal." Professor Gu Baocheng told media that the biggest crisis lay in the country's chronically low birth rate.

Official statistics have showed that China's fertility rate has fallen below the global average for the past 20 years. The internationally accepted standard is 2.1 children per couple. Gu estimates that the population of Chinese women aged between 23 and 30 will drop by 40 percent in the next 10 years, meaning even if every one of those women were to give birth to two children, the birth rate might still continue to fall. According to data from its fifth national demographic census, China's total fertility rate is as low as 1.22 births per couple. In 2010, Beijing recorded 116,000 new births—a fertility rate of 0.71. Shanghai's fertility rate in 2010 stood at 0.74, with 129,000 new births.

In Shanghai alone, the registered population has been in consistent decline since 1993, according to statistics from the Shanghai Municipal Commission of Health and Family Planning. "Today, all the excuses for strictly controlling population growth have disappeared. The situation has completely changed, and it is hard to find a single argument in defense of the One Child Policy," said Professor Wang.

WAY OUT

The adjustment of population policy has been a constant topic of debate during China's annual Two Sessions. In 2015, in addition to He Youlin, a number of NPC deputies and members of the National Committee of the CPPCC, including some government officials working for local health and population commissions, have thrown their weight behind proposals to reexamine the policy.

Guo Yufen, deputy director of the Gansu Provincial Health and Family Planning Commission, also an NPC deputy, told media that before the introduction of the amended policy in Gansu Province, it was expected that more than 30,000 parents would apply to have a second child. However, only 4,000 couples did so, leading her to argue for the swift introduction of a nationwide, universal two-child policy.

In October 2014, Cai Fang, vice president of the Chinese Academy of Social Sciences, China's top government think-tank, told a conference that China is likely to see a two-child policy introduced by 2016. A month later, however, the NHFPC told the media that there was "no exact deadline" for such a move.

Ma Xu, director of the NHFPC Research Center said during the Two Sessions in March that China will not begin trial runs of a two-child policy in 2015 because "it is likely to simply lead to birth spikes in several prosperous areas of the country."

Gu Baochang argues that such theorizing ignores the facts—that it has already been proven by data collected since the introduction of the latest amendment that relaxation of the policy has not created an immediate spike in the birth rate.

As early as 1963, South Korea encouraged couples to have only two children, but as the economy grew rapidly the birth rate experienced a consistent decline. In 1996, the country canceled its population control policy and introduced stimulus packages to encourage couples to have more children. However, neither measure served to reverse the downward trend. In 2005, South Korea's female fertility rate hit a historic low of 1.1 births, close to what international demographers call a "fertility trap." Similar situations have been recorded in Singapore and Taiwan.

"China has missed its best chance to revive its birth rate," Professor Gu told *NewsChina*, adding that 2004 was when the first One Child generation reached marriage age, the prime opportunity to adjust birth policy. However, Gu told *NewsChina*, most people, including academics, failed to recognize the window. "If the current population restrictions continue, the youth of China will, in the near future, pay the economic and social price," he continued.

China's labor pool has been declining rapidly as a direct result of its precipitously falling birth rate. According to statistics from the National Bureau of Statistics (NBS), China was home to a working age population of 937 million people aged between 15 to 59 in 2012, 3.45 million fewer than recorded the previous year, the first recorded decline in the working population. In 2014, NBS data showed that China's labor force dropped 2.44 million on the previous year, indicating that this trend is set to continue.

"It is already a very tough situation now, which allows for no hesitation," He Youlin told our reporter. He continues to appeal to policymakers to take responsibility for overhauling the One Child Policy to address China's aging society and labor shortfall—before it's too late. "Even if challenges and risks abound, the sooner China allows all couples to have a second child, the better," he said. "If the current population restrictions continue, the youth of China will, in the near future, pay the economic and social price."

Migration

Reforming China's Hukou *Policy*

The *Hukou* policy dictates where an individual has his or her permanent residence, typically divided into two categories: rural or urban. It is defined as the household registration record and includes information such as name, spouse, parents, and date of birth. Furthermore, the place of residence will dictate the province and city/township where any and every Chinese citizen can receive education, health care, housing, and other social benefits. For those with a rural *Hukou*, migrating to a city typically means surrendering rights to those basic social provisions, creating a social stratification that many have criticized as reifying class differences and inequality. This system has undergone many revisions over the past decades since its installation as a human migration policy in 1958, which many regard as instrumental in maintaining social stability since that time, with policy relaxations such as those of Henan Province intended to remedy the consequences of an outdated two-tier system that is now the source of social instability in China.

Henan Province is the site of a social experiment, one designed to further grow their metropolitan centers by providing equal rights to new migrants that are enjoyed by existing urban residents. The policy is based on a point system for Henan's 70 million rural residents that includes employment status, education background, payment into the social welfare system, and nine other metrics. Though experts predicted the policy's effects would include a 12 percent increase in urbanization, rural residents apparently did not show up, reluctant to potentially surrender rural landownership and the benefit of either farming that land or contracting it out. Other regions such as Tianjin and Chongqing have provided additional safeguards that allow rural residents to retain their property rights with the option to sub-let or exchange their homesteads for a property in the city. A major issue facing urbanization projects is the financial investment that is required to build up urban infrastructure, such as water works, low-cost housing, schools, and other social services.

Migrants No More

February 2015 Issue of NewsChina | *by Xi Zhigang and Xie Ying*

Henan Province will soon allow rural migrants to apply for urban residence permits, but this seemingly progressive policy has been met with skepticism from the migrant workers themselves.

On November 12, the Henan provincial government issued a new policy relating to *Hukou*, or residence registration, a system often referred to as China's "internal visa." The province announced a plan to grant urban residence permits to around 11 million migrants to the province's cities by 2020. While decades of rapid urbanization have drawn millions of rural people to the cities in search of work, a lack of supporting policies has left them without a social safety net—many are homeless, and few have access to the same welfare and resources as urban residents.

Henan's new policy, according to the government, aims to further encourage surplus rural laborers to move to cities by endowing them with the same rights as their urban counterparts. Analysts said the policy will help raise Henan's urbanization rate to 56 percent, 12 percent higher than that of 2013.

The announcement was met with skepticism, however, from those it purports to help—while the Henan authorities had predicted a boom in applications for urban residence permits, rural people have been reluctant to apply, many worried that an urban residence permit would cost them rights to their rural land. Given that farmland is the primary source of income for China's huge agricultural population, and that the potential acceleration in urban population growth will place yet more strain on the already limited resources available to cities, experts said that the success of the new policy will be determined by the government's capacity to solve the issues surrounding the permit.

NEW POLICY

While other regions have piloted similar policies in the past, Henan's reform plan has stirred the waters nationwide due to the province's huge population—it is home to roughly 8.2 percent of China's citizens. In order to prevent an overwhelming influx of people into its biggest settlements, Henan's pilot program has divided its towns and cities into four categories based on size, with each category imposing different residence requirements. Small towns, for example, only require that applicants are legally employed and either rent or own a house, while bigger cities also set thresholds for how long applicants have worked in the city, and their social welfare payments.

Zhengzhou, Henan's capital and its richest settlement, adopts a point-based system, covering 12 fields, including employment status, education level, social welfare payments and other metrics. Applicants who fall short of requirements will not be considered. "Given that Henan has about 70 million rural people, it is necessary for the government to route the migrant population into different towns and cities, or the capital will be overburdened," Gu Jianquan, vice-director of the Henan Academy of Social Sciences (HASS), told *NewsChina*. "But no matter what the requirements are, application is voluntary," he added. "That is an essential aspect of the new policy."

Geng Mingzhai, director of the Academy of Hinterland Development at Henan University, who participated in the research that guided the province's residence reform, agrees. "The biggest highlight of [Henan's] program is that it is voluntary. Migrants should have the freedom to choose where to register their residence. Past experience in other regions has told us that residence reform that forces people to participate is unsustainable," he told *NewsChina*.

THE LAND ISSUE

Geng's remarks are largely related to what are known as the "three land rights" that apply to rural people's residence permits, namely, the right of using a free housing lot, the use rights to farmland allocated by their village committees—the collective entities that own the land on behalf of the State—and the right to share the benefits from contracted land. However, as Ye Tan, a renowned economics commentator recently pointed out, while Henan's program pledges to protect the "three rights," it fails to go into detail about how it will do so.

Herein lies the primary concern of the migrants at whom the reform program is aimed. During interviews with local media, many asked whether or not the government would take back their land as part of the policy, with some netizens even calling the government's program a "pincer movement" designed to eradicate rural smallholdings and make way for large-scale agricultural production, one of the main goals of China's urbanization effort. "Pound for pound, a rural permit is actually seen to be worth more than an urban permit due to the land rights it grants to the holder," Gao Zhihui, a 63-year-old farmer in a village in the Beijing suburbs, told *NewsChina*. "No rural person would easily give up their land," she added.

China has used a dual-track residence system for rural and urban people since 1958, at which time housing and land for rural residents was allocated by the rural collectives to which they belonged, and jobs and housing for urban people were assigned by the government. While market-oriented employment and residence reform has been going on in cities since the 1990s, the rural system has seen little change. According to current policy, rural residents who obtain permanent urban residence permits, generally via entry into a university or the army, lose the rights to their rural land. While housewife Gao Zhihui has lived in her village for over half a century, she has to rent farmland from one of her relatives, since she transferred to an urban residence permit after her husband took a job as a teacher at a public school over 40 years ago.

Geng Mingzhai insisted that the new policy will not force any applicant to forfeit their land. "Henan is now re-defining and re-registering the land rights of its rural population. Once this process is complete, the land will always belong to the person to whom it is registered, and they will always have the right to share in the benefits from the land, no matter where their residence is," he argued. Zhu Lijia, a professor from the Chinese Academy of Governance, however, believes it would be unfair to urban residents if rural migrants are allowed to enjoy all the benefits of both urban and rural residence permits in perpetuity.

Given the Chinese government's program to promote large-scale mechanized agricultural production, many analysts believe that the new policy aims to pave the way for rural people to transfer or sell their land use rights. The Henan program includes a pledge to "set up a sound compensation system in exchange for farmers' land" and "conduct research into effective ways of marketizing the collectively-owned land," but does not go into details.

Some regions, such as Tianjin and Chongqing municipalities, have taken the lead in land use transactions, allowing rural people to sell or sub-let their land within limited market parameters, or exchange their land for a house in the city. While the reform is generally considered to have been a breakthrough, a lack of legal and policy support has, according to media reports, resulted in an array of problems. Some investors, for example, complained that rural people would often maximize their profits by illegally breaking contracts, while some rural people revealed that they were forced by their village collective to pool their land in order to drive prices up.

"Some of the villagers in our village have exchanged their land for a large sum of money and a house in the city, but many others, including my family, did not," Wang Shuna, a villager in Hebei Province, told *NewsChina*. "I think rural people will be willing to exchange their land for something of equal or higher value. The key is how the government is to convince them that they will be protected in the cities," she added.

THE PRESSURE

Due to similar worries, most migrants in Henan, according to local media, are reluctant to apply for urban residence permits. Worse, due to difficulties in the cities, many have been moving back to villages before the policy is implemented, causing great concern for the local government. As analysts have warned, attracting rural laborers and helping them settle down is not simply a matter of granting them a permit, but requires an array of supporting measures to better accommodate and serve an increased population, an enormous undertaking.

Given that Henan plans to grant new urban residency permits to around 11 million rural people, the local government, according to the 2013 report on the development of Henan Province issued by the Chinese Academy of Social Sciences, needs to invest at least 1.6 trillion yuan (US\$266.7bn) in boosting and improving various forms of infrastructure and public services. Zhengzhou, for example, has suffered two water supply crises this year. If its population continues to expand to seven million by 2020 as planned, the government needs to build at least seven new water plants to ease water shortages. However, there is currently only one such plant under construction.

Funding is an even bigger problem. Experts have proposed to further improve the tax system and introduce private capital into the provision of public services, both of which will require robust, long-term government policy support. "I have two concerns that might obstruct Henan's residence reform. One is that lower-level local governments might misuse the policy to impair rural people's rights to their land, and the other is that the government might drag its feet when it comes to working out supporting policies to guarantee the implementation of reform," said Gu Jianquan of HASS.

Risks and Challenges of Rural-Urban Migration

China has experienced the largest human migration in modern history, with hundreds of millions moving from the rural countryside to burgeoning metropolises—mostly provincial capitals and coastal port cities. In order to deal with diminishing GDP expectations, Chinese leadership is promoting even bigger cities, assuming that increased urbanization will promote domestic consumption, grow the service sector, redistribute wealth, increase labor supply, and revitalize the economy. Officials are deliberating reforms to the *Hukou* system (i.e., household registration system), which limits migrants' access to basic social services such as education and health care—the greatest challenge to effective and healthy urbanization. An alternative solution is to capitalize rural land which officials estimate could create a land market worth $5.6 trillion, though this is criticized by some as a thinly veiled land grab.

Blessing or Burden?

June 2013 Issue of NewsChina | *by Yang Zhongxu and Yu Xiaodong*

A shrinking trade surplus and economic uncertainty are looming over China's new leadership. Their response has been a renewed call for further urbanization to boost domestic consumption. But are even bigger cities the solution?

According to official data, China maintained a steady GDP growth rate of 7.8 percent in 2012. Upon taking office, the country's new leadership set its GDP growth target for 2013 at 7.5 percent. While still enviable, few now doubt that China will fail to sustain the kind of unprecedented economic growth it has managed to maintain through the past two decades. Both domestic and overseas uncertainties including stagnating exports and an aging population have, in the view of all but the most starry-eyed observers, guaranteed an end to China's boom years.

In March, Zhou Xiaochuan, the director of China's central bank, warned National People's Congress (NPC) delegates that the ratio between China's trade surplus and its annual GDP had dropped to 2.6 percent in 2012, a sharp decline from 10.1 percent in 2007, a two-decade low. With Europe still mired in debt crises and the US still struggling to prop up its manufacturing sector, most economists agree that China's surplus, the main driving force behind its GDP growth, is doomed to dwindle further in the coming years.

ALL MATH

In their frantic search for a new source of growth, China's new leadership has long been pushing what its politicians term a "new type of urbanization." The argument goes that urbanization offers a solution to various economic and social challenges by boosting domestic consumption, narrowing the wealth gap by increasing rural income, rebalancing the costs of an aging population and promoting the development of the service sector.

China's new premier Li Keqiang, who assumed Wen Jiabao's mantle in March, is a leading advocate of "new urbanization." In an article published in the State-owned periodical *Qiushi* on February 16, 2012, Li argued that a 1 percent increase in the rate of urbanization translates into 13 million additional urban residents. As urban residents spent 15,900 yuan (US$2,540) per capita in 2011, 3.6 times the consumption of rural residents (4,455 yuan or US$712), these new urban residents would create a 1.5 trillion yuan (US$240bn) increase in domestic consumption, according to Li.

Since China's rural population only contributes 10 percent of national GDP, by transferring surplus rural labor into China's ballooning cities, the government hopes to boost both rural productivity and the declining urban labor force, which has been decimated by China's aging population.

This argument has recently been adopted by experts from various government think tanks, especially those under the National Development and Reform Commission (NDRC), China's top macroeconomic planning agency and one of the most powerful arms of government.

"Massive urbanization will enable China to continue to grow rapidly in the next 10 years," argued Wang Jian, vice-director of the China Society of Macroeconomics under the NDRC. Wang echoed the sentiments of other government pundits, arguing that a massive influx of rural residents will boost demand in the chaotic property market.

Wang's colleague Jiang Kejun added that urbanization can absorb much of China's production surpluses, particularly in the construction materials manufacturing industry, which have increased at an alarming rate as growth has slowed.

Yi Peng, a researcher with the NDRC's Institute of Cities and Towns told *NewsChina* that a potential 300 million new urban residents are currently living in rural areas, contributing less than they might to the national consumption rate.

DISTORTION

However, contrary to the optimistic projections of the NDRC, many independent economists foresee a rocky road ahead for the already-controversial policy of government-initiated urbanization. In a widely-cited commentary published in the *Economic Observer*, economist Xu Xiaonian warned against making urbanization the centerpiece of policymaking.

According to Xu, what the government should do is not to take a proactive approach in promoting urbanization, and instead scale back its interference in the process to allow the market to take over. "Urbanization should be a natural result of the market economy, rather than a policy tool of the government," commented Xu.

Urbanization has been an ongoing process in China. From 1990 to 2012, China's urban population increased from 254 million to 690 million. Correspondently, the percentage of the population represented by urban residents shot up from 22 percent to 52.6 percent, a historic shift which has led to calls for a scaling-back of the pace of government-sponsored urbanization.

The average rate of personal consumption, meanwhile, has barely shifted, confounding the predictions of many economists, who claimed that the new influx of rural residents into urban residents would lead to a consumption boom, as happened in Industrial Revolution Europe and America. China's personal consumption-GDP ratio has remained stagnant at about 35 percent, about half the rate in the US and considerably lower than in most developed and developing nations. Now, analysts are scrabbling to determine why new additions to China's urban class aren't opening their wallets as readily as was predicted.

The blame has largely fallen on a litany of institutional barriers set up by the government which restrict the movement of China's citizens

based on their birthplace. The notorious household registration, or *Hukou* system, has come under particular fire. Effectively an internal visa, it restricts an individual's access to welfare, housing, education, health care and even vehicle ownership to their place of birth.

As a result, rural residents who have lived in cities for most of their working lives cannot access city schools or hospitals, or purchase homes, severely limiting their ability to settle and thus constricting their potential consumption.

Compared to the calculation of the urbanization rate (52.6 percent) officially adopted by the National Bureau of Statistics, which classifies anyone who has lived in a city for more than 6 months as an "urban resident," data from the Ministry of Public Security shows that only 35 percent of the population have an urban *Hukou*. In other words, 17.6 percent of China's population, some 230 million people, are living in areas where they cannot purchase property, obtain subsidized health care, claim welfare or send their children to school. This has forced many migrant workers to leave their dependents in the countryside while working full-time in the cities, further constraining rural development as well as leading to the breakdown of families and the neglect of the most vulnerable in society.

Although it is mandatory for employers to provide basic medical insurance and social security for their employees, this policy is poorly enforced. According to Chen Xiwen, the director of the government's Central Rural Work Leading Group, in 2011 only 18.6 percent of China's floating population were insured by their employer, while only 16.4 percent had access to social security.

UNSETTLING

While rural migrant workers struggle in vain to be fully embraced by the urban environment, the homesteads they leave behind are rapidly being turned into urban land due to the widespread practice of government-led land appropriation. By selling or leasing seized landholdings to enterprises and developers in return for heavy "land grant fees," the Chinese government's revenue stream has outpaced even national GDP growth almost two to one. For this reason, critics have called the government's urbanization drive an effort to urbanize dwindling rural land resources, rather than give impoverished rural citizens the chance of a better life in the cities.

This unbalanced management of limited land resources has led to astronomical increases in housing prices, further limiting the ability of working and middle class Chinese to settle down. In recent years, municipal governments across the country have broken ground on 36 million low-cost housing units, but denied those without an urban *Hukou* the right to purchase any of them.

NEW FORMULA?

It is obvious that China's new leadership, including Premier Li Keqiang, is well aware of these problems. This has prompted economic planners to talk in terms of "humanitarian" urbanization, indicating a shift in focus.

One notable announcement made in the annual government report during the annual NPC session held in March was reform of the *Hukou* system, though no specifics were given. Attempts to reform this hugely unpopular institution have been underway in communities across the country. In 2012, quite a few provinces and several major cities started to allow the children of new urban residents to attend public schools and take the local college entrance examinations, though these young people remained subject to a raft of conditions. Despite being a very small step towards granting new urban residents equal access to public services, local residents, particularly in Shanghai and Beijing where educational resources are most abundant, pushed back, claiming that the influx of "outsiders" was denying resources to their children. "It is just the beginning of a long-term struggle between native and non-native urban residents," Li Tie, director of the Institute of Cities and Towns under the NDRC, told *NewsChina*.

Even some senior officials are pessimistic about the prospect of extending the urban safety net to migrant workers. Chen Xiwen, director of Central Rural Work Leading Group, admitted in 2010 that the State Council had "considered" such measures as early as 2000, but had to drop their plans based on calculations of the potential financial cost of such reforms, which, he claimed, would outstrip even national GDP. It is estimated that extending urban welfare coverage to migrant workers would cost 35 trillion yuan (US$5.6tn). The public purse simply cannot bankroll such a costly reform. The government is hoping to finance this process by modifying a similarly restrictive policy on rural land ownership, allowing residents to trade land on the open market. According to a keynote decree issued by the State Council, this will require local governments to finalize the registration of land rights within their jurisdictions within five years, in order to prevent such a change from causing a legal and administrative catastrophe due to conflicting claims.

Currently, with the exception of a few pilot programs, rural land trading is illegal, due to the official policy that demands that all rural land must be collectively owned. It is estimated that by capitalizing China's rural land market, the government would effectively be creating a land market worth of 40 trillion yuan (US$5.6tn), a figure more than paying for the full "urbanization" of migrant workers. It is hoped that by selling or leasing their collectively owned land back in their rural village, migrant workers will have the resources to properly settle down in cities.

According to a source close to the NDRC, the Commission is drafting a grand urbanization strategy centering around several key issues including granting access to the urban safety net to migrant workers and reforming land ownership policy. Such changes would do away with the unpopular legacies of the planned economy era, but as such will take years to bring to fruition. With a powerful state sector and a predatory real estate industry that have reaped rich rewards from China's State-directed distortion of the urbanization process, it remains a concern whether the country's evermore marginalized rural society will ever genuinely benefit from policies drafted by the very people with the smallest stake in the eventual outcome.

FOR FURTHER STUDY

Response Questions

- What was the One Child Policy in China? When was it first implemented? How has it changed since then?
- What is a *Hukou*? How does it affect migration in China?
- Define the term "Little Emperors". What are common characteristics of "Little Emperors"?
- What is meant by Freestyle Parenting?
- What is a *kenlao*? Why do they exist in China?
- What is the proportion of elderly (defined as those over 60) in China during 2013? What is the expected proportion of elderly in 2020? . . . in 2050?
- What is China's "new demographic normal"?
- What are the three land rights provided to rural residence permit holders?
- What is China's "new urbanization"? What does it expect to solve?
- What do Chinese economic planners mean by "humanitarian urbanization"?

Discussion Questions

- Chinese lawmakers are looking for solutions to both social and economic challenges. As Yang and Xu (2013) pose in their article, "are even bigger cities the solution?"
- What are the factors that lead to higher consumption rates? Do these factors apply to China's situation? What do Chinese analysts and politicians propose as antecedents to higher consumption rates? Do you agree/disagree? Why?
- Urbanization requires a concurrent de-ruralization. How did the US accomplish this? Why does China desire urbanization?
- What is the importance of a *Hukou*? What are the differences between an urban and rural *Hukou*? What is the economic value of an urban *Hukou*? What is the economic value of a rural *Hukou*?
- What were the intended benefits of the One Child Policy? Why are some calling for an end to government control of fertility in China? How would the cancellation of the current Two Child Policy affect the Chinese economy?
- Why is the Chinese social security system at risk of failure? What measures would help mitigate the financial collapse of this system?

Research Exercises

- Which nations restrict the movement of its citizens within their own borders? For example, the United States has several policies which indirectly affect migration from one state to another—lawyers must be barred separately in each state; teachers are credentialed or certified in a single state. As repeated in the articles in this chapter, China implements a household registration system that strictly limits internal migration between regions and cities. What other countries have restrictions on domestic mobility? Make a list of countries (not including China and the US, at least five countries in total) that have such restrictions—describing the requirements or limitations placed on citizens who attempt to move from one region to another.

- As a result of the Chinese government changing the One Child Policy to a Two Child Policy in 2015, there may be an upsurge in the number of babies born in the next few years. Create a list of 3–5 sectors that would benefit over the next 10 years from a baby boom in China. For each sector, search and find at least three listed companies that operate in China today. Indicate each company's current stock market valuation at the time of your research.

- The aging population in China creates challenges for some and opportunities for others. Come up with a brief business plan for a product or service that benefits from a rise in the elderly population in China. Write up a one-paragraph description of the needs of this population, a one-paragraph description of your product/service, and a one/two-paragraph SWOT analysis of your proposed business.

Notes

1 Jie, M. Call to Cancel. *NewsChina*, May 1, 2015.
2 Jones, G. China's Little Emperors. *The Independent*, November 12, 2000.
3 Wang, Y. Second Generation Little Emperors. *NewsChina*, January 1, 2015.
4 Stein, J. Millennials: The Me Me Me Generation. *Time*, May 20, 2013.
5 Wang.
6 Yu, R. Designer Brands for Children. *China Daily European Edition*, July 20, 2015.
7 Steinfeld, J. China's Young People Have Spoken. And What They Want Is Sex. *The Guardian*, July 17, 2015.
8 Bailey, D., Ruddy, M., & Shchukin, M. Ageing China: Changes and Challenges. BBC News Asia. September 20, 2012.
9 Wu, F. Dynamic Demography. *NewsChina*, March 1, 2015.
10 Jie.
11 Xiao-Tian, F., Poston Jr., D.L., & Xiao-Tao, W. China's One-Child Policy and the Changing Family. *Journal of Comparative Family Studies*, 45, 1 (2014): 17–29.
12 Wu.
13 Chen, T. Deadly Nursing-Home Fire Spurs Soul-Searching. *Wall Street Journal Asia Journal*, May 27, 2015.
14 Wang, Q. Graying Area. *NewsChina*, July 1, 2014.

15 Liu, H. The Quality-Quantity Trade-Off: Evidence from the Relaxation of China's One-Child Policy. *Journal Of Population Economics*, *27*, 2 (2014): 565–602.

16 Li, J. Let's Reform the System. *NewsChina*, October 1, 2014.

17 Li, X., Li, E., Li, P.S., Wen, Z., Wen, H., & Abuduhade, R. Integration of Minority Migrant Workers in Lanzhou, China. *Canadian Ethnic Studies*, *45*, 3 (2013): 117–131.

18 National Bureau of Statistics of China. *China Statistical Yearbook*. 2014.

19 Yang, Z. & Yu, X. Blessing or Burden? *NewsChina*, June 1, 2013.

20 Zhang, Y. & Wang, Q. Closing the Divide. *China Daily*, August 21, 2014.

21 Premium Official News. Reforming China's Migration Barriers. January 16, 2015.

22 Xi, Z. & Xie, Y. Migrants No More. *NewsChina*, February 1, 2015.

23 *Global Times*. Rural Residents in Harbin Slow to Embrace New Residence Policies. December 12, 2014.

24 Wen, G.J. & Jinwu, X. The Hukou and Land Tenure Systems as Two Middle Income Traps—The Case of Modern China. *Frontiers of Economics in China*, *9*, 3 (2014): 438–459.

25 Xiaobing, W. & Weaver, N. Surplus Labour and Urbanization in China. *Eurasian Economic Review*, *3*, 1 (2013): 84–97.

26 Jie.

27 Xiao-Tian, F., Poston Jr., D.L., & Xiao-Tao, W.

28 Zhong, H. The Effect of Sibling Size on Children's Health: A Regression Discontinuity Design Approach Based on China's One-Child Policy. *China Economic Review*, *31* (2014): 156–165.

29 Bailey, D., Ruddy, M., & Shchukin, M.

30 Lan, L. Growth of Cities Can Address the Nation's Economic Challenges, NDRC Official Says. *China Daily*, May 14, 2015.

31 Wang, X. Coming or Going, Migrants Alter Dynamics of Labor. *China Daily*, April 13, 2015.

Bibliography

Bailey, D., Ruddy, M., & Shchukin, M. (September 20, 2012). Ageing China: Changes and Challenges. BBC News Asia, retrieved from www.bbc.com/news/world-asia-19630110

Chen, T. (May 27, 2015). Deadly Nursing-Home Fire Spurs Soul-Searching. *Wall Street Journal Asia Journal*.

Global Times (December 12, 2014). Rural Residents in Harbin Slow to Embrace New Residence Policies. *Global Times (China)*, retrieved from www.lexisnexis.com/hottopics/lnacademic

Jie, M. (May 1, 2015). Call to Cancel. *NewsChina*, retrieved from www.newschinamag.com/magazine/call-to-cancel

Jones, G. (November 12, 2000). China's Little Emperors. *The Independent (London)*, retrieved from www.lexisnexis.com/hottopics/lnacademic

Lan, L. (May 14, 2015). Growth of Cities Can Address the Nation's Economic Challenges, NDRC Official Says. *China Daily*, retrieved from www.chinadaily.com.cn/kindle/2015-05/14/content_20715853.htm

Li, J. (October 1, 2014). Let's Reform the System. *NewsChina*, retrieved from www.newschinamag.com/magazine/lets-reform-the-system

Li, X., Li, E., Li, P.S., Wen, Z., Wen, H., & Abuduhade, R. (2013). Integration of Minority Migrant Workers in Lanzhou, China. *Canadian Ethnic Studies*, *45*(3), 117–131, retrieved May 18, 2015 from Academic Search Complete, Ipswich, MA.

Liu, H. (2014). The Quality-Quantity Trade-Off: Evidence from the Relaxation of China's One-Child Policy. *Journal of Population Economics*, *27*(2), 565–602, doi:10.1007/s00148-013-0478-4, retrieved May 18, 2015 from Academic Search Complete, Ipswich, MA.

National Bureau of Statistics of China (2014). *China Statistical Yearbook*, retrieved from www.stats.gov.cn/tjsj/ndsj/2014/indexeh.htm

Premium Official News (January 16, 2015). Reforming China's Migration Barriers. *Premium Official News*, retrieved from www.lexisnexis.com/hottopics/lnacademic

Stein, J. (May 20, 2013). Millennials: The Me Me Me Generation. *Time*.

Steinfeld, J. (July 17, 2015). China's Young People Have Spoken. And What They Want Is Sex. *The Guardian*, retrieved from www.lexisnexis.com/hottopics/-lnacademic

Wang, Q. (July 1, 2014). Graying Area. *NewsChina*, retrieved from www.newschinamag.com/magazine/graying-area

Wang, X. (April 13, 2015). Coming or Going, Migrants Alter Dynamics of Labor. *China Daily*, retrieved from www.chinadaily.com.cn/m/chinahealth/2015-04/13/content_20433714.htm

Wang, Y. (January 1, 2015). Second Generation Little Emperors. *NewsChina*, retrieved from www.newschinamag.com/magazine/second-generation-little-emperors

Wen, G.J. & Jinwu, X. (2014). The Hukou and Land Tenure Systems as Two Middle Income Traps—The Case of Modern China. *Frontiers of Economics In China*, *9*(3), 438–459, doi:10.3868/s060–003–014–0021–1, retrieved May 18, 2015 from Business Source Elite, Ipswich, MA.

Wu, F. (March 1, 2015). Dynamic Demography. *NewsChina*, retrieved from www.newschinamag.com/magazine/dynamic-demography

Xi, Z. & Xie, Y. (February 1, 2015). Migrants No More. *NewsChina*, retrieved from www.newschinamag.com/magazine/migrants-no-more.

Xiaobing, W. & Weaver, N. (2013). Surplus Labour and Urbanization in China. *Eurasian Economic Review*, *3*(1), 84–97, retrieved 18 May 2015 from Business Source Elite, Ipswich, MA.

Xiao-Tian, F., Poston Jr., D.L., & Xiao-Tao, W. (2014). China's One-Child Policy and the Changing Family. *Journal of Comparative Family Studies*, *45*(1), 17–29.

Yang Z. & Yu, X (June 1, 2013). Blessing or Burden? *NewsChina*, retrieved from www.newschinamag.com/magazine/blessing-or-burden

Yu, R. (July 20, 2015). Designer Brands for Children. *China Daily European Edition*, retrieved from www.lexisnexis.com/hottopics/lnacademic

Zhang, Y. & Wang, Q. (August 21, 2014). Closing the Divide. *China Daily—Africa Weekly*, retrieved from www.lexisnexis.com/hottopics/lnacademicThe Effect of Sibling Size on Children's Health: A Regression Discontinuity Design Approach Based on China's One-Child Policy. *China Economic Review (1043951X)*, Dec. 2014, Vol. 31, pp. 156–165.

5

TECHNOLOGY IMPACTS

Introduction

Much as turn-of-the-century India surfaced as the go-to country for Internet-enabled remote services, China a decade later is becoming a giant in online trade. It's the world's biggest Internet marketplace and it's booming. To understand Chinese business, online services and e-commerce must be included, here as well as everywhere else. There are some big players, to be sure, and a lot of new niches being filled.

Alibaba is close to a household name around the world, with its Tmall and Taobao e-commerce offerings, and chief shareholder Jack Ma becoming one of the world's richest men on the firm's NYSE IPO. Runners up Jingdong and even Amazon China are also making a huge impact.

But extending well beyond traditional e-commerce, the Internet is changing China profoundly in areas as diverse as instant messaging, online banking, on-demand transportation, and online dating. As one impressive example, in June 2015 Uber reported making almost 1 million trips a day in its Chinese markets (LATimes.com, June 2015).

The Great Firewall of China

It's no secret that the Chinese Communist Party doesn't want uncontrolled online information flow from abroad. Internet censorship has been prevalent for decades, and is becoming more intensive under the rule of President Xi Jinping. Sites including Google, Facebook, Twitter, Yahoo, Wikipedia, BBC, and Amnesty International are among the over 3,700 blocked[1] by the Great Firewall. And not only are many foreign sites blocked. Over 400 Sina Weibo search terms are also intercepted and dumped. In March 2015, China moved from passive blocking of website access to launching denial of service cyber attacks on some of those foreign sites, particularly those tracking the Great Firewall and those offering workarounds for it[2].

Despite the obvious handicap to the population and to China's economic potential in sharing in the world's knowledge, Beijing continues and intensifies this information blocking apparently out of fear that if the people had access to a free flow of facts and opinions, social instability might result. This fear is not entirely unjustified, as China's history is replete with rebellions, uprisings, and coups. An ancient, ingrained aspect of Chinese culture is the "Mandate of Heaven", which, while granting rulers authority based on their ability to govern well and fairly, also justifies overthrowing them should they fail to do so.

ARTICLES

Rise of the Internet

Mobile Messaging Wars

In a challenge to the high-priced messaging services sold by the three members of China's state-owned mobile phone oligopoly (China Mobile, China Unicom and China Telecom), WeChat introduced an "over-the-top" (OTT) app using Internet data to send texts. This popular app bit so severely into China Mobile's revenue that it started to flex its political muscle to punish WeChat with extra fees. Sun Zhe describes this battle between innovative private enterprise and the SOE dinosaur, with a surprising win-win solution outlined at the conclusion of "Data Discrimination."

Data Discrimination

June 2013 Issue of NewsChina | *by Sun Zhe*

China's State-owned telecom giants have enlisted the help of the industry regulator to impose charges on a hot smartphone app that is eroding their profits

To China's mobile carriers, some data flowing through their networks are different from the rest.

China Mobile, the world's largest mobile carrier, has been leading the country's three State-owned telecom oligopolists in lobbying industry regulators to impose higher charges on data used by mobile messaging app WeChat, claiming that information sent through the app is overloading its network and could potentially cause a collapse.

WeChat, an app developed by China's largest online gaming and social networking company Tencent, is the most popular messenger among China's smartphone users. A free text- and voice-messaging tool that also incorporates social networking and a host of other features, WeChat's popularity is due in part to the fact that it can cut down users' expenditure on phone calls and text messages.

EXTRA CHARGE

Phone calls made through the China Mobile network have seen a severe drop in quality over the past two years, according to Xiang Ligang, CEO of industry portal *cctime.com*. Xiang attributed this to network bottlenecks caused by the large amounts of data sent by WeChat users.

China Mobile, with its user base of around 710 million, has more to lose from overloading than its rivals, said Xiang. He added that China Telecom and China Unicom, the other two State titans whose user bases total 161 million and 239 million respectively, are better placed to adjust their technology.

However, the reduction in call quality does not justify the extra charges China Mobile hopes to impose on WeChat, according to Fu Liang, an independent industry analyst based in Beijing.

"If the telecom carriers cannot handle the data traffic, it's their own problem," said Fu.

Since WeChat users have already purchased data from their mobile carrier, a supplementary charge is unreasonable, said Fu. He added that the company should either upgrade its network or raise the charges for its data service, instead of forcing app developers to charge their users.

The majority of China Mobile's subscribers use the company's 2G GPRS network, a protocol more susceptible to data bottlenecks than modern networks. Only 13 percent of China Mobile users are subscribed to its 3G network, in contrast to one third of China Unicom's and 44 percent for China Telecom, which means China Mobile's revenue is more reliant on charges for traditional phone calls and text messages than its two rivals.

Fu Liang said that the major motivation behind the move by China Mobile, whose profits grew 2.7 percent to 129.3 billion yuan (US\$20.8bn) in 2012, is the threat posed to its revenue streams by the rise of WeChat and other "over-the-top" (OTT) apps, those that enable users to circumvent carrier charges by sending messages via mobile Internet.

According to the Ministry of Industry and Information Technology (MIIT), in 2012, growth in the number of text messages sent by Chinese cell phone users slowed from 6.2 percent to only 2.1 percent, the lowest growth over the past four years. In the first two months of 2013, the number of text messages fell 10.6 percent compared with the same period last year.

Carriers' average monthly revenue per user declined to 68 yuan (US\$11) in 2012, a slip of 5.6 percent from 2011. However, its data traffic almost tripled last year, and data revenues grew by about 54 percent, thanks to the growing popularity of apps like WeChat. Around 12 percent of China Mobile's total revenue now comes from its data services.

"Now, technological progress is pressuring mobile carriers to turn to data services for revenue, but for the Chinese telecom giants, the text message and phone call business could be too lucrative to give up on," Fu said.

WeChat, launched in early 2011, has dealt a fatal blow to Fetion, China Mobile's own messenger app, which has yet to incorporate voice messaging and at present can only be used on phones subscribed to China Mobile.

Fetion used to be the country's second most popular instant messenger service, behind QQ, Tencent's online messenger that boasts a user base of 780 million.

GOING GLOBAL

So far, WeChat has amassed more than 300 million registered users, including more than 40 million overseas, making it one of only a handful of fully Chinese-owned, Chinese-built apps to make a dent in the international market.

The company's international expansion is currently focused on Southeast Asian markets, and WeChat has already become the top grossing mobile app in Thailand and Malaysia.

Tencent has also opened a US office in preparation for a marketing push in the country, although currently, the majority of WeChat users in the US are Chinese people living and studying in the country, who use the app to stay in touch with their family and friends back in China, as well as with other Chinese people in the US.

Miao Wei, minister for industry and information technology, in late March voiced his support for the telecom carriers' plan to start charging WeChat for extra data.

Given that China Mobile is a State-owned oligopolist whose senior management frequently pass through a "revolving door" into high-ranking positions at the MIIT, the regulator has every incentive to side with China Mobile, according to Fu Liang, the industry analyst.

While Tencent is yet to monetize its WeChat service, it is unlikely that potential government-imposed charges will be passed directly onto its users—instead, it might try to sell games or premium services through the app, or integrate e-commerce. For instance, its location-based search feature might enable restaurants or cafes to sell coupons to WeChat users in the area.

"We want to join hands with carriers to offer more value-added services in order to sustain a win-win situation that would help enhance their interests," said Liu Sishan, a spokesperson with Tencent, in an email to *NewsChina*.

The two parties—the telecom operators and OTT developers—should team up to provide better services and create a larger market to generate more profit, rather than attack each other before the market matures, according to Dong Xu, an industry analyst with Beijing-based Analysys International.

In a message sent to all users of WeChat in early April, Tencent vowed that it would never charge for the service.

"If Tencent were to charge for WeChat, its users would turn to other similar free apps, and there are a great many of these," said Dong. "Chinese have become accustomed to free internet products and services."

Dong predicted that Tencent, a giant of the private business world, would pay the carriers a lump sum to settle the case. Tencent's 2012 revenue totaled 43.9 billion yuan (US$7.1bn), 54 percent up from the previous year, and its profits grew about a quarter over the same period to 12.3 billion yuan (US$2 bn).

But even if a cash payoff solves the problem this time, private enterprises may be wondering whether innovation is really worth the risk of angering a State-owned dinosaur. If a giant like Tencent can be punished for creating an internationally successful product, the future does not look bright for smaller private companies, or for the industry as a whole.

Why is Online Video a Loser?

The Chinese appetite for foreign video content is insatiable, particularly for American dramas like *Game of Thrones* and *Breaking Bad*, and Korean melodramas. Despite this, Chinese YouTube lookalike giant Youku-Tudou has lost big money every year since its 2010 NASDAQ IPO. Between licensing fees and increasing government interference, offering prime video content via the Internet has been a losing proposition in China. "Video Killed the Video Stars" by Sun Zhe explains the underpinnings of the online video business in China.

Video Killed the Video Stars

February 2015 Issue of NewsChina | *by Sun Zhe*

Facing cutthroat competition for content and tightening government regulation, China's fast-growing online video services are still far from profitable.

While officially licensed episodes of imported TV shows like *Breaking Bad* have kept Chinese Internet users glued to their computer screens over the past couple of years, China's online video platforms that host such high-profile content have been more concerned with breaking even.

Since online video giant Youku-Tudou listed on the Nasdaq in 2010, it has racked up accumulative losses of about 2 billion yuan (US$323m).

A deal signed late November 2014, which gave Tencent Video the exclusive rights to distribute HBO dramas like *Game of Thrones* and *The Newsroom*, caused a stir among rivals like Youku-Tudou, Sohu Video and iQIYI. Given these shows' immense popularity in China, these worries are not unfounded.

Only a week before Tencent's deal was inked, Youku-Tudou posted a loss of 180 million yuan (US$30m) in the third quarter, triggering the resignation of its chief financial officer. However, this failed to discourage the company from pledging to spend even more money on licensing content in the next year. Copyright purchase now accounts for more than forty percent of Youku-Tudou's operating costs.

CONTENT COMPETITION

Online video is one of the fastest growing sectors in China's tech industry. The user base of China's online video platforms grew by more than a third in 2013, totaling 428 million, or 80 percent of all Chinese Internet users, by the end of that year. This figure is expected to top 700 million by 2017, according to industry consultancy firm iResearch, at which time the market is expected to be worth 40 billion yuan (US$6.5bn).

While the majority of content on China's video portals is uploaded by users themselves, the majority of viewers watch professionally produced TV series and movies, with American and Korean dramas among the most popular. The average online video website user is younger, better educated and wealthier than other Internet users, and platforms rely on advertising revenue from companies eager to reach this sought-after demographic, allowing users to access the majority of content for free.

As advertising revenues are determined by traffic, video platforms must attract users by offering popular shows, and competition for exclusive rights to host the hottest content—particularly foreign-produced TV shows—is becoming expensive.

American drama series are most popular among those with a college education, while Korean soap operas are popular among Chinese females of almost all age groups—China imported 15 times more Korean soap operas in 2014 than in 2013. In early November 2014, Youku-Tudou became the exclusive China licensee for Korean soap opera *Pinocchio* for a record fee of US$280,000 per episode, or US$5.6 million for the whole season.

In addition to big-name foreign content, partnerships with certain domestic entertainment shows have also proven effective in driving traffic.

Video platforms' financial reports show that so far, few content purchases have generated much of a return on investment. In 2013, Sohu Video purchased the rights to *The Voice of China*—the Chinese version of Dutch reality singing competition franchise *The Voice*—for 100 million yuan (US$16.2m). However, the company only generated 200 million (US$32.4m) in advertising revenue from the show, barely enough to cover the operating costs incurred by hosting it.

To make matters worse, the Chinese government has recently tightened up its regulation of the online video market—a move many interpreted to be in defense of China's ailing State-funded television networks.

In recent years, Chinese television stations, all of them State-owned, have been steadily losing advertising revenues to online video services as many people, particularly the young, are watching fewer hours of television in favor of online video. Analysts attribute this trend to the heavy sanitization and censorship of content on State television channels.

In late 2014, China's television regulator, the State Administration of Press, Publication, Radio, Film and Television (SAPPRFT), issued an order prohibiting video platforms from transmitting to television set-top boxes. Video platforms are required to enter into partnerships with one of the seven Internet television content services licensed by the regulator itself, all of which are controlled by large State-owned television stations, on the grounds that Internet content should be monitored and only "healthy" online videos may be played on the nation's television sets. The seven licensed services then take a portion of the revenues from their video partner platform.

When the latest SAPPRFT regulations were issued in June 2014, the share price of LeTV, a major video portal, dropped 20 percent over the next two days of trading.

PRODUCE WHAT YOU PLAY

Though the major market players are yet to see any profit from their online video hosting businesses, investment in the industry has continued to increase, driven mostly by competition between China's three Internet giants Baidu, Alibaba and Tencent.

In April 2014, Jack Ma, president of e-commerce giant Alibaba, acquired about 20 percent of Youku-Tudou's stock to become its second largest shareholder. Baidu, China's dominant search engine, acquired iQIYI, another major video portal, in 2012. Social media giant Tencent's well-monetized online gaming ecosystem provides it with funds to purchase the rights to TV shows, movies and documentaries owned by companies like HBO, Time Warner and National Geographic.

However, there is evidence to show that Chinese Internet giants are not satisfied with relying on expensive content to generate traffic for their video websites—some have begun to move upstream in the industry. After setting up a film production fund in early 2014, Alibaba was also in investment discussions with Hollywood companies shortly after its record-breaking IPO on the New York Stock Exchange in September 2014. Tencent is also reported to have been investing in content production.

Diors Man, a series of online comedy shorts produced by Sohu Video, starring a number of celebrities, has so far been viewed more than 3 billion times. Meanwhile, *Morning Call*, a lecture-style talk show series on a wide variety of topics hosted by a popular folk singer, attracts an average of more than one million views per episode on Youku-Tudou.

However, efforts to produce strong original content have been undermined by scandal. In one recent case, Youku-Tudou allegedly duped a team of young artists into revealing the techniques involved in the production of a video uploaded to Youku-Tudou's platform, in which a small video camera attached to a hot air balloon was used to shoot photographs of the Earth from the stratosphere. Unbeknownst to the artists, the Youku-Tudou production team used the information to re-shoot the video without crediting the original creators.

While Youku-Tudou has since removed the offending video and apologized for the wrongdoing, its public image—like its business model—remains uncertain.

e-Business

The Record Alibaba IPO

Who knew that the 2014 record-breaking NYSE IPO for BABA didn't really float shares in Alibaba at all, but rather in a Cayman-based shell company owned primarily by outside investors, loosely tied to Alibaba through a questionable legal structure called a "Variable Interest Entity?" If the IPO investors knew, it didn't slow them from driving the stock price up 36 percent within hours of the opening. "No Alchemy" by Li Jia details the machinations Jack Ma went through to float Alibaba. Ma rejected Chinese exchanges due to onerous government interference in stock trading and turned instead to a tortuous legal structure created to allow the foreign floatation. Alibaba has made a splash on the NYSE—but will its success affect the reform agenda on the Chinese stock market?

Jumping through tough regulatory hoops, Jack Ma was able to put together what became the largest IPO in history. How he did it may surprise you.

No Alchemy

December 2014 Issue of NewsChina | *by Li Jia*

Why can't Chinese companies innovate like American ones? This perennial question inevitably raises its head whenever Apple releases a new gadget, signaling the commencement of national hand-wringing that sees Chinese media, analysts and officials variously blaming the education system, State banks, foreign protectionism and much else besides.

However, the recent international media attention on Alibaba and its founder, former English language tutor Jack Ma, seems to have put an end to the yearly tradition—Alibaba, the world's largest e-commerce company by some distance, has built its success on hundreds of millions of small Chinese retailers and consumers, changing far more Chinese lives than Apple.

In mid-September, Alibaba raised US$25 billion with its long expected initial public offering at the NYSE, the highest-value IPO in history. The share price of BABA (Alibaba's NYSE stock name) soared by 36 percent in the two-and-a-half hours following its IPO—since then, it has remained at least 22 percent higher than its IPO price, and has at times risen to rival Apple's. Alibaba plans to spend its windfall expanding into China's rural areas and buying up US companies. International investment banks have received huge underwriting commissions. Related industries, such as logistics and packaging, will benefit. As Ma has repeatedly said, Alibaba is a life-changing "ecosystem."

However, swaths of excited Chinese stock investors have found themselves unexpectedly turned away from the party, many of them realizing for the first time that BABA is not the e-commerce platform they know and love, but a foreign-registered company incorporated in the Cayman Islands, the majority of which is owned by Japanese IT company Softbank and US Internet company Yahoo!

Meanwhile, international investors have been continually reminded by analysts that the BABA at which they are throwing money is effectively a shell company that relies on cashflow from the Alibaba mothership in Hangzhou, Zhejiang Province, the majority of which is owned by Jack Ma. In theory, if the Chinese government or the famously eccentric Ma were to change their mind, their shares could become worthless overnight.

BABA, OH REALLY?

In their early days of growth, Internet companies tend to absorb huge investment with little likelihood of making any money. Ma, in his former job as a tutor, had insufficient collateral for a bank loan, and under China's securities rules, a company with no profit record is not eligible for floatation on the stock market. Venture capital, often the savior of new hi-tech, high-risk companies, was basically unheard of in China when Alibaba was founded in 1999, and foreign capital was generally off-limits for Internet-based companies.

The solution for Alibaba and its like was often to register a "variable interest entity" (VIE) and establish an arrangement with an overseas shell company, normally in a low-tax territory such as the Cayman or Virgin islands, allowing access to foreign capital while guaranteeing a license to operate in China.

Alibaba's Cayman shell, held primarily by Yahoo! and Softbank, and the Chinese VIEs owned and controlled primarily by Jack Ma, are linked by three layers of foreign and Chinese companies, a complex tax work-around. So-called "control agreements" within this structure ensure that Cayman Alibaba controls the company's operations, and the profits from Ma's Chinese VIEs return to the Caymans in the form of fees for services and technical support. China's forex controls are also circumvented in the process.

The inherent risk of this business model, as Wang Shuqian of the East Associates Law Firm told *NewsChina*, is that one entity, to circumvent policy restrictions, gives money to another with the requisite license, legally entrusting it to act on its behalf. As a result, the first entity's rights, interests and investment are in the hands of the entrustee. If the second entity sells the first's property without consent, and the entrustee cannot be proven to have illegally colluded with the purchasing party prior to the deal, the first is left either with nothing or, at best, compensation.

The existing law does not specify whether or not using the VIE structure to get around foreign investment restrictions is illegal. A number of Chinese companies, mostly Internet firms but also some in other service and manufacturing sectors, has been using the VIE method since 2000, which many saw as an indicator of tacit approval from Chinese regulators.

However, the development of China's regulatory framework and Jack Ma's behavior over the past few years have accentuated widely held concerns over the dual risks to both legitimacy and reliability inherent in the VIE model, which has underwritten the take-off and boom of China's Internet companies for more than a decade.

TIGHTENING NET

While there is little to indicate that foreign investment restrictions in VIE-oriented areas will be eased anytime soon, there are increasingly clear warning signals that the Chinese authorities are becoming less tolerant of VIEs. In January 2014, restrictions on foreign equity holdings in e-commerce and cloud computing companies were eased in the Shanghai Free Trade Zone, but not enough to allow wholly foreign-owned enterprises like Alibaba in.

In 2011, the Ministry of Commerce required that the acquisition of Chinese companies with foreign investment through control agreements be subject to national security reviews. The same year, the US Securities and Exchange Commission (SEC) disclosed that Buddha Group had withdrawn its application to list in the US after the company's Hebei Province VIE was told by the local government that the arrangement was "in contravention of current Chinese management policies related to foreign-invested enterprises and, as a result, [was] against public policy."

In 2009, the Chinese publications authority prohibited foreign investment in the online gaming industry through "indirect methods of signing relevant contracts or provision of technical support." In 2012, China's Supreme Court ruled that an investment by a Hong Kong company into China Minsheng Bank via one of Minsheng's mainland shareholders was ineffective, on the grounds that the deal aimed to "illegally circumvent" China's restrictions on foreign investment in the banking sector. The case has been widely cited by Chinese and international lawyers as an indicator that VIEs could be defined as illegal for the same reason.

If new rules against VIEs are enacted in the future, say the prospectuses of Alibaba and other companies using Chinese VIEs, the operation licenses held by the VIEs could be revoked, or the flow of revenue from VIEs to their overseas parent companies could be blocked. While few expect VIEs to be completely outlawed overnight, the uncertainty remains a looming risk. Kevin Rosier, analyst with the US-China Economic and Security Review Commission, noted in his recent report that it would be preferable for China to ban VIEs sooner rather than later, since short-term losses would be less trouble than long-term ambiguity.

In 2011, when required by China's central bank to explain the VIE arrangement in order to acquire a license for his third-party payments platform Alipay, Jack Ma voluntarily terminated the control agreement between Alibaba and his Hangzhou-based VIE in control of Alipay, without informing Yahoo! and Softbank in advance. The two foreign companies had no choice but to negotiate with Ma for compensation. Ma responded to questions about his integrity at a press conference, saying that he had to make the "only right, albeit imperfect, decision," in order to avoid the risk of losing the license due to protracted board-room negotiations. His unilateral action, no matter how commercially and legally savvy, has undeniably left foreign investors wary of Chinese VIEs, and Ma's integrity.

A so-called "partnership" arrangement further consolidates Ma's dominance of Alibaba's business operation. A majority of Alibaba's board of directors are nominated or appointed by Jack Ma and his senior managers, minority-stake holders in the company. While this could avoid embarrassing situations like Apple's 1985 ejection of visionary founder Steve Jobs in pursuit of short-term share prices, it also puts investors, particularly small ones, at a significant disadvantage.

NOT EASY

Alibaba's listing has also put Chinese regulators under greater pressure than ever before. Only Chinese companies reporting minimum profit standards set by the existing rules can file to list on the stock market in China. Once they have filed for listing, their ability to profit in future is subject to review by the China Securities Regulatory Commission (CSRC). This system has long been criticized as neither friendly to hi-tech growth companies, nor to market demand for stock. Chinese investors and many analysts blame the system for any and all problems on the market, accounting fraud at listed companies, corruption of CSRC review committees, deterring good companies, and declining share prices. A veteran private equity manager, who asked not to be named, told *NewsChina* they were forced to "give up on" various good companies in sectors that China was keen to develop, such as environmental protection, due to the unreasonable rules governing access to the stock market.

An overhaul of the system was on the CPC's sweeping reform agenda unveiled in November 2013. At the end of that month, the CSRC announced reform guidelines focusing on full and proper corporate information disclosure, leaving the assessment of a company's profit-making ability to investors. Stock exchanges will now review applicant companies. Revision of the Securities Law is scheduled to be tabled at the national legislators' meeting before the end of this year, and a draft of new IPO rules would be unveiled on that basis. It seems that for Chinese stock investors, a lavish investment banquet lies behind this as-yet unopened door.

Some experts warn that this expectation is based on a misunderstanding of the US market which is often used as a reference point. As Professor Wang Xiao at Central University of Finance and Economics in Beijing explained to *NewsChina*, in practice, the US SEC reviews companies by asking thorough questions about business risks that might affect the profitability of the company filing for an IPO, and the three main US stock exchanges exercise final discretion over which companies can trade there after their IPO. The NYSE, for example, revised its rules to accommodate Alibaba's partnership structure, since it believes that Alibaba will bring value. By the same token, a company that meets the stock exchange's standards but is not regarded as valuable would not be allowed to trade. All of this, Wang stressed, is exactly the profitability-oriented "value judgment" that Chinese investors want to remove from the existing Chinese system.

More importantly, some key factors in the US system are either weak or absent in China's case. Exchanges in the US are market-oriented companies, while those in China are quasi-government agencies whose leaders are appointed by the CSRC. Without reform of China's own exchanges, analysts worry that corruption in CSRC-sponsored review commissions today will be replicated on the trading floor tomorrow.

Many lawyers, acquisition-hungry players and short-sellers who profit from share price drops are always on the lookout for chances to take advantage of business and legal vulnerabilities of listed companies. Wang noted that their pursuit of their own interests another powerful market discipline force for investor protection in the US, and a powerful deterrent that forces companies to think twice about going public. This is an important reason, Wang argued, that the number of US listed companies has remained below 5,500 for so many years. Many analysts have pointed out that the risk of lawsuits from overseas brands over counterfeit goods could force Alibaba to improve its business practices. In China, however, short selling is restricted, and the legal procedure for class action lawsuits is lacking.

Developed markets are also cautious about full deregulation without proper conditions. In 2013, the Hong Kong Securities and Futures Commission (HKEx) rejected market pressure to revise its rules to accommodate Alibaba's partnership structure, prompting Alibaba to set its sights on New York. In an article in October 2013 explaining the decision to retain the requirement that shareholders at HKEx-listed companies enjoy equal voting rights—a move that cost the HKEx Alibaba—Charles Li, the stock market's CEO, said that the Hong Kong market was "less institutionalized and less litigious" than the US, and its "checks and balances" were not as strong. In November 2013, HKEx imposed stricter rules on the listing of VIEs. The stock market in the Chinese mainland is even weaker than Hong Kong in both these regards.

Given this, even outspoken deregulation advocates, like Professor Liu Jipeng at China University of Political Science and Law, warned at a forum at the end of 2013 the danger of regarding the reform as an instant and wholesale deregulation, without considering the as-yet undeveloped market infrastructure and legal framework.

Wang Xiao called for steady, consistent steps in order to send clear, predictable signals to market players. For example, the CSRC has suspended IPO reviews from time to time over the years in response to market fears that new stock supply would further drag prices down. Wang suggested that regulators maintain a reliable pace in their reviewing of candidates—regardless of market fluctuations—in order to let traders and candidates know how long the review process is likely to take, and the chances of listing successfully. The CSRC tried this in 2010, announcing that its review process would take 3 months, and about 200 companies would be approved, with roughly a 10 percent failure rate. However, this practice was soon scrapped when it met with resistance from the market. This pandering to short-term interests, he said, distorted both the market and the reform agenda in the long-term.

Alibaba's coup, and the NYSE's flexibility, have made it unprecedentedly difficult for regulators to continue shrugging off the market's hopes of reform.

The e-Giants Do Battle

With Chinese Internet users now numbering a staggering 650 million, nearly half the country's population, and international tech consultant IDC predicting that two-thirds of all retail in China will be online by 2020, the e-commerce space is becoming white hot. Online giants Alibaba and Tencent are locked in a major battle for dominance on many fronts while Internet-related acquisitions occur at a dizzying pace. Zhang Yanan puts the complex and fast-changing landscape of Chinese e-commerce in perspective in his article, "Boom and Boom."

Boom and Boom

March 2015 Issue of NewsChina | *by Zhang Yanan*

Having seen unprecedented growth in 2014, 2015 will likely be another iconic year for Internet businesses in China, the world's largest e-commerce market

The year 2014 was one of the most successful in the history of China's Internet industry. Top of the bill was Chinese e-commerce giant Alibaba, whose record-breaking US$25 billion IPO on the New York Stock Exchange made it the world's largest e-commerce company.

Earlier, in May, China's second-largest e-commerce company JD.com raised US$1.78 billion as it prepared to list on the Nasdaq. In March, Weibo, often referred to as China's Twitter, raised US$500 million. At least eight other Chinese Internet companies also went public in 2014.

Besides these high-profile IPOs, the country's major Internet enterprises experienced exponential growth in 2014. Alibaba's revenue in the third quarter of 2014, for example, reached US$2.7 billion, equivalent to 54 percent year-on-year growth.

2014 IN RETROSPECT

To a large extent, the boom in China's Internet industry has been fueled by the sheer number of Internet users in the country. By the end of 2014, the number of netizens in China reached 650 million, accounting for 48 percent of the total population, a 2 percent increase on the previous year.

In the meantime, the number of mobile Internet users has reached 554 million, with a growth rate double that of PC-based Internet users. As most new mobile users are under 25 years old, a new Internet landscape is reshaping the software and hardware development, as well as the overall business models, of e-businesses.

With the rapid expansion of the mobile Internet customer base, China witnessed unprecedented penetration of mobile Internet companies into many traditional industries in 2014.

Acknowledging the importance of the Internet as a platform upon which to upgrade China's industry, the Chinese government has also launched a number of policies to support the development of Internet companies.

In February 2014, the authorities announced the establishment of the central Internet security and informatization leading group, to be headed by Chinese President Xi Jinping, who has vowed to make China a "strong Internet power." In the meantime, in his government report presented to the National People's Congress (NPC), Premier Li Keqiang launched a policy package he called "broadband China," aiming to increase both the geographic scale and speed of Internet coverage. According to a more detailed plan released jointly by 14 different ministries, the "broadband China" policy package aims to extend Internet coverage to 13,800 villages, covering 30 million more families.

In November 2014, China hosted the World Internet Conference, evidence of the Chinese government's growing interest in promoting its status in the global Internet landscape.

ALIBABA VS TENCENT

The most phenomenal development in China's internet industry in 2014 was the emerging rivalry between heavyweights Alibaba Group and Tencent Holdings, which have established a dominant role in China's Internet landscape in recent years.

Establishing its dominance in the field of e-commerce, Alibaba expanded into various fields through a number of acquisitions throughout 2014. These mergers and acquisitions were not limited to online retail companies such as FirstDibs, a New York-based retailer of interior design and fashion products, but also a variety of fields such as education (Tutorgroup), entertainment (ChinaVision and Wasu Media), travel (Byecity), messaging apps (Tango), online video (Youku), logistics (China Smart Logistics and Singpost), group buying (Meituan) and soccer (Guangzhou Evergrande FC).

To counter Alibaba's dominance in the online retail sector, Tencent Holdings, another Chinese Internet giant, established a strategic alliance with JD.com, China's second largest online retail platform. Tencent sold its own business-to-customer (B2C) platform QQ Wanggou and consumer-to-consumer (C2C) platform PaiPai to JD.com, in exchange for 15 percent of JD in March, and another 5 percent when JD.com went public in May.

However, at the core of Tencent's strategy is its popular messaging and social networking smartphone app WeChat. With more than 600 million users, Tencent launched a host of promotions that succeeded in attracting millions of the app's users to link their bank accounts to its payment function. Meanwhile, Tencent also began allowing vendors to open storefronts on WeChat, turning the app into a powerful tool for traditional businesses.

Although Tencent has embarked into other fields by spending over US$2 billion on US Internet firms like the e-commerce company Fab, as well as gaming companies Riot Games and Epic Games, its acquisitions have focused on promoting its business ecosystem.

Tencent bought a 20 percent stake in Dianping, China's leading crowd-sourced review website, and in June, purchased 20 percent of 58.com, China's Craigslist equivalent, for US$736 million.

In August, Tencent reached an agreement with Dalian Wanda group, China's largest commercial property company, and Baidu, China's leading online search engine, to set up a 5 billion yuan (US$814 million) e-commerce joint venture.

Tencent's efforts in penetrating in the "online-to-offline" (O2O) field pose a serious challenge to Alibaba's dominance in e-commerce, and the competition between the two will be a major theme of China's Internet market in 2015.

LOOKING AHEAD

With new infrastructure investment, it is expected that Internet access will further penetrate into China's third- and fourth-tier cities, aiming to reach the 400 million rural people who are not yet connected to the Internet.

It is estimated that 450 million smartphones will be sold in 2015 in China, accounting for 31 percent of the world's total, or three times the number sold in the US, the world's second largest smartphone market; 71 percent of the smartphones sold in China will be 4G-ready.

With the expansion of mobile Internet, Internet companies will infiltrate into conventional industries on a massive scale. International Internet consultancy IDC predicts that by 2020, 66.7 percent of business transactions in China will be related to e-commerce. In 2015, Internet companies will expand their presence into fields like health care, education, transportation and entertainment.

In the meantime, online retail will remain a major battleground for China's Internet giants. With Alibaba and Tencent locked in a race in developing China's online-to-offline (O2O) market, both will be looking to newly emerging fields. For example, with Chinese demand for foreign products rapidly on the rise, Alibaba and JD.com have been promoting cross-border e-commerce. Currently, quite a few American retail companies, such as Costco, have begun cooperating with Alibaba to sell their goods directly to Chinese consumers.

Another key field will be Internet finance. In March 2014, China launched a pilot project to allow the establishment of five banks owned entirely by private companies. While Tencent has officially launched its Internet bank, Shenzhen Qianhai Weizhong Bank, also known as WeBank, Alibaba is also preparing to launch its own Internet bank, Zhejiang Internet Commerce Bank, which analysts predict may open in 2015.

The changes that private online banking brings to China's financial sector will be a major focus of that industry. Other Internet-related fields to watch include automobiles, wearable technology and Internet security.

Acknowledging the importance of the Internet as a platform upon which to upgrade China's industry, the Chinese government has also launched a number of policies to support the development of Internet companies.

Retail e-Commerce Isn't Easy in China

Doing retail e-commerce in China comes with its special challenges. Selling products at a low price isn't enough. As dynamic CLO Lee Cheng of Newegg explained, a typical Chinese online customer will often order the same product from multiple sites. Since credit cards are relatively scarce in China, the products are usually shipped COD. So the buyer will accept and pay for the first product to arrive, and refuse the rest. As you can expect, this drives up the cost of doing business. Even worse, there are no widespread delivery services such as UPS or FedEx covering the country, so the online retailer has to rely on a network of small operators zipping around on motorbikes to get products into the hands of customers. In short, outbound logistics can be an exceptional challenge for the online B2C firm in China. This and other problems are on their way to being solved. Online retail in China was expected to exceed US$500 billion in 2015, more than doubling the 2012 figure, according to Scott Cendrowski writing for *Fortune.* *

In "When Pigs Fly," Chen Jiying and Li Jia take a further look at Chinese online e-commerce. Black Friday 2014 was a banner day for Amazon in China, which saw a five-fold increase in sales from previous weeks' levels. And this for its inventory of over 150,000 *US-made* products. Yes — US-made. Despite the difficulties of actually getting goods into the hands of customers, and high customs duties, foreign online retailers are beginning to flourish in China.

* *The Week*, p.11 (Oct 16, 2015).

When Pigs Fly

February 2015 Issue of NewsChina | *by Chen Jiying, Li Jia*

China's embracing of e-commerce is bringing global brands to Chinese consumers, but can it successfully integrate itself into the global supply chain online?

While US retailers saw a decline in the numbers of shoppers, and their total spending, over the Black Friday weekend, across the Pacific, history was being made. Within 48 hours of the launch of its first ever Black Friday promotion in China, Amazon saw five times as much sales value on its newly-launched Chinese-language website as it saw during a trial run two weeks before. It currently offers some 150,000 products delivered directly from the US. This milestone was reached in a market home to more consumers than a combination of the US and two EUs.

Nearly all its Chinese competitors, Alibaba, JD and Suning, which are dominating the domestic e-commerce market, immediately joined the fray by partnering with US department stores and doling out coupons to

Chinese customers. All these Chinese retailers are currently scrambling to build a logistics network overseas. The year 2014 was even dubbed in the Chinese media as the dawn of China's era of "buying international."

Chinese consumers, emerging and smaller foreign brands, e-commerce service providers and growth-oriented policymakers are all welcoming this new age of e-retail. Nielsen, a market research company, estimated in a report commissioned by PayPal in September that 18 million Chinese *"hai tao zu,"* a slang term for online shoppers making international purchases, spent a total of US$35 billion in 2013. The report predicted that China would be home to twice as many hai tao zu in 2018, spending 4.6 times as much on international purchases. Hai tao zu represent a very small percentage of Chinese shoppers online, with many seeing this sector as a major area of potential growth. PayPal's October survey projected growth of 52 percent in cross-border online shopping by Chinese consumers for the next 12 months.

Chinese regulators have also underwritten these rosy predictions. Since October 2013, bonded areas facilitating faster delivery and customs clearance have been established in a total of seven cities to provide consumers with easier access to cross-border e-commerce.

Analysts warned interested groups not to lose their minds in this apparent e-trading frenzy, with risks and uncertainties in mind.

DIFFICULTY

In the 1980s and 1990s, Chinese consumers, denied access at home, made shopping a priority in overseas trips. The trend has continued; however, now it is fueled less by scarcity in China and more by concerns over domestic product safety and quality, along with lower prices abroad. An explosion in e-commerce platforms has made it possible to do this online; but a number of barriers have prevented this habit from going fully mainstream.

Zhang Yulin, a 32-year-old accountant with a one-year-old baby, regularly buys Japanese diapers, American cosmetics, and Dutch or German infant formula powder from foreign websites. As direct delivery to China is either not provided by many e-commerce platforms, or is prohibitively expensive, Zhang, like most such shoppers, has to find a "third-party buyer," typically an overseas Chinese, to take delivery from a foreign seller and arrange shipping. She has to wait nearly a month before her delivery reaches her, with no access to after-sales services. Besides all these inconveniences, few third-party buyers will accept responsibility for lost, damaged or incorrectly delivered packages.

Lu Haiping profits from helping those who struggle to search English-language websites or to make time to shop online. "I buy something from the US for US$80, say, then sell it on to domestic consumers for a little more, but still much less than they'd pay in a store in China," he told our reporter.

Despite a good deal being on offer from such third-party sellers, not all customers are completely confident that they're getting what they're paying for. Buyers like Zhang and Lu don't declare their purchases to customs, preferring to take a chance. If they are unlucky enough to be stopped and searched at the border, and their goods are ruled to be for retail and not for personal use, they could be fined or even charged with smuggling. Several sales agents active on Taobao, Alibaba's main online retail platform, were jailed for smuggling in 2013.

Foreign brands are also reluctant to get in too deep in China's cutthroat e-retail market. International luxury brands can retail goods at much higher prices in their entity stores in China than in other markets—partly due to most customers happily paying a premium for status symbols. In a report published in July 2014, Trefis, a securities research team founded by MIT engineers and former Wall Street analysts, explained that the unsuccessful adaptation to Chinese consumer habits by US retailers already in China, including Wal-Mart, Home Depot and Best Buy, had turned bulk purchase giant Costco off the Chinese market.

As a result, people like Zhang and Lu continue to rule the Chinese marketplace.

THINK BIG

Cross-border e-commerce focusing on imports suddenly began to gain momentum in 2014, with large corporations and major investors suddenly wading in. Alibaba's *Tmall.hk*, which manages international purchases for Chinese consumers, launched in February, with nearly all Alibaba's competitors following suit in the subsequent months. S.F. Express, a Shenzhen-based courier company, and the Industrial Bank, a joint stock commercial bank listed in Shanghai, also joined in.

Amazon entered the China market by acquiring *joyo.com*, a Chinese online bookstore, in 2004. It was not until the end of October 2014, however, that Amazon began offering direct delivery to the Chinese mainland from distribution centers in the US, Britain, Spain, Germany, France and Italy. Costco finally linked up with *Tmall.com* that month. In early November 2014, *metao.com*, a cross-border e-commerce platform founded the previous year, received a US$30 million investment from a venture capital consortium, the largest single investment in the e-commerce sector so far. While US$30 million is not a big amount for a major Internet company, the immediate media attention that the Metao deal attracted is a barometer of the current zeal in this particular market.

"Today, it is not difficult for any half-decent international e-commerce platform to attract million-dollar investors," claimed Zeng Bibo, founder and CEO of China's original cross-border shopping platform *ymatou.com* in an article published on *ebrun.com* in June 2014.

Chinese consumers have welcomed the explosion in online cross-border trade. Li Hao, a white collar worker in Beijing, recently made his first purchase directly from Amazon's US website. Before that, he had relied on friends and colleagues to bring his most coveted consumer goods back from their travels abroad. He told *NewsChina* he had little confidence in those overseas "third party buyers" or re-sellers like Lu.

This current enthusiasm for cross-border e-commerce could also prove a boon to those brands seeking recognition in China that lack the resources of Gucci and Louis Vuitton. Mid-range and smaller scale brands are the very products that both Tmall and Amazon are trying to promote to Chinese consumers. Li's order from Amazon, for example, included a pair of running shoes for his four-year old daughter made by a company with no presence in China. He also ordered a second pair of shoes that would have cost him much more in his local department store, as well as a cheap knife sharpener made by a company he'd never heard of.

An annual survey by the China National Network Information Center (CNNIC) shows that in 2013 a majority of Chinese online shoppers were middle-income, a demographic reflected in the most popular purchases that year—baby products and electronics.

Consequently, analysts are expecting drastic changes in market structure, with middlemen like Lu losing their businesses to e-commerce giants with advantageous positioning in the international supply chain. Foreign giants, it is expected, will utilize their already well established international logistics networks to win business from Chinese competitors who, while dominant in the domestic arena, still struggle to compete on a global scale.

FLYING PIGS

It is widely agreed that favorable policies combined with market potential have piqued the interest of corporations and investors. However, going forward, neither factor is a given.

"When the wind's blowing right, even pigs can fly." These widely-cited words from Lei Jun, a prominent Chinese venture capitalist and founder of IT and smartphone company Xiaomi, have become something of a mantra among Chinese investors and business start-ups. In the case of cross-border e-retailing, "while the wind is right, it's hard to find the right pig," said Zeng Bibo in his recent article. He reminded e-retailers that an e-retailer has to prove itself a proper pig for investors by making real efforts on building a global supply chain for itself.

A global supply chain can take years to establish, and is always vulnerable to the changing marketplace. It has taken decades for foreign players to seriously attempt entry into China's e-commerce market. In the US, resistance to foreign players in e-commerce, particularly those originating in China, has made it hard for Chinese companies to make a dent in a crucial overseas marketplace. "The fight for e-fairness is now a war," declared the US Alliance for Main Street Fairness in a statement on October 30, 2014. This group of brick-and-mortar shop owners is lobbying Congress to pass the Marketplace Fairness Act, a law which would grant individual states the authority to order online and catalog retailers to collect sales taxes locally. While claiming victory over their recalcitrant "single biggest threat"—Amazon—which finally endorsed the Marketplace Fairness Act, the UAMSF singled out Alibaba in its statement for seeking to "exploit online loopholes to poach sales from America's local retailers."

In December 2013, the US Supreme Court rejected Amazon's petition for a hearing after New York State demanded that the company properly collect online sales tax. If other states follow New York's lead, or Congress passes the Marketplace Fairness Act, US brands could become even less keen to enter e-retail for fear of increased costs and frustration of their unhappy distribution agents and retailers.

Given the important role e-commerce is playing in achieving the government's goal of a consumer society, Chinese regulators have generally been more receptive to internationalized e-retail than their US counterparts. A new policy from the State Council issued in November described e-commerce for the first time as part of China's effort to expand its imports and reduce a massive trade surplus which has fueled domestic inflation and led to a series of international trade disputes.

Before more measures to encourage the cross-border e-retail can be adopted, however, the new "bonded areas" in Shanghai, Chongqing, Ningbo, Hangzhou, Zhengzhou, Guangzhou and Shenzhen, all launched in 2013, need to show more profit. Customs policies on consumer goods also need to be clarified.

Based on their own data, nearly all major Chinese e-retailers have imported popular products and stored them in bonded warehouses in the seven pilot cities. The volume and value of such orders is also linked to China's customs clearance system, facilitating the efficient collection of relevant taxes. This system, if expanded to cover a broader area, reassures cross-border shoppers who are currently at risk of violations of their consumer rights and even criminal prosecution.

However, only brand names with the resources and reputation to gain a foothold in China's bonded cities can benefit from these new arrangements. Moreover, there remains much debate over the fairness of China's import taxes for personal use, which rank among the world's highest. Imports for personal use are currently subject to import duty of between

10 and 50 percent, and the minimum taxable value was lowered in 2010, expanding the tax to include even more international purchases, in recognition of the rising popularity of cross-border online shopping by Chinese consumers.

Under China's free trade agreements with some economies and the WTO, many imported products are now subject to much lower, or no, taxation, one example being IT products. However, China's customs agency has long argued that imports for personal use should not be equated with imports for trade in terms of taxation. Chinese analysts and even government agencies have questioned whether this current distinction blocking Chinese consumers from lower customs taxes is in line with WTO rules, and, even if it is, if China should consider lowering its import duty to align itself with other major economies.

Quality controls and quarantine checks, when relating to products purchased online from abroad, are also under scrutiny. China's bonded areas have adopted measures to streamline the screening process. However, each zone is free to determine what its quality control and quarantine procedures should be. So far, only Zhejiang Province has published detailed guidelines regarding its customs inspection procedures.

According to these guidelines, aquatic products, meat and dairy (except infant formula) entering Zhejiang do not have to be supplied exclusively by foreign companies registered with China's Certification and Accreditation Administration. Moreover, foreign-made home appliances imported into Zhejiang are not subject to the China Compulsory Certification mark. This has simplified business for e-retailers and foreign producers, as few foreign companies without a China presence manage to secure the relevant certification.

However, without unified regulatory policies, e-retailers in China still struggle to compete on an even playing field. This is why almost all industry analysts are calling on China's General Administration of Quality Supervision, Inspection and Quarantine for a single policy applied equally to all.

China's e-commerce "pigs," it seems, need more than just the right gust of wind to take flight.

Jack Ma Brilliantly Disrupts the State Banking System

Five years ago, Alibaba's Jack Ma vowed that if China's hidebound state-dominated banking industry didn't change, he would change banking for them. As the Internet has disrupted so many other industries, now banking in China is feeling the heat. Using Alipay, its PayPal-like offering, Alibaba now offers access to high-yielding investment products to its online customers. Predictably, this foray into online investing has drawn imitators from other online firms as well as from banks themselves. In "Who Needs Banks," Sun Zhe explains how Jack takes on the banking giants.

Who Needs Banks?

March 2014 Issue of NewsChina | *by Sun Zhe*

Alipay is hoping to change the way the finance game is played in China.

The charismatic founder of Chinese e-commerce giant Alibaba, Jack Ma, vowed five years ago that if China's banks didn't change, Alibaba would change the banks.

Now, he looks close to achieving his goal.

Half a year after launching Yu E Bao, or "leftover treasure," a service allowing customers using Alipay (an online payment system similar to PayPal) to convert cash into highly-liquid investment products with much higher yields than bank deposits, many Chinese banks have attempted to follow suit.

By the end of 2013, Yu E Bao had gathered a user base of 43 million, with combined deposits of 185 billion yuan (US$30.6bn), making it the second largest single wealth management fund in China.

Since June 2013, when Yu E Bao was launched, its annual returns rose from 4.3 percent to about 6.5 percent by early January 2014. Considering the tightening liquidity in China's money market towards the end of 2013, this meant the platform offered more than double the ROI of a benchmark one-year fixed-term deposit, and 20 times the interest of a regular checking account.

Predictably, State bankers expressed concerns that Yu E Bao was chipping away at their deposit base. Unlike their international counterparts who mainly profit from investment, Chinese banks, most of them State-run, rely on the State-controlled interest rate margin for the majority of their profits.

Yao Jingyuan, former chief economist with the National Bureau of Statistics, even mocked the banks' inefficiency and reliance on preferential treatment, joking that they could "appoint dogs as their presidents and still make the same amount of money."

As a result, Minsheng Bank, for example, one of China's few privately-owned banks, unveiled a product that allowed clients to automatically invest money from deposit accounts into funds and promise a return of five percent, while the money could still be withdrawn at any time, an obvious competitor for Yu E Bao.

However, Alipay has retained an edge simply through its liquidity advantage, an area in which State banks struggle to compete. Money can be transferred in real time to an Alipay account for all sorts of payments enabled by the platform—online purchases, taxi fares, water bills and even the public welfare lottery. Within two hours, money can be transferred from an Alipay account back into a deposit account, whereas most banks freeze any invested deposit for months or even years, charging considerable fees for unscheduled withdrawals.

In addition, Yu E Bao sets no investment limit, allowing customers to invest any amount from 1 yuan (US$0.17) upwards. The average State bank investment product necessitates a minimum investment of 50,000 yuan (US$8,260).

BACK TO THE ROOTS

"Finance used to seem mysterious and remote to the masses," said Alipay CEO Peng Lei. "Now, however, buying and selling financial products is a way of life for most people. The Internet enables us to serve the grassroots."

Due to its convenience and lucrative yields, Yu E Bao has lured a great many customers away from the banks, especially young people. Four out of five Yu E Bao users are aged under 35, investing an average 4,300 yuan (US$710) into the fund, a fraction of the average for bank-held investment products, according to industry consultancy iResearch.

Apart from Yu E Bao, Alibaba has also begun brokering financial products on Tmall, Alibaba's business-to-customer online retailing portal, also the country's largest. Other Internet giants such as social media icons Tencent, search giant Baidu and top web-portal Netease, are all competing to offer suspiciously high yields ranging from 8 to even 11 percent.

However, Alipay's expansion in the finance sector has not gone altogether unchecked. In summer 2013, Alipay found it had to remove all its custom POS terminals given to retailers for what it called "reasons known to all" in a statement afterward. It is an open secret that China Unionpay, the State-controlled payment service which provides all the nation's POS devices, was unhappy about losing its monopoly, and pressured the government into forcing Alipay out of the sector.

Alibaba, and other dotcom companies who want to dip their toes into China's hectic but hugely lucrative financial sector might still need to rely on the mercy of State banks, and their masters, if they are to continue to flourish in one of the world's most tightly restricted financial markets.

Disrupting the Taxi Industry

Just as Uber and Lyft have changed the landscape around the world for point-to-point public transportation, online taxi hailing services are disrupting the way the highly regulated taxi industry in China works. Bypassing the taxi companies and their dispatchers, riders can individually hail, direct and pay for cabs. Using a loophole, car rental agencies can also get into the act. See "In the Driver's Seat" for the full story.

In the Driver's Seat

April 2015 Issue of NewsChina | *by Zhou Yao*

The expansion of cab-hailing apps is set to challenge a long-standing State-backed oligopoly in the taxi industry.

While the rapid development of mobile Internet has led to increased competition across China's economy, perhaps the most obvious disruption has been taking place on the roads of China's major cities.

Throughout 2014, Alibaba and Tencent, China's two largest Internet companies, both piled funds into promotion of their respective taxi-hailing apps, Kuaidi Dache and Didi Dache, each aiming to stake its claim as the leader in this nascent market. Meanwhile, international heavyweights such as Uber also entered China in 2014.

But given that the taxi industry has long been subject to strict government control, experts are predicting that the expansion of Internet companies into the sector will inevitably clash with the existing government-backed oligopoly.

FROM HONEYMOON TO STRIKES

Initially, authorities moved to ban taxi-hailing apps, since the payment of a percentage of the fare to the app developer was a direct challenge to the taxi price control imposed by the government. But as cab-hailing apps continued to gain popularity among consumers, authorities in most cities tacitly endorsed them.

Indeed, for much of early 2014, the competition between Kuaidi and Didi saw both companies offering financial rewards to cab drivers for every fare, at no extra cost to the consumer. Although small, these kickbacks boosted the uptake of cab-hailing apps among cab drivers, which in turn improved general market efficiency and, ultimately, consumer satisfaction. According to a survey conducted by a team from Tsinghua University, 55 percent of cab drivers said that their monthly income had increased by 10 to 30 percent since they began using cab-hailing apps.

However, since the apps began to expand their "fleet" beyond licensed cab drivers in mid-2014, the relationship between the Internet companies, taxi drivers and the authorities has become increasingly confrontational.

In early January, 2015, taxi drivers launched a series of demonstrations in several major Chinese provincial capitals, including Nanjing, Shenyang, Nanchang, Jinan, Changchun and Chengdu.

In Changchun, drivers protested on the streets and blocked roads, while cabbies in other cities began a coordinated strike, to protest what they saw as the unfair competition brought about by the use of cab-hailing apps by unlicensed drivers.

RENTAL TO THE RESCUE

The catalyst for the deterioration in the relationship between apps and cabbies was the introduction of new private chauffeur-driven car hire services, Kuaidi One and Didi Zhuanche, launched by Kuaidi (Alibaba) and Didi (Tencent) in July and August of 2014 respectively. Both Kuaidi One and Didi Zhuanche were accessible through the interface of the original apps, as an alternative to the regular taxi-hailing service.

But for taxi drivers and the authorities, the new services appeared to be specially designed to bypass government regulations governing the taxi industry, in terms of number of taxis and the price of a taxi fare.

Through collaboration with rental car companies and private and contracted drivers, the apps were essentially able to roll out a taxi service where drivers wait on call, rather than driving around the city.

Due to tight regulations in China's rental car industry, there is a cap on the number of cars a rental company can own. To circumvent these limits, rental car companies, in cooperation with Kuaidi One and Didi Zhuanche, reached out to drivers of privately owned cars, often through "labor services" companies that supply contract workers for miscellaneous jobs. Effectively, this allowed rental car companies to "rent out" cars that they did not own, complete with drivers.

For example, Liao Kai, a driver who works for Didi Zhuanche through a local rental car firm in Shenyang, told *NewsChina* that although he and most of his colleagues had labor contracts with the rental company, the cars they use are their own, not the company's.

"We signed contracts with the company, but we own our cars," said Liao.

Licensed cab drivers argue that since the cars and drivers being supplied by apps do not belong to rental companies, they directly violate government regulations and should be considered illegal.

Almost immediately following the launch of Kuaidi One and Didi Zhuanche, local authorities in various cities outlawed their use. In Beijing, for example, transportation authorities released a regulation in August, 2014 banning rental car companies from providing drivers.

In the following months, fines have been dealt out to drivers using almost all major cab-hailing apps, including Kuadi, Didi and Uber, in a number of Chinese cities including Beijing, Shanghai and Chongqing. However, given the popularity of the apps, their services remain widely available.

Meanwhile, cab drivers are complaining of a sudden drop in income. In Beijing, a cab driver surnamed Hao told *NewsChina* that his monthly income dropped by 1,000 to 2,000 yuan (US$160–320), or 20 to 40 percent. In Shenyang, a cab driver surnamed Hu told *NewsChina* that his average daily revenue had decreased from 500–700 yuan (US$80–112) to under 500 yuan.

In the wake of widespread strikes, the Ministry of Transport stressed that only licensed taxis could use cab-hailing apps, and that apps' services should be differentiated from public transportation and taxis.

"While we encourage innovation, private cars are prohibited from using platforms to participate in the rental car business," the ministry wrote in a statement released on January 8.

OLIGOPOLY

But for many industry experts, the problem does not lie in cab-hailing apps, but in the State's control over the taxi industry.

The general public agrees. According to an online survey conducted on Weibo, China's Twitter equivalent, 70 percent of 7,505 respondents attributed the strikes to "low income of taxi drivers resulting from a [State] monopoly in the industry." 49 percent said that the new services provided by cab-hailing apps were having a "positive" effect on the development of the industry.

Similar to cities in many countries, the Chinese government imposes strict regulations on the taxi industry, limiting the number of taxis or taxi companies that can operate in an area, dictating rates and setting safety rules for operators.

While this arrangement was designed to protect the safety and rights of consumers, in reality, it has created an oligopoly and a network of vested interests, especially when many cities deny individual drivers direct access to cab licenses.

As licenses are only granted to a small number of companies—often owned by well-connected entrepreneurs—cab firms are able to maintain a comfortable monopoly over the industry, charging drivers monthly rental fees for the use of their car—long a source of resentment among cab drivers.

In Beijing, a cab driver typically pays 6,000 yuan a month to a taxi company, and shares a cab with another driver. Mr. Hao, the cab driver mentioned earlier, told *NewsChina* said that he and his partner use the cab on alternate days. Between them, they pay 6,000 yuan a month to the taxi company, and each works 15 hours per day every other day for a monthly income of 5,000 yuan each.

By contrast, it has been estimated that drivers who work for rental services can earn between 12,000 and 15,000 yuan per month. Many believe that this discrepancy is due to the significant proportion of cabbies' income that goes to their companies, who benefit from the government-backed oligopoly.

Meanwhile, the quota on the issuance of licenses has resulted in a shortage of taxis on the road—exactly the kind of market disequilibrium that mobile apps have proven effective at exploiting in many industries, and a major reason behind the rise of cab-hailing apps in China and worldwide.

While Beijing's population increased from 15 million in 2004 to 21 million in 2013, the number of licensed cabs only increased from 65,000 to 66,000. And since the Beijing authorities imposed a quota limiting the number of new private cars on the city's roads to 20,000 per month, the shortage of taxis has become more and more acute. At peak traffic times in Beijing, it is almost impossible to hail a taxi without using an app.

According to estimates by Kuaidi, the overall nationwide demand for taxis is about 50 million rides per day, of which existing licensed cabs in Chinese cities can only satisfy 60 percent, leaving a market of 20 million rides per day for apps like Kuaidi, Uber and Didi.

REFORM?

Following the taxi strikes, even State media have called for the termination of the government-backed oligopoly in the taxi industry. In an editorial published on January 6, Party mouthpiece the *People's Daily* described the current system as "deformed," and called on the government to allow the market to play a decisive role in the sector.

A mainstream opinion is that the government should liberalize its control over the industry by issuing licenses to individual taxis drivers directly. However, there are still voices urging caution. Zhang Jianfeng, a senior executive at a local cab company in Shenyang, for example, warned that dismantling State control over the sector may simply clear the way for a different form of monopoly.

Zhang pointed out that cab-hailing apps have been taking 20 percent of fares of each ride in Shenyang, which, on average, could amount to 4,800 yuan each month—more than the monthly charges levied by cab companies. According to Zhang, this would be unfair to cab drivers, as ride-hailing apps do not provide drivers with benefits, such as insurance and social security payments, like traditional cab companies do.

So far, authorities in several cities have expressed willingness to reform their taxi policies. On January 11, Beijing's transportation commission told the media that the Beijing authorities are "studying" a plan to issue new licenses to cars that wait to be hailed either through the Internet or over the phone. Authorities in Guangzhou have issued a similar plan.

A draft plan released by authorities in Shenyang proposes to offer taxi licenses to individual cab drivers, although it forbids the private trading of licenses.

But for many experts, these proposed reforms, through which the government appears to be aiming to bring the newly emerged cab-hailing apps under its control, are far from adequate.

According to Peng Peng, an expert from the Guangdong Academy of Social Sciences, the rise of cab-hailing apps has presented the government with both a challenge and an opportunity to address some key problems.

Among the intertwined relationships between cab drivers, taxi companies, Internet companies and government agencies, it remains to be seen if the brute technological power of mobile Internet companies can be a game changer in one of China's most regulated and protected industries.

Virtual Love

Love is not omitted from the e-commerce landscape. No need to actually go out and meet someone. Lonely hearts in China can go online and rent a real live boy—or girlfriend—who will pay them every attention short of physically meeting up. In "Love Virtually," Zhou Fengting explores the business of supplying virtual companionship on demand.

Love Virtually

April 2015 Issue of NewsChina | *by Zhou Fengting*

The Internet has no shortage of solutions to the problems of China's loneliest.

"You can't buy and sell love," goes the refrain of a popular Chinese song "Sales of Love". Thanks to the rapid development of China's Internet, however, love—or at least, its digital manifestation—is now available from all good online retail platforms.

Websites offering "paid-for lovers" have begun employing real men and women to play the role of a romantic partner with a paying customer for a pre-defined period of time. While it may sound like little more than a modern twist on the oldest profession, these paid-for lovers are strictly virtual, their services limited to regular instant messages and phone calls.

"I can't actually help [customers] very much—they just need someone to hear and understand them," Ni Ke (screen name), a self-employed "virtual lover" told *NewsChina*.

LOVE ON TAOBAO

Ni Ke's first experience in the industry was as a customer. Eight months after breaking up with her boyfriend, the lonely Ni typed "boyfriend" into the search box on Taobao, China's largest online shopping platform. To her surprise, she found that there were a number of online stores advertising "paid-for lovers."

Ni clicked onto one of them, and began scanning the product range, from "boys" to "uncles;" from "warm" to "cool;" from "sparky" to "introvert." She opted for the store's best-seller, purchasing the undivided digital attention of a "warm boy," or *nuannan*, for a 24-hour period. Several minutes after the online transaction was complete, her phone rang—when she answered, a pleasant voice said: "Hi, darling. It's time to get up."

After her initial 24-hour contract finished, Ni immediately renewed for a further week, during which time her virtual beau gave her a morning wake-up call every day, chatted with her whenever she wanted, and paid her all the attention she would expect from a real-life boyfriend.

She enjoyed the constant contact so much that she once asked the man whether they could become a real-life couple, but was rebuffed with no hesitation. "We are in the virtual world. I will accompany you until you find a real-life love," he told her.

Ni did not renew the service when it expired. "I didn't want him to feel like he was responsible for me. It would be too much pressure for him," she explained. Instead, she hired another "lover," but kept herself from getting too involved this time round. "The rule is that everything starts and ends in the virtual world," she added.

SELLING "LOVE"

Before long, Ni Ke found herself on the other end of these transactions, advertising her own "paid-for love" services with a post in a forum on China's most popular Internet bulletin board *tieba.com*, reading: "Perhaps you have never been loved, perhaps you have been disappointed in love, or perhaps you no longer feel loved in your boring marriage. You need a platonic lover. We cannot be together for life, but we can share love and happiness in the moment."

Since first appearing on Taobao in July 2014, "paid-for lover" businesses, according to Taobao's statistics, have enjoyed a surge in sales volume over the past seven months.

Yuan Sheng, an online "paid-for lover" shop owner, told *NewsChina* that he has opened three separate stores on Taobao, and employs over 100 lovers, mostly recent graduates.

Another paid-for lover agent on Taobao, who asked to be identified only by his surname Cheng, told *NewsChina* that his shop had served over 2,000 customers since it was established in late summer 2014. "Sales volume has multiplied since media began to report on the business," he said. "On December 12 alone, I earned 8,000 yuan (US$1,333). When I first opened the store, I was only making a few dozen yuan per day," he continued.

"In order to ensure quality, the lovers in my shop serve up to two or three customers per day. My shop has also launched daily, weekly and monthly packages to cater to the needs of different customers," he added.

PROFESSIONAL PRODUCTS

According to Ni Ke, many customers buy her service not for virtual romance, but simply for companionship and a sympathetic ear. "I understand them. After my break-up, I also ate alone, slept alone and cried alone," she told *NewsChina*.

"While comforting others, I'm also talking away my own frustration," she added.

Ni now finds customers through Nannan (literally "chatter"), a popular smartphone app designed to help people find paid-for lovers. Users register as a paid-for lover, and can start doing business after being approved by the app's administrators. Nannan claims to have more than 3,000 paid-for lovers on its roster.

Sensing the huge market potential in catering to lonely Chinese people, Microsoft has also launched a virtual lover service in China. Rather than using real people, however, the tech giant uses a downloadable automated "chat-bot"—a young female avatar named Xiao Bing who chats with users. According to Microsoft's data, Xiao Bing 2.0 has been downloaded by more than 10 million users and has had more than 600 million conversations since its debut in July 2014.

"Our data show that Xiao Bing use peaks at midnight, when many people feel lonely and anxious," Li Di, head of Microsoft's Xiao Bing project, told *NewsChina*.

TRUE SELF IN THE VIRTUAL WORLD

Predictably, not everyone is respectful of boundaries in the paid-for virtual lover business. A-Sang (screen name), a paid-for lover who first worked on Taobao then with Nannan, told *NewsChina* that she had been sexually harassed by some of her customers.

Cheng revealed that he blacklists customers who make improper demands. In order to prevent paid-for lovers becoming prostitution, Taobao's search engine is particularly rigorous when filtering search results for the term "paid-for love," and users of apps like Nannan are encouraged to report any wrongdoing to administrators.

In the face of these restrictions, some customers have begun using software like Peiwo (literally "accompany me"), which connects any two strangers online for a chat about any topic they want. According to Peiwo's data, its most active user has talked for 625 hours since it was launched in September 2014, meaning he or she used the online chat function for an average of five hours every day.

One of users' favorite functions, according to Peiwo, is a three-minute anonymous voice conversation, where neither side is given any information about the other. Once the three minutes are up, the system automatically assigns another random chat partner.

Ye Zi (pseudonym), a married administrator working with a school, is a loyal Peiwo user. He told *NewsChina* that many of his conversations through the app are about sex. "My life is like a train running on tracks, boring and depressing, and the anonymous talk enables me to take off my mask," he said.

Thanks to Peiwo, Ye has talked with strangers for 371 hours, 153 of which he spent in anonymous mode. "Some might think what I'm doing is immoral, but I don't think so. It satisfies me without betraying my marriage. I keep my online and offline lives separate," he told *NewsChina*.

Microsoft chose to launch its Xiao Bing product in China because of the sharp contrast between the online and offline worlds in the country. "Xiao Bing reflects the other sides of netizens," Li Di said, revealing that his company plans to further develop Xiao Bing's artificial intelligence in the style of Scarlett Johansson's character in the 2014 Academy Award-winning movie *Her*.

Ni Ke, however, has grown tired of virtual love. The more time she spends in the "love business," the less enjoyment she gets from it. "'Love' gets worn out in this business. You become numb to your customers' pain and troubles," she said. "This kind of care and comfort are worthless," she added.

"The [paid-for love] business can go some way to easing people's pressure, but it can also lead to addiction, which is damaging in real life," Li Ping, a psychology expert from a psychotherapy school in Nanjing, capital of Jiangsu Province, told Xinhua News Agency.

"No problem can be solved by escaping from the real world, and those with mental troubles should receive professional psychotherapy," she added.

In order to come back to the real world, Ni Ke has turned to social networking apps that encourage strangers to meet face-to-face.

What's In Those Red Envelopes?

Chen Jiying and Xie Ying describe an explosively popular new trend in China, the giving of virtual gifts that simulate the traditional red envelopes. Red envelopes have been given at holidays for years. The new apps, offered by Internet giants Weibo, WeChat, Alipay, and many others, have changed the landscape almost overnight for building online customer bases for many firms. The apps are so insanely popular that many are seeking medical treatment for worn-out eyes and trembling hands from shaking their phones to open the virtual envelopes. This trend, which is all about giving away money, seems so outlandish to the Western observer but has produced eye-popping figures such as over 800 million red envelopes being opened *per minute* during certain TV promotions. The *NewsChina* article "Pushing the Envelope" describes this phenomenon in detail.

Pushing the Envelope

May 2015 Issue of NewsChina | *by Chen Jiying, Xie Ying*

Over the recent Chinese New Year festival, Chinese apps and brands found a way to bring traditional New Year's cash gifts into the online world.

Suffering from dried out, stinging eyes and an uncontrollable tremble in his right hand, Yang, a 22-year-old graduate in Guangzhou, had to take time out of his Chinese New Year vacation to see a doctor. The diagnosis? Too much "red enveloping."

"Red envelopes," essentially cash stuffed inside letter-size crimson-colored packets, are a traditional gift most often exchanged at important festivals, particularly Chinese New Year. As with an increasing range of transactions in the modern Chinese economy, this traditional exchange is moving into the online world via social networking platforms like Weibo and WeChat, and online payment platforms like Alipay. By clicking on a virtual "red envelope" or simply shaking their smartphone, users can open an "e-envelope" sent by a friend or company, and help themselves to the cash or coupons stuffed inside.

During the 2015 Spring Festival Gala, the traditional Chinese New Year's Eve variety show on State broadcaster CCTV, corporate sponsors distributed around 500 million yuan (US$83.3m) in cash through WeChat, with the largest single "envelope" containing 4,999 yuan (US$794). During the five-hour program, around 11 billion virtual envelopes were reportedly opened, around 810 million per minute at the peak time.

"A great number of people have come to the hospital for chronic neck pain, and the 'red envelope' game is believed to be a major cause," Wang Yuling, a medical director at the Sixth Affiliated Hospital of Sun Yat-sen University in Guangzhou, told local media.

"It seems that these red envelopes have become people's only concern during the holiday period. They shake their phones day and night, disregarding their family members. Friends no longer met in the real world, but gathered on a social networking app to scramble for virtual envelopes. Is this new game destroying our traditional festival culture?" questioned a commentary from Xinhua News Agency.

Such criticism, however, did little to quell Chinese people's enthusiasm for red envelopes. Two weeks later, during the Lantern Festival on March 5, 2015, businesses and sponsors were lining up to distribute billions of yuan in virtual red envelopes, with analysts hailing these "lucky money" promotions as the most fashionable new form of social exchange and business marketing.

A NEW CELEBRATION

While some have criticized the game for being a waste of time, since the envelopes often contain little to no cash, others see it more as a quirky pastime than a way of making money.

"In the old days, we made phones calls or sent text messages to pass on festive greetings. Now, these have been replaced by virtual red envelopes, which I find more convenient and fun," Zhang Chao, a 29-year-old white-collar employee in Beijing, told NewsChina.

"While few people would stop to pick up a pile of pennies on the ground, scrambling for red envelopes brings us happiness," he added.

Zhang Jun, assistant general manager of marketing and public relations at Tencent, the developer behind WeChat, agrees. "The main idea of virtual red envelopes is to please our users," he told NewsChina. "It's like playing cards with friends and family members—the gambling chips are not so important," he added.

In order to highlight the entertainment value of virtual red envelopes and maximize the number of participants, the apps offering the game, including Alipay and WeChat, have set an upper limit to the amount of money that can be put in an envelope, and the number of people who can open it. For example, a red envelope offered up by a single user to other members of a 50-member group chat on WeChat can be opened by 30 members, with the app allocating the cash value randomly, from one *fen* (0.16 US cents) to 8.88 yuan (US$1.50). After 30 people have taken a share, the game ends.

"The fun comes from seeing who was the luckiest and quickest, and people get excited by the mystery amount of money in the envelopes," said Zhang Jun. Zhang Chao revealed that during the Chinese New Year vacation, his WeChat feed was filled with posts from friends showing off how much money they had won.

For many people, the red envelope game is a chance to make new friends. Ni Hong, a founder of the Shenzhen Media Association, a journalist association in Shenzhen, told *NewsChina* that red envelopes have helped his organization expand to cities like Beijing and Shanghai— a number of journalists had applied to join after he began giving out red envelopes on WeChat.

"The red envelope served as an incentive for new members to join," he said.

Zeng Junru, administrator of a group of players in the online game *JX3 Online* (a Chinese *World of Warcraft* equivalent) told *NewsChina* that his group had doubled in size since the game incorporated a red envelope function, allowing players to distribute in-game currency to others with a virtual game of chance. "When I started distributing red envelopes in the game, people started calling me 'boss' or 'moneybags,'" he said.

A NEW BUSINESS WAR

As the platforms distributing these red envelopes, apps such as Alipay and WeChat have been the biggest winners in this new game. According to official statistics, Alipay, for example, saw its red envelopes opened 683 million times by over 100 million users on Chinese New Year's Eve. The same day, a total of 240 million "envelopes" were opened, containing a total of four billion yuan (US$630m) in cash and coupons.

"With its sharing and social networking functions, the red envelope game has been a huge boost to Alipay's shortage of user interaction," an insider at Alibaba, developer of Alipay, told *NewsChina*. "Since e-payment apps are used much less frequently than instant messaging apps, we plan to make red envelopes a regular function of Alipay, covering more social events, such as weddings, business banquets, private parties and others," he added. Now, when a user clicks into Alipay's "My Friends" page, they are presented with an option to send anyone on their list a red envelope.

Despite dominance in social networking, Tencent lags far behind Alibaba in e-commerce. Red envelopes, however, have given it a chance to seize more market share by requiring users to link their bank accounts to Tenpay, Tencent's e-payment tool, before sending or receiving a virtual red envelope. According to Tencent's 2014 fiscal report, the company has seen around 100 million users register for Tenpay via red envelope activity on WeChat. Data from Chinese Internet consultancy iResearch showed that Tenpay's market share has risen to about 10 percent from 4 percent since WeChat launched its red envelope function in 2014.

Similar to Alibaba, Tencent has also added a red envelope function to its other services, such as the smartphone app version of QQ (Tencent's hugely popular instant messaging software) and its taxi-hailing app. "With high demand for online payments, red envelopes are of high value to social networking platforms like QQ and will further promote other online payment services, such as online shopping and online lottery, among others," Ying Yu, vice president of Tencent told *West China Metropolis Daily*.

"All online businesses, present or future, are or will have to be based on online payment," he added. According to media reports, Tencent has allegedly nicknamed its red envelope development project "D-Day," indicating that it is a crucial play for Internet market share.

A NEW PROMOTION

While red envelope functions first began appearing in 2014, 2015 has marked the introduction of sponsors. According to Zhang Jun, Tencent's director of marketing, all the cash in red envelopes given out by sponsors on WeChat was supplied by sponsors themselves.

"The two major goals behind our red envelope strategy were to market our brand and to attract more fans," Xu Lei, vice-president of JD.com, a leading B2C online shopping website and also the biggest sponsor of red envelopes on WeChat during the New Year holiday, told *NewsChina*.

Lufax, a finance app, told *NewsChina* that two days after Chinese New Year, it had risen from 30th to 4th place in the iTunes store download chart. Although the company launched many other promotional campaigns during the festival, red envelopes were believed to have played a significant role in the app's rapid growth.

While WeChat remains very cautious about putting advertisements in the app's interface in order to avoid tainting its user experience, red envelopes have provided a soft route to monetization. Although Zhang Jun denied that red envelopes were an advertising ploy, saying that WeChat has received no kickbacks or commission from sponsors, many believe that red envelopes are potentially a more effective marketing method than direct advertisements on WeChat.

The coupons in red envelopes have certainly been helping providers attract more customers, just as many celebrities have boosted their popularity by sending red envelopes on microblogging platform Weibo. According to *Xinhua Daily*, a local Party newspaper headquartered in Nanjing, capital of Jiangsu Province, online red envelope activities have been a boon to offline sales at bricks-and-mortar stores and movie theaters, with sales volume at the city's top two shopping malls, Deji and Golden Eagle, respectively increasing by 11 percent and 8 percent year-on-year by the third day after Chinese New Year.

"There is a lot of space for commerce behind red envelopes … It is a large basket, with each Internet service provider and business taking what he needs. Also, it is urgent to work out new rules to further regulate this new commercial model," said State broadcaster CCTV.

FOR FURTHER STUDY

Response Questions

- List the six major Internet players in China, their principal offerings and what US company each offering mirrors.
- What are hai tao zu?
- What is "Over The Top" or OTT technology?
- In what applications are Alibaba and Tencent competing in China?
- Give three reasons why Youku-Tudou hasn't succeeded in China.
- What are Kuaidi Dache and Didi Dache?
- Chinese consumers do not have access to online shopping at Costco and Amazon. How do Costco and Amazon sell products online in China?
- What are baidu and dianping? What are their US equivalents?
- How many smart phones are expected to be sold in China in 2015? What is the population size of the United States?
- What is Alipay? What is it competing against?

Discussion Questions

- What other opportunities for Internet-based disruptors do you see in China?
- How does Internet censorship in China affect political, scientific, and educational progress?

- What is the tension between officially licensed taxis and ride-booking apps? Should these apps be banned in China? What are the benefits and risks of ride-booking apps? Why is there such a large a market for such apps in China?
- Alibaba, an e-commerce company, had a record-breaking US$25 billion IPO on the New York Stock Exchange in 2014. Nearly a dozen other Chinese internet companies raised a net of several billion US dollars in their US IPOs during the same year. Given China's internet censorship, discuss the reasons for the success of these Chinese internet companies.
- Chinese internet companies whose IPOs in the US stock markets have exceeded expectations have had far stellar results post-IPO. What is your evaluation of the upside and risks involved with investing in Chinese IPOs? Would you invest in Shanghai or Hong Kong over US stock market IPOs? Discuss your rationale.

Research Exercises

- Go to the English-language versions of Amazon.cn and Taobao. How do these sites compare to US-based offerings such as Amazon.com and Ebay.com? How is Amazon's Chinese offering different from its US site? Search for "Sofa" at Taobao.com; select any product on page one of your search; use translate.google.com to translate the webpage into English.
- What are the most important factors for Chinese consumers based on the type of information displayed on Taobao?
- Research and outline some ways a determined netizen in China can bypass the Great Firewall. List websites and providers (either for-pay or free) and indicate their capacity and limitations.
- What are the top three smart phone companies in China? What are the top three smart phones in China? Create a three-column comparison between the top three smart phones in China, including cost, features, and phone company contracts.
- How has Alibaba stock fared since its IPO? Create a graph using stock value data for each month since its IPO. What are analysts writing about the company, and what are their buy/sell/hold recommendations?
- What OTT apps are available for chat in the US, Canada, and Europe? How do they impact cellular companies? What is the major OTT app in China? What services does it offer its users?

Notes

1 GreatFire.org—Bringing Transparency to the Great Firewall of China, retrieved March 31, 2015.

2   Ibid.
3   *Fortune*, February 1, 2015, p. 54.

Bibliography

Chen, J. & Li, J. (February, 2015). When Pigs Fly. *NewsChina.*
Chen, J. & Xie, Y. (May, 2015). Pushing the Envelope. *NewsChina.*
GreatFire.org (March 31, 2015). Bringing Transparency to the Great Firewall of China, retrieved from https://en.greatfire.org
Li, J. (December, 2014). No Alchemy: Alibaba. *NewsChina.*
Sun, Z. (June, 2013). Data Discrimination. *NewsChina.*
Sun, Z. (March, 2014). Alipay—Who Needs Banks? *NewsChina.*
Sun, Z. (February, 2015). Video Killed the Video Star. *NewsChina.*
Zhang, Y. (March, 2015). Boom and Boom. *NewsChina.*
Zhou, F. (April, 2015). Love Virtually. *NewsChina.*
Zhou, Y. (April, 2015). In the Driver's Seat. *NewsChina.*

6

ENVIRONMENT AND LAND

Introduction

As is the all-too-frequent pattern among developing countries, China was a poor steward of its land, water, and air. All three are polluted to a significant degree. Only a handful of China's 500 largest cities meet WHO air quality standards, and air pollution kills over 500,000 Chinese citizens annually[1]. Pollution threatens not only health in China but political stability as well. Over 50,000 environmental protests a year[2] have spurred the CPC to action. As the country progresses from developing to newly industrialized, attention is now being paid to remediating past contamination and reducing levels going forward. For example, in September 2015 President Xi announced a national cap-and-trade program to begin in 2017 which would be the world's largest such program[3].

Beyond natural resource pollution, the quality of China's food has suffered numerous, well-publicized failings. From air to water to land, the environment is fundamental to any nation's economic and physical health. China faces numerous great challenges in these areas, but also has proven remarkably successful at solving challenges that have become the focus of attention and resources.

Legal and economic problems also relate to stewardship of land in China. In the cities, housing prices have been moving up to unsustainable levels, prompting speculation of a coming bubble, while on the farms, inefficient legacy land-owning policies hold down agricultural production while enriching avaricious local developers and officials.

The following articles explore some of the more important of these issues, and how Beijing may be dealing with them in the coming critical decade.

ARTICLES

Protection and Preservation

A Climate Change Milestone

When the November 2014 bilateral climate change agreement between the US and China was announced, President Obama's administration touted this as a breakthrough in the battle to save the planet. Curiously, at least to the casual Western observer, Beijing hardly mentioned this landmark step at all. This despite the serious threat to the Chinese autocracy due to widespread dissatisfaction with the overwhelming pollution of China's air, land and water.

In "China's Climate Change Deal Is a Triumph," the editors of *NewsChina* explain that the reason for this reticence is the fear that the average Chinese might see this agreement as a concession to foreign powers, something the proud population would not approve. To put this view in perspective, history is useful. China suffered gravely at the hands of foreign powers for centuries. The period roughly from 1840 to 1940 is regarded as the "Century of Humiliation," during which China was forced to agree to a series of so-called "Unequal Treaties" ceding control of important parts of its territory, and suffer foreign invasions and even atrocities. A brief timeline is given in Appendix 6.1 at the end of this chapter.

China's Climate Change Deal is a Triumph

January 2015 Issue of NewsChina | *by* NewsChina Magazine

China's leaders are aware that climate change is a major global threat and that China, as the world's biggest carbon emitter, has an international obligation to cut its pollution.

While the international community hailed the climate change deal signed by the US and China during the APEC summit in November as a milestone in bilateral commitment on environmental issues, the domestic response, particularly in the State media, has been muted. Despite China making its first-ever commitment to cap its greenhouse gas emissions by 2030 along with pledges to source 20 percent of its future energy from renewables, little Chinese fanfare accompanied the deal.

Part of the problem could be the context in which the agreement was signed. China's commitment to cap carbon emissions could be seen in some quarters as a major concession to international pressure. Previous arguments that a cap would hamper economic growth have jarred with China's newfound status as both the world's number two economy and its number one polluter. The viewpoint that the new carbon deal has come at a cost to China's own prestige continues to have currency in mainstream political thought within the country, possibly explaining the visible lack of enthusiasm for a deal trumpeted as a triumph by the Obama administration.

China's new economic and political realities have made this viewpoint obsolete and counterproductive. Far from being a concession made under external pressure, this climate change deal is economically, politically and diplomatically beneficial to China.

In the past 30 years, China's economic development has been largely driven by investment and exports, leading to a booming manufacturing sector. However, this growth has been fueled largely by fossil fuels, particularly coal, causing the country's carbon emissions to rocket. China's recent economic slowdown has sounded the death knell for this growth model, with the leadership now advocating a more sustainable, energy-efficient economy.

A changing political environment also makes it crucial for China's leadership to deal with the massive environmental problems that have followed in the wake of rapid economic expansion. The legitimacy of China's government has become tied to its ability to maintain economic growth and improve living standards. Contamination of the country's water, soil and air has shaken this key source of legitimacy, and grievances over pollution have become a major flashpoint for political unrest.

As the Chinese government had to ban drivers from highways and close factories to ensure a blue sky for APEC dignitaries, netizens, their tongues firmly in their cheeks, coined the term "APEC blue," sending the subtle message that the power to secure clear skies rests entirely with the government.

China's leadership cannot ignore this new political reality. During the APEC summit, President Xi Jinping told his guests he hoped that "every day we will see a blue sky, green mountains and clear rivers, not just in Beijing, but all across China so that our children will live in a pleasant environment." As China simultaneously promotes the concept of the "China dream" and "APEC dream," had the administration attempted to sidestep the environmental issue entirely, the reaction from the public would likely have been even more frosty.

Despite their priority being domestic issues, China's leaders are aware that climate change is a major global threat and that China, as the world's biggest carbon emitter, has an international obligation to cut its pollution. Being the first major developing country to make such a commitment, the new deal will boost China's international image, and help allay distrust.

But making a commitment is only the beginning. China must continue to push forward policies and initiatives both at home and abroad to clear skies, mountains and rivers, and, by extension, lead the international struggle against climate change.

Will the New Environment Law be Effective?

There is some hope for improvement in China's environment given the environmental protection law that became effective in January 2015. This law makes polluters subject to more severe punishments than in the past. But as is commonplace in China's distributed power structure, the agency tasked with carrying out this law, the Ministry of Environmental Protection, is given no special authority versus the many other agencies governing land, resources, water, agriculture, and oceans. *NewsChina* points out in "China's Bold New Environment Law Will Likely Remain Hamstrung" the potential failings of this new law, and suggests possible fixes for it.

The ancient and well-known proverb, "The sky is high and the emperor is far away" reflects the relative weakness of central power in China and the strength of regional autonomy. Enforcement of this new law is bound to encounter regional resistance where environmental protection threatens local pet projects or the profitability of major polluters.

China's Bold New Environmental Law Will Likely Remain Hamstrung

April 2015 Issue of NewsChina | *by* NewsChina Magazine

The new law fails to address some major issues behind China's deteriorating environmental situation.

On January 1, China's new environmental protection law came into effect, marking the first time that China has incorporated environmental protection into its legislative efforts to foster social development.

Under the new law, companies that cause pollution will be subject to harsher punishments and tougher fines. The law also stipulates specific measures to safeguard the public's right to environmental information, and to protect from retribution those who report pollution.

However, despite this progress, the new law fails to address some major issues behind China's deteriorating environmental situation. First, as the new law has been given no special jurisdiction, it may conflict with existing laws, including the country's agriculture law, forestry law and water law, which fall under the administration of different ministries. As the environmental law does not take priority, other ministries will be able to challenge perceived contradictions between the laws.

Second, the new law does not address the issue of power structures within these agencies, jeopardizing the effectiveness of the law's implementation. A major issue with China's environmental problems is that the institutional framework regarding environmental protection is fragmented, with a variety of agencies having overlapping authority. Although the Ministry of Environmental Protection is often held responsible for all environmental issues, its power is actually rather limited, as other agencies, such as the Ministry of Land and Resources, the Ministry of Water Resources, the Ministry of Agriculture, the National Bureau of Oceanography and the State Administration of Forestry all have a major stake in environmental policy.

Thirdly, the new law does not clarify whether the public has a basic constitutional right to a livable environment. Although China's new environmental law recognizes that individual citizens and social organizations have a right to access to "environmental information," the right of litigation is limited to a handful of government-recognized social organizations, effectively excluding the majority of the general public from participation in the supervision of the government's environmental protection efforts.

Finally, the new environmental law does not address the lack of independence of environmental protection authorities at the local level, a major contributing factor behind China's environmental problems. As local environmental protection bureaus continue to rely on local governments in terms of personnel and finance, their implementation of the new law may continue to be hamstrung. Despite tougher punishments and higher fines for polluting companies stipulated in the new law, local environmental authorities still need the approval of local governments to implement punitive measures. As polluting companies remain an important source of local revenue, local governments lack the incentive to implement the new law seriously.

To address these problems at their root, China needs to place environmental protection at the core of central policy. In doing so, China would elevate the status of its environmental law to form part of the country's Basic Law. Moreover, it needs to reshuffle the environmental and related agencies to establish a unified and effective environmental protection institution to coordinate environmental authorities at different levels.

Besides legislation, more systemic institutional reform is required to effectively address China's deteriorating environment.

Contaminated Ground

One million square kilometers, nearly 10 percent of China's total land area, has been judged contaminated or heavily polluted by China's Ministry of Environmental Protection. "Soil Justice" by Wang Yan explores how China is waking up to this disaster, deciding who pays for remediation, and how to prevent further soil contamination.

Soil Justice

November 2014 Issue of NewsChina | *by Wang Yan*

While the government has rolled out nationwide measures to cure China's toxic soil problem, prevention efforts remain bogged down.

The fate of Liu Yuying, 57, is inextricably linked to 30 acres of farmland in Miyun County, a northeastern suburb of Beijing, a plot of land in which she has invested all of her family's savings over the past four years.

When Ms. Liu discovered in 2011 that a nearby branch of KB Autosys Co., Ltd, a Korean-owned auto-parts company, had been dumping hazardous waste into more than 30 large pits dug on her property, she embarked on a battle for her livelihood that continues to this day.

"When I noticed truckloads of black powder being dumped, I informed the Miyun environmental protection authorities," Liu told *NewsChina*. "Later, the environmental bureau confirmed that KB had illegally dumped waste [mostly brake dust] on the land, and fined the company 180,000 yuan [US$30,000]." According to the tests carried out by SGS, a multinational inspection, verification, testing and certification company headquartered in Switzerland, the soil was contaminated with highly unsafe levels of heavy metals, including copper and antimony. Worse, the illegal dumping was being carried out just 5 kilometers from a water channel that runs from the local Miyun Reservoir into the Beijing municipal water supply.

Liu filed a lawsuit against KB in 2012, demanding compensation and requiring the latter to remediate the polluted soil in order to make the land safely arable—the lawsuit is ongoing. While the government had the dumped waste and over 500 tons of contaminated soil moved from the site in April 2013, no further action was taken. According to Mao Da, a researcher at Nature University, a Chinese environmental NGO, his tests on September 6, 2014 indicated that parts of the land remained highly polluted with heavy metals, sometimes hundreds of times in excess of safe levels.

Liu Yuying told *NewsChina* that in mid-September, the soil on her land had become barren. Liu has continued to send petitions to various government departments, including the State Council, China's cabinet, to raise awareness of the problem and win justice, but has received no official response. In order to discourage Liu, her landlord, the local village committee, has attempted to terminate her lease, so far unsuccessfully.

POISONED LAND

Liu's case is not an isolated one. Soil pollution has haunted China for over a decade, particularly with booms in manufacturing and mining penetrating even the remotest corners of the country, and the use of fertilizers and pesticides becoming common practice nationwide since the late 1990s. Consequently, heavy metal pollution in particular has poisoned millions of square kilometers of farmland. Entire regional populations have been found to have high levels of lead, cadmium, and mercury in their blood, and dangerous levels of carcinogens like cadmium have been detected in local rice products.

Besides, the government-driven process of industrial restructuring and urban construction since the early 2000s has caused many low-grade, high-polluting industrial enterprises to move from urban regions to suburban areas, leaving behind swaths of toxic soil.

The central authorities have recognized the severity of the situation, and launched a nationwide survey from 2005 to 2012 on about 6.3 million square kilometers of land across the country, more than 65 percent of the country's total surface area. The results were guarded as a "State secret" until their publication in April this year, when the Ministry of Environmental Protection's National Soil Pollution Survey Report, the first of its kind in China's history, revealed that over 16 percent of the country's soil was contaminated, with 1 percent "heavily polluted." "The national soil situation is not optimistic," said the report. "The quality of arable land is especially worrying, and the pollution problem arising from industrial and mining sites is prominent."

The release of the survey results was hailed by media as a step towards greater government transparency, yet detailed data about the location and severity of individual pollution cases remain unknown.

REMEDIATION

As the severity of the situation became more and more obvious, the State Council passed its 12th Five-Year Plan (2011–2015) for Protection of the

National Soil Environment in mid-2012, allocating 30 billion yuan (US$4.8bn) in total for soil remediation around the country, with 14 provinces and autonomous regions listed as priority regions (see "Finding the Source," *NewsChina*, April 2012, Vol. 044). With reference to similar efforts in Western countries, it was calculated that remediation would cost between tens and hundreds of dollars per square kilometer. Considering the vast area of soil pollution within the country (approximately 1 million square kilometers), the total cost would far exceed the 30 billion yuan allocated to remediation efforts in the latest Five-Year Plan.

Fortunately, China's Soil Pollution Action Plan, drafted and passed by the Ministry of Environmental Protection and scheduled for release by the end of this year, aims to further address funding shortfalls and allocate more investment for pollution prevention and remediation. Media reports have revealed that the plan will establish six pilot "soil protection and remediation" projects, each budgeted at between 1 and 1.5 billion yuan (US$160–240m). By 2020, according to the plan, soil pollution will be "generally contained," and arable soil will be effectively protected.

Outside the public sector, the authorities' incentive measures have drawn private investment—a conspicuous number of soil remediation firms have sprung up. However, Gao Shengda, secretary of the China Environmental Remediation Alliance, points out that so far, remediation techniques and management are in need of improvement. Chen Tongbin, director of the Environmental Remediation Center at the Institute of Geographic Sciences and Natural Resources Research, a prominent Chinese opinion leader on the subject, has told the media that the domestic soil pollution remediation industry remains in its infancy.

There are various methods for treating tainted soil, classified into two major categories: ex-situ methods involving excavation of affected soils and subsequent treatment at the surface, and in-situ methods that seek to treat the contamination without removing the soil. Domestically, research into polluted soil treatment and the application of different measures (physical, chemical, biological or botanical) is mushrooming. Even botanical measures, such as mass planting of various forms of vegetation to absorb heavy metals, has been adopted by research groups (see "Silent Killer," *NewsChina*, April 2012, Vol. 044).

Debate on the most suitable method to tackle the problem continues among China's political decision-makers and within its academic circles, with the authorities aiming to come to a conclusion with the publication of the Action Plan.

BLEAK REALITY

Another debate is on who should foot the bill for the soil remediation—the government, or polluters themselves? During a recent interview with

New Century Magazine, Gao Shengda, Secretary of the China Environmental Remediation Alliance, said the most urgent task was to distinguish between "old and new" polluted land. "[In the case of] historical pollution, where the responsible party cannot be identified, the State should pay for remediation. In cases where companies are still causing pollution, the State should use stricter emissions and supervision standards to stop further pollution."

Without strict rules to regulate and punish polluters, the threat of contamination will remain. A recent case in mid-September, in the uninhabited Tengger desert in China's Inner Mongolia Autonomous Region, saw chemical plants continuing to dump untreated waste and sewage water into the desert, despite the scandal coming to light in the media as early as four years ago. While the local government shut down a number of factories, the soil pollution crisis resurfaced, and then worsened. Local government admitted that there were shortcomings in their supervision system.

Calls for a "polluter pays" principle are popular in China, yet the complexity of each individual soil pollution case makes it difficult to define the level of legal responsibility of various interested parties, particularly since the use rights for many plots of land may have been transferred several times.

"Soil remediation costs time and money," Chen Nengchang, vice director of the Soil Pollution and Remediation Committee of the Guangdong Society of Soil Sciences told *NewsChina*. Chen also added that the key to solving the problem lies in prevention rather than a cure, and that related environment protection laws and regulations should be established and strictly implemented.

Many are anticipating the final outcome of the pending Soil Environment Protection Law. The law, according to Wang Shuyi, leader of the team charged with its drafting, "will be formally announced no later than 2017."

A major supplier to auto companies such as Hyundai, GM and KIA, KB continues to manufacture brake pads in Miyun, with an annual manufacturing capacity amounting to over 300,000 units. According to a spokesperson for the company, it has yet to receive notice from the government regarding compensation for the pollution of Liu Yuying's land.

While Liu acknowledges the action the central government has taken to upgrade soil pollution protection, she remains pessimistic about the general situation, and continues to send petition letters—she hopes that someday she will receive feedback. "The policy [on tackling soil pollution remediation] from the central government is inspiring. However, it is local government implementation that is the problem," Liu told *NewsChina*.

Challenges of Managing China's Great River

The Yangtze at 6,300km is the world's third longest river, and drains one fifth of China's land area. The provinces and municipalities along the river generate 42 percent of China's GDP and are home to 200 of the country's 500 largest companies. The Yangtze is also the site of the famous Three Gorges Dam.

In a trio of articles under the heading "River of Gold," Cai Rupeng describes the importance of the Yangtze to commerce and agriculture, and how a coordinated and wide-ranging development plan for the river leading to greatly enhanced economic potential and sustainability could overcome the current mishmash of overlapping agencies which control the Yangtze basin. This plan is known as the YREB—the Yangtze River Economic Belt. Mentioned frequently by Cai is the National Development and Reform Commission, or NDRC. This powerful commission is pushing for the YREB and is an entity that China watchers need to be familiar with.

Arterial Asset

November 2014 Issue of NewsChina | *by Cai Rupeng*

The Yangtze River connects three colossal urban clusters in eastern, central and western China. Through the development of a new economic belt, it is hoped this region could supplant China's industrial eastern coast as the country's principal growth engine.

Chongqing, a vast southwestern municipality directly under the administration of the central government and home to almost 30 million people, is located in the upper reaches of the Yangtze River, and is by far the largest urban center in China's hinterland. On April 28, 2014, Premier Li Keqiang presided over a symposium in the city, which was viewed as almost parallel in its scale and importance to an executive meeting of the State Council.

Themed "building a Yangtze River Economic Belt (YREB) by relying on the golden waterway," the meeting was attended by Vice-premier Zhang Gaoli, Secretary-general of the State Council Yang Jing, and Governor of the People's Bank of China Zhou Xiaochuan. The governors of the seven provinces and two municipalities that sit astride navigable sections of the Yangtze River, along with representatives from Guizhou and Zhejiang, provinces in close proximity to the main waterway, also attended.

The Yangtze River, often called China's "golden waterway," has been a vital commercial lifeline for millennia, and for many, continues to be the country's foremost natural wonder. Alongside its shorter but more fertile cousin the Yellow River, it constitutes a symbol of the nation. Rising from the Tanggula mountain range on the Qinghai-Tibetan Plateau, the Yangtze virtually bisects the country from west to east. Its total length of 6,300 kilometers makes it the world's third longest river. Hundreds of tributaries extend north and south along its entire length, meaning the Yangtze comprises a total drainage area of 1.8 million square kilometers, equaling about one fifth of China's land area.

Since ancient times, the Yangtze has been a central artery for Chinese commerce. It has been the principal waterway serving nine Chinese provinces and, latterly, two municipalities. An economic belt along the Yangtze, if efficiently coordinated and soundly developed, could function as an enormous propeller for China's long-term economic development.

The Chinese government has discussed the idea of an overall development scheme for the YREB for two decades. While sketches have been drawn and theories expounded, implementing such a scheme has been hindered by the generally sluggish economic development of China's inland provinces. Until now, plans for the YREB had been shelved in favor of its more practical rivals—the Western Development Strategy and the Central Rise policy.

Nevertheless, recent signals from the central government have once again created a buzz in provinces and municipalities along the Yangtze River tired of living in the shadow of China's coastal industrial-commercial belt. Intentions to revive the dormant YREB plans have been publicly aired by top officials, and these renewed commitments to turning this overlooked region into a pillar for future economic development have convinced regional administrators that their fortunes are now set to change.

NOCKED ARROW

Before the symposium in Chongqing, Premier Li Keqiang made a three-day tour of inspection of the Yangtze River, traveling upstream after a photo-op on a pier in Chongqing's Wanzhou district. His aim, according to official reports, was to gain an overview of navigation and ecological conditions along the river, as well as to view development projects already underway on its banks.

This year, Li has publicly and repeatedly advocated the development of the YREB. His tour of inspection was therefore viewed as a signal that the zone's establishment is now all but inevitable, with State media referring to the project as "an arrow on the bowstring."

Immediately after the meeting in Chongqing, concept stocks relating to the YREB rocketed in value, with three in particular hitting their daily surge limits. Xiao Jincheng, director of the Institute of Spatial Planning and Regional Economy with the National Development and Reform Commission (NDRC), told *NewsChina* that the NDRC has been busy with fact-finding missions relating to the establishment of the YREB for more than a year.

In September last year, the NDRC, alongside the Ministry of Transportation (MoT), held a mobilization meeting in Beijing to draft their jointly-issued "Guidance for Constructing a New Supporting Zone for China's Economy by Relying on the Yangtze River."

Delegates from seven provinces and two municipalities along the Yangtze River were instructed to attend, and, in a keynote speech, NDRC minister Xu Shaoshi told these dignitaries that planning the YREB was a "holistic strategy" which would "motivate a comprehensive renaissance in eastern, central and western areas of China." The YREB would therefore become "the backbone of China's economy," Xu added.

The general plan, according to Xu, will rely on three urban clusters located in the Yangtze River Delta, the river's middle reaches, and the Chengdu-Chongqing municipal area. Three shipping centers—Shanghai, Wuhan and Chongqing—will enjoy a boost in upriver commerce, and the development of the middle and upper sections of the Yangtze will also be promoted. Plans were also unveiled to dig navigable waterways to link Shanghai on the east coast with Yunnan Province in the remote southwest, forming a trade pattern with "two outlets."

When it comes to the details of implementation of this grand plan, however, plenty of room for maneuver is left to regional administrators.

DELAYS

For some, the NDRC's perspective is too ambitious and aggressive. For many others, the need for such a plan is self-evident, and several officials have argued that developing the commercial potential of China's longest waterway has been deferred for far too long.

Jin Yihua, former director of the Changjiang [Yangtze] River Administration of Navigational Affairs (CRANA), told *NewsChina* that back in the late 1980s, several proposals concerning the overall industrial development of the Yangtze River basin had been brought forward by related experts. One well-known proposal was from economic geographer Lu Dadao, who put forward a "T-shaped" development strategy designed to turn the Yangtze into a lateral axis radiating vertical economic corridors along its length to form a trading grid.

In 1992, the 14th National Congress of the Communist Party of China also saw delegates float the idea of developing the Yangtze River

Delta and the areas along the river's banks upstream of the newly-established Pudong New Area in Shanghai. At the time, however, China's eastern seaboard was experiencing unprecedented breakneck growth, and all eyes were on manufacturing and export-based industries, few of which had much to gain by setting up in the country's remote interior. Pudong bloomed into Shanghai's modern commercial hub, but proposals for developing more inland areas along the Yangtze were largely ignored.

The economy of the Yangtze River basin, particularly in the upper and middle reaches, was poorly developed in the 1980s and early 1990s, lacking the momentum to generate the market demand that would support further investment. Jin Yihua recalled that in the early 1980s, the government had built more than ten 10,000-ton capacity docks along the Yangtze River's banks, a huge investment. However, the river lacked the traffic to warrant such a massive outlay. "There were too few ships coming in. These docks were doing nothing but sunbathing," said Jin.

The river would not remain silent for long. In the 1990s, the Yangtze River's shipping lanes began to catch the attention of local governments, with a few observers noting that they could provide an essential route to inland manufacturing concerns that could operate at much lower costs than those on the coast, which were already experiencing falling profits even as living standards rose. Yet, particularly after 2000, many cities found that the Yangtze River had become a shipping bottleneck incapable of supporting demand for more open lanes, stymieing local development.

"Local governments finally realized that the improved utilization of Yangtze River shipping lanes hinged on cooperation," Jin told *NewsChina*.

In 2006, the first meeting of the "Leading Group of Yangtze River Waterway Development and Coordination" was held in Nanjing, capital of Jiangsu Province, in the Yangtze's lower reaches. During this meeting, seven provinces and two municipalities jointly signed an overall program to promote shipping, an agreement that has held firm until today. However, the ongoing promotional efforts have so far failed to translate into the widespread infrastructural upgrading required to turn the Yangtze into a viable conduit for the bulk of China's inland shipping. The river remains bottlenecked by a shortfall in transportation capacity as its satellite economy, especially manufacturing enterprises situated along its banks, continues to expand.

LOPSIDED

Research from related government departments indicates that, beginning around 2014, cargo volume on Yangtze River's upper reaches peaked at 150 million tons. Yet the gross industrial production of Chongqing Municipality alone is expected to reach 2 trillion yuan (US$324bn) in

2015, requiring an available water transportation volume of 180 million tons. In other words, China's longest river isn't equipped to cope with the shipping requirements of one of the several metropolises located on its banks.

To serve the proposed YREB, the creation of a fully integrated transport system has become a key priority for macroeconomic planners.

Last October, Xu Xianping, deputy director of the NDRC, stressed in his report to CRANA that the construction of an integrated transport system along the Yangtze River would need to incorporate current industrial structures, combine different means of conveyance and optimize the river's transport investment structure.

In Xiao Jincheng's view, the Yangtze River could only become the "golden waterway" referred to by government officials if an integrated, efficient transport network could be established along its entire length.

Last September, the MoT signed an agreement with the seven provinces and two municipalities that straddle the Yangtze River entitled the "Agreement for Cooperation on Promoting Various Important Works in the Development of Yangtze River Shipping." This agreement set a target to raise the average per-vessel tonnage of cargo shipping in the Yangtze River to 2,000 tons along the main waterway and 1,200 tons throughout the entire river basin by 2020.

Currently, since precise guidelines have yet to be issued by the central government, the specific plan to realize the goal of a pan-Yangtze economic development zone remains unclear. However, many anticipate an even more ambitious growth plan from central agencies that will be designed to mobilize provincial authorities to commit significant resources to developing the Yangtze Basin.

Shanghai, Wuhan and Chongqing, as the three main shipping hubs along the Yangtze, remain at the heart of such plans, while the major conurbations of Nanjing, Wuhu, Jiujiang, Yueyang and Yibin have all been mooted as logistics centers to be seamlessly integrated into the region's shipping network.

Meanwhile, the continued construction of high-speed railroads and highways has also been introduced into the YREB development program. According to Chinese media, Beijing has developed a preliminary plan to build a high-speed rail line along the Yangtze River from Shanghai to Chengdu via Hefei, Wuhan, and Chongqing, along with a Shanghai-Kunming high-speed railway that would stretch from China's leading financial center to Yunnan's provincial capital via the strategic commercial centers of Hangzhou, Nanchang, Changsha, and Guiyang. Thus, multiple cities with populations in the millions will be linked directly into a trade network that will flow outwards from the Yangtze Basin.

Meanwhile, a highway network connecting key economic zones, regional central cities, major ports and strategic border ports will be formed around four existing east-west national highways (Shanghai to Chengdu, Shanghai to Chongqing, Shanghai to Kunming, and Hangzhou to Ruili) and fifteen north-south national highways.

Realizing this entire plan will cost trillions of yuan. However, the central government clearly sees this unprecedented investment in infrastructure as preferable to a continuation of lopsided development that has seen the east prosper, albeit rather unsustainably, while the west has largely depended on resource exploitation and shaky investment in real estate, tourism and other privately-led projects.

In April's symposium in Chongqing, Li Keqiang pointed out that in the history of world economics, development often starts from the coast and makes its way inland. In his view, the movement of industrial and commercial development west along the Yangtze is crucial to the government's grand plan for upgrading China's economy, at a stroke weaning the east off dependence on imports and the west off insecure investments such as real estate and the exploitation of dwindling natural resources.

This strategy is a gamble, but one that, most observers agree, has to be taken to ensure breaking the cycle of unbalanced development.

Channeling Success

November 2014 Issue of NewsChina | *by Cai Rupeng*

The diversity and sheer vastness of the Yangtze River Basin makes any attempt at marshaling resources to develop it a gargantuan task. Can even the Chinese government pull it off?

Currently, the "golden waterway" of the Yangtze River accommodates 60 percent of the freight traffic plying China's inland provinces through its main stretch. 85 percent of the country's annual yield of coal and iron ore is produced in the river's basin, and more than 90 percent of foreign trade cargo produced in China's interior is transported via the Yangtze to the nation's ports.

With such economic weight behind the argument, few have doubted the significance of constructing a Yangtze River Economic Belt (YREB). Yet as a regional strategy that would spread across nine provinces and two municipalities, difficulties in implementing any such scheme are also considerable.

While provinces and municipalities along the Yangtze are actively involved in the debate over future cooperation, each one is individually working to carve out its own slice of this promising development strategy. Myriad challenges face those intending to spearhead the development of this vast and diverse section of China's inland territory, not least getting regions locked in competition for resources and investment to work together for the greater good.

Right now, more questions than answers seem to present themselves. How would a YREB stretching for thousands of kilometers across all manner of terrain be effectively formed? How could development projects be coordinated between enormous population centers, scattered rural communities and vast swaths of virtually uninhabited land?

Perhaps the most pressing concern is how to prevent this strategy from further germinating antagonism between a score of provinces that are already in close competition, a situation that has bred mistrust and rivalry between their respective leaderships.

BIGGEST WORRY

Chen Yao, director of the Industrial and Regional Layout Lab of the Institute of Industrial Economics under the Chinese Academy of Social Sciences (CASS), told *NewsChina* that economic relations in areas along the Yangtze River have never been close, with regional development and trade gaps yawning into chasms when one compares these regions with others in eastern, central and western China.

Chen pointed out that after the founding of the People's Republic in 1949, due to the lack of an overall development strategy, the foundation of interaction and integrated development of the entire Yangtze River Basin has been very weak. "There is more competition than cooperation, particularly between the cities," he said.

Hubei, Jiangxi and Hunan provinces, all of which are located along the middle reaches of the Yangtze River, have recently, however, begun to investigate cooperative trade pacts in order to consolidate development opportunities. In 2012, these provinces signed a tripartite development accord aimed at interlinking their economies through greater commercial cooperation between urban centers, using the Yangtze River as a conduit. All three provinces have also been lobbying the central government to elevate their rudimentary "trade triangle" into a national-level strategy, an essential means to acquire central government funding.

However, insiders claim that in most cases, provinces, municipalities and individual cities continue to vie with one another for dominance in regional trade. Xiao Jincheng, director of the Institute of Spatial Planning and Regional Economy with the National Development and Reform Commission (NDRC), told *NewsChina* that local governments along the length of the Yangtze River have been divided over many issues, from navigation strategy to taxation, with the subject of how best to navigate the multiple lockgates of the Three Gorges reservoir a particularly contentious issue.

In 2011, the bidirectional throughput of locks on the Three Gorges reservoir was over 100 million tons, meaning the vast project had hit its intended annual shipping capacity 19 years in advance. This led to countless ships being stranded in the Three Gorges reservoir, with a logjam of 940 ships representing the worst congestion on a Chinese waterway in history.

Currently, it takes about four to five days for a fast container ship to navigate from Chongqing to Shanghai. However, captains complain that two or three of these days are spent waiting to pass through locks, greatly damaging efficiency and increasing costs. These bottlenecks also seriously impact communities and ecosystems along the river through noise, light and air pollution.

It is predicted that in the next 10 to 20 years, annual lockage cargo through the Three Gorges Dam will continue to rise, reaching more than 200 million tons by 2020. This situation has led to a division of opinion between the provinces that suffer most from excess traffic along the Yangtze, and those that produce the bulk of goods that navigate its waters. As a result, Hubei Province recently tabled a plan to establish an integrated transport system that would make Yichang, a city within its borders, a transportation hub that would host shipping waiting to pass through nearby locks. However, Chongqing Municipality and Sichuan Province, both located upstream, have instead demanded the building of additional lock gates in order to facilitate direct navigation.

Many officials have expressed concerns over the administrative barriers that may hinder the establishment of the YREB, though few are willing to speak openly about just how profound these problems might be. "The biggest worry is that the plan won't come off in the end, despite local governments doing their best to appear enthusiastic," one official, speaking on condition of anonymity, told *NewsChina*.

MIDDLE REACHES

The lower reaches of the Yangtze River, currently the greatest beneficiary of the development of the economic hub of the Shanghai Pudong New Area, the Shanghai Pilot Free Trade Zone, and the general boom in China's eastern coastal economies, are often the most reluctant to divert resources upstream. While populous regions and major urban centers such as Sichuan and Chongqing have enjoyed favorable policies that have led to the creation of Chongqing's Liangjiang New Area and Beijing's Western Development Strategy, many areas on the banks of the Yangtze continue to lose out.

Analysts point to Hubei as the province that would benefit most from the establishment of the YREB, likely explaining its officials' enthusiasm in promoting the new strategy.

"[The YREB] is an opportunity that Hubei has dreamed of for a long time, as well as being the biggest, most straightforward and most practical," said a press release by the Hubei's provincial Development and Reform Commission.

Over 2,000 kilometers of the Yangtze's shoreline are in Hubei, and the city of Wuhan has historically been a major stopping point for river shipping, with its municipal officials among the most vocal advocates for the YREB.

In a recent report on the construction of the YREB submitted by Hubei provincial authorities to the NDRC, the province suggested establishing an embassy district in Wuhan to act as a catalyst for foreign investment. The same report also demanded the opening of more international trade routes and boosting international flight traffic into and out of Wuhan's airport in order to both meet rising demand and boost global interest.

However, for every enthusiastic Wuhan official, there is a lukewarm Shanghai equivalent, and until some degree of consensus can be reached on how the further development of the Yangtze Basin can benefit all those reliant on this crucial waterway, more plans are being shelved than implemented.

Uncharted Waters

November 2014 Issue of NewsChina | *by Cai Rupeng*

Could the development of the Yangtze River Economic Belt link the Pacific Ocean to both the Indian and Atlantic oceans? One official is convinced it can, and will.

Xiao Jincheng, vice chairman of China Association of Research into Regional Economies, is also director of the Institute of Spatial Planning and Regional Economy with the National Development and Reform Commission (NDRC)—China's foremost macroeconomic planning agency. A pioneer in the study of China's regional economic development, Xiao has become a leading advocate for the large-scale development and streamlining of the Yangtze Basin economy.

However, Xiao is the first to admit that existing barriers to regional cooperation and the effective establishment of an integrated transportation and logistics network must be overcome before any such plan can be implemented.

> *NewsChina*: What motivated the Chinese government to bring out its first action plan on a Yangtze River economic development zone in 2013?
>
> *Xiao Jincheng*: China's western regions have limited habitable land resources. Even with huge investment, these areas are

unlikely to attract further settlement or industry. However, the river itself, along with its tributaries, has massive potential. The Yangtze River basin is rich in resources and has been a major source of government revenue since ancient times. Yet, compared with eastern coastal areas, the potential of its upper and middle reaches has never been fully exploited. Reform and Opening-up concentrated on the eastern coast, and foreign-funded enterprises have stayed clustered in these areas. The future opening up of China needs to be multidirectional. The new administration hopes to develop the upper reaches of the Yangtze by relying on this "golden waterway."

The development of the Yangtze River belt is also conducive to the progress of urbanization. The central government plans to transfer 300 million people from rural areas into cities within 20 years. It is not possible for all of them to be resettled on the southeastern coast. The area along the Yangtze River has a dense concentration of large, medium and small cities along its banks, giving it great potential for industrial development and for urbanization.

Moreover, in terms of trade, the YREB, when established, will extend to Yunnan Province and even into the Indian Ocean via the economic corridor of China, Myanmar, Bangladesh and India. It will become a link connecting the Pacific and the Indian oceans. Also, it will open China's west to the Silk Road economic belt in a trade route stretching as far as the Atlantic coast.

NC: What are the advantages of the Yangtze basin over other projects, such as interlinking Beiijing, Tianjin and Hebei Province, or the development of the "New Silk Road?"

XJ: Economic and social development requires water resources, land and other conditions. We just have to look at geography to see where development is best situated. In the southwest, there is abundant rainfall but scarce space, ruling out large-scale construction projects. The northwestern regions are mainly composed of the Loess Plateau, the Gobi desert and other arid areas that are tough to settle. In the northeast, we have expansive infrastructure and fertile land, but the long-term exploitation of resources has left these regions resource-poor. Besides, due to the dominance of State-owned enterprises in China's economy, many institutional problems remain unresolved in these areas.

Comparatively speaking, the coast still has the best conditions in terms of location. Since Reform and Opening-up, coastal areas have led the charge of development, starting with the Pearl River Delta, then the Yangtze River Delta, and now Bohai Bay. Right there we have a northward development shift. Why? Because investors are most concerned about land, labor and other production costs, and businesses migrate accordingly.

The biggest difference between the YREB and other projects is that it can serve the dual role of linking existing economic hot zones within China, and connect to Eurasian and South Asian economies.

NC: So what lies in the way of realizing the project?

XJ: The YREB comprises nine provinces and two municipalities directly under the central government. Each of these eleven regions has its own interests and aspirations. They all want to attract industry, but they have to cooperate in order to fully benefit, and this cooperation will require integrated development strategies. Take shipping as an example—all provinces and municipalities want to raise the status of their own ports and attract more ships. None of them care whether more ships dock in a neighboring province.

Pollution stemming from overpopulation is another major issue to consider. Increasing urbanization, particularly in the upper reaches of the Yangtze, has exerted enormous pressure on the environment. We need to move these communities away from areas where their presence threatens entire ecosystems, yet these people need to be accommodated somewhere, therefore we need to build goodwill among local governments further downstream.

Infrastructure in medium-sized and small cities along the river is still very weak, and continues to be a barrier to further investment and urban expansion, putting a damper on potential revenue streams. This is another area where improvement is needed.

NC: Administrative barriers seem to be the biggest obstacles. How to overcome them?

XJ: In my opinion, there should be a central-level coordinating institution overseeing the establishment of the YREB, like the Western Development Office and the Northeast Revitalization Office. Regional cooperation cannot rely on official documents alone. It needs to be pushed forward by higher level authorities. Otherwise, little progress may be made. But such oversight institutions do not need to be permanent— they can be disbanded once they meet their goals.

After establishing such an organ, concrete measures and a scientific and practical plan should be drawn up, and then applied in their entirety. Regions should be prohibited from obstructing such implementation—only through such measures can timely progress be achieved.

NC: Wuhan is a major city located on the central stretch of the Yangtze River. What role should it play in the establishment of the YREB?

XJ: As a large port in the Yangtze River basin, Wuhan has excellent infrastructure and a large population that it could employ to benefit surrounding areas, in order to avoid it simply becoming a prosperous island in a sea of poverty. Nearby historic cities such as Jingzhou and Yichang can also be developed to attract industry and commerce.

NC: Many cities along the river have come up with plans to accelerate development. Which of these should be given priority?

XJ: Not all cities along the Yangtze River may develop into economic growth hubs. In my view, priority should be given to developing small and medium-sized cities into larger conurbations. Then, each urban center needs to be considered in terms of its ability to radiate prosperity outwards and into its surrounding environs.

Currently, overall development of the middle and upper reaches of Yangtze River is sluggish. Yet metropolises such as Wuhan, Chongqing and Chengdu are rapidly experiencing unsustainable population growth due largely to their isolated economic success. Other cities, meanwhile, have struggled to expand, despite every indication being that they should— Nantong and Zhenjiang in Jiangsu, Wuhu and Anqing in Anhui, Huangshi, Jingzhou and Yichang in Hubei, Jiujiang in Jiangxi, Yueyang in Hunan, and Luzhou in Sichuan are all examples of this.

The situation indicates that there is still great potential in China's regional economy, but that it is still not being realized. When the middle and upper reaches of Yangtze River develop to a similar level as its lower reaches, then we will see prosperity truly spread along this "golden waterway."

Food Scandal

McDonalds, KFC, Pizza Hut, and other fast food chains in China were discovered in July 2014 to be serving expired chicken and beef to customers. These products came from the Chinese firm OSI, the world's largest food processor, which had printed fake expiration date labels for its products. Whether the fast food chains were aware of this practice was not then determined, but this scandal is sadly typical of the state of the Chinese food chain. The article "OSI China in Food Scandal" tells the story.

OSI China in Food Scandal

September 2014 Issue of NewsChina | *by* NewsChina Magazine

Shanghai Husi Food Company, a Chinese subsidiary of American firm OSI, the world's biggest food processor, has come under fire after its Shanghai plant was exposed as having processed expired meat.

According to Shanghai Oriental Television, which broke the story, Husi had processed tons of expired frozen chicken to be made into chicken nuggets for Chinese branches of McDonald's. The company also reportedly used beef trimmings that were seven months expired in reconstituted steaks supplied to Chinese KFC restaurants. The report claimed that the company had printed its own expiration date labels in order to evade the attention of food inspectors.

Shanghai's local food supervision authority has so far seized 100 tons of suspect products originating at the Husi plant, many of which were destined for chillers in local branches of McDonald's, KFC, Pizza Hut and 7-Eleven. Parent company OSI, which has set up six other branches on the Chinese mainland in the company's 22 years of China operations, has found its practices under scrutiny, with shockwaves resonating throughout the country's immense fast food industry.

McDonald's CEO Don Thompson argued on July 22 that his company's China branches were fooled by faked quality assurance certificates provided by Husi and that they have ended cooperation with the company. Many other foreign brands affected by the scandal also made similar announcements.

Despite the fact that the plant responsible for the violations was Chinese, the revelations have shaken public faith in what were previously seen as "safe" restaurants operating under foreign brand names. A litany of tainted food scandals have led to mass public outrage at the country's outmoded quality assurance supervision, with critics arguing that only in China could foreign companies get away with selling expired meat products for so long.

Shanghai police have closed Husi's local plant and reportedly detained five employees. An insider revealed that the company's senior executives had encouraged the use of expired materials and the faking of quality supervision documentation. Now the media are digging for evidence that such practices occurred with the full knowledge and complicity of foreign-owned fast food brands operating in China.

Highlighting Food Safety Problems

A more comprehensive rather than anecdotal approach to looking into Chinese food safety was taken by Chen Qiaoling in researching and publishing *China's Compiled Food Safety Incidents.* The book is reviewed by Ma Jing in the following article "Going Public." Its 26 chapters detail how water pollution, unhygienic processing, adulteration and shortcuts taken by small farmers all contribute to this endemic problem.

Though not an attempt at solutions, MBA student Chen Qiaoling's new book is a first try at cataloging China's food safety issues. Interestingly, this effort comes from a self-funded private individual, not, as one could expect, from the government or media.

Going Public

June 2015 Issue of NewsChina | *by Ma Jing*

An academic NGO has published China's first overview of the country's ongoing food safety problems. Their aim is to give ordinary, scandal-weary Chinese information about what is, and isn't, safe to eat.

When Chen Qiaoling first began to write *China's Compiled Food Safety Incidents,* nearly everyone around her voiced their disapproval. Their reason for skepticism towards her project was unanimous: "Nobody will care to read it."

Chen's finished book, 26 chapters in length, took Chen, an MBA student at Tsinghua University, along with her research team, more than two years to finish. *China's Compiled Food Safety Incidents* was published by Jilin University Press in March 2015 at the team's own expense.

While only 200 hard copies of her work rolled off the presses, Chen put a digital version on the website of Yueyaduo, a grassroots food safety research center established by her team of some 20 volunteers, none of whom are food safety professionals.

"China has plenty of food-related research institutions, but food [safety] problems still abound," Chen told *NewsChina*. "We're just trying to find a solution to address these problems from an amateur's point of view."

START-UP

Yueyaduo came into being entirely by chance. In April 2012, when Tsinghua University was celebrating the 101st anniversary of its founding, Chen, then a second-year MBA student, found herself seated beside management graduate Chen Hongrong at a commemorative event. While making small talk about her job prospects, Chen Qiaoling mentioned that what motivated her to study at Tsinghua was her dream to buy a big apartment in Beijing, and a fancy car, after graduation.

Chen told *NewsChina* how her new acquaintance's disappointment at hearing this was "palpable." Instead of lauding her stated goals, Chen Hongrong remarked that "as a Tsinghua graduate, you should aim higher, have more spiritual pursuits, and take more social responsibility."

The conversation quickly turned to China's litany of environmental problems, and then on to food safety, with both parties agreeing that something needed to be done to safeguard public health.

Several months later, Chen Qiaoling suspended her studies at Tsinghua and established the Yueyaduo food safety research center with Chen Hongrong, who declined to be interviewed for this article. Their mission statement included a bid to raise public awareness of food safety while simultaneously providing solutions to farmers and food manufacturers who wanted to enhance the quality of their products.

As Yueyaduo's first published study, *China's Compiled Food Safety Incidents* is being touted as the first major overview of food safety scandals that have affected China's consumers in recent years.

Chen initially aimed to write 50 chapters, but due to staff and funding shortages only managed to publish 26. Each chapter has a specific theme including the impact of water pollution on food, unhygienic food processing practices, and the fatal consequences of adulterating infant formula with chemicals—all themes corresponding to various public outcries in the last decade.

"I am fully aware that present efforts cannot solve these problems immediately," Chen told the official Xinhua News Agency. "My hope is that this record will offer insight into what has happened, and where the dangers are."

Chen said that she was inspired to continue with her research by the story of Harvey Wiley, who caught the attention of the American public and the US government through his research into fraudulent practices in the US food industry; research which contributed to the signing of the

Pure Food and Drug Act of 1906 and ultimately the creation of the US Food and Drug Administration.

"I think China needs someone like [Wiley]," Chen said.

IMMERSIVE

During their two-year research project, Chen and her team visited hundreds of food enterprises, farmers, street vendors and restaurants in nine Chinese provinces to compile a record of how many actually adhered to national food safety standards. Rather than seek to uncover new food scandals, the team's goal was to better inform the Chinese public about their food choices.

Constant exposure to lax food standards has made Chen sensitive to the color, odor and ingredients used in everyday foods. Born into a rural household in Shandong Province, Chen has witnessed first-hand how the weak implementation and the non-adherence to nationally-set food standards, particularly in small-scale enterprises and on farms, is sustained by a combination of ignorance of these standards and a need to reduce costs.

"We realized that food safety is a complicated social problem," Chen told the Chinese daily newspaper *Global Times*. "It involves a number of issues, including soil and water pollution, agricultural produce standards, logistics and public honesty. From an economic perspective, we wanted to find out what motivates food manufacturers and farmers to tamper with food, and possibly provide them with solutions and incentives not to cheat consumers."

Wang Xianzhi, a food safety expert with China's *Economy and Nation Weekly* told *NewsChina* that in the summer of 2014, Chen Qiaoling brought a copy of her manuscript to him and asked for his advice about publishing it. Wang claims he only offered her one piece of advice. "Make sure every source of data is correct and reliable."

"For college students to voluntarily set up this organization to raise the public's awareness of food safety is something that deserves encouragement," Wang added.

Chen's team, most of whom are Tsinghua students, studied and reviewed all the media reports and academic papers that they had mentioned in their book to ensure its accuracy. However, while they comprehensively fact-checked all their research, not one of them expected that a book on food safety would gain widespread public and media attention.

To their surprise, on March 8, 2015 Cui Weiping, a professor with the Beijing Film Academy, mentioned *China's Compiled Food Safety Incidents* on her microblog account, which sparked a surge in demand for copies. Shortly afterwards, Chen and her team were surprised to receive a telephone request for several hard copies of their book from China's Food and Drug Administration, the country's highest food standards authority.

Chen told *NewsChina* that *China's Compiled Food Safety Incidents* is "just the beginning." Her team is now preparing to publish a series of books related to food safety, including a study of China's nascent organic food industry, until a direct platform linking food producers and consumers can be established in China.

Chen has only recently resumed her studies at Tsinghua, and is now trying to recoup some of the 100,000 yuan (US$16,140) of her own savings that she spent on her book. She told our reporter that she has made addressing China's food safety problems, which she sees as being social rather than technical, a worthwhile long-term career goal.

"Previously, I was happy with the returns of my own work," she said. "But now I am trying to create some social value in the area of food safety, even if mine are only minor steps."

Unprepared for Major Earthquake

Tragedy struck Yunnan Province on 3 August 2014, when a 6.5 magnitude earthquake leveled homes, businesses and schools. Over 600 lost their lives and more than 3,000 were injured. Despite the fact that this area was well known to be seismically active, far too little had been spent on reinforcing structures to withstand the frequent temblors. Yang Di describes efforts made there to remedy the situation going forward in the article, "Unpredictable, not Unavoidable." Government subsidies have been available since 2007 for reinforcing buildings in Yunnan, but those renovation projects were somehow not made a priority in Ludian County where the August quake occurred.

Unpredictable, not Unavoidable

October 2014 Issue of NewsChina | *by Yang Di*

Funding shortfalls on housing renovation projects in rural areas, coupled with a lack of basic earthquake safety education, are to blame for the heavy casualties in Yunnan Province's earthquake zone.

On August 3, 2014, a strong earthquake in Ludian County in southern China's Yunnan Province flattened or damaged thousands of buildings, killing at least 617 people and injuring over 3,000.

The 6.5-magnitude tremor struck at 4:30 PM with its epicenter at a depth of 12 kilometers, making it the strongest to hit the province in 14 years and the country's third deadliest quake in the past six years, according to State broadcaster CCTV.

Despite the province's reputation for frequent quakes, however, the tragedy caught both the government and the public off guard. In 2002, Yunnan released a list of regions prone to strong quakes above 7 magnitude, including Ludian, some 366 kilometers east of Kunming, the provincial capital.

After the massive quake in Wenchuan in 2008, the central government sped up the renovation of dilapidated buildings in quake-prone areas, especially in impoverished rural regions. Yunnan's provincial government joined the initiative a year later.

Despite all the efforts and measures, however, the sudden quake in Ludian resulted in heavy casualties in addition to significant economic losses.

DANGER ZONE

According to the China Earthquake Networks Center (CENC), Ludian is a densely populated area of 430,000 people, a density nearly double the provincial average. Besides, it is a relatively poor area, where low construction standards leave buildings susceptible to earthquake damage. Ludian's complex terrain and frequent landslides contributed further to the heavy death toll.

Liu Jie, director of CENC, told *NewsChina* that Yunnan Province, accounting for 4.1 percent of China's land territory, is located in an active earthquake region due to the collision of the Indian and Eurasian tectonic plates. Consequently, Yunnan has become one of China's most notorious earthquake danger zones.

Statistics from the China Earthquake Administration (CEA) showed that in the last century, 377 quakes above magnitude 5 have hit Yunnan Province—the active quake intervals have been reduced from 15 to 10 years. The bureau added that since 2001, Yunnan has seen 41 quakes above magnitude 5, including two in Ludian.

"Currently, Yunnan is witnessing a new active seismic period," Liu told our reporter.

In June 2002, the Yunnan provincial government released a regulation on earthquake prevention and relief work in areas prone to quakes, in which it designated a number of "danger zones." It also required that local governments above county level include quake prevention and relief work in their fundamental economic and social development plans, with specific financial allocations. It also specified that public awareness education on earthquake safety should be made a priority.

281

Nevertheless, it was not until 2013 that the provincial housing and urban-rural development bureau organized a group of experts to compile guidelines on quake resistance for residential buildings in rural areas. 60,000 copies of the document were distributed to township residents for free.

The technical guideline includes details on floor-to-floor height, wall thickness and supporting beam span, specifications that could prevent buildings from collapsing in the event of a strong quake, and would enable residents to continue living at home by making simple repairs after a medium quake.

However, although Ludian is prone to quakes, media reports have showed that many local residents remain unaware of the fact that they are living on an active seismic belt, nor do they know basic anti-seismic measures or how to quake-proof their houses.

"Most victims were killed by collapsing houses," said Ma Zhenxian, head of the civil affairs bureau in Ludian, during an interview with the *Beijing Times*.

Sun Baitao, director of the Institute of Engineering Mechanics at CEA, said that nowadays 90 percent of residential houses in rural areas are not quake-proof, and few rural residents have the foresight to address the problem themselves.

"Earthquakes are unlikely events, and rural residents are reluctant to spend extra money on anti-quake construction," he said.

RENOVATION PROJECT

In 2007, the Yunnan provincial government published a directive to enforce quake-proof building standards in rural areas. In 2008, after the Wenchuan earthquake, the Ministry of Housing and Urban-rural Development, the National Development and Reform Commission and the Ministry of Finance released a joint regulation to expand the renovation of low-quality buildings in rural areas. In 2009, Yunnan Province further revised the project.

According to these regulations, any household in Yunnan Province living in a "relatively dilapidated" dwelling received a subsidy of 2,000 yuan (US$324), whereas those living in "highly dilapidated" houses received 10,000 yuan (US$1,620). Moreover, local governments were encouraged to offer more subsidies within their own capabilities.

On July 4, Luo Yingguang, the province's head of housing and urban-rural development, said during a government meeting that Yunnan is home to 8.43 million rural households, and dilapidated houses made up about 60 percent of that total. The renovation project has so far benefited over 2.25 million households with a total expenditure of 13 billion yuan (US$2.1bn).

"In recent years, the subsidies have been raised to 12,500 yuan (US$2,033) in inland counties and 15,000 yuan (US$2,439) in outlying counties," he said.

Since its inception, the renovation project has played a significant role in certain areas in the province. In Yingjiang County, during the 6.1-magnitude quake on May 30, no deaths were reported, and the rate of collapse was much lower than in other areas of the province.

Yet in Ludian, the renovation project seems not to have been made a priority. According to data released by the Housing and Urban-rural Development Department of Shaotong City in 2013, the implementation rate for renovation projects in Ludian was short of 60 percent, ranking the second lowest among the 11 counties under Shaotong City. In terms of completion rate, Ludian ranked last with under 14 percent.

Remote imaging pictures from China's National Reconnaissance Office show that most collapsed houses in Ludian had clearly been built by local farmers with bricks, mud and wood—materials particularly vulnerable to quake damage.

Chen Guoyong, head of Longtoushan Township in Ludian, said that while he has over 12,000 households queuing up for subsidies for renovations in his town, only a few hundred households would receive them.

"To ensure cash flow to renovation projects, the government normally issues the subsidy in four stages," he said.

A local government official who spoke on condition of anonymity told our reporter that on average, a household has to spend at least 60,000 yuan (US$9,720) to renovate a 60-square-meter house, and that government subsidies are "a drop in the bucket." To make matters worse, the per capita annual income of rural residents in Ludian is 4,300 yuan (US$697).

On the Ludian government website, our reporter found data stating that from 2009 to June 2014, the local government spent 157 million yuan (US$25m) in renovations, supporting 16,610 households, meaning that roughly 85 percent of houses were not renovated.

The auditing bureau in Yunnan also found that during a survey of 20 counties in the province in 2012, most recipients of renovation subsidies were relatively better-off households. For low-income households, whose houses are actually most prone to collapse, the renovation rate was only 13.6 percent.

Moreover, it also found that among the 2,040 households receiving subsidies, over 20 percent had a floor space over 70 square meters, even though the official upper limit for subsidies was set at 60 square meters.

Ye Yaoxian, leading engineer with the China Architecture Design and Research Group, said construction permits are compulsory in quake-proof urban areas, but in rural areas, particularly for residential constructions, the question of permits is a gray area.

"Construction permits should also be implemented for residential houses in rural areas over time," Ye told the *Beijing Times*. "Shouldering the whole burden is beyond the capabilities of the government at present—currently, the problem can only be solved by joint efforts from the central government and local governments, together with rural residents."

No, It's Not Fog

The government used to refer to it as "fog," but everybody in Beijing, Shanghai and dozens of other cities know this is health-damaging smog. It took the courage of Chai Jing, a former TV personality, to highlight the problem. Wang Yan in "Breaking the Silence" describes the February 2015 appearance online of *Under the Dome*, a searing video exposé of the unchecked air pollution in China's cities. Despite being posted on the website of party mouthpiece *People's Daily*[4] and being praised by many public officials, the piece was deleted from most online platforms by censors within a month after it appeared, demonstrating the strange schizophrenia exhibited by Beijing in the face of public dissatisfaction.

Breaking the Silence

May 2015 Issue of NewsChina | *by Wang Yan*

An independent documentary discussing China's air pollution problem, released online in February and erased from most video sharing websites in March, has rekindled debate over how best to tackle the country's most pressing environmental issue.

Chai Jing, a former TV anchor and investigative reporter, produced a self-funded documentary about China's air pollution problem, releasing it online in late February, 2015. The slickly-produced 104-minute film, delivered in the style of Al Gore's *An Inconvenient Truth*, quickly became a sensation, going viral on its first day of release and becoming the top trending topic on Twitter equivalent Sina Weibo.

Within three days, *Under the Dome* received over 150 million views and attracted millions of comments from netizens. Then, on March 6, 2015 the documentary was swiftly removed from most Chinese video sharing websites.

GRUDGE

Over the previous decade, as an investigative reporter for the State-owned China Central Television (CCTV), Chai Jing earned her household-name reputation through coverage of major national news stories including the Severe Acute Respiratory Syndrome (SARS) outbreak in 2004, the 2008 Wenchuan earthquake, coal mine accidents and issues surrounding environmental pollution caused by coal mining in her home province of Shanxi. In 2009, Chai quit reporting and took up a position as an anchor on popular CCTV current events talk show *One on One*.

Chai finally resigned from her job with CCTV in 2014 following the birth of her daughter. *Under the Dome*, named after a US TV series based on the novel by Stephen King, marks her return to the public eye. Chai's "Dome" is the smog that frequently obscures the sky above many places in China.

Under the Dome is presented in the format of a TED Talk, combining a lecture with computer animation embedded with graphical data and animation interspersed with recorded interviews. Chai's film opens with a slideshow demonstrating the PM2.5 (units of particulate matter no more than 2.5 micrometers in diameter found in the atmosphere) curve for Beijing in January 2013, when the city experienced 25 days of unacceptable smog in a single month. Chai discovered her pregnancy that same month, and seeing 25 provinces and cities in China blanketed by heavy smog at that time added to existing fears after her unborn daughter was found to have a benign tumor already growing on her body.

"I'd never felt afraid of pollution before, and never wore a mask," says Chai during her presentation. "But when you carry a life inside you, what she breathes, eats and drinks are all your responsibility, and then you feel the fear."

PM2.5 is widely accepted as being particularly hazardous to public health as it can penetrate the alveolus—the gas exchange region in the human lung. "I perceived smog through my daughter's eyes," Chai recalls, describing how her newborn daughter would be confined indoors on smoggy days, often slapping the window, as Chai perceived, to express her desire to play outside.

"This is a personal grudge against smog," Chai tells her audience, adding that she made *Under the Dome* in order to answer three major questions—what is smog, where does it come from, and what should we do about it.

To back up her claims, Chai interviewed professionals from academic institutes in China and abroad, approached government think tanks, State ministries and environmental departments, took field trips to polluting factories and even former smog hotspots like London and Los Angeles, where she looked at the history of industrial air pollution, and explored potential solutions possibly applicable to China.

Through the use of multimedia platforms, scientific data and interviews with researchers and government officials, the documentary identifies the wide usage of substandard and low quality fossil fuels and the lack of government supervision as the primary contributing factors to China's smog problem. Chai calls for government action in regulating polluters, improving the enforcement power of relevant government departments and individual participation in combating pollution. According to Chai, *Under the Dome* is also an "answer" that she has been preparing for when her daughter grows up. Many attribute the power of Chai's film to her willingness to place her family at the center of the project.

RESPONSE

Chai's film premiered on the website of the *People's Daily*, and swiftly inspired an unusually passionate public and mass media response. Soon, clips were circulating across China's vibrant social media landscape, and Chai was being lauded by users of instant messenger WeChat and microblog site Sina Weibo for funding the project with her own money. Others singled out her bravery in being willing to speak out on issues such as the power of the State energy lobby and bureaucratic obstructions to cleaner air—problems which rarely gain prominence in official media coverage of pollution.

Indeed, Chai's status as a concerned parent rather than a TV reporter was seen as helping her connect with a broad audience. Painting air pollution as a clear and immediate threat to all Chinese people, regardless of social status, Chai struck a chord that few celebrities-turned-activists have been able to. Actor Sun Yizhou commented on his micro-blog account on February 28: "Everyone watch. Regardless of where you are from, whatever your social position, this is a fate that we must collectively face."

"So profound! There has never been such a comprehensive dissection of PM2.5," ran another Weibo post applauding Chai's work.

While the praise was fervent, criticism also emerged as Chai's film became increasingly ubiquitous. Some questioned the morality of Chai explicitly linking her daughter's tumor to air pollution. Others accused her of being a lackey of the State, given the official support afforded her project by numerous government organs, particularly Party mouthpiece People's Daily Online. Peking University professor Wu Jing called the film a typical example of celebrities "promoting themselves" for commercial gain or to obtain public funding while masquerading as concerned citizens.

Some even accused Chai of hypocrisy for "pretending to care about China's problems" even though she chose to have her baby delivered in the US. Others spread rumors that Chai was a smoker, and chose to drive a gas-guzzling SUV.

When most links to Chai's film in its entirety were expunged from the Chinese Internet, however, much of this criticism subsided. In professional circles, environmental advocates, including China's new minister of environmental protection Chen Jining, sent personal messages to Chai to thank her for raising public awareness of environmental issues. Nevertheless, certain scientists and industrialists pointed out factual inaccuracies in *Under the Dome*, while others accused Chai of singling out the coal and oil industries for attack while neglecting other major contributors to the pollution problem.

RIPPLES

The ongoing debate surrounding *Under the Dome* has come alongside a major leadership reshuffle in China's Ministry of Environmental Protection. Minister Chen Jining, a former president of Tsinghua University, even likened the documentary to *Silent Spring*, ecologist Rachel Carson's landmark exposé of profligate use of synthetic chemical pesticides which helped inspire a generation of environmental activists in the 1960s.

The film's release, which just preceded the annual gathering of the National People's Congress and the Chinese People's Political Consultative Conference, popularly referred to as the "Two Sessions," was interpreted as a bid to have China's smog problem become a leading item on an agenda dominated by the economy and the Party's ongoing anti-corruption campaign.

Despite being removed from most Chinese video sharing websites, the film's social impact has already been felt in a number of fields. An environmental protection hotline mentioned in the film, which allows members of the public to notify the authorities of illegal emissions, was flooded with calls following the film's release. Although this national hotline has existed since 2001, many have claimed that if it weren't for *Under the Dome*, few members of the public would have known about its existence.

"The hotline does play an effective role in supervising local environmental protection bureaus taking action to combat pollution," Beijing resident Yan Yan, 35, told *NewsChina*. A passionate environmentalist, Yan has personally called the hotline on a number of occasions since 2005 to report air and water pollution issues in her community. According to Yan, all these cases were followed up on by her local environmental protection bureau.

According to Zhong Chonglei, head of the Beijing Environmental Monitoring Team, all calls made to the hotline are recorded and forwarded to relevant local departments within 24 hours, with a follow-up by government personnel also guaranteed.

On March 1, 2015 the Ministry of Environmental Protection also launched a new public WeChat account to allow users to upload photos and written descriptions of pollution, with all reports accessible to local authorities who can then inform users of any follow-up action taken.

Chai's documentary has even been credited with helping boost the share price of many "environmentally friendly" companies. On March 1, more than a dozen stocks in the fields of pollutant treatment, air quality monitoring and green technology saw huge increases, with several stocks jumping 10 percent or more to reach their daily trading limits.

PROSPECTS

In her documentary, Chai Jing tells the audience how "smog" was once described by weather reporters as "fog," with most ordinary Chinese citizens, herself included, barely noticing the horrendous air pollution blanketing their towns and cities. "Smog" as a concept only really entered the Chinese psyche in 2012, when the US embassy in Beijing publicized its PM2.5 monitoring data to indicate the local air quality. Under pressure from social media, the municipal government began to publish its own data, and a rash of record-breaking readings in recent years have turned smog into a national issue.

According to a report by the World Health Organization, it is estimated that 2.8 million of the premature deaths caused worldwide by air pollution in 2012 were clustered in China and the Western Pacific region. Statistics from China's Health Ministry indicate an annual number of premature deaths due to air pollution of 350,000 to 500,000.

Zhang Jin, deputy managing editor with Caixin Media, commented that Chai's delivery, not her source material, was what made *Under the Dome* groundbreaking. "Frankly speaking, the content and viewpoint presented in the documentary are not new. . . [yet] its influence is much stronger than ours. We can only learn from Chai's technique in delivering information."

While air pollution was a leading topic of discussion in the State media in 2012 and in the first half of 2013, the Party's national security and anti-corruption agenda soon took precedence, with coverage of environmental issues being softened or sidelined even as face masks and air purifiers rapidly become features of everyday life.

Action has, however, been taken. A new environmental protection law enacted on January 1, 2015 was hailed as China's toughest environmental law yet. In late February this year, inspectors from the Ministry of Environmental Protection summoned mayors from two northern cities, urging them to crack down on violators of the national environmental law. However, grassroots activism, despite being showered with outward praise, remains unwelcome in the corridors of power. Days after *Under the Dome* was erased from China's video sharing websites and online media outlets, minister Chen Jining called for "greater transparency" in the fight against pollution, and encouraged greater public participation in anti-pollution efforts.

Although Chai Jing's efforts have kept the pollution debate alive, the fact that the same government supporters who gave her a platform have since attempted to mute her message shows that China's political establishment remain sensitive to criticism when it comes from the general public. The long-term effectiveness of *Under the Dome* to engender real change on a national level will hinge primarily on whether or not Chai's work can be rehabilitated into mainstream discourse.

Real Estate and Land Rights

Real Estate Bubble—Slowdown or Collapse?

China's real estate market had been flirting with the stratosphere for years. Fearing the catastrophic effects of a real estate bubble bursting, and with one eye on the spectacular failures of US regulators in the years leading up to 2008 to keep the underpinnings of the market sound, Beijing took a number of steps to keep the market from skyrocketing too fast. Among these measures were limits on bank mortgages, limits on second home ownership, and others.

In "End of an Era," Xie Ying and Zhou Zhenghua carefully dissect the recent cooling of the real estate market in China. Authorities had to walk a fine line between too much cooling and too little, as land sales and construction make up a significant portion of the GDP, and Beijing is committed to keeping GDP growth above 7 percent.

When reading about "homes" in China, think modest apartments, not the standalone single family dwelling on a tree-lined suburban street. Even then, purchasing such an apartment is well beyond the financial reach of most young people in China. This is especially sad for young men, who, due to widespread selective abortion and female infanticide, find themselves competing for mates with too many other men. For them, eligible young women in general consider a potential mate who does not own a home (and a car) to be out of the running.

End of an Era

December 2014 Issue of NewsChina | *by Xie Ying and
Zhou Zhenghua*

China's real estate market has been on a downward spiral since early 2014. Although stimulus policies may be helping sales in some areas, most analysts believe that market is simply weaning itself off price hikes.

Spurred by local stimulus policies, such as loosening controls on the purchase of second homes and reducing mortgage rates, many Chinese cities have seen a slight warming in real estate sales since September.

However, compared to last year, growth, according to analysts, remains far from being sufficient to bring the entire market out of its current slump. Beijing, for example, sold 472 new apartments over the "Golden Week" National Day vacation (October 1–7), nearly 40 percent fewer than were sold in the same period in 2013. Similarly lukewarm figures emerged from the other key markets of Shanghai, Guangzhou and Shenzhen. Although Hangzhou, the so-called "barometer" of the Chinese real estate market, saw a rise in year-on-year sales volume during Golden Week, analysts warned that this was largely due to promotions and price cuts—bad news for those pinning their hopes on a turnaround.

On September 30, just one day before the National Day holiday officially began, China's central bank announced that it would offer the families that had paid off loans for their first homes up to 30 percent off their next mortgage, indicating that the Chinese government is keen to boost the country's real estate market. Many developers and investors voiced optimism at the news, but with early gains reportedly "consumed in advance" by previous price hikes, the "golden age" of the Chinese housing market might already have passed.

TURNDOWN

The sudden freezing of China's previously white-hot real estate market, according to analysts, originated in second- and third-tier cities from late 2013, and soon spread to even the country's most robust markets in Shanghai and Beijing.

According to the National Bureau of Statistics, nearly all Chinese cities have seen both average house prices and sales volume decline in the first eight months of 2014, with some even suffering particularly sharp falls. For example, average house prices in the key economic centers of Hangzhou, Wenzhou and Ningbo (all in Zhejiang Province) plummeted to below those of four years ago, leading some homeowners to riot against developers.

Despite sales growth in September, Su Xuejing, a top real estate analyst with China Securities, told *NewsChina* that sales "cannot catch up with the increase in housing stock." According to China's Ministry of Housing and Urban-rural Development, Beijing currently has nearly 80,000 unoccupied housing units, which according to current projections will take at least 18 months to sell. 2014 sales in the capital peaked in August with 10,163 new apartments sold, but these retailed at an average 25 percent discount on the previous year.

Second-tier cities like Hangzhou were even harder hit, with housing bubbles caused by reckless investment leading to prices even more inflated than those in Shanghai and Beijing, where demand has somewhat tempered the fallout from the downturn. Despite having only about one third of the population of a first-tier city, this small eastern resort town had stockpiled nearly 130,000 unoccupied housing units by June 2014.

Now, the sluggish market has seemingly halted developers' thirst for new land to build upon. Data from the China Index Academy showed that land-transfer revenue had decreased nationwide by about 22 percent over the past eight months, with the figure halved in some key cities. Despite slightly improved housing sales, September was a low point for land sales, with revenue dropping by 70 percent year-on-year. Many cities, including Beijing, Shanghai and Hangzhou, frequently go months without closing a deal.

This data was a bitter blow to local economies that are heavily reliant on land sales and construction. Many analysts have voiced concerns that dismal market projections might drag GDP growth in some cities below the 7 percent demanded by the central government.

REGULATION

Pressured by the downturn, most cities had already moved to rescue the market before the central bank issued its new policies on September 30. According to Chinese media reports, by the end of September, all Chinese cities excepting Beijing, Shenzhen, Shanghai, Guangzhou and the resort town of Sanya, Hainan Province had loosened previous restrictions on homebuyers, such as provisions preventing people from taking out a mortgage on a second home. The hope is that this will revitalize the market and prevent developers and buyers from hedging currently stifling growth.

Hangzhou, for example, has re-opened the purchase of second homes to non-locals since July, 2014. Though keeping its own restrictions, Shanghai has eased the terms under which local residents can take advantage of public reserve funds to apply for mortgages.

Amid calls from developers to break capital chains, the central bank also attempted to bolster the market by relaxing lending restrictions on State banks. An anonymous insider told NewsChina that the relevant departments are planning to work out a new policy allowing unlisted developers to issue company bonds at the Shanghai Stock Exchange. While discussed in terms of being a bold step, many listed developers have already rushed to take this course of action. In July, Citychamp Dartong, a real estate developer in Shanghai, issued US$300 million in company bonds. The same month, Jiangsu Future Land issued US$330 million in bonds, followed in quick succession by another three big developers whose issuances added up to US$700 million in total value.

"These bonds have performed well so far, and stimulus policies issued by the central bank and local governments will further help reduce the risk of developers breaking contracts in case of a fragmentation of their capital chain," Xu Hanfei, chief analyst from Guotai Jun'an Securities, told NewsChina.

END OF AN ERA

A variety of successful stimuli have marginally improved real estate sales volume since the end of September, but the kind of growth developers hoped for has failed to materialize. Data from Essences Securities showed that out of 20 second-tier cities observed, only an average 6 percent month-on-month growth in sales volume was recorded, despite stimulus measures being in place as early as June.

Investors and developers have attributed the slow turnaround to poor implementation that failed to comply with the requirements of the central bank. The September 30 policy statement from the People's Bank of China (PBoC) thus came as a reassurance that central support would improve market outlook. However, analysts and developers have remained conservative in their forecasts, most citing the housing surplus as a reason to be wary of the prospects for growth.

The most typical example of the plight of China's real estate sector is Hangzhou, where an orgy of land snatching made the local government's 2013 land sales revenue 40 percent higher than the total financial budget for that year. Supposing that Hangzhou had maintained the breakneck pace of selling 8 million square meters of new housing every year, it would take a minimum of five years to clear surplus land resources.

Shao Changjian, a real estate developer in Hangzhou dubbed "the housing prophet" by Chinese media, refused to call the slowdown a "collapse," but instead, "a return to normalcy." In past years, Hangzhou's housing price has grown on average 20–30 percent faster than annual municipal GDP. Shao believes this to be an abnormal state of affairs.

This idea is shared by many well-known developers, such as Vanke, China's biggest real estate firm, which in 2014 purchased only one fourth of the total land resources they amassed in 2013. The Evergrande Group, another leading real estate developer, also claimed that they would not buy new landholdings until they had cleared surplus stock.

As early as in 2012, Zhang Baoquan, president of Antaeus Group, a major real estate developer in Yunnan Province, warned that the traditional residential apartment market in China was becoming saturated. According to statistics published by the Ministry of Housing and Urban-rural Development, China had built around 260 million residential housing units nationwide by 2013, a total of 1.1 homes per household on average, while the number of the young people aged 25–35, the largest demographic for first-time buyers, is declining year on year. Although some analysts believe that the government's intensive urbanization program will create new demand, especially in major cities, stagnant wages and what many see as inflated house prices are a major threat to future growth.

"It is good for the market that the government has lifted its former administrative controls on home purchases, but this does not mean that the market will enjoy an immediate turnaround," Tian Shixin, a chief analyst at BOC International, an investment company under the Bank of China, told *NewsChina*. He believes that real estate investment may return to a slow stable pace in the future, even more potential demands are released.

When attending an IMF conference in Washington in early October, Zhu Guangyao, China's deputy finance minister, told media that the Chinese government is keeping a "close eye" on the real estate market, but will be very "cautious in launching any big stimulus package."

"I don't think a turndown in the market is a problem, since the previous prices were too high," he said. "We should allow the market to self-regulate."

His words, however, did not allay confusion over the tendency of China's real estate market, especially in the longer term, to expand and contract according to China's reform agenda. Controls on home purchases, the much-hated residence registration permit or *Hukou*, the spotty construction of low-income housing and back-and-forth over land sales regulations have all served as destabilizing factors in the market. Until clarity on these issues is achieved, real estate developers, investors and ordinary homebuyers are likely to remain bewildered and yet beholden to the vicissitudes of one of the world's messiest marketplaces.

How to Modernize the Farm?

China is the world's largest agricultural producer, feeding nearly 20 percent of the global population from 10 percent of the world's arable land. "Flipping

Farmland", by Zhou Zhenghua and Yu Xiaodong, highlights a fundamental problem for China and its nearly 300 million small farmers. That is, per Marxist prescription, farmland is held in the name of the collective, or village, not by the person or family who actually farms it. So the land cannot be sold by the tenant, which hypothetically could provide a stake for the farmer to move to a city and start a small business or find employment. Since the average farm size is a mere 1.5 acres (0.6 hectares), economy of scale is impossible and China's agricultural output is thereby limited. Even worse, with such small plots to farm, the temptation to skirt pollution and food adulteration laws is high. Furthermore, this arrangement incentivizes collective officials to sell farmland out from under the tenant farmers at great profit. Some solutions are being suggested by high officials, but predictably, firm resistance at the local level is being felt. As so often in China, "the sky is high and the emperor is far away." The center cannot readily control the distant parts.

Flipping Farmland

June 2013 Issue of NewsChina *| by Zhou Zhenghua and Yu Xiaodong*

While China's new leadership has stated its aims to liberalize rural land policy as a part of a grand urbanization strategy, it seems reluctant to proceed.

"It is now time for China to transition its traditional agriculture into modernity," Xu Xiaoqing, director of the Department of Rural Economic Research at the Development Research Center of the State Council told *NewsChina*, referring to fragmented messages sent out by the State Council, China's cabinet, pressing for the introduction of market forces into China's countryside.

In a keynote white paper released in February, the State Council called for the development of "family farms," encouraged enterprises to "go rural," and promised that the government would finalize the registration of rural land rights, an ongoing task, within five years.

Following the announcement, China's new Premier Li Keqiang, the alleged mastermind behind the white paper, remarked during an inspection tour of the Yangtze Delta that some of China's family farm units should transition towards larger-scale production. On April 7, the State Council approved agricultural reforms in northeastern Heilongjiang Province aiming to consolidate farmland into large-scale plots.

Observers believe that these developments signal the beginning of long-term reform of China's rigid system of rural farmland rights, reform expected to end with market-based land trading. Others, however, are not so sure.

DILEMMA

China's agricultural policies, particularly those regarding land rights, have long been under scrutiny from experts and officials. Under China's current rural land policy, which has its roots in communist ideology, China's rural land is collectively owned by villages, rather than individuals. Since China kicked off economic reforms in the late 1970s, collectively-owned land was made available for lease to rural households, but the right to sell or trade land remained in the hands of the collectives.

These policies restricted all farmers, regardless of productivity or efficiency, to tiny plots of land. According to official data released in 2006, each rural household works an area of a farmland averaging 1.5 acres, a fraction of that farmed by their peers in India and Japan. The result is stagnation in terms of both productivity and rural income growth, which has in turn driven hundreds of millions of rural laborers into China's burgeoning cities in search of a better life.

The economic boom led by a prosperous manufacturing industry only served to exacerbate the urban-rural income divide, leading farmers to cut even more corners to turn a profit, resulting in food safety crises and the widespread pollution of arable land. However, urbanization, the cause of many of these ills, is now being touted as a potential solution.

NEW ERA

With millions of rural residents abandoning the countryside for the cities, experts believe that rural populations have reduced sufficiently to safely liberalize the rural land policy and promote larger-scale agriculture without risking either food security or a complete collapse of the socialist system. However, despite initiating a number of pilot land exchange programs in the past few years, the government has balked at rolling out provincial or national-level reforms.

While political conservatives are worried that a shift in land policy would represent the final abandonment of Marxist doctrine in favor of economic pragmatism, the biggest concern for academics is that China's small farmers would be rapidly marginalized in a free land market hijacked by special interest groups. Many point to the urban slums that have emerged from the process of urbanization in other developing regions such as India and South America, warning that liberalizing land trading could spur the disenfranchisement of millions, resulting in political and social turmoil as the indigent converge on the cities.

The fact that 250 million rural migrants are still denied access to urban public services shows that these concerns are well-founded. Were these people to lose access to their existing rural safety net, effectively making them and their families both stateless and penniless, the results could be catastrophic.

"China should not promote consolidating farmland until it can genuinely turn rural migrants into urban residents," Professor He Xuefeng, director of the China Rural Governance Research Center under Huazhong University of Science and Technology, told *NewsChina*.

China's new cabinet seems to have adopted a new line of thinking on this problem. Relating the rural reform to a grand plan for promoting "human-based urbanization," Premier Li Keqiang has offered an ambitious and comprehensive solution to a number of problems challenging today's China.

According to Li and his supporters, by making land a tradable asset, rural residents can tap into credit allowing them to become businesspeople or build a new life in one of the country's cities without relying on government handouts. In Li's view, such reform would create a steady flow of labor into developing urban areas while also enabling larger-scale modern agriculture, generating more income for farmers and narrowing the urban-rural income gap while greatly boosting productivity.

BLOODLINES OR BUSINESSES

While there is agreement at the administrative level on this general strategy, what appears to have divided the new leadership is the potential speed and extent of its implementation. In the aforementioned white paper, two concepts were raised in this regard, "family farms" and "capital going rural."

Family farms, or the consolidation of several family homesteads, are both common concepts in modern China, as many rural residents rent their land to relatives and fellow villagers when they go to work in cities. According to the Ministry of Agriculture, officially recognized family farms in 33 pilot areas number 6,670. Unofficially, more than 2.7 million rural households operated a plot larger than 16.5 acres by the end of 2012.

As a more moderate solution, family farms, which can help a rural household to boost its income, also have their limits. A larger operation also means a bigger risk for farmers trading in specific commodities. Moreover, consolidating farmland alone cannot bring much-desired capital and technology into the countryside. Farmers in areas initiating pilot land transfer schemes have already been complaining about the rising price of land and a shortfall in skilled agricultural labor that has held back attempts at greater mechanization.

As a solution, the government has been encouraging the development of rural cooperatives. Data from the Ministry of Agriculture shows that the number of rural cooperatives has reached 600,000, meaning that 18 percent of farmers nationwide are part of one. However, according to Professor Han Jun, vice-director of the Development Research Center of the State Council, the majority of these cooperatives only exist on paper, with farmers operating as individuals in practice while using their certification as a cover.

With the stagnation of the development of rural cooperatives, the government is now sending tentative signals encouraging enterprises to "go rural," a concept anathema to Marxist doctrine which has raised alarm among conservatives and rural activists.

In the past decade, urban capital has developed a strong foothold in the countryside, often colluding with local governments to appropriate land and evict farmers in order to construct development projects. To allay fears of a complete takeover of rural land resources by big business, the government has pledged to keep enterprise out of the rural land market.

"By encouraging enterprises to go rural, the government should only encourage them to bring capital, technology and market forces to the countryside," said Xu Xiaoqing. However, as central policies are often distorted at the local level, few believe Xu's pledge to end the illegal appropriation of land will be delivered in practice.

Consensus on these sensitive issues, which tap into the heart of China's political ideology as much as into the heart of her agriculture, remains elusive even in a consensus-led government.

RIGHTS REGISTRATION

No matter which direction the government ultimately takes, one action now appears unavoidable—the full recognition of the land rights of farmers. Only such an acknowledgement could give individual households a clear link to their holdings and thus place a verifiable value on such property. In its white paper, the State Council required local governments to finalize land rights registration within five years.

Many have called this deadline overoptimistic. The State Council made a similar demand in 2010, and progress has been slow in a country with no recent history of extending land rights to individuals. According to Professor Zhao Junchen from the Academy of Social Sciences of Yunnan Province, governments at county and village level have been very passive in implementing the policy, most likely because the appropriation of rural land remains the primary source of income for local governments across China. Indeed, the vague legal status of collective rural land ownership has proven hugely lucrative for rural officials, allowing them to claim to represent both individual farmers and rural collectives in deals with developers.

The State Council is painfully aware of the difficulty they face in getting local governments to surrender their powers to appropriate and sell land, but are nonetheless experimenting with reforms in this area. According to one experimental reform in Shenzhen, for example, local governments will be cut out as middlemen, allowing farmers to deal directly with developers. However, this is no guarantee of a square deal, and it is unlikely officials will have no hand whatsoever in such tricky negotiations.

Professor Zhao said that it would require great political determination for the central government to overcome local resistance in pushing forward the task of land rights registration.

Fragmented and hesitant messages on the issue of land rights are no longer any use—nothing less than a concrete plan for overhauling rural land rights, and its vigorous enforcement, even at the expense of political capital, will do.

Treating Farmers Fairly

Another take on the issue is given by the editors of NewsChina in "Land Reform Must Redress the Systematic Bias against Farmers." Here the political aspects of the problem are also discussed, both at the local collective level and the national level, where an increasing number of newly landless farmers creates political unrest. And in the spirit of the "Mandate of Heaven," the unelected Communist hierarchy fears nothing more than grassroots dissent.

Land Reform Must Redress the Systematic Bias against Farmers

February 2015 Issue of NewsChina | *by* NewsChina Magazine

The government must realize that a major root cause of dissatisfaction is not the collective ownership of rural land, but the abuse of power and a failure to protect farmers' rights.

One major item on China's economic reform agenda has been an overhaul of agricultural policy. For years, there have been calls for land reform in order to liberalize the strict restrictions on rural land ownership.

Recently President Xi Jinping endorsed an experimental program to permit farmers in certain localities to transfer land use rights to other farmers for a rental fee. It is believed that liberalizing the land use rights system without eliminating the collective ownership policy in rural areas will remain the focus of the government's agenda.

For a long time, land use has been the single main contributing factor to a variety of social problems in China. As land use rights are split between households, with holdings collectively owned by entire villages, farms tend to be very small in China, averaging just 1.6 acres (0.6 hectares), compared with an average of 400 acres in the US. The result has been low yields and low incomes. In the meantime, rapid urbanization has led to the massive appropriation of rural land resources, sometimes forcefully, and almost always with the complicity of village administrators but little input from individual farmers. This state of affairs not only exacerbates urban-rural income inequality, but has become a major source of political dissent.

With its proposed land reforms, the government aims to achieve multiple goals, including further urbanization, by increasing the supply of land and labor to China's cities, narrowing urban–rural income disparity, and fostering the development of modern agriculture.

The Chinese government also aspires to achieve the capitalization of land resources, and thus awaken so-called "sleeping wealth," which economists argue would enable farmers to acquire property income and give a boost to China's economy.

However, there are conflicts of interest inherent in these goals. These conflicts could derail reform unless they are addressed by the government.

For example, many experts have argued for the privatization of rural land resources, which they argue to would allow market forces to create bigger farms, increasing agricultural productivity and facilitating further urbanization. However, such an approach also risks exacerbating income disparity, as farmers who sell up and move to the city might struggle to establish themselves in an urban environment.

Therefore, the government should take a prudent and balanced approach to any reform of land ownership rules. Instead of the complete privatization of rural land resources, the future of China's rural society lies in the "privatization of collective ownership," allowing farmers to genuinely enjoy their land rights and seek collective prosperity.

In the meantime, the government must go beyond the ownership issue to address some systematic bias against farmers. The government must realize that a major root cause of dissatisfaction is not the collective ownership of rural land, but the abuse of power and a failure to protect farmers' rights.

In recent years, local governments, plagued by endemic corruption, have played a dominant role in the land market. With no effective cooperative mechanism established among farmers, village councils often merely serve as agents of local authorities, rather than a collective management body. Farmers face various institutional barriers when attempting to exert their collective land rights. Lacking necessary skills, capital and collective organization, it is unsurprising that farmers have found themselves marginalized in recent years.

In order to achieve its multiple goals and deliver a mutually beneficial land reform agenda, the government must focus on addressing these institutional barriers within the current system, which has so far prevented farmers from effectively seeking collective prosperity.

Most importantly, the government needs to retreat from the land market to allow the market to do its job. By removing institutional barriers between urban and rural society, and allowing farmers to exercise their collective rights, the center can foster cooperation between urban capital and rural ownership. While urban capital can maximize the efficient use of rural land and introduce modern skills into rural society, farmers, as primary stakeholders, need to see the benefit of surrendering the only items of value most of them possess.

FOR FURTHER STUDY

Response Questions

- What 2014 bilateral environmental treaty was signed by China and the US, and why is Beijing keeping relatively quiet about it?
- What firm is the world's largest food processor?
- What is the YREB and why is it important to Chinese commerce?
- How do small farm plots in China lead to food adulteration?
- What is the "Mandate of Heaven," and how does it affect Chinese governance?
- What is the "sleeping wealth" of China?
- Name at least five drawbacks to collective farming as practiced in China today.
- What are the major causes of soil pollution in China?
- Name one natural disaster that is affecting Yunnan Province? What is the level of risk there?
- List examples of food scandals in China and the US companies involved.

Discussion Questions

- What does "The sky is high and the emperor is far away" imply in China? Give some examples. How does this concept benefit businesses? In what ways is this concept harmful to society?
- Many Chinese and a few foreign investors have become wealthy investing in—and oftentimes flipping—real estate, with double-digit growth year-on-year for most of the past 30 years. What are the indicators of a real estate bubble? Which of these indicators do you see evidence for in China? Do you believe there is a Chinese real estate "bubble" or do you foresee a "soft landing" for real estate? Support your position.

- China's leaders see the necessity of consolidating and privatizing farmlands in order to create efficiencies that countries like the US have enjoyed. However, attempts to do so have been met with resistance by farmers who claim unfair treatment. How are they being treated unfairly? What are some possible solutions or compromises that would result in a fair system of land consolidation? What practical considerations prevent Beijing from privatizing all farmland?
- China is a modern economic miracle, raising its standard of living and GNP by leaps and bounds since the 1970s. It has been able to do so at the expense of its environment. Discuss the necessity of sacrifices to China's water, air, and land quality in order to achieve its current world economic power status. Compare this to the environmental sacrifices made by the US during the 19th and 20th centuries to secure its future economic prosperity. Should countries be restricted from making such sacrifices? Consequently, should those same countries be restricted from economic growth and poverty alleviation?
- China has more housing units than families. This has resulted in "ghost cities" — real estate investment projects that were either undersold or held by investors without occupancy. How do these projects affect the environment? What economic purpose do they serve? What social purpose do they serve? What is the relationship between these "ghost cities" and the basic principles of communism?

Research Exercises

- Describe three Chinese food contamination scandals in the last 10 years. Write a summary that includes those affected by the food contamination (including the number of deaths), the date and location of the scandal, the causes of the food contamination (including names of companies or individuals involved), and what was done to solve the problem.
- Each year, Beijing is rated one of the most polluted cities in China. What is the pollution level of Beijing compared to New York and Paris? What steps is Beijing taking to alleviate severe air pollution in the cities? What steps are citizens taking to protect themselves?
- As a percentage of national territory, compare the Yangtze and the Mississippi River drainages. Also compare the percentage of GDP coming from US states in that drainage to that of the Yangtze provinces. How does the Tennessee Valley Authority (TVA) compare to the YREB in scope and objectives? Or choose similar questions for Germany and the Rhine or Brazil and the Amazon.
- Compare the per-square foot (or meter) housing prices in Shanghai with those of Los Angeles and London. What is the average apartment size in each city? What is the average income of individuals living in Shanghai,

London, and Los Angeles? If they saved 100 percent of their income each year, how long would it take for an average resident in each city to purchase an average apartment/house in their respective city?

- Watch Chai Jing's *Under the Dome* on youtube.com, and prepare a 1–2-page summary review. Describe the situation being portrayed and potential solutions.

China "pie" divided up by foreign powers, ca.1898
(UK, Germany, Russia, France, Japan dividing the pie—China behind)

By Henri Meyer [Public domain], via Wikimedia Commons

Notes

1   *The Week*, October 16, 2015, p. 11.
2   Ibid.
3   www.nytimes.com/2015/03/19/opinion/why-under-the-dome-found-a-ready-audience-in-china.html, retrieved May 17, 2015.
4   *Fortune*, April 1, 2015, p. 79.

Bibliography

Cai, R. (November, 2014). River of Gold—Three articles on the Yangtze. *NewsChina*.
Ma, J. (June, 2015). Going Public. *NewsChina*.
NewsChina Magazine (September, 2014). OSI China in Food Scandal. *NewsChina*.
NewsChina Magazine (January, 2015). China's Climate Change Deal Is a Triumph. *NewsChina*.
NewsChina Magazine (January, 2015). China's Bold New Environment Law. *NewsChina*.

NewsChina Magazine (February, 2015). Land Reform Must Redress the Systematic Bias against Farmers. *NewsChina*.

The Week (October 16, 2015). China's Green Revolution. *The Week*.

Wang, Y. (November, 2014). Soil Justice. *NewsChina*.

Wang, Y. (February, 2015). Breaking the Silence. *NewsChina*.

Xie, Y. & Zhou, Z. (December, 2014). End of an Era. *NewsChina*.

Yang, D. (October, 2014). Ludian Quake—Unpredictable, not Unavoidable. *NewsChina*.

Zhou Z. & Yu, X. (June, 2013). Flipping Farmland. *NewsChina*.

Appendix 6.1

Table 6.1 Why China Distrusts Foreigners

Year(s)	Event	Comments
1279–1368	Mongol conquest of China	China ruled by Kublai Khan and his successors
1644	China seized by the Manchus	Last Han dynasty ends
1839–1842	First Opium War	China loses to British and French, forced to sign Treaty of Nanking: foreign concessions, Hong Kong ceded to Britain beginning the "Century of Humiliation"
1856–1860	Second Opium War	China loses to British, French, and US Forced to sign Treaties of Tientsin, further "Unequal Treaties"
1858–1860	Treaty of Aigun Treaty of Peking	China forced to cede Outer Manchuria to Russia
1862–1877	Dungan Revolt	Russia occupies the city of Kuldja in Xinjiang
1883–1885	Sino–French War	French win control of Vietnam and Cambodia, formerly under Chinese domination
1899–1901	Boxer Rebellion	Eight countries seize Beijing to protect foreign concessions
1894–1895	First Sino–Japanese War	China loses to Japan; Korea becomes independent
1931	Second Sino–Japanese War begins	Japan invades Manchuria, seizes control of much of coastal China
1937	Rape of Nanking (Nanjing)	200,000–400,000 Chinese citizens killed; 20,000–80,000 Chinese women raped by Japanese soldiers
1939 to present	International support of Taiwan	Beijing regards Taiwan as a renegade province
1989	Tiananmen Square massacre	Widespread Western condemnation including arms embargos, foreign loans terminated, trade curtailed; CPC maintains actions necessary to control disturbances that threatened national stability

7

LEGAL CONSIDERATIONS

Introduction

Doing business in China has always been fraught with legal dangers, both for the foreigner and the native. Vague laws, arbitrary officials, and a weak judicial system encourage graft and an over reliance on *guanxi*. Clearly, this hurts China's economic future and leaders are taking notice. Many powerful forces resist change, as is always the case, but Xi Jinping may just have the strength of position and mind to start moving in the direction of rule of law.

Intellectual Property protection has probably been the foremost sore point for foreign businesses in China, and some progress is being made there. Clearly China's indigenous IP industries such as software, pharmaceuticals, and entertainment won't truly prosper until IP is better protected there.

Areas within the Chinese economy that have been unregulated, lightly regulated, or poorly regulated are highlighted here, taking the fine art market and airspace control as representative examples. Problems abound, and Beijing has yet to take definitive steps to cure them.

ARTICLES

Rule of Law

Fighting Corruption and Vested Interests

Fortune magazine calls President Xi Jinping the strongest leader of China since Deng Ziaoping[1]. He's punished over 250,000 Party members for corruption, while advocating for strengthening rule of law. In fact, the Chinese Communist Party, hardly known as being a friend of fair and consistent legal practice, chose *fazhi*, or rule of law as the theme of its 2015 annual plenum. How Xi will implement this mandate is the subject Yu Xiaodong covers in the *NewsChina* article "Legally Bound."

Yu points to the rather ambiguous pronouncements of Xi regarding how rule of law will be implemented, whether in the Western style of adherence to written constitutions and statutes, common law, or, seemingly favored by Xi, by following Confucian principles of leadership and governance. Rule of law is critical for business in China. From the well-known abuses of intellectual property rights, poorly protected in practice by Chinese courts, to frequently changing and vague regulations subject to varying interpretation by officials, businesses pay a price for being in China.

Surprisingly, though, this can cut both ways. Carrefour, the French retail giant, got its foothold in China by ignoring national law regarding foreign ownership of stores while being supported by local governments happy to see its superstores built in their jurisdictions. Eventually Beijing came down on Carrefour, but the nominal punishment was well worth the early and substantial market penetration achieved (Fernandez and Liu, 2007).

Legally Bound

December 2014 Issue of NewsChina | *by*
Yu Xiaodong

The Party's decision to choose "rule of law" as the theme of its annual conference reflects important shifts in its approach toward economics, law and ideology.

Since the central leadership under Chinese President and Party Chief Xi Jinping announced in late July that *fazhi*, loosely translated as "rule of law" would be the theme of the Party's Fourth Plenum, heated discussion has raged among Chinese academics and officials, with many hoping that the plenum would lead to a fairer legal system.

While analysts continue to debate the significance of the reform guidelines issued in the wake of the meeting, there is a consensus among experts that the success of legal reform will be crucial for China both in terms of sustaining its economic development and maintaining political stability, given the massive social problems that continue to result from the stagnation of political reform.

"REFORM DIVIDENDS"

Much of the discussion has been conducted in the context of "reform," a topic that has dominated China's policy agenda ever since China launched its reform program more than 30 years ago.

As reform is generally seen as the driving force behind China's rapid economic growth over the past three decades, many experts attribute the lack of rule of law to the failure of the government to agree upon a reform agenda.

In the late 1970s, in the aftermath of decades of political turmoil, the late Deng Xiaoping, the Chinese leader often credited as the architect of China's reform, outlined an ambitious blueprint for economic and political reform that called for the separation of the government and the Party.

But after the restoration of basic law and order following the Cultural Revolution, the emphasis on economic growth soon eclipsed the shortcomings of the country's political and legal systems. Indeed, since the previous Maoist-era legal system had outlawed private property, the first steps toward market economy were, in the eyes of many, illegal. Effectively, this made law-breaking not just a necessity for a market-oriented reform, but a form of innovation to be encouraged.

For example, the bold experiment in 1978 conducted by villagers in Xiaogang Village, Anhui Province, who rejected the collective ownership of farmland, a landmark event that for many signaled the beginning of China's economic reform, was at the time technically a capital crime.

In the past three decades, with slogans such as "Cross the river by feeling the stones," and "Try boldly, and if you fail, correct your errors," Chinese leaders have adopted a policy of "trial and error" that is effectively a ceaseless flirtation with law-breaking.

"[Try and see] fosters disregard for the law among many officials," said Xu Yaotong, a legal expert from the Chinese Academy of Governance, a mentality Xu warns has become prevalent, especially since economic growth has long been prioritized in officials' performance criteria.

This mentality is so deeply rooted that the ongoing anti-corruption campaign President Xi launched two years ago, which has brought down dozens if not hundreds of senior officials, has, some have argued, discouraged officials from "innovating," as many fear being punished for overstepping blurry legal boundaries.

VESTED INTERESTS

However, since rapid economic growth creates powerful vested interests, the argument that the law should bend to accommodate reform—rather than vice versa—is often manipulated to serve the interests of local officials and their associates, resulting in widespread abuse of power. Perhaps the most obvious example of this is land appropriation, which often ends in forceful eviction of those who resist, a major source of public discontent.

The lack of rule of law is also believed to be the fundamental reason behind most of China's problems, such as environmental pollution, ailing food security and a spotty welfare state. The consensus is that China's current model, which is based upon unlimited State power, is a dead end.

In a widely cited article written in September 2013, Wu Jinglian, a respected economist, warned that without a market based on rule of law, vested interests would transform China's economic model into "crony capitalism."

The Party's pledge to allow the market to play a "dominant" role in the economy during the Third Plenum held in 2013, and this year's focus on "rule of law," are both seen as efforts to avoid that outcome.

In the meantime, the Party has stepped up its anti-corruption drive, which has increasingly targeted interest groups within several State-dominated sectors. In a Party meeting held on October 8, President Xi reiterated his warning against the formation of "vested interests and factions" within the Party.

On the next day, Party mouthpiece the *People's Daily* explicitly identified five major "interest groups" including those in the oil sector associated with fallen former Politburo Standing Committee member and security tsar Zhou Yongkang, and senior officials in coal-rich Shanxi Province, who have also fallen under investigation in recent months.

Experts now hope that tackling vested interests and establishing a fairer legal system, which economists say would lead to lower business costs and reduced uncertainty, would provide new "reform dividends," making China's economic growth more sustainable.

For example, in a survey conducted by Bloomberg News, a group of 17 economists estimated that Xi's anti-corruption campaign would boost GDP by 0.1 to 0.5 percent by 2020, equal to a dividend of about US$70 billion.

MEANS OR ENDS?

But for many liberal experts, discussion of legal reforms should go beyond the issue of reform dividends, and genuinely solve the fundamental issue—the power structure within China's political system.

Chen Jian, vice-president of the China Society of Economic Reform, for example, argues that the establishment of rule of law should not just be a tool to fight corruption and drive economic reform, but the overall goal of China's reform agenda.

According to Chen, the fundamental problem with China's legal system is that the Party has placed itself above the law, allowing senior leaders such as Zhou Yongkang to abuse power on a national scale for an entire decade.

Chen argues that China's legal reform should take a two-pronged approach. On one hand, the Party should confine its power within the framework of the constitution and the law. On the other, the government should take concrete measures to ensure that the various civil rights guaranteed in China's constitution, such as the rights to free speech, protest and demonstration, as well as freedom of the press, are respected and protected.

But so far, protection of civil rights has been entirely left out of the proposed legal reforms, with minimal discussion among experts and officials—the Party has sent mixed messages regarding the limiting of its own power.

After assuming power, President Xi has repeatedly vowed that the Party's power will be exercised "within the cage of regulations." Moreover, by announcing the "rule of law" theme of the Fourth Plenum at the same time as the announcement of the investigation into Zhou Yongkang, the most senior Party official ever to fall under investigation, the Party has also shown itself willing to subject individual top leaders to punishment according to the law.

In recent months, the Party has taken measures to grant more independence to local courts to guard them from the political influence of local officials, in an attempt to bring some fairness at the local level, where social conflicts are most serious.

On September 7, all seven members of the Politburo Standing Committee attended a ceremony celebrating the 60th anniversary of the establishment of China's top legislature the National People's Congress (NPC), an unusual move which many took as a sign that the NPC's role will be strengthened.

According to the Fourth Plenum's decision, the Party will adopt the principle of "rule according to the constitution," establishing a supervision mechanism over the implementation of the constitution within the NPC.

Prior to the opening of the Fourth Plenum, a book authored by 18 leading Chinese legal experts, entitled *The State's Bottom Line*, delineated an initiative for constitutionalism, calling for the establishment of a constitution committee within the NPC, with the power to interpret the Chinese constitution, investigate constitutional violations and impeach national leaders.

Although details of the legal reforms are yet to be unveiled, the fact that the book was published by the Central Compilation and Translation Bureau (CCTB), an influential agency directly subordinate to the Central Committee of the Communist Party of China (CPC), indicates that constitutionalist initiatives are at least on the agenda of the central leadership.

Despite all the optimism, few expect the Party to relinquish its legislative and judicial decision-making power, something Professor Chen and many others deem to contradict the principle of rule of law.

In an earlier speech in 2012 calling for respect for the constitution and legal reform, Xi reaffirmed that the Party must retain control over the country's legal system. "The Party will lead the people in legislation and law enforcement, and will be the first to abide by the law," said Xi.

The approach is not only in line with that of the ongoing anti-corruption campaign, an effort to boost the Party's reputation and legitimacy, but also appears to be a part of Xi's overall governance strategy based on his ubiquitous buzzword, "the Chinese dream."

"CONFUCIAN SOCIALIST CONSTITUTIONALISM"

Instead of adopting "rule of law" as it is understood in Western democracies, Xi has repeatedly cited classical Chinese literature and philosophy, including the ancient sage Confucius, who advocated harmonious social order maintained by a righteous and virtuous ruler. Xi has also quoted Han Fei, a legalist thinker and contemporary of Confucius, who argued for uncompromising legal order maintained under a strong ruler.

In a keynote speech made just days prior to the Fourth Plenum, Xi again drew upon ancient Chinese wisdom to justify the proposed legal reforms. Among the key concepts Xi raised in the speech were "the combination of ethics and law" and "virtuous rule with the supplement of punishment," quotes from Xunzi and Dong Zhongshu, two later Confucian philosophers.

Stressing that "the Chinese nation trod a development path that was different from other countries' for several thousand years," Xi argued that China should see "the experiences of other countries"—a phrase usually used to refer to Western democracies—as reference points, while also learning from China's own cultural and historical heritage.

Xi's literary rhetoric has sparked debate as to whether he is more of a ruthless, Mao Zedong-style ruler, or a liberal, Deng Xiaoping-style reformer. His apparent endorsements of a variety of ideological concepts since assuming power, ranging from Marxist-Leninism, to socialism with Chinese characteristics, to constitutionalism and Confucianism, have left China-watchers puzzled.

Although Xi has vowed to "remain fully mindful of the experiences, lessons and warnings of history," many remain skeptical about his seriousness in pushing forward meaningful political and legal reform, given the long tradition of authoritarian rule in China.

But according to Professor Zheng Yongnian, director of the East Asian Institute at the National University of Singapore, Xi's rhetoric may reflect a broader strategy aiming to transcend the heated ideological debate within China in recent years, primarily between "leftists" arguing for a stronger, more orthodox socialist State and liberal "rightists" advocating Western-style democracy. Many see both approaches as recipes for chaos and, ultimately, disaster.

Zheng argues that by avoiding becoming tied up in ideological debates, Xi will be able to take a more pragmatic and institutional approach to solving the various challenges China is facing.

Zheng's view is partially echoed by Kang Xiaoguang, a professor of public administration at Renmin University, who argues that Xi's emphasis on classical Chinese thought indicates a genuine interest in promoting a cultural change to re-establish China's traditional value system after decades of economic growth that has encouraged naked materialism.

In the last couple of months, in pushing forward with the anti-corruption drive, China's State media has frequently called for respect and restoration of Confucian ethics among officials and Party cadres.

Professor Kang argued that Confucian values are a more cohesive and inclusive force than most political ideologies, and by blending Confucian values with elements of both socialist and Western values into what he calls "Confucian socialist constitutionalism," the Party can not only accommodate the seemingly contradictory historical legacy left by Mao and Deng, but also allow it to take a non-confrontational approach towards Western political concepts.

For Kang and many others, with its new focus and new theories, the Fourth Plenum will have a significant impact on China's development as the Party strives to establish a new platform for national governance.

Enforcing the Law

"Laws Are Useless If They Can't Be Enforced," by Yang Yingjie hails the new budget law, which after 10 years of debate puts on the books all sources of revenue and all expenditures of local governments. Previously, land sales and other dubious revenues were invisible to Beijing. And local governments are now permitted to legally issue bonds in some cases, whereas until now they were prohibited from taking on debt. This despite the mountains of debt they actually carry from dealings with China's vast shadow banking system. But Yang despairs of seeing these laws actually enforced, given the highly entrenched power structure in the localities and the weakness of enforcement structures.

Laws Are Useless If They Can't Be Enforced

November 2014 Issue of NewsChina | *by Yang Yingjie*

The grand ambitions of the new Budget Law need to be supported by effective and systemic reform.

Ten years after revisions to China's Budget Law began to be debated, a draft amendment has finally been passed by the National People's Congress (NPC). China's existing budget statute, which went into effect in 1995, has long been criticized as having engendered widespread corruption within the government. However, in the last 10 years, attempts to revise the Budget Law have met with stiff resistance, with two previous amendments shelved by national legislators.

The NPC's recent approval of the revised budget law at the height of the ongoing anti-corruption campaign spearheaded by President Xi Jinping has now been hailed as a major step towards the establishment of a modern fiscal administration.

To some extent, this is accurate. First, it overturns the existing "general budget" code that allows government agencies to defray expenses via unregulated fundraising channels, most notoriously land sales. The revised act takes all government revenues and expenditures into account, including the general budget, budgets for government-managed funds and those of State-owned enterprises and the welfare system.

This amendment has also approved the sale of government bonds by provincial-level governments, though it tightly restricts both their quantity and how the funds raised may be spent. Under the existing law, local governments were forbidden from issuing bonds even as a means to rebalance a budget deficit. In practice, however, governments issued "stealth bonds" in the country's vast shadow banking sector, running up huge debts out of sight of central government supervisors.

It is argued that by assuming jurisdiction over local government debts, the revised budget law will lead to increased transparency and improve local fiscal management. However, without a strong legislature with the power to challenge, supervise and, when necessary, launch enquiries into government budgets and expenditures, it will remain impossible to tackle China's most looming fiscal problems. Debt mountains in many localities, despite it being technically illegal for any Chinese administrative unit to accrue any amount of debt, are proof of just how little laws drafted in Beijing mean when they clash with local pragmatism.

The new Budget Law will be meaningful only if it is followed up with further institutional reform that will allow genuine supervision of government expenditure. For example, one progressive area noted in the amendment has been detailed guidance on the publication of budget information, including the scale of disclosure and the ideal channels for its release.

If the public and the media had the power to hold the government to account for its fiscal policy, transparency might be achievable. Without such measures to include the general population in the oversight of decision-making, backroom deals and the fudging of data will continue to be daily occurrences.

Instead of viewing this amendment as an achievement, the government should take it as a starting point for genuinely systemic change. The new Budget Law will be meaningful only if it is followed up with further institutional reform that will allow genuine supervision of government expenditure.

The author is a senior commentator for *NewsChina*'s sister publication *China Newsweek*.

Why Corruption Isn't Just a Legal Problem

"An Effective Anti-Corruption Drive" offers *NewsChina's* approach to getting to the root of the graft issue, rather than attempting to merely take down the worst offenders. The current approach to ending corruption is bound to fail, but asolution is possible. The problem, as the editors see it, is that Chinese officials and even the public are driven solely by materialism and cannot see any moral value in acting lawfully with respect to bribery and abuse of power. China's is a shame-based culture as opposed to the guilt-based culture of the West. That is, a Westerner hesitates to do wrong based on the guilt associated with transgressing. In China, if you don't get caught, there is no punishment, but if you do, there is shame. Morality needs to be taught at the earliest levels of education in order to permeate the society in the future.

An Effective Anti-corruption Drive Needs a Three-dimensional Approach

November 2014 Issue of NewsChina | *by* NewsChina Magazine

What has been largely ignored in the discussion is the need to foster a political culture in which corruption is politically intolerable.

Amid his ongoing high-profile anti-corruption campaign, President Xi Jinping said in a speech at an event celebrating the establishment of the National People's Congress that the government will strive to create a system in which government officials will be "unwilling, incapable and afraid" of becoming corrupt. The pledge reflects not only the leadership's long-term approach in its anti-corruption efforts, but also all three dimensions of the anti-graft mechanism the government must establish to eradicate the corruption currently endemic in Chinese officialdom.

There is no doubt that China's current anti-graft drive, which has witnessed the fall of dozens of ministerial-level officials and several Politburo members, has brought with it a discernible atmosphere of fear, causing what observers called "political earthquakes," as entire leaderships in certain sectors and localities fall under investigation. Hailing the crackdown as a method of "addressing the symptoms" of corruption, Wang Qishan, the Party leader spearheading the anti-graft drive, has long pledged that the government will also strive to address the "root causes."

The consensus among experts is that the key to eradicating corruption is an institutional approach, establishing a system in which officials, in President Xi's words, would be "incapable" of corruption.

But what has been largely ignored in the discussion is the need to foster a political culture in which corruption is politically intolerable not just among the public, but also among government officials themselves. Without such a culture, political institutions, no matter how sound their design, are doomed to defeat in their fight against corruption, as all have to be staffed with individuals, with regulations enforced by people.

Unfortunately, the moral aspect of the anti-corruption drive has not only been ignored, but has even been met with cynicism and derision. Many consider efforts to appeal to a sense of morality either too abstract or simply meaningless, given the prevalence of materialism among both officials and the general public.

A healthy political culture and value system is indispensable in systematically eradicating corruption. Cynicism is exactly the reason why more efforts need to be made in this regard.

By emphasizing the need to build a system that would discourage officials from becoming corrupt, the central leadership is clearly aware of the problem. To achieve this goal, the government should not simply resort to empty conceptual rhetoric on morality, but should take concrete measures to reform its recruitment processes and the appraisal of government officials.

More importantly, the government should drastically rethink its approach to the country's overall civic and national education to nurture a value system that can reverse the prevailing tendency toward materialism.

Anti-corruption Watchdogs Outranked

Su Xiaoming, Hua Xuan, and Xie Ying look inside some of China's largest SOEs in their article "Pulling Rank." What they see is not only the expected rampant corruption, but watchdogs appointed to catch the wrongdoers who have little authority and are outranked by those they are to monitor. Recent crackdowns on various "tigers," as President Xi calls the big fish caught in the anti-corruption net, give some hope that the watchdogs will be given expanded powers to actually do their jobs. Testimony of an inside anonymous source gives a revealing insight into how and why corruption persists in the SOEs.

Pulling Rank

September 2014 Issue of NewsChina | *by Su Xiaoming, Hua Xuan, and Xie Ying*

Executives at China's State-owned enterprises often hold a higher administrative position than those charged with their supervision. Unless the government can find a way to keep tabs on State-sector leaders, corruption will remain rife.

On June 5, Li Lang, former general manager and Party secretary of the Zhangzhou branch of China Telecom, one of China's three telecoms giants, was detained by police for "severe violation of law and Party discipline," becoming the 47th high-ranking State-owned enterprise (SOE) executive to come under investigation for corruption this year.

Following the 18th National Congress of the Communist Party of China (CPC) in November 2012, China launched an ongoing nationwide anti-corruption campaign, an effort that has so far seen a total of 180 high-ranking SOE "tigers" (President Xi Jinping's buzzword for powerful corrupt officials) jailed, with bribery, embezzlement and abuse of power being the three most common charges. Repeated exposures of systemic corruption within China's monolithic SOEs, including in core fields like energy, telecommunication, press and construction, have left China's population with little faith in the government's supervision of SOEs.

"It has become evident that [the government's] various layers of supervision on SOEs are largely ineffective. In other words, SOE officials are not subject to supervision by their subordinates, and are beyond the control of their superiors," Ji Xiaonan, chairman of the Supervision Commission of Key SOEs told the media following the arrest of Jiang Jiemin, former president of CNPC (China National Petroleum Corporation).

In 2014, the Disciplinary Inspection Commission of the CPC Central Committee has so far held four separate conferences on the subject of SOE corruption, and has issued an array of new policies to tighten both internal and external supervision on SOEs, such as setting up a dedicated office for the supervision of the State-owned Assets Supervision and Administration Commission (the SASAC), the department responsible for overseeing the SOEs, and expanding the range of investigations. However, these efforts have been met with skepticism—critics called for a loosening of the relationship between administrative powers and SOE management, which many have referred to as the "soil" in which corruption germinates.

POWERLESS SUPERVISORS

China is now reportedly home to over 150,000 SOEs, most of which fall under the jurisdiction of the SASAC or its local counterparts which are responsible for supervising the assets, operations and human resources— including top-level personnel—of SOEs.

It is generally believed that this management structure has led SOEs to bear a closer resemblance to government departments than enterprises, with many SOE leaders enjoying immunity from supervision due to their high administrative rank.

Of the 113 SOEs managed directly by the SASAC, 54 are designated "deputy ministries" whose top-level leaders are appointed by the State-level Organization Department of the Central Committee of the CPC, China's highest determining body for official appointments. This means that many leaders at these SOEs hold a higher administrative rank than their supposed supervisors at the SASAC, let alone those at local supervision organs. Former president of China Three Gorges Corporation Cao Guangjing, for example, was a deputy ministry-level official with status equal to that of the mayor of Chongqing Municipality where the gorges are located. Even more ironically, Jiang Jiemin, the former CNPC president now under investigation, had been promoted to director of the SASAC before his arrest.

"[Due to the ranking issue,] the SASAC cannot exercise its right of supervision," Zhou Fangsheng, deputy director of the China Enterprise Reform & Development Society under the SASAC, told *NewsChina*, adding that many SOEs have been known to bargain with the SASAC over their annual performance appraisals.

Worse still, the administrative ranking system has effectively allowed SOE officials to set their own budgets. While the SASAC's financial approval system, ostensibly an internal anti-corruption measure, sets specific thresholds for the amount of public funds different levels of SOE leaders are authorized to use, this has seldom restrained senior leaders, especially those in big State-owned monopolies. Many believe this to be the reason why SOE corruption is often most rife in finance-heavy business activities like investment, procurement and bid solicitation.

For example, both Li Lang and Jiang Jiemin are accused of having accepted bribes during purchases of telecoms and petroleum facilities, respectively. Jiang was also accused of controlling overseas assets valued in the billions of yuan. Sources within the CNPC are reported to have criticized him for making the corporation into a "walled kingdom," requiring private enterprises to offer substantial kickbacks in exchange for contracts.

"The so called 'chairman' of an SOE actually serves as both competitor and referee, usually dominating the decision-making with his sizable power," Zhao Huxiang, president of SinoTrans & CSC, a State-owned logistics giant, told political journal *Nanfengchuang*.

In 2000, China's State Council set up a separate supervision commission, the Supervision Commission of Key SOEs, in an effort to tighten supervision of large, listed SOEs by bringing in third-party auditing firms, sitting in on SOE board meetings, and calling ad-hoc talks with top leaders. However, since many SOEs form a part of the same administrative structure as the various supervisory departments, many of them enjoying an equal footing with their supervisors, the new measures have failed to guarantee independent supervision.

Official data show that the Supervision Commission in 2012 submitted a total of 283 briefs about their supervision of SOEs, proposed 730 pieces of advice and revealed 222 problems, most of which analysts have dismissed as irrelevant.

INSPECTORS MARGINALIZED

A force of "disciplinary inspection secretaries," government-appointed internal supervisory personnel for SOEs, are even less effective, Chen Wei (pseudonym), one such secretary for a large SOE directly under the

SASAC, said in an interview with *NewsChina*. He said that his position, in the eyes of many, is "nothing but an empty shell."

"As subordinates to the top leaders, it was hard for us to get involved in their work, let alone to supervise them," said the source. "Sometimes, [leaders] would get irritated because I was asking too many questions."

Having been involved in SOE disciplinary inspection for 18 years, the source told *NewsChina* that he spent most of his time reading newspapers and official documents. "The position was commonly known as a job for idle workers, or a substitute for retirement," he said.

Gao Zhikai, a former deputy president of a large SOE, China National Offshore Oil Corporation (CNOOC), agrees. He attributed the limited remit of disciplinary inspectors to the lack of legal rights of detection and investigation. "They have neither the right to monitor the calls and emails of those under suspicion nor to get involved in company operations. Simply 'looking around' at SOEs does little to fight corruption. Corruption is never obvious," he told *NewsChina*.

"Even if the inspectors find evidence of foul play, the SOE leaders would either try to push them aside or drag them into the wrongdoing," he added.

"'No abnormalities were detected' is our most frequently used term in reports to upper-level departments," said Chen Wei. "Although SOE corruption has been expanding in recent years, the number of reports of corruption we receive from the public is declining sharply, even to zero in the case of some SOEs. This proves that the public no longer trusts us," he continued.

HOW FAR TO GO?

Luckily for Chen Wei, since 2014 the Party's central disciplinary inspection commission has expanded the powers of its disciplinary inspectors within SOEs, such as increasing their say over things like human resources and remuneration. According to Chen, the new policies have enhanced his status in the enterprise, and he is now receiving corruption reports from the public again. However, corruption remains endemic.

"I still feel reluctant to report a suspect to the higher authorities [for further investigation]. If I do not do so, I have failed to fulfill my duties, but if I do, I might lose my job," he said. "I had never dared to refuse an SOE leader's request for leniency on a suspect he wanted to protect."

Chen's worries are understood by many analysts and experts who believe that anti-corruption efforts based entirely on short-term campaigns will not be effective. Some now hope that the recent spate of shocking corruption scandals will press the government to deepen reform of SOEs, with measures such as breaking SOE monopolies and improving information disclosure to the public.

These hopes were given new momentum when the CNPC issued a new draft policy on June 26, allowing private businesses to participate in the nation's petroleum network—a move that some have suggested may be a byproduct of anti-corruption work.

However, many remain pessimistic, claiming that the government's supervision of the SOEs is similar to a parent disciplining their children—favoritism is unavoidable.

"I would much rather own a State-owned enterprise than have shares in one, as it's the only way to have any say in how they are run," Zong Qinghou, chairman of the private food and beverage giant Hangzhou Wahaha Group, commented on the government's bid to tempt private capital into State sector.

"The root cause of SOE corruption is that the true stakeholders—the public—are kept out of supervision," CNOOC former deputy president Gao Zhikai said. "If an SOE were to draw a map of its vested interests, it would start with bodies like the State Council, the SASAC and the Ministry of Finance, before moving onto things like the industrial and commercial sectors. The public wouldn't be a factor," he continued.

"If this system can't be broken, it will be impossible to uproot corruption."

Intellectual Property

Xiaomi Imitates Apple

Sun Zhe's article "Outsmarted" outlines start-up Xiaomi's success in imitating Apple's iPhones in the Chinese market. The company went from zero to a value of US$4 billion in two years by selling clever imitations of Apple products, down to building an Apple-like cachet and slavish imitation of CEO Lei Jun's idol Steve Jobs. Xiaomi may have trouble expanding beyond China, where IP protection is more robust. Since this article was written, both Xiaomi and Apple have enjoyed phenomenal success in China, and Apple is now the number one smart phone seller there. In the first quarter of 2015, International Data Corp. put Apple ahead with 14.7 percent of the total shipments, just ahead of Xiaomi (13.7 percent) and Huawei (11.4 percent). Samsung (9.7 percent) and Lenovo/Motorola (8.3 percent) rounded out the top five[2].

Outsmarted

November 2012 Issue of NewsChina | *by*
Sun Zhe

As China draws towards overtaking the US as the world's largest smartphone market, manufacturers of China's high-spec, low-cost cell phones are aiming to take their brands overseas.

Dressed in a black polo shirt and jeans during an unveiling of his company's latest market-storming cell phone in August, Lei Jun, CEO of Chinese phone manufacturer Xiaomi, struck a somewhat familiar image. In Chinese tech circles, he's known as "Leibs," a reference to his dutiful mimicry of his role model, the late Apple CEO Steve Jobs.

Comparisons between Lei and Jobs are not unwarranted. In the two years since his company was founded, Lei has made Xiaomi a formidable competitor in China's booming cellphone market, packing his products with enough technology and cult cachet to rival Apple, as well as current handset market leader Samsung, in the domestic market.

As the scale of the Chinese smartphone market advances on its US equivalent, local brands are catching up with their foreign rivals, competing on the full range of cell phone purchase factors: price, quality, specs and even the elusive "cool factor." In the second quarter of this year, international brands accounted for less than 40 percent of smartphone shipments in China.

SMART BOOM

Shipments of Apple, ranked first or second in almost all other regional markets, placed a disappointing seventh among smartphone brands in the first half of this year in China, lagging behind local brands Lenovo, Coolpad, Huawei and ZTE. Nokia came in fifth, while Samsung held onto its top spot.

While shipments of international-branded smartphones saw significant growth, totaling 16.7 million units in the second quarter this year, a 67 percent rise, those of domestic brands increased at a much quicker pace, growing more than fivefold to total 25.6 million, according to research firm Canalys. A total of 160 million smartphones, or a quarter of the world's total, are expected to ship for the Chinese market this year, 141 percent up from last year, overtaking the US as the world's largest smartphone market, according to industry consultancy IHS iSuppli.

Sales statistics reveal that when it comes to smartphones, traditionally seen as a luxury product, China's consumers remain particularly responsive to price. Over the second quarter of this year, smartphones priced below 2,000 yuan (US$314) made up about 70 percent of total sales in terms of units, according to research firm iiMedia Research. The low end of the market is largely ignored by international brands like Samsung and Apple, whose products are generally concentrated above 4,000 yuan (US$630).

Chinese handset manufacturers have been pumping out 3G smartphones priced under 1,000 yuan (US$157), or about half the price of their primary models a year ago. Aside from their increasing affordability, their close cooperation with carriers has also helped expand the market share taken up by homegrown smartphones.

Since last year, the country's three telecom operators—China Mobile, China Telecom and China Unicom—have been offering generous subsidies to smartphone buyers in order to expand their base of 3G mobile service users. Chinese smartphone user numbers reached 290 million by the end of the second quarter, and the user base is expected to see average annual growth of about 26 percent over the next five years due to the expansion of budget handsets, according to market research firm IDC.

RISE OF THE XIAOMI

Of China's domestic smartphone contenders, Xiaomi is undoubtedly the most promising—Lei Jun, a former angel investor and dotcom entrepreneur, recently became China's newest billionaire, and Xiaomi is now valued at US$4 billion, about half the value of declining giant Nokia.

The MiOne (MI), Xiaomi's first model, sold for 1,999 yuan (US$316), less than half the price of its international-branded rival models of similar specs, and has sold over 3 million units since it was introduced a year ago, with 200,000 orders taken in its first half hour on the market.

"The handset caters to smartphone enthusiasts on low budgets," said Kevin Wang, an industry analyst with IHS iSuppli.

The biggest selling point of the MI2, Xiaomi's latest model unveiled this August, also priced at 1,999 yuan (US$310), is its 2GHz quad-core Qualcomm processor, the fastest ever adopted on a smartphone.

A self-confessed Apple imitator, it comes as no surprise that Lei Jun plans to take Xiaomi global. He announced earlier this year his ambition to introduce devices into overseas markets in the second half of this year, with India and Russia as its first destinations.

However, Lei will need more than a black polo shirt and a pair of blue jeans to repeat his success outside of China. Xiaomi has yet to sell a single device in any foreign country, according to the company's spokesperson Liu Fei, who declined to elaborate on Xiaomi's expansion plans with regard to other markets. Rumors circulating on various tech blogs point to a push into Europe as early as 2013.

"Lei's fame might have earned him a crowd of Chinese fans, but Indians and Russians would have no idea who he is," said Wang, the industry analyst.

GOING GLOBAL

Other Chinese tech brands are also gearing up to expand their smartphone presence in overseas markets. However, when it comes to smartphones, foreign consumers are particularly brand-conscious.

Lenovo, the Chinese company that builds 14.9 percent of the world's PCs, said late August that it plans to move its smartphones into India, the Philippines and Indonesia. But while it took the second-biggest share of the domestic handset market in terms of units in the second quarter, the Lenovo smartphone brand remains unknown outside of China.

Huawei, a world-leading Chinese telecommunications equipment maker, has already unveiled multiple cell phones in the US market, and has enjoyed moderate success with low-cost handsets sold through major carriers, such as its Impulse model, which sold for US$29 with AT&T. However, Huawei is struggling to shake off its reputation as a manufacturer of carrier-branded phones for Western operators and establish itself as a brand in its own right.

"Stepping out from underneath the carriers will require significant investment on branding and marketing, meaning a heavier burden on their already suffering margins," said C.K. Lu, an analyst with Gartner, a tech research firm, in an email exchange with *NewsChina*.

Legal and patent threats will also be a major risk for Chinese brands once they build a significant presence overseas, according to Lu. Apple's recent patent lawsuit victory over Samsung should strike a chord with China's phone makers, many of whose products bear more than a passing resemblance to some Samsung phones.

Lu believes that ZTE, Huawei, Coolpad and Lenovo all have the potential to be significant players in the global smartphone market in terms of unit sales. "But if we look at profit margin and innovation, I don't think they can reach the level of Apple and Samsung anytime soon," Lu added.

How Poor IP Protection Hurts China Too

Also by Sun Zhe, in "Failure to Kickstart," the lack of IP protection also figures in the general lack of success of crowdfunding in China, especially when compared to the US. Other barriers cited are lack of Chinese originality, government regulation regarding public fundraising, and the desire of the Chinese investor for a monetary return versus a product sample. Crowdsourcing has become an important tool for innovative start-up financing in the US, and its poor performance in China will hinder the country's desired move from manufacturing to invention.

Failure to Kickstart

August 2014 Issue of NewsChina | *by Sun Zhe*

A lack of original ideas and concerns over intellectual property protection are standing in the way of crowd-funding's successful transplantation to the Chinese market.

In China's IT circles, C2C means "copied to China" just as often as it means "customer-to-customer." Both have proven a fairly safe bet—provided they make adjustments to meet local tastes and policy requirements, most popular foreign dot-com models boom soon after their transplantation. Success stories have emerged in various fields, including e-commerce (Taobao), social networking (Renren), web portals (Sina), microblogging (Weibo) and group buying (Lashou).

There is one notable exception, though—crowdfunding. In the West, crowdfunding sites allow users to post their venture proposals—anything from documentaries to flying bicycles—and solicit cash from Internet users, who then receive a pre-determined gift if and when the project reaches its funding goal.

Three years after the first Chinese crowdfunding knockoff was launched, crowdfunding remains largely unpopular in the country. The funds raised over the last year by Chinese crowdfunding sites are estimated to total about 1.2 billion yuan (US$194m), less than half the US$480 million raised in 2013 by Kickstarter, the US pioneer and one of the world's most prominent crowdfunding portals.

CREATIVITY BYPASS

Some believe that a lack of originality—the very reason why Chinese web entrepreneurs copy from Silicon Valley in the first place—is stalling crowdfunding's development in the People's Republic.

He Feng, co-founder and former CEO of Demohour, China's first crowdfunding portal, has said that the lack of great original ideas is the most important reason behind the industry's sluggishness.

It does not take an investment expert to determine that projects posted on Chinese crowdfunding sites are far less attractive than those on Kickstarter or Indiegogo, another major US crowdfunding site.

While projects launched on Kickstarter have included the world's first full 360-degree high-definition video camera and a movie that was later nominated for an Academy Award, on China's largest crowdfunding site, the "projects" on offer tend to be conventional commercial ventures—business schools selling MBA programs, or farmers touting oranges —that use the site to promote pre-sales. On some portals, the proposals are so conventional that the user experience is no different to a group buying or e-commerce site.

Concerns over intellectual property protection may be discouraging those with real creative ideas from posting their projects on the crowdfunding portals, said Sun Hongsheng, CEO of *zhongchou.com*, by far the largest player in the Chinese crowdfunding market, which currently occupies about half of the market.

"In the worst cases, pirated products were already on sale on Taobao [the country's largest C2C e-commerce website] before the original projects got fully funded," said Sun. "There is a high probability that the project's initiator will be driven out of the market even before they manage to file a lawsuit against the infringer."

Though fraud has been reported since the inception of crowdfunding in China, a lack of faith in the protection of intellectual property rights is no doubt an obstacle to the development of crowdfunding in the country, according to Sun.

A lack of basic business skills among venture teams in China also adds to the challenge of creating growth, accounting for the slowness of the industry.

"Unlike their counterparts in the US, Chinese venture teams are often naïve when it comes to funding, financial management, marketing and other skills vital to the success of a startup," Sun said.

Crowdfunding sites find themselves acting as entrepreneurship and financial consultants for venture teams, making their business model far more challenging than that of their US counterparts, who have no need to train venture teams.

"When you're heavy, you're slow," Sun said, who revealed that though the industry has grown more than 100 times larger over the past year in China, it is still nowhere near the size of the US market.

POLICY SETBACKS

Li Zichuan, industry analyst with IT research consultancy International Analysys, thinks that there are also cultural factors at play—he believes that the "Chinese mindset" is also another factor preventing the industry from booming.

"Chinese have yet to become accustomed to paying for a product that has yet to materialize. They prefer mature products that have been approved by the market." He added that Chinese people are more likely to be interested in investments that result in monetary gains, rather than a product.

Consequently, crowdfunding projects that offer equity make up more than 80 percent of the market in China, according to Sun Hongsheng of *zhongchou.com*, with a total funding of about 1 billion yuan (US$162 m) over the past year. In contrast, in the US, the majority of donors to crowdfunding projects donate a small amount of money and are rewarded with anything from a product—an electronic gadget, a film ticket, or a DVD for example—to a "thank-you" in the credits of a film or the sleeve notes of a CD.

However, the model of rewarding crowdfunding donors with equity was confronted with policy setbacks as soon as it became popular in China, since unlisted companies are forbidden from selling equity to more than 200 individuals. This sets a funding limit for project initiators, who usually aim to solicit a small amount from as many contributors as possible in order to expand the reach of their idea.

Regulation measures are reportedly under consideration at the China Commission of Securities Regulation, and the entire industry is looking forward to measures similar to the JOBS Act in the US, a regulation on crowdfunding for small businesses and start-ups that took effect in September 2013, allowing ventures to launch general solicitation from qualified investors.

"So far, the lack of clear regulation measures is making industry players, as well as potential players, hesitate to make any aggressive moves," said Li.

Aside from legal uncertainty, a lack of trust in strangers is another obstacle Chinese crowdfunding sites need to overcome.

"To prevent fraud and put the contributors at ease, we wire money to the project initiator part by part, in accordance of the progress of the project," said Sun.

IP Protection Best Practices

The US-China Business Council (USCBC), comprised of major US multinationals doing business in China, has long experience combatting the loose protection of IP there. Its web site www.uschina.org is an invaluable resource for any foreign firm operating in China. Its report "Best Practices: Intellectual Property Protection in China" lays out a plan of attack to address this problem while still doing profitable business in the world's largest marketplace. Beginning with a six-point corporate strategy, the report goes on to detail understanding the legal landscape, adopting protective measures, balancing global protection with China market opportunities, designing the manufacturing process to protect IP, utilizing information technology to track and protect information, and focusing on human resources and business partners among many other worthwhile ideas.

Best Practices: Intellectual Property Protection in China

US-China Business Council
February 2015

Intellectual property (IP) is a longstanding, critical concern for companies operating in China. IP enforcement has consistently placed among the top handful of issues raised by US-China Business Council (USCBC) member companies every year in USCBC's annual membership survey. Concern about IP enforcement remains a major factor influencing company strategies and operations in China. China's IP laws and regulations increasingly reflect international standards, and China has indeed made steady efforts to better protect and enforce IP rights. However, challenges remain, including lingering issues with China's IP legal framework in areas such as trade secrets, uneven enforcement, and significant procedural barriers that frustrate company efforts to protect IP in China. At the same time, counterfeiters and infringers in China are increasingly sophisticated. They often exploit procedural loopholes, proactively seek to invalidate legitimate patents and trademarks, deploy advanced techniques such as reverse engineering, and find new ways to infiltrate legitimate distribution networks and build their own parallel networks.

Decades in the trenches have equipped multinational corporations with hard-won expertise and a set of strong preventive best practices, including internal controls and external engagement with key stakeholders. To be successful in China, companies should develop an integrated IP protection strategy that reflects the nature and extent of the IP problems they face and is grounded in a realistic assessment of internal goals and resources.

This best practices document lays out key strategies and tactics that companies should adopt in their attempt to identify and protect their IP in China, both to prevent IP problems before they occur and to tackle IP infringement once discovered. To protect their IP in China, companies should follow several steps:

CRAFT AND IMPLEMENT A CORPORATE IP STRATEGY IN CHINA

- Conduct an initial audit of the company's China operations to determine IP assets, IP risks, and assign appropriate levels of protection to those assets based on the risk of infringement.
- Review the company's internal IP controls to determine whether they provide sufficient protection. Make adjustments based on the IP audit, and dedicate resources in alliance with the company's IP protection goals.
- Classify IP-relevant information according to its level of sensitivity, and integrate that classification into information control and operational procedures.

- Make IP protection a core responsibility of the entire China management team, not merely a function of the legal or brand protection teams, and adjust internal information flows and reporting structures to reflect those responsibilities.
- Regularly communicate the value of IP protection—and the appropriate ways to handle IP—to key stakeholders, including government officials, employees, contract manufacturers, business partners, and customers. While the level of IP consciousness among Chinese citizens is growing, regular communication of the importance of IP is critical to instill a sense of ownership of company IP among key stakeholders.
- Take clear steps to document company IP protection policies and efforts as such documentation can play an important part in infringement disputes, particularly in areas like trade secrets.

UNDERSTAND THE IP LEGAL LANDSCAPE

- Review not only China's core IP laws and regulations, such as the Patent, Trademark, Copyright, and Anti-Unfair Competition laws, but the growing body of other laws and regulations that impact China's IP environment, including (but not limited to) the Corporate Income Tax, Antimonopoly, and Labor Contract laws.
- Ensure that the legal protection the company is seeking for its IP in China is available. For example, many software products that are eligible for patent protection in other jurisdictions are not in China, and are more commonly protected as copyrighted products.
- Monitor laws, regulations, and judicial interpretations to ensure that the company's IP enforcement strategies are valid under Chinese law. Examples of areas that may require scrutiny include employment contracts, IP licensing arrangements, and evidence collection procedures.

ADOPT PREVENTIVE MEASURES TO PROTECT IP

REGISTER IP IN CHINA

If a company doesn't file its copyrights, patents, and trademarks in China, its IP has no formal protection there. Companies should register (or record) eligible IP in China as early as possible. Companies should also understand the full range of IP for which they might file, including multiple types of patents (utility model, design, and invention), as well as trademarks and copyrights.

- **Patents:** Companies should file applications with the State Intellectual Property Office (SIPO) for IP that they view as valuable to their business for both core and fringe technologies. Companies should ensure that their patents are properly translated before filing. Filing can be done directly with SIPO or via international patent arrangements such as the Patent Cooperation Treaty.
- **Trademarks:** Companies should broadly register their core trademarks with the China Trademark Office, including the English name, Chinese character name, and Chinese pinyin name for core brands with the China Trademark Office. When filing, companies should carefully select the product categories and sub-categories in which to file, and check China's online trademark database for similar trademarks filed by competitors and infringers, including marks filed in categories outside a company's core products. Many companies have experienced challenges in which a local competitor registers a very similar trademark in a different product category, a practice allowed under the Trademark Law.
- **Copyrights:** Though registration is not required, entities should consider registering their works with the National Copyright Administration, since registration provides a public record and can serve as useful evidence in copyright disputes.

BALANCE GLOBAL IP PROTECTION NEEDS WITH CHINA MARKET OPPORTUNITIES IN TRANSFERRING OR LICENSING IP

- Conduct a realistic assessment of the business risks and benefits of transferring IP to China. For many companies, this means keeping vital designs and latest-generation technologies overseas while bringing to China IP that supports their business in country.
- Negotiate clauses in technology transfer and licensing contracts to address company needs on royalty rates and ownership of improvements. Companies should recognize differences in how China's legal framework treats ownership of improvements and liability, and that negotiated royalty rates in China are frequently lower than in other markets.
- Register technology licensing contracts as required under the Ministry of Commerce's Technology Import and Export Administrative Regulations.

DESIGN THE MANUFACTURING PROCESS TO PROTECT IP

- Compartmentalize critical steps in the design and production processes for IP-intensive products—and the equipment used to manufacture these products—to limit the likelihood that any one employee has access to all the information needed to copy IP.

- Consider incorporating into the production process technologies and techniques that are difficult to copy, such as chemicals, foils, inks, labels, papers, stamps, and threads.
- Incorporate IP protection needs into facility design. Some companies, for example, limit IP exposure by ensuring that sensitive information is kept in low employee traffic areas or behind unmarked doors.

UTILIZE INFORMATION TECHNOLOGY TOOLS TO TRACK AND PROTECT INFORMATION

- Consider tracking data flows and employee file transfers (both paper and electronic), engage internal stakeholders such as the human resources department in early conversations about developing and implementing policies that monitor employees in this manner.
- Closely monitor or prohibit the use of flash disks, portable hard drives, laptops, cell phone cameras, and other devices that could be used to capture and transmit sensitive information.
- Establish IT mechanisms to limit employee access to sensitive information, such as separate computer terminals or specialized passwords.

FOCUS ON HUMAN RESOURCES

- Run background checks on key hires to check for any IP-related "red flags," and include noncompete and nondisclosure agreements in employee contracts.
- Educate employees regularly about the firm's confidentiality requirements, and about the practical and reputational consequences of IP violations.
- Delineate based on job title and function which employees have access to what types of information.
- Control and monitor employee access to sensitive equipment and facility areas based on job title and function.
- Conduct exit interviews with departing employees to recover any sensitive materials and remind them of confidentiality obligations.

CAREFULLY SELECT, MONITOR, AND ENGAGE WITH BUSINESS PARTNERS

- Conduct comprehensive due diligence on suppliers and distributors prior to any agreement and on a regular basis thereafter. As part of that due diligence, investigate how those companies view IP, including IP they access through business partnerships and their own IP.

- Include IP protection clauses in all contracts and agreements. Regularly engage business partners to share the importance of those clauses to the ongoing business relationship, and ensure that partners fully understand what those obligations mean for both parties.
- Regularly engage business partners to reiterate the importance of IP protection, and, where appropriate, partner to boost IP protection efforts, such as supplementing monitoring resources or jointly engaging with government officials.
- Manage supplier, vendor, and distributor relationships through multiple personnel to limit the ability of local staff to abuse business networks.
- Review information that could be sent to third parties before transmission to ensure that it is not sensitive, or that the benefits of sending it outweigh the risks of it being leaked.

BUILD INTERNAL LINES OF COMMUNICATION ON IP

- Establish an anonymous internal hotline, as well as an outside hotline for confidential communication with suppliers, distributors, customers, and other third parties to report IP infringement.
- Build a database of company infringement cases and infringers and make it available to key employees across the company's China offices. Such a database can help educate staff about the types of infringement that a company may face, and increase the likelihood of spotting future problems.

ENGAGE IP ENFORCEMENT BODIES

- Build relationships with government officials at multiple levels in IP-related government agencies and courts relevant to the company's industry, before any problems arise. Key agencies include not only core IP agencies like local branches of the State Administration of Industry and Commerce and the Ministry of Public Security, but also agencies that could impact a company's IP protection efforts, such as the General Administration of Customs and local branches of the General Administration of Quality Supervision, Inspection, and Quarantine.
- Educate local officials responsible for allocating the resources for and enforcing IP protection about the company's IP protection needs. For companies facing problems with exported counterfeits, this includes recording IP with Customs in Beijing and educating local customs officials about the company's products in order to monitor for counterfeits.

- Engage with industry associations, including IP-, industry-, and country-specific associations, to exchange best practices for IP protection, identify cases of infringement, and (if appropriate) develop collective strategies and actions to advocate on concerns.
- Build ties with, and conduct due diligence on, IP service providers and investigative firms to identify enforcement resources that fully comply with relevant Chinese regulations.
- Work with local and national media as appropriate to address negative publicity that could accompany an IP case against a domestic company.

ACTIVELY MONITOR FOR INSTANCES OF INFRINGEMENT

- Send representatives to look for counterfeiters at industry trade shows and trade fairs, such as the Chinese Export Commodities Fair (Canton Fair).
- Review distribution networks at all levels regularly for weak links and possible entry points for counterfeit products.
- Monitor IP publications, including the PRC Patent and Trademark gazettes, for new patents and trademark applications to see if they infringe on the company's IP.
- Establish and publicize clear reporting channels for outside stakeholders to report cases of IP infringement.
- Check the Internet regularly for infringing domain names and for websites that are used as platforms for counterfeit products. These include e-commerce sites such as Alibaba and Taobao.

CONFRONT IP INFRINGEMENT WHEN DISCOVERED

CONTACT INFRINGERS AND THEIR SERVICE PROVIDERS

- Send cease-and-desist (C&D) letters to infringers. C&D letters can be a cost-effective way to stop infringement in some cases, especially those involving small infringers. These letters, however, also alert infringers that a company is aware of their presence, which could prompt them to move, change names, or otherwise alter their operations in ways that could inhibit a company's ability to gather evidence.

- Work with Internet marketplaces and Internet service providers, such as Alibaba and Taobao, to remove infringing goods or pirated materials from websites, and to take down websites providing infringing products or content.

BUILD CLEAR CASES AGAINST IP INFRINGERS

- Conduct a careful review of internal documents that can demonstrate infringement, including physical and electronic evidence. Companies should be aware that documentary evidence (as opposed to oral testimony or non-official documents such as marketing materials) carries more weight with Chinese officials.
- Work with vetted IP investigative firms to collect evidence on the company's behalf, monitoring firm activities to ensure that evidence is collected legally.
- Consider possible locations where the company could file an infringement case, and collect evidence accordingly.

UTILIZE OFFICIAL ENFORCEMENT CHANNELS TO PURSUE INFRINGERS

- Weigh various channels available to halt infringement in China, including administrative, civil, and criminal channels. In determining a course of action, companies should consider company resources, timelines for action, and the strengths and weaknesses of each channel. (For more on the pros and cons of various enforcement channels, see the next page.)
- Engage with local government officials to convince them to conduct enforcement proceedings. Consider using a company's contributions to local development or tying the case to larger goals such as product safety or public health, to illustrate to local officials the value of pursuing a case. Such ties can sometimes give companies access to additional penalties under other laws, such as the Food Safety or Environmental Protection laws.
- Consider "venue shopping," or bringing infringement proceedings in jurisdictions (and through enforcement channels) with a better record of IP enforcement.

Policies and Regulations

Flight Delayed? Look to the PLA

Delays and cancellations of regularly scheduled commercial flights in China are endemic. Even the published 80 percent on time record is misleading as this reflects only whether cabin doors were closed on time, not the possible subsequent hours spent on the ground awaiting takeoff. A good deal of the problem lies with China's military, which controls some 80 percent of the country's airspace. Li Jia and Xi Zhigang describe this problem in "Air Traffic—Flying Blind." With air travel burgeoning, and many shiny new airports under construction around China, it seems time that Beijing reprioritize airspace usage.

Air Traffic—Flying Blind

October 2014 Issue of NewsChina | *by Xi Zhigang and Li Jia*

Thousands of Chinese air travelers remain stranded at airports on a daily basis, victims of the worst airport delays on Earth. What will it take to modernize the use of China's restrictive airspace?

On July 24, an announcement on the website of the Civil Aviation Administration of China (CAAC) told travelers that flights bound to or from some major eastern cities including Shanghai, Wuhan and Qingdao would be delayed or canceled due to "thunderstorms and regular military drills." Stranded travelers immediately swamped the east coast's rail infrastructure as they attempted to secure seats on high-speed trains.

By August 1, when CAAC announced that flight schedules were back to normal, according to the administration's own data, air traffic in the same airports was down by 65 to 75 percent. CAAC went on to warn that a comparable situation would likely arise in August due to similar reasons. This was the first time that passengers had been informed in advance of possible delays and cancelations by CAAC, as well as the first time that military drills had been publicly cited as a contributing factor.

Chinese airlines are notorious for delayed departures, and regular air passengers are accustomed to lengthy, unexplained waits either at boarding gates or in their seats in a grounded aircraft. The default reason for delays usually given by operators is either "bad weather" or "traffic control issues," a term deliberately designed to be ambiguous.

The cited 80 percent annual punctuality record in CAAC logs since 2005 is equally misleading, as the punctuality of a departure is only measured from the moment the cabin is closed, not when the aircraft actually takes off. As a result, an aircraft that takes off four hours after its scheduled departure time is considered, for statistical purposes, as having taken off on time provided the exterior doors were closed on schedule.

Perhaps unsurprisingly, this situation has led to unpleasant incidents during the most serious delays. Physical assaults on ground staff and cabin crew and even minor riots at airports have occurred, with footage captured on cell phones and spread via social media.

Moreover, in the past two or three years, Chinese air passengers have been made aware of why they are so often stranded for hours despite clear skies and open air corridors. The People's Liberation Army (PLA) Air Force, according to widely cited data, is believed to exercise exclusive jurisdiction over 80 percent of the country's airspace, leaving only about 20 percent open to civilian carriers at normal times, a percentage that is further reduced during regular military drills.

The notice that appeared on CAAC's website in July turned this imbalance into headlines across the country. During a Ministry of Defense press conference on July 31, the issue of how to improve the allocation of airspace supplanted questions about military drills and maritime disputes as the leading subject of press inquiries.

MILITARY FIRST

After China's civil aviation industry was released from military control in 1980, several reforms were made within the new civil aviation system to build a business-oriented market by establishing and reshuffling the division of airspace between State-owned airlines, and the market was gradually opened to private carriers.

However, the dimensions and allocation of air corridors remained mostly under the direct control of the country's military. According to the existing rules in effect since 2000, the sphere of operations for China's civilian air traffic is controlled by a committee jointly established in 1986 by the State Council, China's cabinet, and the CPC Central Military Commission (CMC), which presides over this committee.

When air travel was still the exclusive privilege of senior government officials, and later the country's tiny middle class and foreign tourists, this situation presented few problems. There were simply too few civilian aircraft in the skies to create major bottlenecks even in the most heavily trafficked of China's air corridors.

Since 2005, however, passenger and freight volume in China's airspace has risen by an average of 15 percent annually, giving China the second largest volume of air traffic in the world (after the US) since 2007. Airspace allocated to civilian aircraft, meanwhile, only increased by 2.6 percent annually between 2007 and 2012.

International carriers, too, have also been hit by increasing delays and ongoing restrictions, adding their voices to calls for reform. The US

Chamber of Commerce and other business associations have been particularly vocal, and companies such as Boeing and Airbus routinely complain about a lack of adequate access to China's domestic market.

REFORM IMPERATIVE

While passenger numbers have continued to rise, and violent incidents caused by lengthy delays at airports are increasing in both severity and regularity, the economic costs of the current allocation of civilian airspace are also cause for concern, as many of the worst delays affect key economic zones, particularly the area on the east coast surrounding Shanghai and the Hong Kong–Shenzhen–Guangzhou trade triangle in the south.

CAAC's pointed reference to military drills in its warning to passengers shows just how resentful China's civil aviation authority feels towards the military's retention of the bulk of available airspace.

Ten years ago, Yang Yuanyuan, former head of CAAC, submitted a report to the State Council demanding reform of China's national air traffic control policy. Unhappy about this challenge from a civilian agency, the military made things even harder for civil aviation operators who applied for access to more routes, according to several CAAC insiders who spoke to *NewsChina* on condition of anonymity. Senior CAAC officials speaking to State media repeatedly refer to the gap between limited airspace and China's expanding air traffic volume, though most do so without explicit reference to the military.

Now, even the military has broken its silence on the issue. In recent press conferences and online announcements, the Ministry of Defense admitted the effect of drills on civil aviation, but promised to push for reform of the existing system to allow for "more efficient use" of China's airspace.

The military, however, is already upset about the attention being drawn to its role in restricting civil aviation, with the Ministry of Defense issuing denials that the military was a major cause of flight delays and cancelations. Yin Zhuo, a well-known military commentator, told media that "bad weather and bad management" were far more culpable, as the bulk of military drills, he claims, are conducted at sea, not in civilian airspace.

On its official microblog account on July 29, the *PLA Daily*, official newspaper of the Central Military Commission, criticized some Chinese and Western media coverage for "highlighting" the effect of drills on civil aviation, accusing offenders of possessing "either lack of common sense or ill intentions."

With decision-making power out of its hands, the CAAC is virtually powerless against the military. Its own spotty track record hasn't helped its case—indeed, its own reports attest to frequent and major disruptions regularly caused by bad weather and poor airport management. Passenger complaints, according to the passengers themselves, are typically less to do with the actual delays and more the indignities stranded passengers are regularly subjected to by ground staff and airline officials—conflicting or incorrect flight information, refusal to compensate delayed or stranded passengers, and ground staff abandoning gates rather than dealing with irate customers are all common complaints.

Apparently the public are growing weary of an absolute failure of the government to take discernible action, though provision for reform of the air traffic control exists in the government's 12th Five-Year Plan (2011–15). If such provisions fail to lead to change, however, growth in China's civil aviation industry could soon plateau, a scenario with economic consequences likely to be felt across the world.

Counterfeit Art

The largest market for fine art since 2010 has been China's. But it's not been without problems. "Masterful Mock-Ups," by Yu Hua and Yi Xiaohe exposes the vibrant market in China for counterfeit art. Since real estate investing was restricted by the state, lots of investor money has flowed into art. With an average return on investment of 30 percent per year, fine art has a lot of appeal. No longer dominated by serious collectors, the market is rife with speculators, money launderers, and fraudsters. The government has laid out some guidelines for auction houses to help clean up this situation, but, lacking the force of law, the guidelines are unlikely to change things significantly.

Masterful Mock-Ups

January 2012 Issue of NewsChina | *by Yu Hua and Yi Xiaohe*

Counterfeiting, driven by booms in speculation and investment, has now become endemic in China's nascent art market.

In late May, an ink-and-wash painting sold for 425.5 million yuan (US$65m) at the China Guardian auction house, setting a national record. However, less than a day later, rumors emerged that the painting was in fact a forgery.

The art work in question was a study of an eagle perched upon a pine tree entitled *Towering Pines and Cypress*, with an accompanying calligraphic couplet which translates as "A Long Life; A Peaceful World." The piece was said to be the work of Qi Baishi (1864–1957), one of China's best-known 20th century masters of ink-and-wash, who allegedly completed *Towering Pines and Cypress* in 1946 to commemorate the 60th birthday of Chiang Kai-shek, China's former paramount leader.

China Guardian's management was less than pleased with media reports that they had auctioned a forgery to an unsuspecting buyer, responding with an online statement on September 30 on one of China's major art portals, which read: "We reserve the right to pursue the media outlets which concocted inaccurate reports and people who made irresponsible remarks through the appropriate legal channels." The auction house accused the media's allegations of "lacking an academic and factual basis." However, four months later, the painting's buyer, the Hunan TV & Broadcast Intermediary Co. Ltd (TIK), had still failed to pay for its latest acquisition, according to various sources. China Guardian refused to comment on whether or not they had received payment for the artwork.

As with many such cases, it wasn't long before other auction houses came under scrutiny for allegedly peddling fake artworks. In September, a group of artists from the Central Academy of Fine Arts graduating class of 1984 claimed in an open letter that an oil painting of a female nude attributed to Xu Beihong (1895–1953) which sold for 70 million yuan (US$11m) at the Jiuge auction house in June 2010 was actually painted as a practice canvas by one of their classmates. Despite Xu's son Xu Boyang vouching for the work's authenticity, the letter was accompanied with photos of similar paintings depicting an identical nude from various angles, seemingly supporting the claims of forgery.

These two high-profile incidents have embarrassed China's auction houses and, according to observers, proven that counterfeit artworks are being knowingly sold to unsuspecting buyers on the open market.

INFERIOR IMITATIONS

Mou Jianping, an art critic specializing in counterfeit artworks, was the first to allege that *Towering Pines and Cypress* was very likely a fake, in an interview with CCTV, China's main State television network. Mou also told *NewsChina* that while the painting itself could be classed as a "mid-level forgery," the accompanying calligraphy was barely up to the standard of "inferior imitation."

Mou's allegations were supported by the discovery of a similar painting by Qi Baishi. Part of a collection belonging to Le Manyong, the wife of a former Kuomintang official, the painting bears a striking resemblance to the piece auctioned by China Guardian. However, Liu Wenjie, a prominent collector of modern Chinese ink-and-wash paintings, came to the defense of the auction house, saying that 20th century Chinese painters would often produce copies of their own works. However, an art historian speaking on condition of anonymity told NewsChina: "Qi Baishi created many paintings featuring similar images, but he never executed two pieces with exactly the same composition. If two of his works have the same composition, one of the two must be fake."

China Guardian emphasized its "strict" vetting procedures to our reporter. According to Kou Qin, vice-president of the auction house, the company has adopted a "four-step, three-dimensional method" for distinguishing genuine artworks from fakes. China Guardian claimed that every artwork they receive has to undergo a primary appraisal, followed by internal research, consultation with experts outside the company and a final assessment prior to auction. The auction house's "three dimensions" refer to assessment of individual pieces, historical research and comparison with similar works, and the use of modern techniques to determine the authenticity of each artwork.

However, China Guardian has found itself struggling with issues such as non-payment, which is especially pronounced when dealing with government-affiliated agencies. "The auction houses operate in the light, whereas buyers operate in the dark," Kou Qin told NewsChina.

The auction of Towering Pines and Cypress is a case in point. Originally intended as a lucrative deal for the painting's seller, real estate mogul Liu Yiqian, chairman of Shanghai Sunline Group, the artwork has proven to be something of a false economy. Liu bought the painting in 2005, and the couplet in 2010, at a total cost of 17 million yuan (US$2.6 m). Yet, despite selling for 25 times that price at auction, Liu and China Guardian have yet to see a cent as the buyer continues to hold out on payment.

COLLECTION OR SPECULATION

The Chinese classical painting and calligraphy market entered the so-called 100-million-yuan era in 2009 with the auction of Eighteen Arhats by the 16th century Ming Dynasty painter Wu Bin, which sold for 168 million yuan (US$24.8m).

Following that, Aachensee Lake, a landscape by the 20th century master Zhang Daqian (1899–1983) fetched 101 million yuan (US$15.9m) in 2010. In the same year, Xu Beihong's Baren Jishui (The Sichuan People Draw Water) sold for 180 million yuan (US$28.4m), while the fourth century calligrapher Wang Xizhi's cursive-hand scroll Ping'an Tie (Peace Note) sold for 308 million (US$46.4m). In a spring 2011 auction, Zhichuan Resettlement by the Yuan Dynasty (1271–1368) painter Wang Meng sold for 402.5 million yuan (US$62.1m). Towering Pines and Cypress merely set the latest record.

Mou Jianping sees 2009 as a watershed year for China's fine art market. According to Mou, before that year people were mainly buying artworks for collection. However, investment and speculation have since become the principal driving forces behind a market boom. Now that Qi Baishi's work has set a record price at auction, many observers have begun to count down to the first 1 billion yuan (US$157m) price tag.

Since the latter half of 2009, hot money, already a well-known phenomenon in China's other commodities markets, has become a keyword in art circles. The business volume of auction houses in China has grown explosively, tripling from 21.25 billion yuan (US$3.27 bn) in 2009 to 58.87 billion yuan (US$9.06 bn) in 2010, quickly recovering from a brief lull during the 2008 financial crisis. According to a report released earlier in 2011 by *artprice.com*, a leading world art data portal based in France, China had overtaken the United States and Britain to become the world's largest fine arts market by 2010.

Experts believe the explosive growth of the art market is largely attributable to the influx of hot money from other sectors. The Chinese government stepped up its regulation of the real estate market in order to put a brake on runaway housing prices at the end of 2010, sealing off the country's foremost channel for private investment. Eager to find an outlet, hot money soon flowed into the largely unregulated art market. In late 2011, among the leading auction houses in China, Poly's auction turnover had reached nearly 6.2 billion yuan (US$976m), China Guardian's stood at 5.3 billion yuan (US$835m), Hanhai's at nearly 2.5 billion yuan (US$394m) and Council's at over 2 billion yuan (US$315m).

Though the profusion of counterfeit artworks continues to threaten the stability of this emerging market, investor confidence seems robust. Industry insiders told *NewsChina* that with the well-embraced theory of "liquidity before authenticity," recent scandals over counterfeit works are unlikely to derail the boom. But why would buyers of fine arts not care if they were sold a lemon?

WHO CARES?

"Authenticity is very important to collectors but matters little to investors [and speculators]," said Ma Weidu, one of China's best-known fine art collectors. "Selling counterfeit goods has become common practice, and I think this ambivalence is reflective of society in general."

Conservative assessments from anonymous insiders suggest that only about half of the buyers in the Chinese art market are collectors and investors. About 20 percent are short-term speculators, 20 percent get in the art market for bribery purposes and 10 percent to participate in money laundering. Sources told *NewsChina* that in many cases, a buyer pre-sells an artwork at a "special price" to someone they wish to bribe, usually a government official, and then outbids all comers at auction, making a loss on the purchase but gaining a foothold with their ultimate buyer.

It is this market atmosphere that has allowed a complete supply chain for counterfeit artwork to become well established across the country. In Beijing, for example, counterfeiters are reputedly particularly good at faking paintings of Qi Baishi and Xu Beihong as well as other 20th century masters. In places with better access to pre-revolutionary artworks like Henan Province and Xi'an, capital city of Shaanxi Province, their peers focus on local ancient masters.

The vagueness of China's legal statutes also allows counterfeiters to flourish. Article 61 of China's 1996 Auction Law decrees that unless the auctioneer and seller declare some doubt over the authenticity of a lot prior to auction, they cannot be made liable for any defect. In short: buyers beware.

The clause has been criticized for favoring sellers and auction houses over buyers. "I think it's unfair," said Zhang Xinjian, former vice chief of the Cultural Market Department of the Ministry of Culture, told *NewsChina*. "It's difficult for the buyers and bidders to obtain comprehensive and accurate information about the artworks on sale. How can a potential bidder tell a fake from the genuine article through a glass case?"

As a result of the recent counterfeiting scandals, the government has begun to strengthen supervision of the market. On July 1, *Heritage and Artwork Auction Procedures*, the first set of standardized industry guidelines for China's auction houses was finally published. Though concrete in content and practical in application, the *Procedures*, as an industry guideline, is only a government regulation, not a law, and is therefore not legally binding.

Prior to the *Procedures*, the China Auction Association (CAA) also released the Self-Discipline Convention of Heritage and Artwork Auction Enterprises, urging auction houses to stop selling counterfeit goods. Yet, the association itself has long been criticized for inaction in response to the practices it is set up to prevent. Mou Jianping said that several high level CAA officials actually work for auction houses. "They are both athletes and referees," he told our reporter. However, the vast profits and widespread practice of bribery means there is little motivation for China's art market regulators to get tough on the tricksters.

In 2010, the average rate of return in China's financial industry was around 15 percent, and around 20 percent in real estate. By contrast, the average rate of return in the art market stood at 30 percent, according to sources. There's little sign that China's billionaires are losing their taste for luxury goods. Liu Yiqian, the seller of *Towering Pines and Cypress*, spent more than 800 million yuan (US$123m) on art in 2009.

"It's difficult to tell how long the art investment craze will last. Whether the bubble will continue to expand or burst is hard to tell," Liu remarked in a recent media interview.

FOR FURTHER STUDY

Response Questions

- How is rule of law being implemented in China today?
- What are the fundamental Confucian principles of leadership and governance that are part of the fabric of Chinese culture?
- Describe how someone might use the Chinese fine art market to bribe an official.
- Name the top five smart phone sellers in China.
- How does Apple protect its intellectual property in China?
- What was the common unregulated fundraising channel used by government agencies to defray expenses under the previous general budget code?
- What are the three dimensions of the anti-graft campaign that President Xi Jinping has highlighted as necessary to the eradication of political corruption?
- What is the default reason for delays given by airline operators in China? What is most likely the reason for flight delays in China?
- Define C2C in both ways that it is used in China.
- What are the legal limitations of crowd-funding in China?

Discussion Questions

- Is President Xi Jinping taking an ideologically rightist (Marxist/Maoist), leftist (Western Liberal Democratic), or pragmatic (experimental and anti-ideological) stance on the issue of corruption and rule of law? Discuss the pros and cons of each ideology as an approach to China's current legal system.
- In the case of flight delays, China has the longest delays for airline departure and arrivals because commercial airlines only occupy 20 percent of the total airspace, and even less than that when there are military exercises in play. Should national interests always take precedence over individual interests? Discuss possible solutions that would preserve both military priorities as well as civilian needs?

- What is the relationship between the legal protection of intellectual property and innovation, creativity and entrepreneurship? Discuss this question in reference to each of the following sectors: film and music; technology; medicine; furniture.
- Through a combination of example-setting, high-profile arrests, and systematic policy changes, the current Chinese administration is attempting to reverse centuries old traditions of graft and *guanxi* (a system of relationships that are mutually beneficial to those inside it). Discuss the implications of each of these approaches to battling corruption in China? How do these affect foreign companies operating in China?
- Protectionism is an economic strategy practiced by any government, regardless of ideology. However, nations vary in their degree of protectionism, both in terms of foreign policy, such as tariffs and quotas, but also in regards to domestic practices such as immigration laws and foreign incorporation. Discuss China's right to set laws that protect and advantage Chinese companies. Include in your discussion of the following topics (in addition to others of your choosing): minimal/selective protection of intellectual property; currency value manipulation; subsidies and dumping.

Research Exercises

- Check out the published conclusions of the CCP's 2015 annual plenum. How do you predict these conclusions will affect China? What specific business sectors will these political decisions will affect most?
- Look into the history of Carrefour in China. How did the firm get established there? How is it doing now vis-à-vis its competition? What recommendations might you have for Carrefour management in the "New Normal" environment?
- Review the USCBC recommendations on IP protection. Pick a company you are familiar with, and describe how that company should implement the applicable recommendations in an effort to market their products in China.
- Research China's public debt structure. How does it compare to that of the US, Japan, or Germany with respect to national GDP, and local versus national components? What steps should Beijing take to avoid a debt crisis in the future, given that land sales, which have propped up local governments for years, are to be curtailed?
- In 2012, Apple won a patent lawsuit over Samsung whose phones and tablets were deemed imitations of technology and form that Apple owned. Xiaomi is a self-described imitator of Apple and Samsung, and their products are often near copies of iPhones and Galaxy smart phones. Compare iPhone and Galaxy products to phones produced by

Xiaomi. If you were lawyers representing both Apple and Samsung, what patent infringements would you pursue against Huawei in international courts?

Notes

1   *Fortune*, April 1, 2015, p. 79.
2   http://techcrunch.com/2015/05/10/apple-top-but-chinese-smartphone-market-shrinks/#.qpumm0:qNTd, retrieved May 11, 2015.

Bibliography

Fernandez, J. & Liu, S. (2007). *China CEO: A case guide for business leaders in China*. Singapore: John Wiley & Sons.

Li, J. & Xi, Z. (October, 2014). Air Traffic—Flying Blind. *NewsChina*.

NewsChina Magazine (November, 2014). An Effective Anti-Corruption Drive. *NewsChina*.

Sun, Z. (November, 2012). Outsmarted. *NewsChina*.

Sun, Z. (August, 2014). Failure to Kickstart. *NewsChina*.

USCBC (February 15, 2015). Best Practices: IP Protection in China. *The US-China Business Council*.

Xie, Y., Su,X., & Hua, X. (September, 2014). Corruption Crackdown: Pulling Rank. *NewsChina*.

Yang, Y. (November, 2014). Laws are Useless if they can't be Enforced. *NewsChina*.

Yu, X. (March, 2015). Legally Bound. *NewsChina*.

Yu, H. & Yi, X. (January, 2012). Masterful Mockups. *NewsChina*.

INDEX

Taylor & Francis eBooks

Helping you to choose the right eBooks for your Library

Add Routledge titles to your library's digital collection today. Taylor and Francis ebooks contains over 50,000 titles in the Humanities, Social Sciences, Behavioural Sciences, Built Environment and Law.

Choose from a range of subject packages or create your own!

Benefits for you

» Free MARC records
» COUNTER-compliant usage statistics
» Flexible purchase and pricing options
» All titles DRM-free.

Benefits for your user

» Off-site, anytime access via Athens or referring URL
» Print or copy pages or chapters
» Full content search
» Bookmark, highlight and annotate text
» Access to thousands of pages of quality research at the click of a button.

eCollections – Choose from over 30 subject eCollections, including:

Archaeology	Language Learning
Architecture	Law
Asian Studies	Literature
Business & Management	Media & Communication
Classical Studies	Middle East Studies
Construction	Music
Creative & Media Arts	Philosophy
Criminology & Criminal Justice	Planning
Economics	Politics
Education	Psychology & Mental Health
Energy	Religion
Engineering	Security
English Language & Linguistics	Social Work
Environment & Sustainability	Sociology
Geography	Sport
Health Studies	Theatre & Performance
History	Tourism, Hospitality & Events

For more information, pricing enquiries or to order a free trial, please contact your local sales team:
www.tandfebooks.com/page/sales

 Routledge Taylor & Francis Group | The home of Routledge books

www.tandfebooks.com